HORMONE REST DIET

40+ Muffins, Pancakes and Cookie recipes designed for a healthy and balanced Hormone Reset diet

TABLE OF CONTENTS

This document is geared towards providing exact and reliable information in regards to the topic and issue covered. The publication is sold with the idea that the publisher is not required to render accounting, officially permitted, or otherwise, qualified services. If advice is necessary, legal or professional, a practiced individual in the profession should be ordered.

- From a Declaration of Principles which was accepted and approved equally by a Committee of the American Bar Association and a Committee of Publishers and Associations.

Introduction

Hormone reset recipes for personal enjoyment but also for family enjoyment. You will love them for sure for how easy it is to prepare them.

BREAKFAST

PINEAPPLE PANCAKES

Serves: **4**

Prep Time: **10** Minutes

Cook Time: **20** Minutes

Total Time: **30** Minutes

INGREDIENTS

- 1 cup whole wheat flour
- ¼ tsp baking soda
- ¼ tsp baking powder
- 1 cup pineapple
- 2 eggs
- 1 cup milk

DIRECTIONS

1. In a bowl combine all ingredients together and mix well
2. In a skillet heat olive oil
3. Pour ¼ of the batter and cook each pancake for 1-2 minutes per side
4. When ready remove from heat and serve

ALMOND PANCAKES

Serves: **4**

Prep Time: **10**   Minutes

Cook Time: **30**   Minutes

Total Time: **40**   Minutes

INGREDIENTS

- 1 cup whole wheat flour
- ¼ tsp baking soda
- ¼ tsp baking powder
- 1 cup almonds
- 2 eggs
- 1 cup milk

DIRECTIONS

1. In a bowl combine all ingredients together and mix well
2. In a skillet heat olive oil
3. Pour ¼ of the batter and cook each pancake for 1-2 minutes per side
4. When ready remove from heat and serve

Serves: **4**

Prep Time: **10**   Minutes

Cook Time: **20**   Minutes

Total Time: **30**   Minutes

INGREDIENTS

- 1 cup whole wheat flour
- ¼ tsp baking soda
- ¼ tsp baking powder
- 1 cup mashed apple
- 2 eggs
- 1 cup milk

DIRECTIONS

1. In a bowl combine all ingredients together and mix well
2. In a skillet heat olive oil
3. Pour ¼ of the batter and cook each pancake for 1-2 minutes per side
4. When ready remove from heat and serve

Serves: **4**

Prep Time: **10** Minutes

Cook Time: **20** Minutes

Total Time: **30** Minutes

INGREDIENTS

- 1 cup whole wheat flour
- ¼ tsp baking soda
- ¼ tsp baking powder
- 1 cup strawberries
- 2 eggs
- 1 cup milk

DIRECTIONS

1. In a bowl combine all ingredients together and mix well
2. In a skillet heat olive oil
3. Pour ¼ of the batter and cook each pancake for 1-2 minutes per side
4. When ready remove from heat and serve

PEAR PANCAKES

Serves: **4**

Prep Time: **10**   Minutes

Cook Time: **30**   Minutes

Total Time: **40**   Minutes

INGREDIENTS

- 1 cup whole wheat flour
- ¼ tsp baking soda
- ¼ tsp baking powder
- 2 eggs
- 1 cup milk
- 1 cup mashed pear

DIRECTIONS

1. In a bowl combine all ingredients together and mix well
2. In a skillet heat olive oil
3. Pour ¼ of the batter and cook each pancake for 1-2 minutes per side
4. When ready remove from heat and serve

LETTUCE OMELETTE

Serves: *1*
Prep Time: 5   Minutes

Cook Time: *10*   Minutes

Total Time: *15*   Minutes

INGREDIENTS

- 2 eggs
- ¼ tsp salt
- ¼ tsp black pepper
- 1 tablespoon olive oil
- ¼ cup cheese
- ¼ tsp basil
- 1 bunch lettuce

DIRECTIONS

1. In a bowl combine all ingredients together and mix well
2. In a skillet heat olive oil and pour the egg mixture
3. Cook for 1-2 minutes per side
4. When ready remove omelette from the skillet and serve

ZUCCHINI OMELETTE

Serves: *1*

Prep Time: *5*   Minutes

Cook Time: *10*   Minutes

Total Time: *15*   Minutes

INGREDIENTS

- 2 eggs
- ¼ tsp salt
- ¼ tsp black pepper
- 1 tablespoon olive oil
- ¼ cup cheese
- ¼ tsp basil
- 1 cup zucchini

DIRECTIONS

1. In a bowl combine all ingredients together and mix well
2. In a skillet heat olive oil and pour the egg mixture
3. Cook for 1-2 minutes per side
4. When ready remove omelette from the skillet and serve

JICAMA OMELETTE

Serves: **1**

Prep Time: **5**   Minutes

Cook Time: **10**   Minutes

Total Time: **15**   Minutes

INGREDIENTS

- 2 eggs
- ¼ tsp salt
- ¼ tsp black pepper
- 1 tablespoon olive oil
- ¼ cup cheese
- ¼ tsp basil
- ½ cup jicama
- 1 cup red onion

DIRECTIONS

1. In a bowl combine all ingredients together and mix well
2. In a skillet heat olive oil and pour the egg mixture
3. Cook for 1-2 minutes per side
4. When ready remove omelette from the skillet and serve

MUSHROOM OMELETTE

Serves: **1**

Prep Time: **5**   Minutes

Cook Time: **10**   Minutes

Total Time: **15**   Minutes

INGREDIENTS

- 2 eggs
- ¼ tsp salt
- ¼ tsp black pepper
- 1 tablespoon olive oil
- ¼ cup cheese
- ¼ tsp basil
- 1 cup mushrooms

DIRECTIONS

1. In a bowl combine all ingredients together and mix well
2. In a skillet heat olive oil and pour the egg mixture
3. Cook for 1-2 minutes per side
4. When ready remove omelette from the skillet and serve

BASIL OMELETTE

Serves: **1**

Prep Time: **5**   Minutes

Cook Time: **10**   Minutes

Total Time: **15**   Minutes

INGREDIENTS

- 2 eggs
- ¼ tsp salt
- ¼ tsp black pepper
- 1 tablespoon olive oil
- ¼ cup cheese
- ¼ tsp basil
- 1 cup tomatoes

DIRECTIONS

1. In a bowl combine all ingredients together and mix well
2. In a skillet heat olive oil and pour the egg mixture
3. Cook for 1-2 minutes per side
4. When ready remove omelette from the skillet and serve

MUSHROOM OMELETTE

Serves: *1*

Prep Time: 5   Minutes

Cook Time: *10*   Minutes

Total Time: *15*   Minutes

INGREDIENTS

- 2 eggs
- ¼ tsp salt
- ¼ tsp black pepper
- 1 tablespoon olive oil
- ¼ cup cheese
- ¼ tsp basil
- 1 cup mushrooms

DIRECTIONS

1. In a bowl combine all ingredients together and mix well
2. In a skillet heat olive oil and pour the egg mixture
3. Cook for 1-2 minutes per side
4. When ready remove omelette from the skillet and serve

Serves: *1*
Prep Time: 5   Minutes

Cook Time: 5   Minutes

Total Time: *10*   Minutes

INGREDIENTS

- 1 cup corn cereal
- 1 cup rice cereal
- ¼ cup cocoa cereal
- ¼ cup rice cakes

DIRECTIONS

1. In a bowl combine all ingredients together
2. Serve with milk

SAUSAGE BREAKFAST SANDWICH

Serves: **2**

Prep Time: **5**   Minutes

Cook Time: **15**   Minutes

Total Time: **20**   Minutes

INGREDIENTS

- ¼ cup egg substitute
- 1 muffin
- 1 turkey sausage patty
- 1 tablespoon cheddar cheese

DIRECTIONS

1. In a skillet pour egg and cook on low heat
2. Place turkey sausage patty in a pan and cook for 4-5 minutes per side
3. On a toasted muffin place the cooked egg, top with a sausage patty and cheddar cheese
4. Serve when ready

BREAKFAST GRANOLA

Serves: 2
Prep Time: 5   Minutes

Cook Time: 30   Minutes

Total Time: 35   Minutes

INGREDIENTS

- 1 tsp vanilla extract
- 1 tablespoon honey
- 1 lb. rolled oats
- 2 tablespoons sesame seeds
- ¼ lb. almonds
- ¼ lb. berries

DIRECTIONS

1. Preheat the oven to 325 F
2. Spread the granola onto a baking sheet
3. Bake for 12-15 minutes, remove and mix everything
4. Bake for another 12-15 minutes or until slightly brown
5. When ready remove from the oven and serve

PANCAKES

BANANA PANCAKES

Serves: **4**

Prep Time: **10**   Minutes

Cook Time: **20**   Minutes

Total Time: **30**   Minutes

INGREDIENTS

- 1 cup whole wheat flour
- ¼ tsp baking soda
- ¼ tsp baking powder
- 1 cup mashed banana
- 2 eggs
- 1 cup milk

DIRECTIONS

1. In a bowl combine all ingredients together and mix well
2. In a skillet heat olive oil
3. Pour ¼ of the batter and cook each pancake for 1-2 minutes per side
4. When ready remove from heat and serve

PINEAPPLE PANCAKES

Serves: **4**

Prep Time: **10** Minutes

Cook Time: **20** Minutes

Total Time: **30** Minutes

INGREDIENTS

- 1 cup whole wheat flour
- ¼ tsp baking soda
- ¼ tsp baking powder
- 1 cup pineapple
- 2 eggs
- 1 cup milk

DIRECTIONS

1. In a bowl combine all ingredients together and mix well
2. In a skillet heat olive oil
3. Pour ¼ of the batter and cook each pancake for 1-2 minutes per side
4. When ready remove from heat and serve

ALMOND PANCAKES

Serves: *4*

Prep Time: *10* Minutes

Cook Time: *30* Minutes

Total Time: *40* Minutes

INGREDIENTS

- 1 cup whole wheat flour
- ¼ tsp baking soda
- ¼ tsp baking powder
- 1 cup almonds
- 2 eggs
- 1 cup milk

DIRECTIONS

1. In a bowl combine all ingredients together and mix well
2. In a skillet heat olive oil
3. Pour ¼ of the batter and cook each pancake for 1-2 minutes per side
4. When ready remove from heat and serve

APPLE PANCAKES

Serves: **4**

Prep Time: **10** Minutes

Cook Time: **20** Minutes

Total Time: **30** Minutes

INGREDIENTS

- 1 cup whole wheat flour
- ¼ tsp baking soda
- ¼ tsp baking powder
- 1 cup mashed apple
- 2 eggs
- 1 cup milk

DIRECTIONS

1. In a bowl combine all ingredients together and mix well
2. In a skillet heat olive oil
3. Pour ¼ of the batter and cook each pancake for 1-2 minutes per side
4. When ready remove from heat and serve

STRAWBERRY PANCAKES

Serves: **4**

Prep Time: **10** Minutes

Cook Time: **20** Minutes

Total Time: **30** Minutes

INGREDIENTS

- 1 cup whole wheat flour
- ¼ tsp baking soda
- ¼ tsp baking powder
- 1 cup strawberries
- 2 eggs
- 1 cup milk

DIRECTIONS

1. In a bowl combine all ingredients together and mix well
2. In a skillet heat olive oil
3. Pour ¼ of the batter and cook each pancake for 1-2 minutes per side
4. When ready remove from heat and serve

PEAR PANCAKES

Serves: **4**

Prep Time: **10**   Minutes

Cook Time: **30**   Minutes

Total Time: **40**   Minutes

INGREDIENTS

- 1 cup whole wheat flour
- ¼ tsp baking soda
- ¼ tsp baking powder
- 2 eggs
- 1 cup milk
- 1 cup mashed pear

DIRECTIONS

1. In a bowl combine all ingredients together and mix well
2. In a skillet heat olive oil
3. Pour ¼ of the batter and cook each pancake for 1-2 minutes per side
4. When ready remove from heat and serve

COOKIES

BREAKFAST COOKIES

Serves: *8-12*

Prep Time: 5   Minutes

Cook Time: *15*   Minutes

Total Time: *20*   Minutes

INGREDIENTS

- 1 cup rolled oats
- ¼ cup applesauce
- ½ tsp vanilla extract
- 3 tablespoons chocolate chips
- 2 tablespoons dried fruits
- 1 tsp cinnamon

DIRECTIONS

1. Preheat the oven to 325 F
2. In a bowl combine all ingredients together and mix well
3. Scoop cookies using an ice cream scoop
4. Place cookies onto a prepared baking sheet
5. Place in the oven for 12-15 minutes or until the cookies are done
6. When ready remove from the oven and serve

FIG SMOOTHIE

Serves: *1*

Prep Time: 5   Minutes

Cook Time: 5   Minutes

Total Time: *10*   Minutes

INGREDIENTS

- 1 cup ice
- 1 cup vanilla yogurt
- 1 cup coconut milk
- 1 tsp honey
- 4 figs

DIRECTIONS

1. In a blender place all ingredients and blend until smooth
2. Pour smoothie in a glass and serve

POMEGRANATE SMOOTHIE

Serves: *1*

Prep Time: *5*   Minutes

Cook Time: *5*   Minutes

Total Time: *10* Minutes

INGREDIENTS

- 2 cups blueberries
- 1 cup pomegranate
- 1 tablespoon honey
- 1 cup Greek yogurt

DIRECTIONS

1. In a blender place all ingredients and blend until smooth
2. Pour smoothie in a glass and serve

GINGER-KALE SMOOTHIE

Serves: **1**

Prep Time: **5** Minutes

Cook Time: **5** Minutes

Total Time: **10** Minutes

INGREDIENTS

- 1 cup kale
- 1 banana
- 1 cup almond milk
- 1 cup vanilla yogurt
- 1 tsp chia seeds
- ¼ tsp ginger

DIRECTIONS

1. In a blender place all ingredients and blend until smooth
2. Pour smoothie in a glass and serve

BERRY YOGHURT SMOOTHIE

Serves: **1**

Prep Time: **5**   Minutes

Cook Time: **5**   Minutes

Total Time: **10**   Minutes

INGREDIENTS

- 6 oz. berries
- 2 bananas
- 4 oz. vanilla yoghurt
- 1 cup milk
- 1 tablespoon honey

DIRECTIONS

1. In a blender place all ingredients and blend until smooth
2. Pour smoothie in a glass and serve

COCONUT SMOOTHIE

Serves: **1**

Prep Time: **5**   Minutes

Cook Time: **5**   Minutes

Total Time: **10**   Minutes

INGREDIENTS

- 2 mangoes
- 2 bananas
- 1 cup coconut water
- 1 cup ice
- 1 tablespoon honey
- 1 cup Greek Yoghurt
- 1 cup strawberries

DIRECTIONS

1. In a blender place all ingredients and blend until smooth
2. Pour smoothie in a glass and serve

RASPBERRY-VANILLA SMOOTHIE

Serves: **1**

Prep Time: **5**   Minutes

Cook Time: **5**   Minutes

Total Time: **10** Minutes

INGREDIENTS

- ¼ cup sugar
- ¼ cup water
- 1 cup Greek yoghurt
- 1 cup raspberries
- 1 tsp vanilla extract
- 1 cup ice

DIRECTIONS

1. In a blender place all ingredients and blend until smooth
2. Pour smoothie in a glass and serve

CHERRY SMOOTHIE

Serves: *1*

Prep Time: *5*   Minutes

Cook Time: *5*   Minutes

Total Time: *10* Minutes

INGREDIENTS

- 1 can cherries
- 2 tablespoons peanut butter
- 1 tablespoon honey
- 1 cup Greek Yoghurt
- 1 cup coconut milk

DIRECTIONS

1. In a blender place all ingredients and blend until smooth
2. Pour smoothie in a glass and serve

CHOCOLATE SMOOTHIE

Serves: **1**
Prep Time: **5**   Minutes

Cook Time: **5**   Minutes

Total Time: **10**   Minutes

INGREDIENTS

- 2 bananas
- 1 cup Greek Yoghurt
- 1 tablespoon honey
- 1 tablespoon cocoa powder
- ½ cup chocolate chips
- ¼ cup almond milk

DIRECTIONS

1. In a blender place all ingredients and blend until smooth
2. Pour smoothie in a glass and serve

TOFU SMOOTHIE

Serves: **1**

Prep Time: **5** Minutes

Cook Time: **5** Minutes

Total Time: **10** Minutes

INGREDIENTS

- 1 cup blueberries
- ¼ cup tofu
- ¼ cup pomegranate juice
- 1 cup ice
- ½ cup agave nectar

DIRECTIONS

1. In a blender place all ingredients and blend until smooth
2. Pour smoothie in a glass and serve

ORANGE SMOOTHIE

Serves: *1*
Prep Time: 5   Minutes

Cook Time: 5   Minutes

Total Time: *10*   Minutes

INGREDIENTS

- 1 orange
- ½ cup orange juice
- ½ banana
- 1 tsp vanilla essence

DIRECTIONS

1. In a blender place all ingredients and blend until smooth
2. Pour smoothie in a glass and serve

RAISIN DATE SMOOTHIE

Serves: **1**

Prep Time: **5**   Minutes

Cook Time: **5**   Minutes

Total Time: **10**   Minutes

INGREDIENTS

- ¼ cup raisins
- 2 Medjool dates
- 1 cup berries
- 1 cup almond milk
- 1 tsp chia seeds

DIRECTIONS

1. In a blender place all ingredients and blend until smooth
2. Pour smoothie in a glass and serve

MUFFINS

SIMPLE MUFFINS

Serves: **8-12**

Prep Time: **10** Minutes

Cook Time: **20** Minutes

Total Time: **30** Minutes

INGREDIENTS

- 2 eggs
- 1 tablespoon olive oil
- 1 cup milk
- 2 cups whole wheat flour
- 1 tsp baking soda
- ¼ tsp baking soda
- 1 cup pumpkin puree
- 1 tsp cinnamon
- ¼ cup molasses

DIRECTIONS

1. In a bowl combine all wet ingredients
2. In another bowl combine all dry ingredients
3. Combine wet and dry ingredients together
4. Pour mixture into 8-12 prepared muffin cups, fill 2/3 of the cups

5. Bake for 18-20 minutes at 375 F
6. When ready remove from the oven and serve

GINGERBREAD MUFFINS

Serves:	*8-12*	
Prep Time:	*10*	Minutes
Cook Time:	*20*	Minutes
Total Time:	*30*	Minutes

INGREDIENTS

- 2 eggs
- 1 tablespoon olive oil
- 1 cup milk
- 2 cups whole wheat flour
- 1 tsp baking soda
- ¼ tsp baking soda
- 1 tsp ginger
- 1 tsp cinnamon
- ¼ cup molasses

DIRECTIONS

1. In a bowl combine all wet ingredients
2. In another bowl combine all dry ingredients
3. Combine wet and dry ingredients together
4. Fold in ginger and mix well
5. Pour mixture into 8-12 prepared muffin cups, fill 2/3 of the cups

6. Bake for 18-20 minutes at 375 F
7. When ready remove from the oven and serve

CHERRIES MUFFINS

Serves: *8-12*

Prep Time: *10*   Minutes

Cook Time: *20*   Minutes

Total Time: *30*   Minutes

INGREDIENTS

- 2 eggs
- 1 tablespoon olive oil
- 1 cup milk
- 2 cups whole wheat flour
- 1 tsp baking soda
- ¼ tsp baking soda
- 1 tsp cinnamon
- 1 cup mashed cherries

DIRECTIONS

1. In a bowl combine all wet ingredients
2. In another bowl combine all dry ingredients
3. Combine wet and dry ingredients together
4. Pour mixture into 8-12 prepared muffin cups, fill 2/3 of the cups
5. Bake for 18-20 minutes at 375 F
6. When ready remove from the oven and serve

BLUEBERRY MUFFINS

Serves: *8-12*

Prep Time: *10*   Minutes

Cook Time: *20*   Minutes

Total Time: *30*   Minutes

INGREDIENTS

- 2 eggs
- 1 tablespoon olive oil
- 1 cup milk
- 2 cups whole wheat flour
- 1 tsp baking soda
- ¼ tsp baking soda
- 1 tsp cinnamon
- 1 cup blueberries

DIRECTIONS

1. In a bowl combine all wet ingredients
2. In another bowl combine all dry ingredients
3. Combine wet and dry ingredients together
4. Fold in blueberries and mix well
5. Pour mixture into 8-12 prepared muffin cups, fill 2/3 of the cups
6. Bake for 18-20 minutes at 375 F

BERRIES MUFFINS

Serves:	*8-12*
Prep Time:	*10* Minutes
Cook Time:	*20* Minutes
Total Time:	*30* Minutes

INGREDIENTS

- 2 eggs
- 1 tablespoon olive oil
- 1 cup milk
- 2 cups whole wheat flour
- 1 tsp baking soda
- ¼ tsp baking soda
- 1 tsp cinnamon
- 1 cup berries

DIRECTIONS

1. In a bowl combine all wet ingredients
2. In another bowl combine all dry ingredients
3. Combine wet and dry ingredients together
4. Pour mixture into 8-12 prepared muffin cups, fill 2/3 of the cups
5. Bake for 18-20 minutes at 375 F
6. When ready remove from the oven and serve

CHOCOLATE MUFFINS

Serves: *8-12*
Prep Time: *10*   Minutes

Cook Time: *20*   Minutes

Total Time: *30*   Minutes

INGREDIENTS

- 2 eggs
- 1 tablespoon olive oil
- 1 cup milk
- 2 cups whole wheat flour
- 1 tsp baking soda
- ¼ tsp baking soda
- 1 tsp cinnamon
- 1 cup chocolate chips

DIRECTIONS

1. In a bowl combine all wet ingredients
2. In another bowl combine all dry ingredients
3. Combine wet and dry ingredients together
4. Fold in chocolate chips and mix well
5. Pour mixture into 8-12 prepared muffin cups, fill 2/3 of the cups
6. Bake for 18-20 minutes at 375 F

RASPBERRIES MUFFINS

Serves: *8-12*

Prep Time: *10*   Minutes

Cook Time: *20*   Minutes

Total Time: *30*   Minutes

INGREDIENTS

- 2 eggs
- 1 tablespoon olive oil
- 1 cup milk
- 2 cups whole wheat flour
- 1 tsp baking soda
- ¼ tsp baking soda
- 1 tsp cinnamon
- 1 cup raspberries

DIRECTIONS

1. In a bowl combine all wet ingredients
2. In another bowl combine all dry ingredients
3. Combine wet and dry ingredients together
4. Pour mixture into 8-12 prepared muffin cups, fill 2/3 of the cups
5. Bake for 18-20 minutes at 375 F
6. When ready remove from the oven and serve

THANK YOU FOR READING THIS BOOK!

CPSIA information can be obtained
at www.ICGtesting.com
Printed in the USA
BVHW031400150321
602550BV00001B/398

SWORD AND WIG

Robin Dunn

SWORD AND WIG

Memoirs of a Lord Justice

ROBIN DUNN

Quiller Press
London

First published 1993 by
Quiller Press Limited,
46 Lillie Road,
London SW6 1TN

ISBN 1 870948 88 2

Front cover artwork and design
by Tim Jaques.

Production in association with
Book Production Consultants Plc,
25-27 High Street, Chesterton,
Cambridge.

Typeset by Cambridge Photosetting Services.

Printed by St Edmundsbury Press,
Bury St Edmunds, Suffolk.

Jacket illustration: *'Run-in shoot'* reproduced by
kind permission of 24th(Irish) Battery RA.

CONTENTS

Maps

PART I

THE ARMY

CHAPTER I

Childhood and Schooldays, 1918–36

In our family there was never any discussion about what I would do when I grew up: I would be a soldier like my father, both my grandfathers and my Dunn great-grandfather, who served in the Horse Artillery in the Peninsular War and became a major-general. Not only was soldiering in my blood, but I was a child of the regiment, born and brought up on the barrack square or in the gun park. Throughout my childhood and adolescence my parents never owned their house: we lived in quarters or in rented houses near the barracks – at Newbridge in Ireland, Weedon, Woolwich, Catterick and finally Aldershot. Perhaps, as a result, I have never felt any deep attachment to bricks and mortar or to possessions. Home to me was where my parents lived. My earliest recollections are of the trumpet calls, reveille, officer's mess, last post, the shouts of words of command, the stamping of feet and the smell of ammonia in the troop stables.

I was a shy and nervous little boy with a pale face and very light-coloured hair, anxious to please and do the right thing, and longing to be 'grown up'. My brother Teddy, who died of meningitis in 1922 at the age of three, although a year younger than me, was the stronger character. He was tough and robust with a wicked sense of humour. My sister Barbara was born in 1924. With a six year age gap, although strongly attached to one another, we did not share our interests and were not companions. So I was brought up effectively as an only child.

My father Keith never served in India, where in those days nearly half the army was stationed. He used to call it a first-class country for second-class people. I suspect that the real reasons were his passion for fox-hunting in England and because he did not wish to be separated from his children. The climate of India was considered unsuitable for children after the age of about seven and most service children spent their school years at boarding schools in England and the holidays with relations here: there were no jumbo jets to ferry children back and forth. Rudyard Kipling vividly describes the traumatic effect this separation had on him during his formative years and my parents were determined it should not happen to me. Fortunately, as a gunner, my father had a choice. There was a 'foreign service roster' for the whole

Royal Regiment and there were those who preferred service in India to service at home. So, when my father reached the top of the roster he bought an exchange with a recently returned officer, taking his place at the bottom. He did this twice between the wars, involving a payment each time of £100. I am sure it was worth it for the sake of the whole family.

Although my father had little besides his army pay and my mother had virtually no private means, we lived in considerable comfort not to say style. We always had a resident cook, house parlourmaid and nanny. In addition my father's soldier servant spent the day in the house. Our nanny was Elsie Sturman, one of thirteen children brought up in a railwayman's cottage near Northampton. She left school at the age of 13 to go into service, but she wrote with style in a clear and round hand and read aloud to us with feeling and expression. She was an expert needle-woman and used to make most of Barbara's clothes. She was completely calm with a wonderful big soft lap, very gentle but with a strong sense of right and wrong. I never saw her put out or angry or flustered.

We spent much of our childhood with my maternal grandparents, Horace and Emily Kays, at their small house at Murrayfield in Edinburgh. She was the daughter of Sir Auckland Colvin, who had been Governor of Bengal in the 1870s and was later Financial Secretary to Lord Cromer in Egypt.

My Kays grandmother was quiet and kind and very easy-going. She was dominated by Horace, who had retired from the army as a brigadier-general. After Harrow he joined the Highland Light Infantry which he ultimately commanded. I had some marvellous times with my grandfather. He used to take me round the sights of Edinburgh, and his great delight was to go to some place where the public was not allowed or to get in somewhere without paying for a ticket. One of our most exciting escapades was to stand in Princes Street between the two tram tracks with moving trams passing on either side of us which was strictly forbidden. His study was like a regimental museum with military tools, pictures, shell cases and weapons of all kinds, where I used to spend enchanting hours. Every night he used to change for dinner into his HLI mess kit, with green jacket and McKenzie tartan trews.

My grandfather was a fine shot and an accomplished fisherman. But after he retired he was induced to put most of his capital into a business venture which failed. So he gave up shooting and fishing and took up golf. He moved from a large house in one of the Georgian squares in Edinburgh to the small house in Murrayfield, although he too employed a resident cook and house parlourmaid. He always said that it was a great mistake to be over-housed and that it was better to have a sovereign in your pocket. Certainly he was never short of cash. As well as being a member at Muirfield he joined the Royal and Ancient at St. Andrews and took rooms there for a month every summer. He and my father used to play a round on the Old Course in the morning and on the New Course in the afternoon, while Barbara and I spent the day on the beach with nanny. After tea we used to play with the grown-ups on the long putting course. My grandfather was friendly with the great professional,

James Braid, who taught me to swing a golf club.

My mother, named Ava after her godmother the Marchioness of Dufferin and Ava, wife of the Viceroy of India at the time of my mother's birth, had a host of relatives some with unusual pet-names: Aunt Fluffy, my grandmother's sister and wife of General Sir Bindon Blood, and her daughter Cara, wife of Colonel Hugh Brocklebank; my mother's sister Sibyl married to her cousin Ragnar Colvin; a Kays cousin, Johnnie Crosbie of the Rifle Brigade; and my mother's Long cousins, Tootie, Beady and Tuppy who married Lady Leverhulme after her divorce from the first Lord Leverhulme. My mother loved being with all these people, who were very warm and relaxed and full of fun.

We also saw a great deal of our paternal grandmother Constance. Her father was General Erskine, who had been seconded from the army for twenty years to undertake the survey of the Indian Province of Oudh. This involved a survey of every holding to assess it for tax.

Unfortunately my grandmother suffered from asthma, and for most of her married life she had been a semi-invalid. She spent the winter in her flat in Basil Street and the summer in a converted Elizabethan school house in Guilsborough in Northamptonshire. She had great taste and her homes were beautifully furnished.

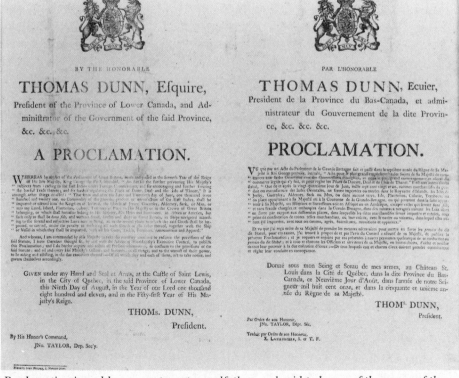

Proclamation issued by my great-great-grandfather, and said to be one of the causes of the Anglo-American war of 1812, since it prevented U.S. ships from trading to Canada.

She always said with pride that she and my grandfather had furnished their first house entirely out of income. He had died the year before I was born leaving his money 'to my dear wife who knows my wishes'. This provision caused trouble between my father and his only sister Margery, who had married Ross de Wend Fenton. The de Wend Fentons were an old Yorkshire family with a small estate near Sheffield. My mother always said that Ross was too proud to work and used his energy to extract money from my grandmother – whatever the rights and wrongs of this assertion it did not prevent me from being fond of my cousin Rosemary de Wend Fenton and her brother West, a colourful character and one of the few people to have escaped from the French Foreign Legion.

My grandfather (Robin) served after Eton in the Royal Welch Fusiliers in India and the Burma War and after the Boer War commanded the Depot at Wrexham. He sent in his papers when he was posted to India, and the family moved to a house on Bangor racecourse. He was tall, with the typical Victorian military moustache, and by all accounts quiet and gentle, though rather gruff in manner. He loved shooting. My father told me that once his school report from Wellington described him as 'gentlemanly', to which my grandfather retorted, 'I don't need a bloody school-master to tell me that my son is a gentleman!' My father said it was the only time that he had seen my grandfather angry.

My father served in France from 1914 until 1916, when he was hit on the head a glancing blow from a machine-gun bullet on the first day of the battle of the Somme. Fortunately he was wearing his newly issued steel helmet, but was badly concussed and served in a training establishment at Trowbridge until shortly after I was born in 1918. He was then posted to the HAC in Palestine and took part in Allenby's final cavalry advance through Syria to Aleppo. He kept a fascinating diary of this campaign, describing the difficulties the guns had in keeping up with the cavalry through the hilly, biblical country of Judea.

After the war we all went to Ireland, of which I remember nothing, except that my mother drove a dog cart with a pony called Paddy, although the 'troubles' were at their height. In 1921 my father went on a course at the equitation school at Weedon. He was an accomplished horseman, and an even better instructor, and became an instructor immediately the course ended. Part of the course at Weedon was to go hunting three or four days a week in the winter with the Pytchley, Grafton, Warwickshire and Bicester and I loved to hear my father's accounts of the hunts. He used to read aloud to me John Masefield's *Reynard the Fox* and even before I wholly understood the words I was fascinated by the metre and rhythm of the poem. I also became addicted to Surtees and knew many of Jorrocks's sayings by heart.

In 1926 my father became adjutant of the Royal Military Academy at Woolwich (known as the Shop) where 'gentlemen cadets' were trained for the sappers, gunners and signals. Our house was on the front parade, where a ceremonial parade with the R.A. band took place every Saturday morning. I used to hang out of the night-nursery window watching every movement of the parade. Then I used to dress up in uniform and hold my own parade in the garden.

We were at Woolwich for four years, so my father knew all the gunner officers of that generation. Many have told me how much they admired him. He was always immaculately turned out and a great believer in what he called the 'minor military virtues': punctuality, cleanliness, orderliness and attention to detail. To many he was the *beau idéal* of a gunner officer. But he was not a martinet and was a kind and loving father.

While we were at Woolwich I went to my prep school, St. Aubyns at Rottingdean. One of the instructors at Weedon, Alwyne Pelly, had been there and his son John and I went together on the same day and have remained life-long friends. The headmaster was R. C. V. Lang who Wilfred Thesiger, the explorer, describes in his autobiography as a homosexual sadist. If he was I never noticed. He completely dominated the school which was run by him through the senior boys. Although the classes were small, never more than ten, St. Aubyns won few scholarships and the common entrance results were no more than adequate. My parents, who were very fond of Lang, said that this was because he did not believe in pushing small boys too hard at their work.

My time at St. Aubyns was undistinguished, although I opened the batting for the cricket XI and became vice-captain of football. I paid little attention in class because I was always dreaming. I was in my imagination Sir Nigel leading a band of knights, exploring vast tracts of Africa with Rider Haggard or leading a French cavalry charge with Brigadier Gerard or the Three Musketeers. I even had my own imaginary island to which I could retire when the rigours of Latin grammar became too demanding. This island had a small but extremely efficient army. At first, since it was an island, there was no one for the army to fight. So I incorporated a mountainous region inhabited by a race with similar characteristics to those of the Scots, who were great fighters and enjoyed raiding the settled parts of the rest of my island. That at least gave my army something to do.

My mother told me that one of the other mothers had told her that she had sent her son to St. Aubyns because the boys were taught to fear God and honour the King. We were all entirely innocent of sex. When I left Lang explained to me 'the facts of life'. When I arrived home I told my mother. She asked what he had said. I replied, 'Never spill the seed.' She told me this years later amid gales of laughter. I had no recollection of the occasion.

About a year before I left St. Aubyns we moved to Catterick where my father was in command of one of the newly mechanised field batteries. In spite of this all officers had two chargers and a groom. The official reasons for this concession were that the artillery in India was still horsed and all officers were supposed to keep up their riding, and also that hunting was considered good training for war, developing an eye for country and quick courageous decisions. Certainly there was no lack of opportunity for hunting at Catterick, since the Bedale and Zetland were both within reach, and enjoyed good countries and good packs of hounds.

I have often wondered since how my mother occupied her time during the long dark northern winters at Catterick. She did not hunt, regarding horses as dangerous unpredictable animals. She was gregarious, full of high spirits, a marvellous mimic and able to illuminate the most ordinary experiences with flashes of wit and humour. She was excellent company and one of her friends told me that to be with her was like drinking a glass of champagne.

She had a pretty though small singing voice. As a young woman she had sung solo at public concerts and we loved to hear her sing sentimental Edwardian ballads, her favourite being *And when I told them how wonderful you were, they wouldn't believe me.*

She was also an enthusiast. Once, on coming home for the holidays, she suggested that I should give up meat and take up a vegetarian diet. When I asked how long this would continue she made it clear that it was to be a new and marvellous way of life and that I would be much better for it. 'You can eat as much as you like of any one thing,' she said, 'but don't go mixing different kinds of food. It is very bad for you.' So I started by eating twelve bananas for supper, which caused havoc to my digestive arrangements. That was the end of vegetarianism so far as I was concerned, but Barbara was brought up on the diet and nanny used to say, 'Poor Barbara, her little stomach just won't take a proper meal. She needs feeding up.' My mother never tried to make my father diet, which was just as well as he was a good trencherman who enjoyed traditional English food, especially roasts and steamed puddings. Usually my mother was wholly uncompromising: she saw things very clearly; everything was either black or white. But on this issue she did not press her point.

My mother was also interested in religion and she always had a collection of religious books by her bed. She was attracted to Christian Science, to which she had been introduced by two friends in London, General Tom and Mrs. Esther Holland, who were prominent members of that Church. She was a great believer in 'right thinking' and used to say, 'If you think right you won't get ill.' But that did not prevent her from sending for a doctor if either Barbara or I was off-colour. Esther Holland's daughter, Doris Pease, lived near Catterick and was also a Christian Scientist. Once Doris had a fall out hunting and broke her arm. She refused to see a doctor and went to the hunt ball that evening.

My mother was devoted and passionately loyal to my father. She entertained his hunting friends and was full of interest in his doings, although she once said to me, 'I don't mind talking hunting in general to my neighbours at dinner. But I do get a little bored when the conversation is confined to that day's hunt, when I have not been there and do not know the country.'

Although I had had a pony at Weedon and been blooded at the age of seven by Frank Freeman, the famous huntsman of the Pytchley, it was not until we went to Catterick that I started to hunt on a 13.2 hands dun pony called Leo – named after Lucy Glitters's hunter Leotard. At first I did not really enjoy hunting: sooner or later we came to a fence, bigger than usual, and were faced with the dilemma of either trying to jump it and falling off or pulling up and missing the hunt. It was not until I was old enough to ride a larger animal which could negotiate all the obstacles that I acquired the necessary confidence. From that time I enjoyed hunting as much as my father, whom I always followed.

With some help in mathematics, always my weak subject, from a local schoolmaster, I managed to pass into the bottom form at Wellington in January 1931.

My first impression of Wellington was how much more friendly the boys were to one another than at St. Aubyns. Boys of prep school age are very cruel, but the boys at Wellington were helpful and thoughtful, especially to New Men as we were called.

My great friend was Ronnie Coaker, who lived near Wiveliscombe in Somerset and later became a major-general. It was while staying with him that I first rode over Exmoor and I remember thinking how rough and broken the ground was and that I would not want to hunt there. We were encouraged to make our friends among those of our own year in our own dormitory, the Combermere, a limit of about ten or a dozen people. This did not prevent me from making two other friends who qualified. Digby Tatham-Warter won the DSO at Arnhem. He later went farming in Kenya and commanded an irregular mounted posse of settlers during the Mau Mau rebellion. He wrote saying he had not enjoyed himself so much since Arnhem. My other close friend was Pat Weldon whose elder brother Frank rode in our Olympic three day event team and for many years ran the three day event at Badminton. Frank was Head of the Combermere and played rugger and boxed for the school. We all used to stay regularly in one another's houses during the holidays. I was lucky to have such people about me during my time at Wellington.

I was small for my age and, although I played scrum half, no good at rugger. I was never able to bring myself to make a flying tackle, the acid test of physical courage. This caused a dramatic change in my athletic prospects. One day the dormitory captain of rugger detailed me to run in the Little Side, a cross-country race for those under sixteen, saying that I was not good enough for the dormitory colts XV so I might as well try to run. Although I was only just fourteen, I finished in the first ten and for the first time realised that I had the ability and stamina to run. So I went into hard training and the following year won the Little Side. Later I won the Big Side, the Big Kingsley, which involved wading the River Blackwater, and all the middle distance events on the running track, in due course becoming master of the hunt or captain of cross-country and captain of athletics. All this gave me a standing in the dormitory and later the school which I never expected in view of my poor performance on the rugger field.

When I was about sixteen I was approached by an usher (as the assistant masters were called) called 'Boosie' Gould. E. G. Gould was not addicted to drink; his nickname was caused by the colour and texture of his face. Boosie said he was going to raise a cricket team called 'the Occasionals' which would include a few ushers and senior boys and would play away on Saturdays against local villages and regiments at

Aldershot. Would I be captain? I was astonished as, although I had won my colours at St. Aubyns, I did not regard myself as a serious cricketer and as Boosie was a house tutor I was surprised that he had not chosen one of his own boys. But of course I accepted with alacrity and remained captain for three seasons.

The ushers at Wellington were a mixed lot, with some eccentrics but mostly good teachers in their own way. My first dormitory tutor was H. G. V. Civil, soon to be replaced by Herbert Wright. He was a classical scholar who had served in the gunners in the war and a charming and most understanding man. He and his wife set the tone in the Combermere and treated us as part of their family. I found the younger ushers more sympathetic than some of the older, who had taught my father. Cecil de Saumarez of an old Channel Island family became a great friend. He felt wasted as a schoolmaster, having failed the examination for the Foreign Office, diplomacy and international politics being his passion. He used to console himself by quoting from Kipling's *A School Song*:

Wherefore praise we famous men
Men of little showing
They that put aside Today
All the joys of their Today
And with toil of their Today
Bought for us Tomorrow!

'Bouncey' Brown, an Australian, first interested me in English literature. The most formidable was Wanstall known as 'the Hun' who taught German. He was a great believer in learning by rote and maintained strict discipline in his classroom. When answering a question one had to stand up in one's place. The army boys were taught French by Albert Noblet who always wore the ribbon of the Legion of Honour in his buttonhole and deplored what he saw as German influence in the school. He was Master in Hall and used to smother his food with Worcester sauce, saying, 'When eating English food one thanks God for chemicals.' But towering above them all was the Master F. B. Malim, an alarming figure as he hurried through the quadrangles in his mortar board and gown. He was a considerable orator with a precise manner of speech emphasising the consonants. He used to say that English as spoken in America consisted of a series of mispronounced vowels interspersed with inaudible consonants. He was not only a classical scholar, but was also a great administrator: a Victorian head of a Victorian school. I once heard him say, 'Public schools are so called because we train boys for the public service.'

Preferment among the boys at Wellington was based almost entirely on seniority in the school and as I had been the youngest boy in the school my first term it was inevitable that during my last year, when all my contemporaries had left, I should be at the top. I was Head of the Combermere and a school prefect. I enjoyed that last year immensely. There was so much to do at Wellington.

After School Certificate I spent two years in the Army VI. Those destined for the Shop spent most of our time doing mathematics and science, my two weakest subjects. The minimum pass mark for each of them in the army examination was 125 out of 300. I got 128 in maths and just 125 in science. When he saw my results James Wort, who had struggled to teach me maths, said, 'The reward of true merit.'

I look back on Wellington with affection and gratitude. It brought me out. I was no longer shy and I made many friends and developed many interests. My time there coincided with the rise of Hitler in Germany and in those days there was much to admire in the physical fitness and commitment of German youth, but there were also disturbing signs. A team from a German school came to play hockey. Before they left they lined up in front of the Great Gate and shouted 'Sieg Heil' three times in unison, at the same time giving the Nazi salute. Cecil de Saumarez said to me, 'Those people frighten me, especially when you see the newsreels of them marching by torchlight at the Nüremburg Rally. Where is it leading Europe?'

CHAPTER II

Pre-War Soldier, 1936–39

About a year before I left Wellington my father was awarded his 'jacket'. That is to say he was posted to the Horse Artillery in command of 'D' Battery at Aldershot, which formed part of the 1st Cavalry Brigade still with horses. My father was delighted and his feelings were summed up in the couplet: 'And some would say that they'd reached the height of a soldier's wildest dreams; if it weren't for the nasty professional guns which spoil the look of the teams.' My mother was also delighted for different reasons. She was back in the south with her relations nearby. The Walpole Kays lived in Farnham and my mother's first cousin Pam had just married 'Strafer' Gott of the 60th Rifles. He became a legendary figure in the desert, was appointed Commander of 8th Army and was killed almost immediately thereafter in an air crash. He was a charming gentle man.

My father missed his hunting in Yorkshire and, as the hunting round Aldershot was not good, sent his horses to the stables at Childrey, which he had just inherited from an uncle, to hunt with the Old Berkshire twice a week. I joined him during the holidays. The Old Berkshire is a vale country carrying a good scent. Every fence had a ditch on one side or the other, so one needed a horse that would gallop on at its fences. I thoroughly enjoyed it.

In 1936 I joined the Shop as a snooker, as first term cadets were called. In a way it was like coming home. The first morning we were addressed by the Commandant, General Jumbo Goschen. He said, 'Three qualities are required of an officer: courage, physical fitness and brains – in that order.' I often thought of that remark during the war years. The discipline at the Shop was strict, even stricter than the RMC Sandhurst where the cavalry and infantry were trained. After the war the two establishments were amalgamated to form the RMA Sandhurst. This had a bad effect on gunner officer recruiting. Before the war it was considered to be an achievement to pass into the Shop and schoolmasters encouraged their more intelligent army boys to take the Shop examination. But once the two were amalgamated many cadets found the glamour of a cavalry regiment more appealing than life in the gunners and recruiting suffered accordingly. Most of the sons of my gunner contemporaries who joined the army went to the cavalry. Before the war there were many old gunner families, like my own, who were attracted by serving in a mounted arm, but could not afford the private means demanded by most cavalry regiments. We were said to be 'poor, proud and prejudiced'. After the war, when army pay was increased, this did not apply in the same way and the gunners suffered accordingly.

We lived in Houses, about a dozen GC's to a House with two House corporals. Ours were Philip Tower and Alastair Mann, who unfortunately later caught polio, which did not prevent him from riding to hounds as joint master of the South Oxfordshire. Philip was to have a distinguished military career, serving in the 1st Airborne Division at Arnhem and becoming a major-general responsible for extricating our forces from Aden. They were both keen horsemen and understanding to the snookers. We slept two to a room and the day started with House Parade when we were inspected before breakfast. A piece of fluff on our uniform meant a 'hoxter' or extra drill, which involved parading under one of the drill instructors at 7 am in full uniform with rifle and bayonet and spending half an hour marching and turning at double quick time on the gun park. During the mornings we had frequent changes of clothes, the ability to change quickly from PT kit into full uniform including breeches and puttees being apparently considered an essential attribute for an officer.

During our first term we did infantry drill and PT every day. Our drill instructor was Sergeant-Major Hennessy of the Grenadier Guards. In spite of his name he was a real cockney with a biting wit concealing a kind heart. He preserved the conventions by always referring to us as 'gentlemen', even after some gem of invective. At the annual ball Hennessy in his scarlet tunic was at the door to introduce us and our partners to the Commandant. When he announced my name he hissed in my ear, 'And swing that right arm, sir.'

After lunch, preceded by lunch parade, when we were again inspected, the afternoon was free, although we were expected to take exercise four times a week. I gravitated to the running track. After tea we had two hours of lectures before dinner when we wore blue patrols. I have never been so fit as at the end of my first term at the Shop, but it was exhausting. As Philip Tower said, 'By the end of term you will have to start using your legs on yourself.'

One of the horrors of our first term was the snooker boxing. Every snooker had to box in the gymnasium after dinner in a knock-out competition, with all the instructors and the whole Shop sitting round in a haze of blue tobacco smoke.

During our second term at the Shop we started riding at the RHA riding establishment at the Woolwich depot under Robert Vining. We used to bicycle down as a formed body in half sections after the usual parade to inspect our boots and leggings. Although by then the Royal Regiment was in the course of being mechanised, the second term rode twice and the third term three times a week, mostly in the riding school.

During the term I represented the Shop at athletics, although I was beaten in the mile by Bobby Spiller my old rival from Wellington. We competed against Oxford

University and I set a cracking pace relying on my stamina to exhaust the opposition. However, entering the final straight, the Oxford first string suddenly 'kicked' from behind me and passed me like a rocket to win comfortably. I realised then that in that class I was no more than a plodder, so decided to give up running and concentrate on riding.

During our second term we lined the route for the Coronation of King George VI and Queen Elizabeth, King Edward VIII having abdicated the previous year. We were positioned alongside Sandhurst opposite the entrance to Westminster Abbey, dressed in our blue patrols. We were to have gone to London by coach, but there was some hitch and we had to march in the early morning to Woolwich Arsenal station and crowd into the train. Consequently we were late, to the ill-concealed derision of Sandhurst who were already in position. That evening we all changed into plain clothes and went to join the crowd outside Buckingham Palace. It was a long day.

At the end of our second term we and the snooker term all bicycled through the suburbs of London to a week's camp at Aldershot. I had been made one of a dozen corporals for camp. On our return to the Shop the adjutant, Bob Mansergh, announced the promotions for our senior term. All seniors automatically became corporals except four Under Officers and the Senior Under Officer. When we were all assembled Bob looked me straight in the eye and said, 'The new SUO will be G.C. Dunn.'

At what should have been a time of rejoicing for all of us, the whole family was hit by crisis. My father's brigade, 3rd Royal Horse Artillery, was under orders for Egypt in the autumn. For him it was not likely to be for very long since he was due for promotion to lieutenant-colonel within the year. At first my mother was looking forward to a winter in Cairo. During the summer, however, she became increasingly unwell and when the brigade sailed in October she was in a nursing home at Hampstead.

Fortunately for me Ragnar Colvin was Admiral President of the Royal Naval College at Greenwich, where I used to go alternate weekends during my last term at the Shop.

The day-to-day running of the Shop was in the hands of the adjutant working through the SUO. Bob Mansergh had been born in South Africa. He was tall and immaculately turned out and believed in exercising command by persuasion and suggestion rather than by direct order. I never had a disagreement with him. He became a full general and Master Gunner of St. James's Park, the Head of the Royal Regiment.

I spent most of my spare time at the Shop riding. I was in the Saddle Ride under 'Sailor' Kitcat and in addition to three days a week riding parades we went voluntary riding on a further two afternoons a week. We were occasionally allowed to go out with the RA Drag, which had lines in Kent, and across the river in Essex where the country was much bigger with large yawning ditches, although I never enjoyed the artificiality of drag hunting. I was captain of the Shop riding team against Sandhurst. The competition consisted of a mini one day event with school work or dressage, cross-country and show jumping. I already knew several of the Sandhurst team, who came to the Shop for the event. Sandhurst won; besides George Rich, who was an outstanding horseman, they had several very competent performers and our team was just not good enough.

During the term we put on the traditional Seniors' Concert, which was a revue consisting mostly of skits on the various instructors. We decided to do a burlesque of a riding parade, which had never been done before and in which I played a prominent part. All the instructors, including the riding instructors, were of course present. Next morning we arrived at the riding school to find all the instructors, including the NCOs, assembled, a line of large jumps in position down one side of the school and a magnificent looking 16-hand young horse, which Robert Vining had been schooling, standing in the middle of the school with no saddle. I knew it had a terrific buck in it. Robert said, 'The SUO will vault on to that horse and ride it over the jumps without reins.' I jumped on and set off down the jumps which the horse sailed over in great style. Before I could pick up my reins it put its head down between its front knees and produced three enormous bucks, at the last of which I ended up on the tan amid roars of laughter from all present. As I was picking myself up Robert said, 'That, Mr. Dunn, will teach you not to poke fun at the Riding Establishment.' But I knew that he was delighted by the show the previous evening.

I was determined to win the Saddle, the riding prize, which my father had won in 1910. I had worked hard in the riding school during the holidays with the 'D' Battery Roughrider (as the NCO instructors were called) trying to improve my school work, which was my weak point. The competition consisted of the same three phases and at the end three of us were picked out, changed horses, and made to do the cross-country course again. Then the placings were announced: John Hunter was the winner and Hugh Hamilton, who became a sapper, and I were equal second. I reconciled myself to never being a top-class horseman, although I knew that I would always ride well enough to enjoy myself and do all I wanted.

At the end of term I won not only the Sword of Honour, but also the Tactics and Military History prizes and the prize for the gunner with the best marks in military subjects. One of my mother's relations wrote, 'We were not surprised that our dear Robin won the Sword of Honour, but we never knew he was a swot!'

My father had suggested that I should spend my Christmas leave with him in Cairo. I was very doubtful as, although it would be a marvellous opportunity, I was torn at the prospect of leaving my mother whose condition was deteriorating and not spending Christmas with Barbara. I agonised for some time but finally Sibyl Colvin said firmly that I should go; so not without misgivings I went. I had never been abroad before and was fascinated by the strangeness of everything. I woke up in the train crossing the Lombardy Plain and was enchanted by the red-roofed houses, the extensive cultivation and the clear blue sky after the grey clouds of England. I embarked at Genoa on Christmas Day, although the only sign of Christmas was a fir tree lashed to the mast of a German warship in the harbour. A few days later we arrived at Alexandria.

The most obvious thing about the army in Egypt was the string of polo ponies which daily perambulated from Abbassia to the Gezira Club. We used to go there most afternoons to play tennis and watch the polo and then on to Groppis or the Turf Club, which was sacked and burnt down by the mob in the fifties, for tea or a drink before dinner. Cairo was a striking mixture of a modern city with a strong French influence and a dirty dilapidated Arab town with terrible signs of poverty. All the car drivers habitually drove with their hands on their horns and the noise, interspersed with the shouts of the vendors of the evening newspaper, the *Bourse*, was appalling.

My chief and abiding memory of Egypt is of the antiquities. We visited the pyramids and Sphinx and travelled by the night train to Luxor to see the Temple of Karnak by moonlight, the Valley of the Kings and the Tombs of the Nobles. Here were the remains of a civilisation five thousand years old, which spoilt me for any subsequent sight-seeing. I was especially moved by the Tombs of the Nobles with their splendid murals displaying a way of life not unlike that of Europe in the 18th century. There were pictures of the Lord and his Lady riding out into the fields to watch the harvest being gathered in and conversation pieces of domestic scenes showing men and women of assured dignity and grace.

All too soon it was time to go home. I sailed from Alexandria in an Italian ship to Venice. In the evening, boarding a Pullman car on the Orient Express, which had come from Istanbul via Sofia and Belgrade trailing the mystery of the east as it steamed into the station, I travelled in comfort to London in time to join the School of Artillery at Larkhill for my Young Officers' course.

Soon after the course started I was called to the telephone to be told that my mother had died. I had seen her once since I returned and had been distressed to find her very ill. I sent a telegram to my father and was given indefinite leave as there was much to be done. I went straight to London to the house of my father's uncle Bobbie Erskine in Thurloe Square. Sibyl had already gone to Australia. Bobbie and his wife Ruby treated me with the greatest kindness and consideration. I do not know what I would have done without them. My father arrived after a few days, having flown from Egypt by Imperial Airways. The funeral was at St. Peter's, Eaton Square, where my parents had been married nearly twenty-five years before. My father went up to the Peases to be with Barbara, who was living with them in Yorkshire, and then returned to Egypt. I went back to Larkhill. I felt my youth was over. One of her friends had written of my mother, 'She certainly was one of the sweetest and most fascinating of God's creatures.'

The Young Officers' course was a comprehensive specialised course in field gunnery. By the end of the course we had performed the function of every member of a field battery from battery commander to gun ammunition member. The Royal Regiment ended the war with a greatly enhanced reputation, much of the technique of massed artillery fire which won so many battles having been developed at the School of Artillery.

My term from the Shop was joined by a few university candidates from Oxford and Cambridge, including John Dill whose father was later CIGS and a field marshal. John became a great friend and was best man at my wedding. My other great friend was Tony Wainwright whose father was a gunner and commanded a division in Burma. Tony lived near Larkhill and taught me to fish in the chalk streams. He was a born soldier winning the MC at Dunkirk and becoming a major at the age of twenty-two. Sadly he was killed in a motor accident in England in 1943, a great waste as he would have had a brilliant career. Another friend from the Shop was Marcus Linton, who became a brigadier and was killed in an aircrash in the Far East.

My term retained the high spirits they had shown at the Shop. Once after a guest night we dismantled a 25 pounder gun, took its parts into the ante room, assembled it and carried out some very smart gun drill. By that time nobody wanted to dismantle the gun again, so it was pushed through the door and down the steps causing some damage, which proved expensive even when divided among those taking part.

As our four months' course drew to its close there was much discussion as to where we should apply for our first posting. Vacancies were allotted on choice, depending on where one passed out. The whole empire was our oyster and the criterion was sport. Should one go polo playing and duck shooting in Egypt or pig sticking at Muttra or big game shooting at Lucknow? Or should one go fox-hunting in England? Not surprisingly I chose the latter and John Dill, Tony Wainwright and I, together with Dick Chartres whose father owned a big farm in Northumberland, were posted to 7th Field Regiment, then at Bulford but under orders for Catterick in the autumn.

After Larkhill I went on a six weeks driving and maintenance course at the Military College of Science, then at Woolwich. We lived in the magnificent gunner mess at Woolwich with its superb silver and spent the day in overalls with our heads inside engines. I was never mechanically-minded and hated the course. At the end of the course I had some leave which I spent with my father, Barbara and Nanny at Le Touquet. By that time he had returned from Egypt and was commanding 17th Field Regiment at Woolwich. He did not move into the Commanding Officer's house and lived as a bachelor in the mess. We used to go to the casino, which had been the hospital in the Great War to which my father had been taken after being wounded on the Somme.

My father and I visited the Somme battlefields and Vimy Ridge, also Ypres where he had spent the first year of the Great War. Little did I think that I would soon be fighting Germans again near some of those same places.

The army was in a deplorable state when I joined 7th Field Regiment (brigades having by then been re-designated regiments) in the late summer of 1938. There were only two fully-equipped infantry divisions and practically no tanks or anti-tank guns. 7th Field was part of 3rd Division, ear-marked for the first wave of the Expeditionary Force. But the horses had only just left as I arrived and the guns were in ordnance being re-bored from 18 to 25 pounders. The regiment was reduced for the winter to a cadre of a hundred officers and men, in common with other artillery regiments in the 3rd and 4th Divisions. When we arrived at Catterick I walked into the mess to find the Colonel, Sir Ivor Twistleton-Wykham-Feinnes, drinking tea and eating hot buttered toast. 'What is the first thing you do, Robin, when you arrive at a new station?' he asked. Thoughts raced through my head to find the right answer, but before I could reply he said, 'I will tell you. Find the quickest way to get out of it. Give me the railway timetable.' The next day he went off to Boughton Castle, his house in Warwickshire, and we did not see him again apart from a few days over Christmas when he came up to hunt.

Shortly after we arrived the Munich crisis broke. Flying columns were organised to go to the northern industrial towns to deal with the civil unrest and looting which were anticipated after the expected air raids. Elaborate air raid precautions were taken in our barracks. Slit trenches were dug, buildings sand-bagged and a gas decontamination centre set up in the bath house. If war had broken out then only the two divisions at Aldershot would have been able to take part. The Munich agreement gave us a breathing space.

Militarily there was little for us to do. With no guns and very few men training opportunities were minimal. It could have been demoralising for us, who had just completed two years of the most rigorous and intensive training in our profession. So I threw myself into hunting and was far from demoralised. Tony Wainwright and I each sent a horse with one of our grooms to a pub on the River Tees from which we could hunt on the Durham side of the Zetland, a glorious hunting country which, in those days, was all grass, with plenty of well cut-and-laid fences and very little barbed-wire. We called it 'the Elysian Fields'. We hunted in Yorkshire from barracks. I had four horses, two chargers and two of my own and they were all kept at government expense. The regiment had a quota of free forages but, as several officers did not hunt, I was able to benefit. In those days the pay of a 2nd lieutenant was 10/- a day. In addition I had a scholarship from the Shop of £150 a year and an allowance from my father of a further £150. My mess bill was about £10 a month (I hardly drank anything and did not smoke) and I was able to run a car and hunt as much as I liked. The annual subscription for serving officers was £10 to each pack.

I have never felt so well as when sitting on a horse. The outside of a horse is the best thing for the inside of a man. And in those days I enjoyed the thrill of galloping and jumping over natural country. I also enjoyed the social side of hunting. I met on easy, friendly terms people from all walks of life whom I would never have met if I had just stayed in barracks, playing golf and squash with my brother officers. And I enjoyed the feeling of physical tiredness and well-being at the end of the day, with the prospect of a hot bath and poached eggs for tea. Many of my contemporaries whom I had known as a child when we were at Catterick were still living nearby and I spent a busy winter dining in their houses and enjoying their hospitality. That season I had fifty-three days hunting.

One of our few military tasks was to write an essay on a subject set by the Brigadier. That year it was, 'The primary role of the British army is imperial policing. Discuss the organisation and handling of a field regiment in carrying out this role.' This seemed extraordinary to me at the time, with Munich just behind us and the prospect of a European war in all our minds and I could not work up much enthusiasm for the set subject. The Brigadier wrote on my essay, 'This was obviously written without much thought after a long day's hunting.'

In the spring I was sent as range officer to the artillery practice camp at Redesdale in Northumberland, with a range party from the regiment. My task was to run the ranges, maintain the targets including the moving targets for anti-tank shooting and organise the safety arrangements. A series of territorial regiments from the north each came to the camp for a fortnight's live firing on the ranges during the summer. The TA had just been doubled in strength, each regiment forming a second line. The response had been enthusiastic, and all the regiments were up to strength and full of keenness. Conscription had also been introduced for the regular army and the conscripts, or militiamen as they were called, went straight to regiments instead of the depot for their primary training. The country being what it was (and still is) much publicity was given to the home comforts which were to be enjoyed by the militiamen. I never saw many.

In April 1939 the Germans, in breach of the Munich agreement, invaded Czechoslovakia and occupied Prague. We all felt then that war was inevitable and this view was confirmed in August by the Soviet-German Pact, made at a time when we and the French were negotiating a defensive alliance with the Soviets. Our feeling was that if war was to come the sooner the better. There was an air of fatalism. We tried to lead a normal life, riding and fishing and playing tennis, but in our minds we knew that we would soon be at war.

When I returned to the regiment at the end of August everything was different. Our guns were back. The reserves had been called up. This was a magnificent body of men, all trained soldiers, many of them experienced NCOs who formed the backbone of the regiment throughout the war. Then there were the militiamen, mostly more intelligent and very keen. The officers were a mixture of the very young and inexperienced like myself, a few more senior who had been on leave from India and the supplementary reservists. We also had a new Colonel, Jock Wedderburn-Maxwell, recently promoted from the RHA. He was a live wire and his personality raced through the regiment like an electric current.

The regiment was almost wholly untrained. We never did fire our guns, except to calibrate them, until we met the enemy. Before we left England we had never even exercised as a battery. But the discipline was good and the men soon acquired the individual skills required for the new equipment.

CHAPTER III

France and Belgium, 1939–40

On 1st September, while I was checking stores in the gun park, the Sergeant-Major came up, saluted and said, 'Major's compliments, sir. General mobilisation has been ordered, so there will have to be a parade after tea.' It took us a week to mobilise and we then drove down to Dorset where 3rd Division was concentrating. The Divisional Commander was Major-General B.L. Montgomery, known throughout the division as 'Monty'.

We started at once with a digging exercise on the Dorset Downs. The whole division dug itself into trenches, dug-outs and gun pits. Even Monty could not forget the Great War. Then we moved to France. To avoid air raids the guns and vehicles sailed from Falmouth to Brest. The rest of us went from Portsmouth to Cherbourg. As our ship glided out of the harbour a group of stevedores on the quay shouted, 'Are you down-hearted?' to which our troops roared back, 'No.' 'Well you f-ing well soon will be,' was the cheerful response. We travelled by train from Cherbourg to near Le Mans where we met up with our guns and vehicles. Then we drove for two days of pouring rain through northern France to our billeting area near Lille. The subalterns all rode motor-cycles to keep the column moving and very wet and uncomfortable it was.

We were billeted at Thumesnil, a suburb of Lille, the officers in private houses and the men in large buildings such as schools or church halls. The battery officers all messed together in a large private house. I was billeted with Ian Syddall, another subaltern just joined from the Shop, in the house of the Carpentiers, the owners of the local dairy, from whom I learnt to speak French with a Lillois accent. Latterly Ian and I used to join their large luncheon party on Sundays. They could never understand why we used always to go for a walk after luncheon, instead of following their example of going to sleep with their heads on the table.

Our first task was to fortify our stretch of the Belgian frontier. The Maginot Line did not run north of Sedan and was to be extended along the frontier to the sea. An anti-tank ditch was dug, concrete 'dragons' teeth' constructed as a further anti-tank obstacle, and behind these we and the infantry dug our defences. We used to drive the ten miles or so from our billets to the frontier every morning and worked on the gun positions until evening when we returned. All positions were camouflaged and linked by dug-in telephone wires and targets were fixed. The whole tactical approach was defensive, based on the methods of 1918. Even our Commander Royal Artillery (CRA), Brigadier Rowland Towell, who had been my father's best man and later became a most successful commandant of the School of Artillery, set the tone in two lectures, 'The handling of artillery in defence' and 'The preparation of gun positions'. But Monty soon made his presence felt. The strategy of the BEF was that if the German army invaded Belgium we, and the French armies on either side of us, would advance from our prepared defences and occupy a line facing north-east covering Brussels. So every month our division moved an equivalent distance south-west to the area of St Pol, where we fought a defensive 'battle' on a river line and then withdrew about twenty miles to another river line for another defensive 'battle' culminating in a counter-attack supported by tanks, which in the event were not available since there were only two tank battalions in the whole BEF. These were the first of the famous Monty exercises of large formations. They were carefully stage-managed, followed by a post-mortem attended by all officers of the division and conducted by Monty himself. The operations were analysed and the lessons brought home with no lack of criticism. Sometimes the Corps Commander Alan Brooke, a former gunner and later CIGS, was invited as an observer and summed up the exercise. I never saw a more impressive man. He exuded controlled power and intellectual stature. He once said to us, 'Every commander should from time to time take off his earphones, stand back from the battle and think.' I believe he was the only one of his superiors for whom Monty had any regard. Certainly he treated him with deference. We learnt the techniques of long moves at night in motor transport, of occupying defensive positions at short notice and of that most difficult of operations, withdrawing in face of an active enemy, and worked out appropriate drills for all of them.

During the winter we were visited by the Prime Minister, Neville Chamberlain, and the War Minister, Hore-Belisha, who inspected our defences, accompanied by a bevy of very senior officers. When he was introduced our Colonel Jock at once launched into a monologue, listing all the shortages of equipment and amenities from which the regiment suffered. The Prime Minister looked pained, the War Minister embarrassed and the senior officers outraged. Only Monty appeared pleased. It was a diverting interlude for us. One episode is typical of military bureaucracy at that time. I developed German measles and was evacuated to the Casualty Clearing Station about ten miles away. In a few days I was fit and told I was to be evacuated to the RA base at La Baule on the Atlantic coast. I went to see the OC (a mistake which I would not have made later) and said, 'Would it help if I rang up my regiment and asked for a truck to take me back?' 'It would bugger everything,' I was told. So I set out on a two-day rail journey to the base, where I found myself in a pool of reinforcements liable to be posted to any regiment. I managed to get in touch with the Colonel and after a not unpleasant week by the sea received a posting order to 7th Field Regiment. So back I went to Lille in another French troop train with square wheels. The whole trip must have been quite expensive for the taxpayer.

Soon after we arrived in France our battery commander, a dear old boy, was sacked by the Colonel and replaced by Humphrey Drew who had been my company commander at the Shop. He was a charming bachelor, who knew what he wanted and usually managed to get it by the exercise of charm rather than direct order. During the winter I was given command of a troop of four guns and about sixty men, although I was still a second lieutenant. John Dill commanded the other troop. Troops were supposed to be commanded by captains, but there was a shortage of that rank and there were no acting ranks in those days. In action the troop commander occupied the OP or Observation Post and the control of the guns was under another officer called the Gun Position Officer or GPO. My GPO was Marcel Hudson who was older than me and a supplementary reservist. It was a bitterly cold winter and the engines of all vehicles were started up by the guard every two hours throughout the night to prevent their radiators from freezing. An example of the 1918 syndrome was that we collected the stores necessary for the preparation of a gun position: sandbags, corrugated iron and stakes for revetting and when we moved into Belgium these were loaded on to the gun towers. Unfortunately we had overlooked the increase in weight and suffered badly from broken springs on arrival at our destination.

At that time we did not believe that the Germans would attack in the west or, if they were so foolish as to try, that they would have any chance of success. True they had overrun Poland in a few weeks, but the French army would be a very different proposition from the Polish. We were taught that the French army was the best in Europe and what we had seen of it confirmed that view. A DLM or Light Mechanised Division was billeted near us and we were impressed by their equipment and the bearing of their troops. One or two of our officers had attended short courses at the French School of Artillery during the winter and returned impressed by the professionalism of their French comrades. And we had lived among the French people for several months and grown to admire their practical outlook on life and their attitude towards the war. Above all we noted their hatred of the Germans (Lille had been occupied throughout the Great War) and their apparent determination that this should not happen again. They always referred to Germans as 'les sales Boches'.

So it was a surprise to us when, early in the morning of 10th May 1940, we heard on the wireless that the Germans had invaded Belgium and Holland. Our Colonel was on leave, Humphrey Drew was commanding the regiment and nearly half our officers were away either on leave or on courses.

Within three days of arriving in England from Dunkirk I wrote an account of the campaign in the form of a daily diary, which appears in full in Appendix 1 – page

251 (see also map page 252). I felt at the time that this, my first campaign, was the culmination of everything that had happened in my life up till then and indeed from long before, since I was the fourth successive generation of my family to face the ultimate test of a soldier, in battle.

The popular conception of Dunkirk is of the final evacuation from the beaches, portrayed in photographs showing lines of men waiting on the beach to embark in the ships of all shapes and sizes which were anchored off-shore, with German aircraft bombing and machine-gunning ships and men. But my principal recollection is of the three weeks of retreat from Louvain, through Brussels, across the French frontier to our final stand at Furnes. The weather was glorious, day after day of warm sunshine and a cloudless sky. This was in one way an advantage from the point of view of our physical comfort and well-being; but a serious disadvantage in another, since it enabled the Luftwaffe to take full advantage of their complete air superiority. It was not until we had nearly reached the coast that, for the last few days, clouds appeared overhead, British fighters came from England and we were spared the worst attentions of the German air force. Until then we were continually bombed by Heinkels and JU 87s (the dreaded Stuka dive bombers) and machine-gunned by Messerschmidt fighters. Strangely enough these attacks, in which we suffered no casualties, did not affect us as much as the shellfire, which was unpleasantly accurate and which I always disliked. It was not so much that one was frightened but rather that one felt a kind of heaviness of spirit, with the feeling, 'Oh not again. Why can't they stop?' But as soon as the shelling did stop, there was a feeling of relief, an uplifting of the spirit and no long-term consequences – until the next time.

I was much affected by the effect of war on the civilian population. The country round Louvain had been evacuated at short notice leaving abandoned houses and unmilked cattle in the fields. The pleasant university town of Louvain itself was almost deserted and it was sad to see damaged houses and devastated avenues and public parks. The effect of this policy of evacuation was that the roads were jammed with refugees heading for the French frontier. These unfortunate people not only impeded our retreat, but their plight was pathetic, since the Germans bombed and machine-gunned them indiscriminately. By the time we got back to the French frontier the industrial towns of Lille, Roubaix and Tourcoing were cut off by the Germans from the rest of France and the people were frightened, bewildered and very short of food. The RAF had been built up as the main British contribution to the war, but as one French civilian with whom I shared a ditch during a dive-bombing attack said to me, *"Où est le Royal Air Force, monsieur?" "Où?"* indeed.

Throughout the retreat we just could not believe what was happening and until the last few days refused to accept that we would have to run for the coast. It was unthinkable that the French army should have collapsed and that we were no match for the Germans. Indeed, whenever we had stood to fight we had beaten them off. We remembered that in March 1918 the Germans had nearly reached Amiens and had been defeated six months later. We were convinced that this would happen again.

Nor, in a strange way, did I ever feel that we were alone. We were in the cockpit of Europe, where British armies had marched and fought for hundreds of years and I was always conscious of the spirits of our predecessors all round us like an invisible cloud. The soldiers of Marlborough's wars must have used the same roads and seen the same sights as us – we even passed through Oudenarde; we were close to Waterloo where so many had died; and towards the end we drove along the Messines ridge, close to Ypres, and saw Hazebrouck and Dickebusch where soldiers used to rest from the 'line', and the cemeteries with their serried ranks of tombstones. So we were just continuing the history already made by those others; we were part of their armies and they were still part of ours.

There was no sign of panic until we were approaching Furnes. Then we saw many abandoned vehicles and small groups of soldiers trudging back without arms or equipment and thumbing lifts on our vehicles and guns. In the midst of this flotsam we passed a battalion of Grenadier Guards, marching slowly in step on either side of the *pavé*, carrying their weapons with their equipment all in place. There was cheering at the head of the column and there, beside the ditch, stood Monty his hand at the salute. It was like Napoleon reviewing his Old Guard. This campaign brought out the finest qualities of the Guards. I shall never forget sitting at Battalion HQ of the 3rd Grenadiers in Furnes, in the cellar of a house which eventually collapsed under shell fire on top of us. There was an atmosphere of complete calm and confidence, no excitement, no shouting. Everyone talking quietly, mostly of things unconnected with the war.

When we reached our final position in the sand-dunes near La Panne, John Dill said to me, 'I can't see how any of us will get out of this alive.' I said, 'Well, what they ought to do is to collect every small boat from the south coast of England and ferry us home. But of course they won't.' Well, they did.

Wading out to the naval cutter off the beach at La Panne, I met Peter Miller-Munday, who was standing up to his chest in water, helping us on board. His regiment, the 12th Lancers, had been dismounted from their armoured cars and ordered to take charge of the embarkation. I asked him how long he had been there. 'Two days,' he said. I replied, 'How awful.' 'Not at all,' he said. 'I have never met so many friends before.' I had last seen him at his 21st birthday party the previous year, when he had dived head first through a plate-glass window into the ballroom.

There were many stories of Dunkirk. My favourite was of a soldier who had appeared on the beach without his trousers. He was asked by an officer what he had done with them. At first he would not say but eventually, looking extremely embarrassed, explained, 'Well to tell the truth, sir, I spent the night with a woman in La Panne. I had to leave in a hurry and left my trousers behind.' That night La Panne had been a blazing inferno, continually bombed and shelled, and it was a remarkable tribute to the resilience of the British soldier that he should have ventured into the place at all, especially for that purpose.

Looking back after over 50 years my first impression is still one of surprise at the small number of casualties suffered by the regiment. This was, I am sure, due to the training of the division by Monty and to the high quality of the regular infantry battalions in front of us. We were, I believe, the only division never to have our front broken, partly perhaps because we retreated so fast in our motor transport! My principal recollection of the campaign is of shortness of sleep. We were in action most days and driving most nights. On arriving in England I slept whenever I could for about a fortnight. I also vividly remember our surprise at the way we were treated by the civilian population in England. We had expected to be shunned as objects of derision after our humiliating defeat. A bedraggled army, rescued by the navy, having abandoned all our equipment. When I had gone on board a destroyer off Dunkirk a sub-lieutenant R.N. had said to me, 'I don't understand you bloody Pongos. When we are surrounded we shoot our way out. We don't call on another service to rescue us.' But in England we found the civilians treated us as heroes who had won a great victory.

It is ironic that the Blitzkrieg tactics of fast-moving armoured columns closely supported by low-flying aircraft, which had defeated us and the French army, had been invented after the Great War by British writers and military thinkers, such as Liddell Hart, 'Boney' Fuller and Hobart. But a combination of a financially parsimonious British government and a conservative military establishment had produced an army equipped and trained to fight a 1918-style battle, with far fewer tanks than then existed. First Armoured Division landed in France in the latter part of May with no artillery and their highly trained motor battalions were sent to cover themselves with glory in the static defence of Calais. Apart from the two tank battalions, our only armour consisted of a handful of Light Armoured Regiments used as divisional reconnaissance regiments. No wonder we were outclassed. However the operation of 27–28th May, described in my diary from the point of view of a subaltern at p264, was in fact a remarkable operation of war, as shown by Lord Alanbrooke in his memoirs. 3rd Division successfully withdrew in the face of the enemy from the frontier defences at Roubaix, side-stepped behind 5th and 50th Divisions who were holding the line of the Ypres canal to our left, and took up position on their left or northern flank to fill the gap left by the Belgians, who had suddenly surrendered.

CHAPTER IV

England, 1940–41

3rd Division concentrated near Frome in Somerset. Within a week we had been re-equipped down to the last split-pin and told that we were to return to France as a token support for the French army. Monty held a conference for all officers of the division in the cinema at Frome. He walked onto the stage and after the usual ban on smoking and coughing ('If you must cough, cough now, and not when I am speaking') he said, 'I have told the War Office that the division must go back to France to support the French. Now I shall tell you how to beat the Germans.' At that there was a roar of laughter from the assembled officers. We had just suffered one of the most complete defeats ever suffered by British arms and now, a week later, we were expected to beat the same formidable adversary. At first Monty looked nonplussed. Then he saw the joke and laughed himself. Three years later when he made such a claim everyone hung on his words like holy writ. But not in 1940. Fortunately for us the French surrendered shortly afterwards and our move to France was cancelled.

We were inspected by the King. By this time we had a new Colonel, 'Boy' Selby-Lowndes, who, wherever he had been stationed before the war, had always managed to hunt a pack of hounds. He was telling the King that he had brought his favourite hunt terrier back from Dunkirk. 'You must miss him being in quarantine,' said H.M., not knowing that the terrier was curled up in the back of the Colonel's staff car.

As we were the only fully-equipped division in the country, we were sent to defend the coast at Brighton, which was regarded as the most likely place for a German invasion as it was so close to London. The infantry fortified the front, the piers were demolished, the guns were in action on the Downs behind the town and I established an OP in the attics of the Metropole Hotel, which was still occupied by visitors. Many of them could not understand and were resentful of the warlike preparations we were making, saying we were spoiling their holiday. While we were at Brighton we heard that Monty had been promoted to command South-eastern Army being formed in Kent to withstand the expected invasion there. He visited the regiment to say 'good-bye'. I had been recommended for the MC but only received the consolation prize of a 'Mention in Despatches', entitling me to wear an oak leaf on my chest. However, acting ranks had been introduced and so, as a troop commander, I was promoted straight from second lieutenant to captain. I never wore two stars on my shoulder. When Monty was inspecting my troop he stopped opposite me, looked at my shoulders and said, 'Quick promotion, Dunn.' I had never spoken to him before and it was a good example of his style of command and the meticulous briefing he must have received before visiting the regiment.

We heard that a large-scale parachute drop by German airborne troops was expected on the Cotswolds, so the division was moved to Gloucestershire. We were split up into three brigade groups, each with a regiment of artillery as well as three infantry battalions. Our group was commanded by Brian Horrocks, who had recently been promoted from command of the Divisional Machine-Gun Battalion. He was a charismatic leader who, two years later, was commanding a corps in 8th Army. Our whole tactical doctrine changed. We read everything we could about the methods of the German army. Defence went out of the window. Horrocks said, 'If any Germans land they must immediately be attacked and hit hard from the outset.' He organised what he called a 'Forward Body', consisting of three bren gun carrier platoons, mortars, medium machine-guns and a company of lorried infantry with our regiment in support and this mini-armoured force was exercised over the Cotswolds.

We expected to spend the winter in our billets round Wooton-under-Edge, so 'Boy' Selby-Lowndes collected a few hounds and arranged with the Duke of Beaufort and the master of the Berkeley to hunt the unfashionable hill country along the Cotswold escarpment. Tony Wainwright and I were to whip-in. Unfortunately in late August we were ordered to move to the Tiverton area, as there was said to be a German threat to invade in the south-west and cut off the south-western peninsula. So no hunting in Gloucestershire.

It would require the pen of a Homer or Shakespeare to write an epic poem describing the atmosphere in England during the summer of 1940. There was a feeling of unity in the country which would be inconceivable today. We were alone, facing the most powerful military machine in the world. We could not be defeated – the navy and air force would see to that. But we did not know how we could win. Sustained and encouraged by Churchill's broadcasts on the wireless, we lived at a level of excitement and mental awareness which I have never subsequently experienced. Every experience was vivid and life was exciting. Patriotism was not just a word or a duty; it permeated our lives. Nothing was certain, the future wholly unknown. We felt it was a truly heroic time.

Soon after we arrived in Tiverton in this highly charged atmosphere I was told that I was to go for the winter to Minehead as gunner instructor at the newly formed divisional battle school, which was to be set up to train on Exmoor. As soon as I arrived at Minehead I hired a horse from Joe Collings at Porlock to go hunting with the Devon and Somerset Staghounds. The meet was at Hawkcombe Head and we finished at Culbone. I asked the master, Mrs. Flo Hancock, my best way back to Porlock. 'Oh,' she said, 'Judy Pilcher will be going back that way; she will show you.' She introduced me to a very pretty girl with laughing eyes and a voice like an angel, whom I had already admired sailing across the moor at the top of the hunt on a thoroughbred horse. So we rode home together. As we crossed Porlock Hill Judy pointed with her whip to a long grey house under the woods in the valley ahead and said, 'That's where I live. Why don't you come in for some tea?' So I did.

At first I missed jumping fences on Exmoor, although there were plenty of other hazards from bogs to holes in the ground. Judy had already broken her back in a fall, the effect of which remained for the rest of her life. I suggested we should have a day with the West Somerset, a more traditional hunting country. Judy said, 'You won't enjoy it' – but we went. We rode the five miles to Minehead, boxed the horses on the train to Williton, whence we hacked to the meet. Judy was quite right. The country was very hairy; horses had to scramble through the fences rather than fly over them and we were exhausted after our long journey home. After that we stuck to hunting on Exmoor.

By Christmas we had agreed to marry, but told no-one, although Judy's parents must have guessed as I was invited to stay at Lynch for Christmas. The house belonged to Mrs. Allan Hughes, Judy's grandmother, always known as 'Googie'. She was beautifully dressed in dark clothes and she had a mass of pure white hair and a very erect carriage. In spite of an incisive way of talking she had the sweetest character of anyone I ever met. Her two great interests were the gardens at Lynch, which she had created herself when the house was built in 1913 in the Lutyens style by her husband Allan Hughes, and her collection of porcelain. Judy's mother Jane was living in the house for the duration of the war. Their house in Rutland Gate had been emptied of furniture and was being used as the HQ of the London AA defences. Judy's father Toby was a KC and had recently become legal adviser to MI5, although we were not allowed to know this at the time, the very existence of MI5 being shrouded in mystery. Judy's brother John, a year younger than her, also came on leave from the guards depot at Caterham where he was training for a commission in the Grenadiers. He was going on to the RMC Sandhurst as an officer cadet.

Soon after Christmas a stray bomb from a German aircraft, returning from a raid on London, was dropped on to John's room at Sandhurst, killing him instantly. It was a cruel blow. He was a great countryman, a good shot and a fine fisherman who enjoyed hunting, although he had not Judy's passion for horses. Judy was much affected by his death, as they had been particularly close, spending hours together on the river and ferreting on the hill behind Lynch. So far as I was concerned John's death meant that any marriage would be postponed indefinitely.

In the spring of 1941 I was awarded my 'jacket' and posted from 7th Field to an RHA regiment, the 11th HAC stationed in Surrey. The HAC was a territorial regiment, the oldest in the army and based in the City of London. It had been an officer-producing unit and on the outbreak of war 80% of the soldiers including almost all the NCOs had been granted commissions. The War Office offered the regiment three hundred regular reservists, but the HAC refused to take them, saying that they would prefer to recruit their own men. This meant that when I joined them even the senior NCOs had no more than one year's service. After Dunkirk the regiment had become the artillery of 1st Armoured Division and had been sent on a firing practice camp at Larkhill, attended by some very senior gunner officers, including Alan Brooke who at that time was Commander-in-Chief Home Forces. The camp was a disaster. Everything went wrong and it was decreed that either the HAC should be replaced in 1st Armoured Division by a regular RHA regiment or most of the senior TA officers should be replaced by regulars. The latter course being decided, I arrived with half-a-dozen other regulars with the regiment. At first nothing could have been more difficult. The HAC were a proud regiment with a long tradition and a good record of service in the Great War and they resented what they saw as a bunch of young regulars being sent to teach them their business.

In July, 1st Armoured Division was put under orders for the Middle East. By this time the regiment had moved to Hungerford and Judy and I had announced our engagement. What were we to do? It was a difficult decision. Prudence suggested that we should wait to marry until after the war, but Judy thought that if the worst happened she would prefer to be a widow rather than someone whose fiancé had been killed. So after much heart-searching we decided to marry as soon as the arrangements could be made. The regiment was visited at our camp at Chilton Foliat near Hungerford by the King and Queen. After inspecting the regiment they both had tea with us in the mess. I was lucky enough to sit at the same small table as the Queen. The Germans had just invaded Russia and for the first time we saw how we could win the war; if the Russians could hold and maul the German army. The Queen said, 'I dislike them both intensely. I hope they do beastly things to one another. I am sure they will.' This was the general feeling at the time. She also said that the King loved a day visiting the army. She said that visiting bombed towns and cities exhausted him.

Judy and I were married at Selworthy Church on 23rd August. John Dill, my best man, and I stayed the previous night at Dunster Castle with the Luttrells. It poured with rain all the morning and at luncheon Mrs. Luttrell said in her deep voice, 'If you marry a West Country girl you must expect to be married on a West Country day.' But as we left the church the sun came out in time for the reception at Lynch. My father's place was taken by his cousin Duncan Dunn, who proposed the health of the bride. Duncan should have reached high rank in the army, but developed an ulcer while commanding his battalion at Dunkirk. After the war he became commandant of the police college at Bramshill. His watchword for police work was 'Softly, softly', which was adopted as the title of the famous television series.

Molly Brine, a cousin of Judy's mother had lent us her house at Winchester, where we spent the weekend and then went to the Dorchester for a few days. There was a lull in the air-raids but London looked battered and tired with very little on sale in the shops. The blackout was one of the minor horrors of war. There was no lighting on the streets and the prostitutes stood in doorways in Piccadilly shining torches on their legs. Masks were fitted to the headlights of all cars, which dimmed the lights so that they were little better than sidelights. It was almost impossible to find a taxi. The tube stations were full of bunks where people slept during air-raids and the smell was appalling. But behind the blacked-out windows the restaurants and night clubs were in full swing. Most had floor shows and Judy and I went to the most popular: the Café de Paris, later demolished by a direct hit which killed or wounded most of the people there, including the famous singer, 'Snake Hips' Johnson; Quaglino's and the 400. The food was good, although we did not inquire too closely into the source of the meat. There were no bored-looking fat cats dining on expense accounts. Everybody was young, most of the men and some of the women in uniform. There were always people you knew and the atmosphere was vivacious, cheerful and full of real enjoyment.

Judy came back to Hungerford with me. We had found rooms in a charming little house about a mile outside the village, appropriately called Hidden Cottage. And there we lived until 23rd September, exactly one month after our marriage, when the regiment entrained in the evening at Hungerford for Glasgow to embark on our great adventure. Poor Judy stayed the night with friends of Sibyl Colvin's who lived near Hungerford and next day drove back to Lynch in my Hillman Minx. Our parting was far worse for her than me, for I had much of interest to look forward to and plenty to occupy my mind.

CHAPTER V

Convoy, 1941

As dusk was falling on 1st October we sailed down the Clyde and early next morning joined our convoy which was assembling off Northern Ireland. It was an awe-inspiring sight under the low clouds. There were merchant ships in all directions as far as the eye could see, forming into five or six long lines. Our naval escort consisted of an aircraft carrier, an AA cruiser and numerous destroyers and frigates. The German U Boat campaign was reaching its zenith and our convoy consisted of the whole 2nd Armoured Brigade group, the men in troopships and the armoured cars, tanks, guns and vehicles in fast cargo ships. For this was a fast convoy, much safer than the slow-moving ten-knot convoys of old merchant ships which were suffering terrible losses in the North Atlantic. We sailed in zig-zags to confuse the U boats, and were to go almost to Greenland before turning south and east across the North Atlantic.

Our ship was the *Samaria*, an old Cunarder built for the North Atlantic run, so that she had little deck space, which we found inhibiting when we reached the tropics. She was of course completely blacked out at night. I was embarrassed by the contrast between the accommodation available to the officers and the men. We were four to a cabin, with comfortable berths, and had access to all the first class accommodation, including the dining room with lavish menus which astonished us after wartime rations in England, spacious lounges and well-stocked bars. The men on the other hand lived, fed and slept on the troop decks. These were bare deck spaces with wooden tables and benches bolted to the deck and hammocks for sleeping. The food was plentiful but unappetising, mostly stew and no alcohol except for beer. For the first few days out the sea was rough and the ship pitched and rolled in the Atlantic swell. I have never been a good sailor and my frequent trips to the troop decks were purgatory. The atmosphere there was appalling, a mixture of stale sweat, bad air and vomit. Amazingly the troops were cheerful and accepted their conditions with a kind of resigned insouciance. I have always admired British soldiers, but never more than on board SS *Samaria*. One day I saw one of my troop sitting in the hurly-burly of the troop deck reading the bible.

We soon settled down to a regular routine on board. The mornings were spent doing what training we could, PT, medicine ball, morse code and lectures on desert warfare. But the rest of the day we spent sleeping, reading, playing chess and drinking in the evenings. We wore life-jackets all day and kept them handy at night. Amazingly by the end of the voyage we were very fit and the morale of the troops was high. I wrote to Judy every day an instalment of a long letter which I posted whenever we reached port.

We were a fortnight at sea before we saw land. The convoy called at Freetown for oiling and although we were not allowed ashore the sight of land delighted us. The North Atlantic is very monotonous at that time of year. The harbour was full of ships and native craft and our troops cheered and shouted and whistled at every one as we passed. We stayed four days at Freetown and towards the end it became hotter with spectacular thunderstorms inland at night.

When we sailed most of our escort had left us, as the U Boats had not penetrated in any numbers to the South Atlantic. We had the usual ceremony of 'crossing the line' as we passed the Equator. The party ended with a free-for-all water fight. It was astonishing that nobody was hurt, except for the odd scratch.

After about ten days we arrived at Cape Town where half the convoy was to stop for a week, while we sailed on to Durban. A band was playing as we arrived, with a line of motor cars drawn up on the quay. As soon as we stepped on shore we were welcomed by one of the lady car drivers, who drove us to her home and entertained us. 'Convoy week' at Durban was regarded by the locals as a form of war work and their hospitality was overwhelming. We were allowed ashore each day, returning to sleep on board. I spent most of my time on the beach or at the Durban Club playing tennis. By that time we were in our khaki drill tropical kits, ill-fitting baggy shorts and tropical pith helmets which did not make the troops look very imposing. The helmets were thrown away as soon as we reached our destination.

After our welcome break at Durban the other half of the convoy rejoined us and we sailed on up the east coast of Africa. By that time war with Japan was imminent and surface raiders were expected in the Indian Ocean. So the great battle cruiser HMS *Repulse* escorted our convoy. One glorious Sunday morning she left for Singapore with some ceremony. She sailed up and down the lines of the convoy manning ship, her Marine band playing on the deck. We were at boat stations. As she passed each ship her ship's company gave 'three cheers' and we cheered back. Little did any of us think, as she sailed away towards the east, that within a month she would be at the bottom of the sea with HMS *Prince of Wales*, both sunk by Japanese bombers off the coast of Malaya, and we would have lost most of our tanks and guns.

We called at Port Sudan and Aden, at both places being allowed ashore. Port Sudan was a hot dusty place, which smelt of the east. Inevitably we gravitated to the club, where they still played polo, and watched a game between one of our cavalry regiments and the local club, all mounted on Somali ponies and umpired by our colonel. The native town was teeming with people who, as I wrote to Judy, all seemed busy 'either saying their prayers or cooking their supper'. I was impressed by the Moslem practice of prayers, noting that while our ship was being oiled by a local tanker, one of the crew knelt down and prayed, banging his head on the deck as he did so.

At Aden I took my troop ashore for marching and swimming and afterwards lunched at the Crescent Hotel. I wrote to Judy, 'Everybody in the East does a lot of talking. The natives all sit round in their cafés talking hard and the white men sit round in their clubs and hotels doing the same thing. I can quite see why anybody who has lived for long in these countries is never quite the same afterwards. They are absolute lords of creation and I can imagine how they must feel about retiring to a villa in Camberley or Cheltenham after living here with perfect servants and clean linen every day!' Aden was then a well-laid-out town, with well-planned streets and houses. But it was hot and dusty with very little green vegetation. We went to an open air cinema, with privet hedges dividing the different castes; natives, Lebanese shopkeepers, British soldiers and a wooden pavilion with small tables between the chairs for the British officers and officials. 'What should they know of England who only England know?'

The convoy dispersed at Aden, each ship sailing alone up the Red Sea to avoid bombing. We arrived at Port Tewfik on 5th December, over two months since we had left England. We were all relieved to leave the ship and looked forward to doing the job for which we had been trained and for which we had come so far.

By the time we left the *Samaria* I felt I had been accepted by the HAC. Our regular Colonel Ebbels, always known as the 'Baron' for his distinguished appearance and gracious manner, was a horse gunner of the old school who had served for some years with the Egyptian army. He always smoked Egyptian cigarettes. He was very popular with the regiment and got the best out of everyone. Our 'A' battery commander was John McDermid, a pre-war HAC officer who was a born leader of men. He was to lose an eye at Mersa Matruh. I had two excellent subalterns, 'Slogger' Armitage and Quentin Drage, who had both joined the regiment from OCTU early in the war. They were tall, Slogger with fair curly hair who affected a rather grand manner. We all three became great friends. Slogger was killed in circumstances which I shall describe shortly. Quentin was killed at the end of the war in an attack on the Gothic Line in Italy. The most able of the HAC officers was the battery captain, Geoff Armstrong, who ended the war with a DSO and MC as a lieutenant-colonel commanding a field regiment in Burma. He was a born soldier. The other troop commander was the charming Gerry de Boinville, who proved to be an outstanding forward observation officer (FOO) and later commanded a regular RHA battery. Another friend was Mark Wathen who, with his wife Rosemary, had welcomed Judy when she arrived as a bride at Hungerford. Mark took Holy Orders after the war and lives in a remote manse on the Isle of Skye.

There was an RAF detachment in the *Samaria* including Michael Judd, who had fought in the Battle of Britain and was on his way to command a fighter squadron in the desert. He had had a brilliant academic career and spent the voyage reading Proust in French. I liked him very much. He introduced me to the works of Damon Runyan.

My soldier servant was Frank Cook, who had joined 7th Field Regiment after Dunkirk and joined me thereafter. He came with me to the HAC. He had been valet to the South African millionaire Solly Joel and was the perfect 'gentleman's gentleman'. He even laid out my clothes on my camp bed in the desert. He adapted well to army life and was very popular with the other gunners. With me he managed to create an atmosphere of discreet omnipotence and to produce the aura of gracious living into the desert.

When we landed we found our mail, our first contact with home since we had left. Amongst it was a cable from Judy saying that she was expecting a baby in June. I have never experienced such a thrill of pleasure and delight. She later told me that she had overheard her mother and my father, who was staying at Lynch, discussing the event. Both agreed that it was a most irresponsible thing to have allowed to happen. But in those heady days life was too exciting and romantic to think of consequences. Anyway we both felt that the baby would be something for her to remember me by. All our letters were of course censored and we were not supposed to say where we were. Judy and I had however evolved a simple code: we each had an identical map of the Eastern hemisphere. When I wished to tell her where I was I would write a particular sentence in my letter, put the map over the corner of the notepaper and stick a pin through the place where I was. Judy had then only to put the letter over her map, and stick the pin through the hole so that it pierced the map. It worked well.

A day or two after we arrived I was given forty-eight hours leave to meet my father who had come down from Palestine. He had obviously done well and been awarded the CBE for his work in the Syrian campaign and afterwards commanding a horsed cavalry brigade. Then he fell ill and was medically down-graded so that he could not command troops in action. It was a sad blow as he was well placed for a senior gunner command or perhaps even command of an armoured brigade. Now he was awaiting a ship to take him home via South Africa to an administrative post in England.

We stayed at the Hotel Cecil in Alexandria and I developed gastric flu – so instead of forty-eight hours I remained there for about ten days.

Meanwhile the regiment had already been equipped and had left for the desert. The 'Crusader' battle had started in mid-November, Tobruk had been relieved and 2nd Armoured Brigade was to follow up the advance and join in the battle. I managed to get a lift with Tishy Benson, our second-in-command who had also been ill and had commandeered a staff car. He was a typical horse artilleryman, small and neat, who had achieved success race-riding before the war. He was also as brave as a lion. We set off from Alexandria along the only road, a single carriageway which ran along the coast, and spent the first night at a transit camp at Mersa Matruh. The first person I saw was Tim Llewellyn-Palmer dressed in suede desert boots, corduroy trousers, a knee-length tweed covert coat and an Old Etonian silk scarf round his neck to prevent desert sores from the sweat. The only indication that he was a soldier was a very battered Herbert Johnson service dress hat with a 7th Hussar badge. This style of dress was affected by 7th Armoured Division and we soon adopted it. Next day we drove on to Sidi Barrani. The Germans were still holding the pass at Halfaya over which the road ran, so we were obliged to turn off across the desert and my desert war began.

CHAPTER VI

Desert War, 1942

By the time we rejoined the regiment they had crossed the rusty barbed-wire fence, known as 'the Wire', which marked the frontier between Egypt and Libya, and were near the recent battlefield of Bir El Gubi, where our Yeomanry Brigade, 22nd Armoured, had had their first action about a month before against the Italian Ariete Division. When they viewed the enemy the gallant Yeomen had metaphorically drawn their swords, stood up in their stirrups and charged the enemy. The result was clear for us to see as we crossed the battlefield. A confused column of about fifty British tanks were sitting stationary and derelict in the sand with, at their head, a battery of damaged Italian guns with trenches and abandoned equipment lying around them. Some tanks were about a thousand yards from the guns and the column extended to within fifty yards of them. It was a sobering sight and described the battle better than any words.

2nd Armoured Brigade consisted of the Queen's Bays, 9th Lancers and 10th Hussars all in Crusader cruiser tanks with a 2-pounder gun, our regiment of towed 25-pounders, 1st (Motor) Battalion of the Rifle Brigade and a regiment of 2-pounder anti-tank guns mounted on unarmoured portees. My battery was with the Bays, commanded by Tom Draffen, in which my old friend George Rich was a captain. We moved in desert formation in three groups, each consisting of an armoured regiment (about fifty tanks), a battery of eight 25-pounders, a motor company, and an anti-tank battery of twelve guns. It was a splendid sight. The stream-lined tanks in a horse-shoe formation with the sand flowing up like bow waves on either side as they moved, the 25-pounders with their ungainly 'Quad' gun-towers in the centre and the motor company and anti-tank guns covering the rear. Because of the activity from the enemy air forces all tanks and vehicles moved widely dispersed, about a hundred yards apart and remained dispersed in 'open leaguer' when we halted during the day. At night we moved into 'close leaguer', closed up nose to tail in lines, with the tanks on the perimeter and the guns and 'soft-skinned' vehicles in the centre and Rifle Brigade listening posts at the corners of the leaguer. It was at night that we were replenished with food, petrol and ammunition by the supply echelon and it always seemed to me a miracle how they found the leaguers in the trackless desert.

All our vehicles had been fitted with sun compasses, which we had learnt to use on board the *Samaria*, but we soon abandoned them in favour of ordinary prismatic compasses, with the necessary adjustment from magnetic to true north. This method of navigation, using the milometers on our vehicles, was surprisingly accurate and we always seemed to reach the right place on our maps.

The regiment drove in this way seven hundred miles from the Delta to Saunu, training and manoeuvring as we went, getting to know our armoured regiment (ours was the Bays) and learning to overcome the problems of living in the desert. The desert is not flat, it is mostly rolling country interspersed with dry water courses or wadis, with prominent landmarks in the form of wells or birs and piles of stones marked on the map as 'Dancing Men'. The going varied from good gravel surfaces to hummocks of camel grass and soft sand. There were no trees and very few birds. As we moved west the going became worse and in some places there were rocks and boulders which made driving difficult. Every vehicle was equipped with sand tracks and spades, which we used if the vehicle became stuck in soft sand. The Quads were all supplied with winches.

We passed no buildings and the only signs of human habitation were the occasional bedouin encampments, with their black tents surrounded with camels, donkeys, emaciated looking goats and chickens. We were surprised at the amount of wildlife in the desert – as well as camels there were gazelle, which we would occasionally chase in our pick-up trucks or scout cars, although we never bagged one. It was a welcome contrast to fighting in Europe. No damaged buildings, no dead or wounded cattle, and above all none of the heart-rending scenes of frightened refugees which had been such a distressing feature of the retreat to Dunkirk. War in the desert was a paradise for the tactician and a nightmare for the quartermaster. Movement was uninhibited by natural features such as rivers or woods or built-up areas and wheeled vehicles were not confined to roads. The armies moved and fought more like naval fleets at sea than armies in European countries. But our railhead at that time was back near Mersa Matruh and all our supplies including water had to be brought across the desert in lorries, either from there or from the port at Tobruk when it was re-opened.

Because of our long communications our rations consisted of bully beef, biscuits, jam and the occasional tin of bacon, with half a gallon of water per man per day for all purposes. This meant three pint mugs of tea a day, the remaining pint being used for shaving and the dirty water went into the radiators. The weather was cold, especially at night, and we wore greatcoats over our battle dress. We managed a cheerful Christmas of bully beef and bacon washed down with beer after church parade. A ration of Christmas puddings arrived two days later.

When we reached Saunu we were told that we were to leave our armoured regiments, with whom we were beginning to form a close liaison, and move forward eighty miles to Agedabia to take over the front from 7th Support Group. We were

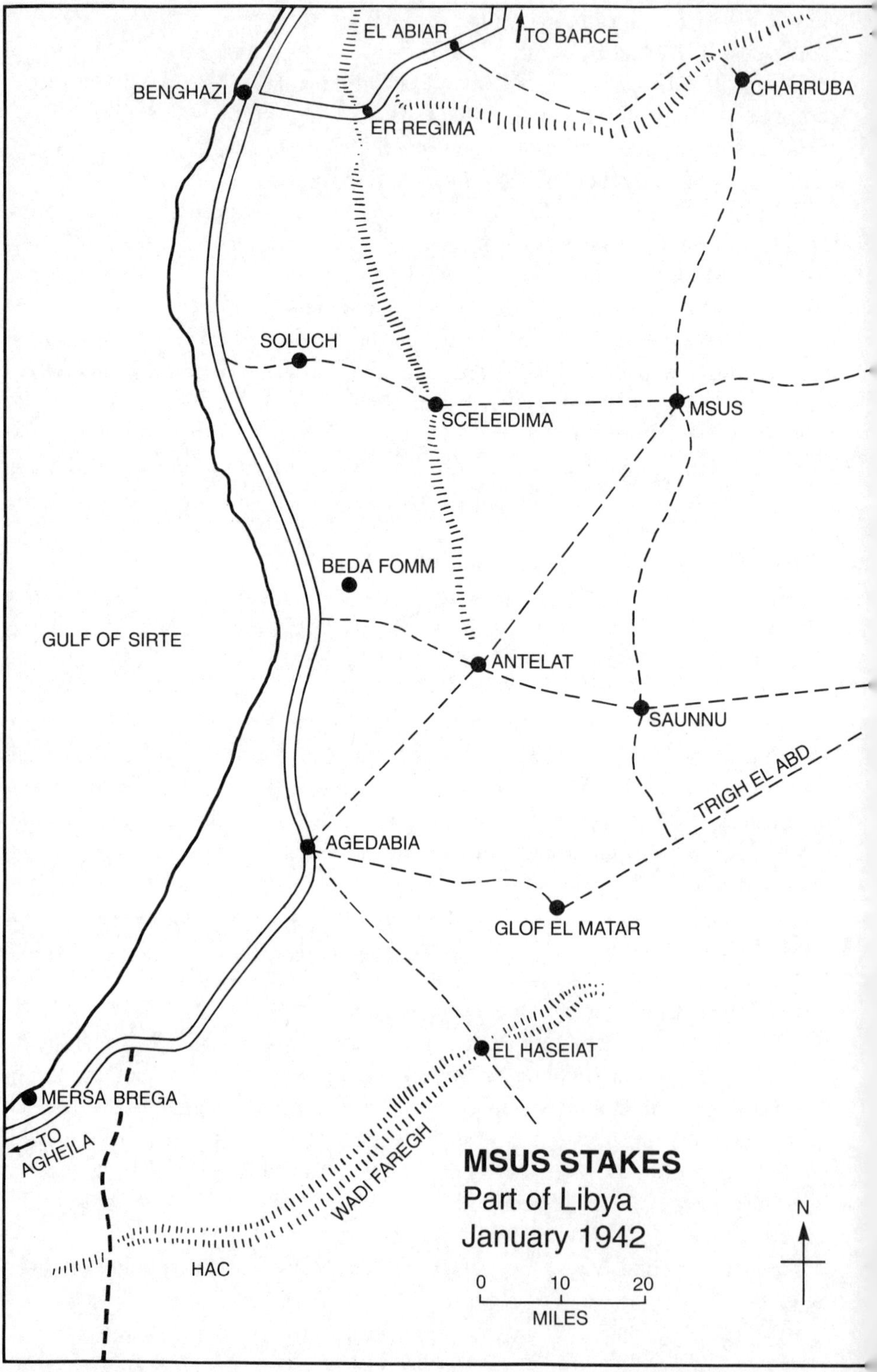

EL ABIAR

↑ TO BARCE

BENGHAZI

CHARRUBA

ER REGIMA

SOLUCH

SCELEIDIMA

MSUS

GULF OF SIRTE

BEDA FOMM

ANTELAT

SAUNNU

TRIGH EL ABD

AGEDABIA

GLOF EL MATAR

EL HASEIAT

MERSA BREGA

TO AGHEILA

WADI FAREGH

HAC

MSUS STAKES
Part of Libya
January 1942

N

0   10   20
MILES

to form 'Jock' columns. These had been invented by Jock Campbell, a horse gunner, in the early days when there was very little armour in the desert. Each column was based on a 25-pounder battery, with a motor company, anti-tank guns and armoured cars. Their function was to dominate selected parts of the desert and to harass the Italians in their fortified camps. They had been very successful, but were unable to compete with tanks. If tanks came out in any strength the column would withdraw leap-frogging back by troops each covering the other and trying to avoid getting pinned. The effect of this change of plan was that the armour lost their artillery and motor infantry and we lost our tanks.

The country where we were to operate between Agedabia and the Wadi Faregh consisted of some of the worst going in the whole desert. Rolling dunes of soft sand interspersed with hummocks of camel grass extended for about thirty miles. The armoured cars sensibly refused to drive in it and we were given a squadron of tanks from 22nd Armoured Brigade for our protection, but as soon as the battle started they moved off to the east and we never saw them again.

We were told that the Germans had lost almost all their tanks and were covering Mersa Bregha with light forces. The plan was that as soon as the ports of Tobruk and Benghazi were operating our division, consisting of 2nd and 22nd Armoured Brigades and 20th Guards Brigade together with the South African infantry division, would advance to Tripoli. But shortly before Christmas a column of German tanks had appeared at Antelat and given 22nd Armoured Brigade a bloody nose. So we were wary.

When we took over from 7th Support Group I visited their HQ with messages from my father to Jock Campbell, their brigadier. He had just been awarded the VC for his inspired leadership at Sidi Rezegh. I arrived in a sandstorm and the HQ looked like a bedouin camp – and the men like scarecrows. I found Jock sitting under a tarpaulin looking clean and well-dressed in his battledress, brimming with confidence. His staff told me that he had won the VC three times over, driving about the battlefield standing up in his open staff car and leading tanks into the attack waving a flag. He implied that we should have little difficulty in occupying Tripoli. 'They have had the stropping of their lives,' he said. 'Keep them on the run.'

Our first two days on column were very quiet. The guns were in action in the sand-dunes south of Agedabia and I occupied an OP from which I could see occasional movement of the enemy. On the morning of 21st January while we were cooking breakfast I heard from behind the dunes in front the throbbing of tank engines and soon afterwards shells started falling round my OP. Then I saw odd tanks appearing over the dunes ahead. After a few minutes I counted about forty. I reported to John McDermid over the wireless and a few minutes later he ordered, 'Tank alert. Prepare to withdraw.' By this time I was under machine-gun fire, so got permission to move back. The tanks followed. Soon I saw our guns. They were trying to move back, but movement was very slow. Vehicles were repeatedly having to be dug out of soft sand

and the Quads could in some cases only move the guns by winching. We tried to carry out an orderly retreat, moving from one position to the next and delaying the enemy as much as we could by fire. But this was almost impossible, the gun platforms buckled in the soft sand, the tie-bars broke, radiators boiled and half-shafts fractured. The guns soon came under fire. One after another the guns were hit or their tyres punctured. In the afternoon, by the time we were clear of the sand dunes, the battery had lost five out of its eight guns and many vehicles, but by this time we were clear of the enemy tanks – probably they had had as much difficulty with the going as we had. After a few miles of good going we came to a depression of soft sand and the same process of winching and digging started again. As the men worked to keep the vehicles moving two groups each of about fifteen Stuka dive bombers appeared overhead and came screaming down releasing their bombs on our stricken battery. By this time the tanks had closed up again and although we engaged them over open sights from the depression where we were stuck, yet another gun received a direct hit, leaving us with only two guns. Eventually we managed to get clear of the depression and after driving for a further ten miles formed close leaguer at about 6.30 pm. It had been a disastrous baptism of fire for the HAC.

The next day was quiet and we moved north-east for about thirty-five miles over good going to near Saunu. We hoped that what we had experienced the day before might have been a reconnaissance in force, or Rommel Flurry, a tactic he had previously employed against the Jock columns. But never before in soft sand so that they could not get away. But it was not to be. Next day, the 23rd, as we were continuing our retreat north-east I saw about forty-five enemy tanks moving to attack our supply echelon which was ahead of us. We were ordered to delay the tanks to enable the echelon to get clear. It was late afternoon when we dropped into action with some 25-pounders of the Transvaal Horse Artillery who had joined us. I normally travelled in my wireless truck a mile or two behind the battery to keep a lookout to the rear, but was driven into the guns by about thirty-five tanks which moved towards the guns from hull down positions with the setting sun behind them, closing in and probing round our flanks.

When I arrived at the guns the colonel was standing behind them wearing a red and blue RHA forage cap. He told me that the South Africans were not firing and to find out why. I drove over to their position (there was a full battery in action) and found them lying behind their guns with the tanks moving in. I asked the officer in charge why the hell they were not firing. He said they had not been trained to fire over open sights. I said, 'It's not very difficult. I will show you.' I got into the layer's seat of one of the guns, told the sergeant to load, lined the telescopic sight up on a German tank, estimated the range and fired. By the grace of God the round hit the tank first shot. I got out of the layer's seat and said to the South Africans, 'Now you get on and do it.' By the time I drove away from them the South Africans were banging merrily away at the tanks.

When I got back to our two guns the colonel was still standing calmly in the same place, with machine-gun bullets and bits of armour-piercing shot flying all round. I am sure they were aiming at his red hat. I told him about the South Africans and immediately afterwards was hit on the right ribs by a piece of armour-piercing shot. It was only a glancing blow, but painful. The colonel said, 'There are too many officers here already. Collect all the men and vehicles you can and rally a thousand yards behind the gun position. And get that wound dressed.'

As I left the gun position I could see the German tanks closing in on our two guns, firing their machine-guns. I heard later that one gun was soon knocked out and that Slogger Armitage the GPO had got into the layer's seat and fired the one remaining gun. Quentin Drage and Tishy Benson, who had no business to be there, acted as ammunition numbers, the whole detachment having been killed or wounded. Although the gun had been hit, jamming the elevating gear, and all the armour-piercing shot had been used, Slogger continued to fire high explosive at the approaching tanks. Eventually he was hit, saying to Tishy, 'Sorry Major, I'm no good now – I can't feel my legs.' He was lifted out of the layer's seat. By this time the tanks were on the gun position and Quentin and Tishy, both of whom were wounded, lay beside the gun feigning death. The tanks drove through the position, machine-gunning as they went, and as soon as it was dark Quentin and Tishy hobbled and crawled away. They met some friendly bedouin next morning and were eventually picked up by 10th Hussars. Slogger was posted missing but must have died on the gun position.

This was a desperate action, comparable to that of 'L' Battery at Néry in 1914, 'K' Battery at Hondeghem in 1940 and other Horse Artillery epics. Like so many military epics it had arisen from bad generalship. To have separated us from our tanks and sent the guns into the sand dunes were acts of criminal folly, which cost many lives and much loss of equipment.

Next day a Dodge truck arrived driven by George Buchanan who had been in charge of the supply echelon on the first day. They had been overrun and George and others had been captured. As an officer George had been kept for interrogation. He was put into the Dodge which had been captured from us and was being used by the German fitters. They were part of the Marcks Group which were leading the German advance against us and George was with them for two or three days. Because of their rapid advance there was no chance of interrogation. He said they were good people to be with. The rations were plentiful and varied and came up on time; above all the mail from Germany only took ten days. Their morale was very high and their discipline strict, the officers wearing riding breeches and field boots. At night the leaguers were lit up by constant flares and lights. After a few days the Dodge stuck in some soft sand. The sergeant fitter, who was driving, got out to supervise the digging out, leaving George sitting in the passenger seat with the engine still running. George slipped across into the driver's seat, engaged the gears and drove off at speed across the desert. Immediately there was a clatter of machine-gun fire behind him, caused by two co-axially mounted machine-guns in the back of the truck which had jammed – but started firing as soon as he drove off. The effect on the German fitters of their truck disappearing over the horizon, with its guns firing at them over the tail, must have been alarming. George, wearing an Afrika Korps cap, drove on past the column of tanks, edging away from it as he drove. The Germans must have become suspicious as he was chased by an armoured car which fired a bullet through the door which fortunately passed under George's legs. Eventually he caught up with what was left of the battery – and became my GPO in place of Slogger. He was utterly imperturbable with a dry sense of humour and ended the war in command of a regular RHA battery. We took the Dodge on to the troop strength – and very useful it was in spite of the bullet-hole in the door, which we left unrepaired as a talisman.

The next two days remain confused in my memory. The MO dressed my wound and I did not have to leave the battery. Second Armoured Brigade deprived of their artillery support had been badly mauled at Saunu and lost many tanks. We drove east across the desert in small groups of mostly soft-skinned vehicles, with the German armoured columns swooping like packs of wolves among flocks of sheep. We felt particularly vulnerable – gunners without guns. The retreat became known as the Msus Stakes compared with the Benghazi Handicap of the previous year. Many legends grew up around it. My favourite was of the petrol lorry which was told to drive due east on a compass bearing of 90°. When they ran out of petrol they filled up from the store they carried. After several days they reached a metalled road and soon saw a town with a sign 'Khartoum'.

Eventually we reached Gazala where a front had been formed behind a minefield running from the sea to Bir Hacheim. My troop was ordered to escort some prisoners back to the railhead. There were a few Germans and hundreds of Italians, who were completely demoralised, sitting in the sand crying, 'Aqua – Aqua.' There was a feldwebel or sergeant-major with the Germans, whom I put in charge. He failed to salute me and I said, 'Don't they teach you to salute in the German army? I thought you were professionals.' Whereupon he shouted, 'Jawohl, Herr Kapitan', threw me a terrific salute and took complete charge of the prisoners, making them dig slit trenches at night to avoid air attack and explaining exactly what they were to do each day. He was a very high-class NCO. Among the Germans was an officer who had escaped twice; we kept him tied to a stretcher since he had already shot two of his guards and we were taking no chances. We then went to a camp by the sea east of Tobruk, where in a remarkably short time we were re-equipped and brought up to strength with drafts from the base depot and our own wounded back from hospital. Our rations improved dramatically. Tinned fruit was especially popular, until everyone developed bumps and boils over their bodies caused by a sudden increase of sugar in our diet. Soon we moved back into the desert to rejoin the regiment and 2nd Armoured Brigade, which was in reserve behind the Gazala line.

There followed three months of desert training, digging gun positions and columns. The enemy had not closed up to the minefield and there was an open flank to the south. The batteries of the regiment took turns to patrol these open spaces with armoured cars, a squadron of tanks and the usual motor company and anti-tank guns. There was little serious fighting (although one troop was over-run in a Rommel Flurry) and we gradually became desert-worthy. We lived and messed on our vehicles with our crews. We slept beneath the stars, the officers on camp beds, the men on the ground. There were no latrines. We simply walked out into the desert with a spade. Our main pleasure was to receive our mail, which took up to three months for sea mail, although air mail letters took three weeks and an airgraph, which was a photographed air mail letter reduced to the size of a postage stamp and then enlarged on arrival, took only ten days. We were allowed a ration of cables.

We felt very isolated from our homes and families; we had no idea how long we would be in the desert, or how long the war would last, or when we would see our families again – if ever. We were serving an indeterminate sentence and unlike serving in France there was no home leave. We acquired a kind of jocular self-pity. The letters MEF ('Middle East Force') were translated into 'Men England Forgot'. There was a popular story of the soldier who said to his chum, 'Isn't it wonderful. I've been out here eighteen months, and my wife has just had a baby.' But reading my letters to Judy I am astounded that in almost every one I said that now that the Russians and Americans were both in the war it would soon be over and I would be home by the end of 1942. Perhaps a triumph of hope over reality.

The 8th Army was quite small in those days, only three British divisions with Indians, Australians, New Zealanders and South Africans together with a few Free French making up the majority. We felt that we were in a way a race apart, with our own customs and language and standards. Every article of equipment was important. 'Scrounging', or stealing by finding to put it more accurately, was our principal diversion. Derelict vehicles were cannibalised and an unguarded vehicle was soon 'won' by some scrounger. After the January débacle we did not have much confidence in our leaders or our equipment; we admired Rommel and had respect for the Afrika Corps as clean fighters. But we had immense pride in our own regiments and those of our brigade and in our ability to 'see off' the enemy in spite of everything. We were pretty bloody-minded.

During this time Jamie Shiel joined the battery as my driver. He had originally been a Durham miner who like so many others had joined the army during the depression of the 1930s. He became my father's soldier servant at Catterick and followed him through his various promotions and moves. When my father was invalided home from the Middle East he arranged for Shiel to be posted to the HAC. It was good to have an old family friend with me.

We hardly ever changed our clothes and only very occasionally bathed in the sea. One day, when we were near the Trigh Capuzzo I managed to 'scrounge' a tin bath and enough water to fill it. As I was enjoying my bath a truck stopped on the Trigh beside me and out stepped a girl in corduroy trousers and a shirt. It was Kit Tatham-Warter, sister of my old school friend Digby and a successful point-to-point rider. Women were not allowed by the British in the forward areas, but she had joined Lady

Spears's ambulance unit attached to the Free French, who were not so particular about such things. I was so surprised to see her that I stood up in my bath stark naked. 'Oh please, Robin, do sit down,' she said, and told me she had been visiting her brother John who was adjutant of the Bays and had told her that I was nearby. John was killed shortly afterwards during the Knightsbridge battle.

With the spring came a few showers of rain, causing the desert to bloom into life. A profusion of brightly-coloured wild flowers appeared in the Ghatts or low-lying places. At the same time we were plagued by the dreaded Khamsin, a hot wind which blew from the Sahara causing frequent sand-storms. The more the surface of the desert was broken by our vehicles, the more the sand whirled and eddied round us. Everything became impregnated with sand – our boots, our clothes, our food, our hairbrushes and worst of all our toothbrushes. To be in the Khamsin was like sitting in the path of a large and continuous blow-dryer.

In April I had a week's leave in Alexandria. I booked in to the Hotel Cecil and rang up Dorothy Peel who at once asked me to stay. Bobbie Peel had been a gunner and served in Ireland with my father before the Great War. The family were old, established cotton brokers in Alexandria and they lived in a most comfortable house with a large garden. It was marvellous to feel really clean again after four months in the desert, to sleep between sheets and to eat fresh well-cooked food. The Peels kept an open house to friends from the desert and their visitors' book seemed to contain the names of everyone in 8th Army from the GOC to the latest joined subaltern. I had hardly recovered from the desert and was just beginning to enjoy civilised life when it was time to return to the regiment.

When I arrived it was obvious that something big was about to happen. Each of our armoured regiments had been equipped with a squadron of the new American General Grant tanks, much superior to anything they had had before. The Grant carried a 75-mm gun with limited traverse mounted in the hull and a 37-mm anti-tank gun with all-round traverse in the turret. Our regiment had been given General Stewart or 'Honey' tanks for our OPs in place of the unarmoured wireless trucks in which we had been expected to move with the tanks in an armoured battle. About a hundred of the new 6-pounder anti-tank guns, much superior to the 2-pounder pop-guns, had been issued to the anti-tank regiments and the motor battalions. 4th Armoured Brigade of 7th Armoured Division, two-thirds of whose tanks were Grants, had returned to the desert. And there were two tank brigades with Valentines and Matildas which, although they only carried 2-pounders, were comparatively heavily armoured, in addition to our own 2nd and 22nd armoured brigades.

Malta was blockaded and under heavy bombardment from the air and I had heard in Alexandria of the terrible casualties suffered by the navy in trying to keep the sea lanes open. It was obvious that we must capture the Axis airfields in the Jebel country east of Benghazi, both to deny them to the enemy and to use them ourselves to provide air cover for our coastal convoys between Tobruk and Malta. At the same time we knew that, despite the efforts of the navy, Rommel had been reinforced and was expected to attack us to try to capture Tobruk and destroy 8th Army.

CHAPTER VII

The Battle of Knightsbridge and South Africa, 1942

K nightsbridge was the name given to the point at which the desert track from Acroma to Bir Hacheim crossed the Trigh Capuzzo. A large area of desert round the cross-tracks had been made into a strongpoint or Box, an unfortunate name since the defenders were in the end literally boxed in. Tactically it was a good position, standing on the top of an escarpment to the north, with extensive views over the whole desert in all directions. It was held by our Guards brigade with the 25-pounders of the 2nd Horse Artillery, anti-tank guns and a battery of Bofors light anti-aircraft guns. Everyone was dug deeply into the sand and the defences were surrounded by barbed-wire and mines. The box had two functions: to act as a long stop behind the Gazala minefield, which was held by two infantry divisions, and to form a pivot on which our armoured brigades could manoeuvre in the event either of an Axis breakthrough along the Trigh Capuzzo towards Tobruk, or of a wide turning movement by Axis armour to the south of Bir Hacheim directed north behind the minefield (see map p. 271).

As during the retreat to Dunkirk I kept a daily log of the battle, which I wrote up in diary form a month or two later. I have quoted extensively from my diary and relied entirely upon it in writing a detailed account of the battle, which appears at Appendix 2 (p. 270).

Knightsbridge was a battle of missed opportunities. Its loss led to the fall of Tobruk and the long retreat by 8th Army to within sixty miles of Alexandria. On the night 26th/27th May the Afrika Korps moved round the south of Bir Hacheim, brushing aside 4th Armoured Brigade who had been taken by surprise and were moving into their battle positions, and by 9 am had reached Rigel, and the Knightsbridge box. Thereafter we had the best of the battle for the next three days, but gradually lost the initiative, which passed to the Germans on 5th June. Then it was only a question of time before we were beaten. Re-reading my diary I am struck by how late in the day we always seemed to move. The mornings passed relatively quietly, we did not usually move until after midday at the height of the mirage when observation was difficult, and were not in position until about 4 p.m, leaving only a couple of hours before the light started to fade.

On 27th May, although the tanks of the Afrika Korps were reported on Rigel by 9 am, we did not move until midday so we were unable to complete the destruction of the lorried infantry before dark. On 28th, instead of following up our success of the previous day at first light (we heard later that the German tanks on Rigel were out of petrol), we did not move until the afternoon, although we could see the unarmoured column to our west, and achieved virtually nothing that day. By 29th the Germans, though caught off balance, had refuelled and reorganised themselves and were able to withstand our armoured attacks of that day and 30th. If the night attack by 5th Indian Division had gone in as planned on the night of 31st May or even 1st June it might well have succeeded. But it was postponed for no less than five days, by which time the Axis forces had firmly established their bridgehead at Bir Aslag, had overrun 150th Brigade and opened a gap for their supplies through our minefield.

When the attack eventually went in on 5th June it was against the whole of the Afrika Korps and the Ariete Division in prepared positions. At the time we could not understand why the threat to Tobruk posed by that force could not have been masked by infantry, our two army tank brigades and the 6-pounder anti-tank guns, while our armoured brigades either attacked in the north due west across the minefield or made a wide circling movement south of Bir Hacheim, striking north into the enemy's rear areas. Jock columns of 7th Motor Brigade from the south and South African armoured cars from the north did in fact operate in those areas, causing considerable havoc among the Axis rear echelons. Our three armoured brigades used in this way could have cut the enemy's communications and forced his armour to withdraw across the minefield. But we simply butted our heads against the strongest part of the enemy's position without any attempt at manoeuvre.

The contrast between our movements and those of the Germans is striking. Although they were undoubtedly surprised by the effectiveness of our Grant tanks and 6-pounder anti-tank guns during the first three days fighting, they soon regrouped and organised a strong bridgehead over the minefield. When we attacked on 5th June, Rommel was not content just to beat off the attack. He reacted immediately, sending 15th Panzer Division to the north and 21st Panzer Division to the south to encircle and destroy the attacking force. This was the turning point of the battle, although we did not realise it at the time. Then Rommel overwhelmed the gallant and unsupported Free French at Bir Hacheim and once that southern bastion of our defences had been eliminated pushed his armour rapidly north-east, defeating our remaining armour on 12th June at Point 169 leaving his way clear for Tobruk.

Rommel was always in touch with the changing situation. He travelled on the first day just behind the Afrika Korps, east of the minefield, and was in the bridgehead himself throughout. The system of command in 8th Army was very different. Command was exercised through a triumvirate consisting of the GOC Neil Ritchie recently appointed from the staff of GHQ Cairo, and the two Corps Commanders Willoughby Norrie and Strafer Gott, both of whom were senior to him and more experienced in command. Their headquarters were located close together and well east of the battlefield, south of El Adem. While Rommel was bold and enterprising, sometimes to the point of rashness, they were cautious and determined not to take any risk which might uncover the road to Tobruk. Instead of initiating moves they reacted to those of Rommel. By the time they had received reports of the situation in the morning, decided what action to take and transmitted orders to the fighting troops, it was too late for those orders to be put into full effect.

Willoughby Norrie believed in relying on the man on the spot. That is to say leaving difficult decisions, whether to withdraw or surrender or stand and fight, to brigade and even lower commanders directly involved. Strafer Gott had a reputation in the desert second only to Jock Campbell who had been his immediate subordinate, but by this time had been tragically killed in a motor accident just after obtaining command of 7th Armoured Division. Strafer had been in the desert continuously commanding 7th Support Group, 7th Armoured Division and finally 13th Corps, since the Italians declared war in June 1940. When I saw him shortly before the battle he appeared exhausted. Willoughby relied much on his judgement and experience and was reluctant to move without his approval.

I found it intriguing that those two should have been so closely associated in such influential and important positions at this time. Sibyl Colvin had told me that before she married Strafer Pam had been very fond of Willoughby and would gladly have married him had he not already been happily married. If that formidable woman had been with them in the desert at Knightsbridge I cannot help feeling that there would have been more decision in the command of 8th Army. I heard after the war that Strafer had 'told' Pam from the grave that when he was appointed to command 8th Army he was very tired and could never have achieved what Monty achieved at El Alamein. I fear he was right.

My own feelings and reactions to the battle are described in my diary. Unlike war in Europe we could see the enemy and the fighting was fast-moving, so that our experiences were more like those of 18th- and 19th-century battles, except that with our long range weapons we were operating thousands of yards from the enemy instead of hundreds. And there was a certain sense of chivalry between 8th Army and the Afrika Korps, which was lacking in Europe. I found the battle exhilarating. There was virtually no fighting or movement at night, so we were not short of sleep, and even at that time of year the desert air was clean and fresh and gave a feeling of well-being. Nor was the holding of ground of itself of prime importance. It was a battle of movement and if things became unpleasant one could always move somewhere else. I enjoyed the technique of an FOO, finding my way alone across the desert to a suitable OP, watching the fall of shot and correcting the fire on to the target. Above all I enjoyed the easy companionship of my tank crew and the feeling of relaxation when at night we moved into close leaguer.

Ever since I had been wounded in the knee on 14th June as described in my diary, I had suffered agony of mind over Judy. Her baby was due on 15th and we were incommunicado. Amazingly during the battle our mail had arrived regularly with the rations, but now my mail would not come through. I realised that she would know that I was in the battle and would have heard of the fall of Tobruk on 20th June – so she would be worrying. I sent a cable giving my address as soon as I arrived at the base hospital near Tel-El-Kebir, but it did not get through, so I sent another which did not arrive until 1st July. At last on 6th July I received a cable, 'Your daughter arrived 19th – Midday – Weight 7 lbs 11 ozs – Very good – both well.' I cannot describe my delight at this news. When the baby was born Judy did not know where I was or even if I was alive, so she called the baby Jennifer Robin Allan in case of the worst. I had ordered a sapphire and diamond eternity ring from Tessier, the Bond Street jeweller, to be sent to Judy's mother to be given to her when the baby arrived. Once we were again in touch airgraphs and cables came through regularly. It was a great relief.

One morning in the hospital I was sitting up in bed eating a boiled egg for breakfast when a large white maggot crawled out of the top of my plaster. I screamed for the nurse who hurried me into the theatre where my plaster was removed. My wound looked like a clean piece of butcher's meat, with a small colony of fat white maggots inside it. This was just before the days of pennicilin. The surgeon told me that in the Great War I would not have been in plaster, but have had dressings which had to be changed twice daily, a most painful process. During the Spanish Civil War a wounded soldier had lain out for several days and when he had been recovered his wound had been cleaned by maggots. So the technique was developed of fertilising maggots inside a plaster and leaving the cleaning of the wound to them. I had noticed a smell of putrid flesh coming from my leg for several days, and said to the surgeon, 'You might have told me.' He said it was better not, as most people did not like the idea of maggots in their wounds. Usually the plaster was removed before the maggots had cleaned the wound completely and so run out of food.

On 10th July I was told that I was to be evacuated to South Africa next day. Rommel was only sixty miles from Alexandria and it was the time of the 'big flap' when all the secret files at GHQ in Cairo were burnt and all seriously wounded were evacuated. We were taken on board an old British India boat which had been converted to a hospital ship.

We sailed down the Red Sea with a following wind so that it was very hot on board; mercifully there was no blackout, although we were dubious whether the Japanese, said to be operating in the Indian Ocean, would respect the Red Cross we carried. We stopped at Aden. It always amused me that whenever a troopship came into port our troops would line the rails shouting and whistling and making ribald remarks to anybody in a skirt or sari. As we glided into harbour we passed close to a US troopship crammed with American troops, the first we had seen. They were standing on deck, absolutely silent watching our men on their crutches, some without limbs or in body plasters. One of our boys shouted across the narrow stretch of water between us, 'Look what's f – ing coming to you.'

There were several kindred spirits on board. Ralph Campbell of the Cameron Highlanders had a shattered arm. He was tall and fair with the air of a highland laird, and always wore his tartan kilt.

Then there was Michael Halsted of the Bays who had lost an eye on 27th May who we called 'The Parson' and Michael Hawkins of the 10th Hussars who had lost an arm with the squadron which had lost all their tanks on 29th. He became Equerry to the Duke of Gloucester. Finally there was Roy Farran of the 3rd Hussars who had had a machine-gun bullet through his wrist. Although he was only twenty-one Roy had already won the MC and bar and had been wounded four times. Roy was excellent company, always laughing and making outrageous remarks. He was very attractive to women and enjoyed many escapades when we reached South Africa. He was also highly intelligent, as well as being brave and resourceful.

On 25th July we arrived at Mombasa where we were allowed ashore. We went to the club, overlooking the harbour, where we met a series of people out of Africa who might have been characters in an Evelyn Waugh novel. They were extremely hospitable and good company. A lady called Jane, with whom we lunched the following day, was said to be the only woman in the RAF. She had been flying with the local Auxiliary Squadron and when war broke out had been commissioned into the RAF by mistake due to a clerical error. The authorities had tried to persuade her to take a commission in the WAAF but she had refused, saying, 'My commission in the RAF is signed by the King, and unless he throws me out in the RAF I stay.' It was difficult to know who was married to whom and they all had a prodigious capacity for alcohol. One man told us with pride that he had been court-martialled seven times. We were sorry to leave and all collapsed into our cots and fell asleep before the ship sailed. It had been a memorable interlude.

About three weeks after leaving Suez we arrived at Durban and were taken by ambulance to Oribi Military Hospital at Pietermaritzburg. This was an enormous complex built on a hill overlooking the town. It was staffed by a collection of beautiful girls, all very smart in their uniforms, who were not supposed to fraternise with the patients, a rule more honoured in the breach than in the observance. The exception was our ward sister, who was a splendid down-to-earth woman with a biting wit and a kind heart. She was a Canadian and wore the smart blue uniform of the Canadian nursing service. The South Africans were incensed by the fall of Tobruk where a South African division had surrendered. They particularly blamed its commander, who they said had a German wife and had always been pro-German, even suggesting that he was a traitor. There was at that time a strong pro-German element in the Nationalist Party. We did not see much of the country, but the road to Durban through the valley of a thousand hills was in those days particularly beautiful. It was a Zulu native reserve with superb views and trees coming right down to the road on either side. At nights, staying outside Durban, we could hear the beautiful rhythmic singing of the natives floating across the darkness and proclaiming the soul of Africa. Although it was winter the garden flowers, especially azalea and bougainvillea, were full of colour.

These were pre-apartheid days, but I remember thinking that fearful problems faced the country after the war. Most people in Natal were of British descent and they despised what they called 'the Boers' or Afrikaners. Most of the shopkeepers, some very affluent, were Indian. But I was told that they were not allowed entry to the club and that if an Indian bought a house in one of the smart suburbs everyone in the street would put his house up for sale. Then, all around, was a sullen shabby mass of blacks who were called Kaffirs, most of whom were in fact Zulus – that proud military race. The domestic servants were excellent and well treated, but the others were regarded as part of the indigenous wildlife, though of less interest.

In September I had a medical board. The doctor said, 'You would like to go home, wouldn't you?' He told me it would be several months before I was passed A1 and I might just as well convalesce at home with my wife and daughter as in South Africa, or at a desk job in the Middle East. A humane man. Roy Farran was also posted home and I determined that if we were torpedoed I would join the same life raft as Roy, as whatever the vicissitudes we would somehow survive.

We went by train to Cape Town and, after a couple of days seeing Table Mountain and the other sights of that beautiful city, we boarded a spacious Union Castle boat which had been converted to accommodate large numbers of troops. There were only one hundred and fifty on board, all wounded, and we were to run the gauntlet of the submarines unescorted, relying on our speed to evade trouble. The holds were full of oranges for the babies of Britain and a few days out the OC troops asked Roy and I to organise a guard over the oranges as there had already been much pilfering by the crew. One night after dinner Roy suggested that we should go down to the holds to see what was happening. We sat behind some crates of oranges and after a little heard footsteps. Roy whispered, 'Give me your crutch.' A figure then appeared round the corner of the stacked crates and Roy brought the crutch down on his head with all his strength. The man dropped like a felled ox and lay breathing heavily on the deck. I said, 'I do hope you haven't killed him.' Roy was completely calm and replied, 'Oh no. He'll be alright.' So we left and returned to the bar leaving him where he had fallen. But there was no more pilfering of oranges.

In the event we had an uneventful voyage, although a submarine was spotted west of Gibraltar, and arrived at Liverpool a little over a year after we had left in the *Samaria*, so full of hope and anticipation. It had been an eventful year for the HAC and for Judy and me.

CHAPTER VIII

Preparing for Invasion, 1943–44

Since the Gulf War I have heard of the so-called 'separation syndrome' said to have affected the families of those who served in that war, involving as it did three months' separation and three days' fighting with minimal casualties. The returning men were said to be 'different', their wives finding it difficult to 'relate' to them, and the situation so serious that teams of 'counsellors' were set up to assist the troubled couples to 'come to terms' with and 'accept' the changed situation. My first reaction was one of disbelief, until I read an article in *The Times* by the wife of the commanding officer of one of our famous regiments saying that 'things would never be the same again' between them. She may have meant that the short separation and prospect of danger had brought them closer together, but then why call it a 'syndrome'? Assuming, however, that such a recognisable condition existed as to warrant the description, I am astonished. Human nature must have changed greatly in fifty years. Judy and I suffered no such problem and I never heard of anyone who did – unless, of course, there had been some reason, such as infidelity, apart from and additional to mere separation, which put the marriage under strain.

Our reaction on my return was of unalloyed pleasure at being together – if only for a comparatively short time – a determination to be together as much as possible, a feeling of thankfulness that I had survived and was not still in the Middle East and the delight of my seeing Jennifer and being able to spend some time with her. Jennifer until then had been entirely surrounded by women, apart from the occasional friendly 'coo' from the Lynch gardeners (one of whom she always called 'Coo-Coo') and at first she was nervous of me and did not want to come to me. It was not until after the war that I felt she was really relaxed and at home in my company.

Assisted by some robust physiotherapy (the beauties at Oribi had been too kind) my knee improved much quicker than expected. I was soon passed A1, posted back to 7th Field Regiment and promoted Acting Major in command of my old 16th Battery. All this pleased me very much. I had been recommended for the MC at Knightsbridge, but once again had been mentioned in despatches. But it was much better to be a major at the age of twenty-four in command of a regular battery.

Soon after I rejoined the regiment at Christchurch we moved to Kent as part of the anti-invasion force. There had been many changes since I left. Most of the regulars had left on promotion or for the staff. They had been replaced by a large batch commissioned from the HAC and some very good young officers from the OCTU (Officer Cadet Training Unit). Two of these, Richard Harrison and Bill Pakenham Walsh, obtained regular commissions after the war and reached high rank. The second-in-command was Mike Head, an old friend from Catterick, whose best man I later became. Mike was one of the very few pre-war gunner officers who was not interested in horses.

Shortly after I rejoined a new colonel arrived, Nigel Tapp, who had spent the war on the staff. Before the war he had served with the Sudan Defence Force, like many others who went 'bush whacking' to save some money after life in an expensive station. Nigel's quiet almost diffident manner concealed a will of steel. He did not know much about gunnery, having never commanded a battery, but he knew the basic essentials of training a regiment, and had the determination to put them into practice. He was an educated soldier and particularly keen on the training of officers, saying, 'There are no bad regiments, only bad officers' – and his first task was to weed out any whom he did not regard as suitable, including a battery commander. This at first caused some dismay in the regiment, but as we settled down to hard training he became more and more popular. He allowed us battery commanders great freedom in running our batteries, but insisted on his orders being obeyed to the letter. He was to prove an outstanding battle commander, completely calm and unruffled whatever the circumstances, and always clear and decisive in his orders. He eventually became a major-general and was knighted. It is a tribute to his personality that until his death almost fifty years later the regimental officers' dining club 1939–45 still attracted about twenty members at our annual dinner.

My battery sergeant-major was Arthur Lacey. His father had been RSM of the Cheshire Regiment and, on their fourteenth birthdays, each of his several sons were taken to the recruiting officer and enlisted for their 'boy service'. This service produced a high proportion of the warrant and non-commissioned officers who were the backbone of the pre-war regular army. They received a good education as well as being subject to strict discipline and learning all the basic military skills (often including a trade) until they were 18, when they could 'sign on' for up to 21 years 'men's' service. Arthur was a typical product of this system. He was in his uniform the smartest soldier I believe I ever saw. He had a fine athletic figure and had been middle-weight boxing champion of the army in India. Although no great intellect – he would never agree to go on a course – Arthur understood how to manage soldiers and was a strict disciplinarian. There was practically no 'military' crime in the battery largely due to his influence in maintaining the highest standards. I suspect that occasionally defaulters were given the option of being brought up before the major on a charge, or having three rounds with bare fists with the BSM behind one of the barrack huts. The troops called him 'Sandbag'.

In the spring of 1943 we were told that our division was to be one of the assault divisions for the invasion of the coast of north-western Europe and that we were to go to Scotland for intensive training in Combined Operations.

Soon after we arrived in Scotland we exchanged our towed 25-pounders for Priests, self-propelled American 105 mm guns mounted on a Sherman tank chassis, since no wheeled vehicles were to be allowed across the beach on 'D' Day. We also developed the technique of firing from our landing craft. A troop of four guns was loaded on to a tank landing craft (LCT) and the whole divisional artillery, consisting of seventy-two guns in eighteen LCTs, was to sail towards the beach firing and dropping the range as they 'ran in'. The regimental fire was observed by an officer (Hendrie Bruce) from a small personnel landing craft anchored before 'H' hour a mile or so from the beach. We practised this unique method of fire in the River Clyde, firing on a deserted part of the coast of Argyll. We stayed on the Isle of Bute at Rothesay, where Judy joined us and thoroughly enjoyed herself as the mess was established in a very good hotel which was still open. The whole procedure was extremely inaccurate, but it meant that before 'H' hour the beach would be covered by shellfire as well as bombs from the RAF. The principle was that everyone with a weapon should fire it as his landing craft approached the beach. The effect on the German's morale must have been considerable.

The SPs all had to be 'water-proofed' before loading on the LCTs in case of a 'wet landing', the water-proofing being blown off with a small charge once on shore. The exhaust gases were directed up a kind of chimney or shute which was fitted to the back of the vehicle so that they escaped vertically into the air, so as to avoid the danger of water entering the normal exhaust pipe below the vehicle. All this, especially on new guns with their different sights and their tank engines and tracks, required much hard training and practice before we mastered them. Also we continually practised our communications and fire and movement techniques and were constantly out training on the moors, firing our guns.

In the early spring of 1944 we moved to Fort George near Inverness for our final combined operations training. Even Judy failed to join me there, as we were obliged to sleep in the fort, so she sadly returned to Lynch. My grandfather had commanded the 1st Battalion of the HLI at the fort before the Great War and I found it a fascinating place, one of the few 18th-century fortresses, built at the height of European fortress-building, which exists in this country. While we were there we were visited by Monty. The whole brigade was formed up in hollow square on the parade ground. It was a bitterly cold though bright day and we wore no greatcoats. Monty alighted from his staff car wearing a leather fur-lined RAF jacket. As soon as he saw our dress he removed his jacket and handed it to his ADC Johnny Henderson of 12th Lancers, an old friend of mine. Johnny did not remove his British Warm and as he passed my battery I said quietly, 'Take off your greatcoat, Henderson.' Monty first ordered that all ranks remove their headgear saying, 'I want to have a good look at you. I can't see you properly under your hats.' Then he slowly inspected the whole brigade, speaking to many of the men and being introduced to the more senior officers. A jeep was positioned in the centre of the square, on to which Monty climbed after the inspection. The brigade was ordered to break ranks and gather round. Monty spoke through a loud-speaker. What he said was quite short and very simple. After explaining that he had come 'to have a good look at you and so that you can have a good look at me', he went on to say that we were the finest, best trained and best equipped troops in the world, man to man more than a match for the Germans. He said that we should have air cover 'from the decks of your landing craft to 20,000 feet'. He said that we would be working to a good plan (he knew because he had made it) and that he would be there personally to see that everything went according to plan. He said finally that it would be one hell of a party and that we would give the Germans one hell of a beating. He spoke quietly in that strange high-pitched voice with difficulty in enunciating his Rs. He appeared completely relaxed and confident in himself and in us. It was a most impressive performance and had a lasting effect on us all. We felt that if we had to go to war, Monty was the man to go with, as he would look after us, and that we would do the job with the minimum of casualties.

By this time our division had been joined by an assortment of what we called 'funnies'. There was 27th Armoured Brigade, one regiment of which (13th/18th Hussars) was equipped with amphibious or DD tanks. These were Sherman tanks surrounded by a kind of collapsible boat which when extended allowed the tank to float on the water, propelled by a propellor attached by a shaft to its engine. These tanks would actually lead the assault, being launched from their LCTs two or three miles from the beach and touching down just before 'H' hour. They would be accompanied by a squadron of flail tanks of 22nd Dragoons, also Shermans with a flail mounted in front, which would drive up the beach flailing the mines as they went. Then there were the Crocodiles, Churchill tanks mounted with flame-throwers which would land with the leading infantry and direct their flame into the embrasures of the pill-boxes. Finally there were the AVRES, manned by sappers, Churchill tanks which carried a bombard with an explosive charge which was to be laid against the pill-boxes and exploded by remote control from inside the tank. All these fearsome appliances had been developed and the crews trained by General Hobart, a pre-war tank expert and the first commander of 7th Armoured Division in Egypt. Had he not been so irascible towards his superiors, who regarded him as a crank, he would undoubtedly have achieved high command in the war. As it was he was ideally placed commanding 79th Armoured Division which contained all these specialist units. The Americans scorned such devices, preferring to rely on the assault techniques they had developed with their marines and infantry in the Pacific. I believe that they regretted that decision.

While at Fort George we carried out our first rehearsal of the divisional invasion plan. We loaded on board the LCTs in which we would actually sail and sailed by night sixty miles into the North Sea, turning back and landing in the Moray Firth.

The plan had been produced at a seminar consisting of the staffs, all commanding officers and their adjutants which had lasted for a week soon after Christmas, and been approved by the corps and army commanders and no doubt by Monty. Basically we were to land on a one brigade front, with a commando on each flank of the assaulting brigade which had all the funnies in support. The brigade which we supported (185th) with an armoured regiment was to land three hours later and push rapidly inland to our divisional objective some ten miles inland. Finally the third brigade with another armoured regiment was to move, after landing three hours later, to the right of the bridgehead so as to extend it, and then advance on bicycles to a position just behind the right flank of 185th Brigade.

In late March we moved down to Bolney in Sussex to our concentration area. This had been proclaimed a security zone and no civilians except residents were allowed to enter. However, Judy was not prevented from joining me there and we stayed on a duck farm plagued by fleas. Judy was again pregnant, as we thought that Jennifer should not be brought up as an only child, and the baby was expected in October. Looking back I suppose we did not choose very good times for her babies.

While at Bolney we had our final rehearsal of the invasion on the south coast near Arundel, although we did not go so far into the Channel as we had gone across the North Sea. We had a new divisional commander, Tom Rennie, who had commanded a brigade of 51st Highland Division with distinction in 8th Army and had a high reputation. The commander of 185th Brigade was Brigadier K. P. Smith, who had been with the brigade for some time and had so far in the war seen no action. He was a good trainer of troops who had worked us hard during our training in Scotland. But he did not fully accept the role of the brigade in the divisional plan. We had heard that 21st Panzer Division had been identified as having recently arrived about thirty miles inland of our landing beach. The presence of this division became a fixation in K.P.'s mind. He was haunted by the idea that, if 185th Brigade pushed too boldly inland, 21st Panzer would come round our right flank, which was in open country and cut us off from the beaches. There was wooded country on the left and K.P. wished to infiltrate his infantry through the woods beside the river and approach the objective in that way along the divisional left flank. During our final rehearsal he attempted this manoeuvre, which involved keeping one battalion on our original thrust line and passing the other two round their left flank in a wide turning movement. The result was chaos. The battalions became separated from one another and the Brigadier lost communication with the flanking force which lost all momentum. I was at brigade HQ when Tom Rennie arrived and said wearily, 'You won't let this happen on the day will you K.P.' It would have been better, even at that late stage, if he had sacked K.P. on the spot.

At the end of May Judy returned to Lynch and we started our final preparations in earnest. All the vehicles were water-proofed and we duly set off for Portsmouth down the deserted Sussex roads. On arrival we went to a camp on the outskirts of the town surrounded by wire, which we were not allowed to leave. They were aptly called 'sealed camps'. We drove to the harbour and loaded our SPs and half-tracked vehicles from 'hards' especially constructed sloping concrete wharves, from which the vehicles could drive on to the LCTs. Then we returned to camp to await the lorries which would finally take us on the first part of our great adventure.

Finally on 4th June we loaded, and were greeted by our naval friends who we had already met on the two exercises. They were most hospitable, giving our officers the use of their diminutive cabin so that the men could use the shelter aft of the tank deck, the only cover on board. We in return provided them with whisky and other offerings. But we soon had an unpleasant shock. Due to bad weather the operation was postponed for twenty-four hours. So for the whole of 5th June we sat in our LCT impatiently waiting for news. Fortunately there were diversions. Naval launches and cutters manned by WRENS spent the day busily crossing and re-crossing the harbour, the WRENS in their white shirts and sailor hats carrying out impeccable boat drill, one always standing with a raised boat-hook in the bows, showing off her figure to the troops watching in the LCTs, which certainly kept up their morale.

Just as light was fading we moved slowly out of harbour to assemble in Spithead. At last we were off.

CHAPTER IX

Normandy and After, 1944

A few days after we landed the Colonel asked all officers to write an account of their experiences during the first two days of the invasion. This narrative is based on my account.

A high sea was running as we formed up in Spithead, with a naval motor launch harrying us like a sheepdog herding a flock. The ML seemed to be rolling at least 45° in each direction, her captain in a duffle coat with his hair streaming in the wind shouting at our LCT skippers through a loud-hailer to keep closed up. We had a rough night. Fortunately Judy had given me some tins of Brand's Essence, a beef extract now I believe off the market, as she knew I was a bad sailor. It was all I could eat for two days and I was grateful for it.

Reveille on 'D' Day was at 05.45 hours in the gun LCTs. The gunners had passed a rough night, and there was a long list of names chalked on the shute of an SP under the heading 'Those not requiring a greasy breakfast'. The sea was coming green over the ramp, as breech and muzzle covers were removed and ammunition finally checked. George Haigh, GPO Fox Troop, stood on the bridge alternately giving orders over the tannoy system and making good use of a large bucket which stood conveniently near him.

The wireless net was opened and checked, miraculously every station reported OK and at 06.50 hours the run-in shoot began. Standing on the bridge one could see the shells sailing away into the blue and looking like cricket balls as the guns fired.

We, in the gun LCTs, must have had as good a view as anyone of the assault. At 'H' hour, 07.35, we were about four thousand yards from the beach. We could just see the turrets of the DD tanks above the waves, with tracer flying inland from them; the AVREs crawling up the beach and little figures running among them, and the hundreds of little twinkling lights as the air force bombed the various strong-points.

We turned away and out to sea after our shoot, passing bobbing assault landing craft full of steel-helmeted infantry and infantry landing craft with waving, green bereted commandos on board. All was bustle in the LCTs – cartridge cases to be

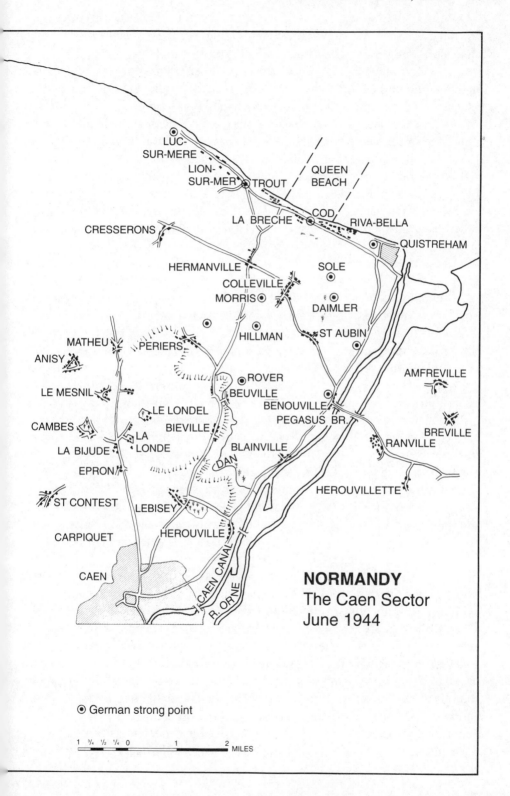

LUC-
SUR-MERE

LION-
SUR-MER   TROUT

QUEEN
BEACH

COD

LA BRECHE

RIVA-BELLA

CRESSERONS

QUISTREHAM

HERMANVILLE

SOLE

COLLEVILLE
MORRIS

DAIMLER

ST AUBIN

HILLMAN

MATHEU
PERIERS

ANISY

AMFREVILLE

LE MESNIL

ROVER
BEUVILLE

LE LONDEL

BENOUVILLE
PEGASUS BR.

BREVILLE

CAMBES

BIEVILLE

LA
LONDE

BLAINVILLE

RANVILLE

LA BIJUDE

EPRON

DAN

HEROUVILLETTE

ST CONTEST

LEBISEY

CARPIQUET

HEROUVILLE

CAEN

CAEN CANAL

R. ORNE

NORMANDY
The Caen Sector
June 1944

⊙ German strong point

1 ¾ ½ ¼ 0   1   2
                              MILES

thrown overboard, SPs to be stowed for landing, breakfast (for those who could stomach it) and a shave. The absolute lack of response from the Germans was almost uncanny. Here and there the odd shell fell among the bombarding squadron on our left, but there was no sign of movement or gun-flashes from the shore. One or two LCTs were on fire and a ship of some kind had her back broken.

About an hour after 'H' hour the first report came through, the assaulting infantry were progressing steadily and the Airborne Division had captured the bridge over the Orne. This was given out by loud-speakers and was good news for all ranks.

We were due to land at H + 195 minutes, and shortly before that the signal to beach appeared at the masthead of the flotilla officer's craft. Our skipper ordered Emergency Full Speed Ahead and the old LCT went in with her bows out of the water like a speedboat; LCTs were beached the whole length of the beach, like a pack of hounds with their noses in the feeding trough, and we were only just able to squeeze ourselves between two of them. We ran a good ten yards up the beach, the ramp fell down and we drove off to a dry landing. It was an anti-climax after months of learning how to water-proof and days spent in water-proofing, and the gunners' comments on the time thus spent were unusually pungent. The chaos on the beach was indescribable. Only one exit appeared to be being used and the traffic through it was stationary. Another exit, almost opposite where we landed, was almost complete but impassable for carriers, so I directed George Haigh to lead his guns through it. There was only about ten yards of sand between the waterline and the back of the beach, so many vehicles had to remain for some time on the craft.

John Plowman, our adjutant, whose craft was alongside ours, and I walked through the beach exit and up the road to see if we could get the traffic moving. The trouble was caused by the North Staffordshire Yeomanry, our armoured regiment, who would not leave the road for fear of mines and were halted nose to tail blowing off their waterproofing, removing motor-bikes from their tanks and brewing up. We walked about half a mile to where 76th Field Regiment were in action and eventually the traffic began to move slowly forward. The only sign of hostile activity was one troop of 88 mms which was shelling the beach area in a rather desultory manner.

I was in charge of the regimental gun group and responsible for getting the guns clear of the beach to Hermanville, where they would meet their battery reconnaisance parties, who had landed an hour before, to be taken to their gun positions. I led the guns through Hermanville where I saw Nigel Tapp with the General and other senior officers. He told me afterwards that he had never been so relieved in his life as when he counted all twenty-four guns following me. I had been told that our gun position, just south of Hermanville, was not yet clear of the enemy, and that if we liked we could come into action north of the village, but the traffic was moving so slowly that I decided to push on. The sight of 16th Battery would probably make up the Germans' minds for them in any event. At the cross-roads just south of Hermanville I met Colin Fergusson in charge of our battery reconnaissance party and one of our best subalterns, sadly killed later in Normandy. He told me that the situation was somewhat confused, several snipers had been caught in the buildings flanking the road, our tanks were only about four hundred yards ahead and did not seem to be able to get forward. Odd shells were falling on our gun position, about eight hundred yards to the east of the cross-roads and south of the lateral road to Colleville. I considered putting the guns north of the road where there was an orchard which gave cover, but at that moment George Haigh and his troop drove up. I explained the situation to him and asked him what he thought. He at once said, 'What are our tanks and SPs for?' – and led his troop into action on the exact spot upon which we had decided from air photographs during our briefing. This action of George's galvanised the infantry. We came into action about a hundred yards in front of one of our assault battalions, who were lying in the ditch beside the lateral road and did not seem inclined to move forward. No doubt they had had a nasty time on the beach. But when they saw the battery deploying in front of them, with signallers running out land lines, all the impedimenta of a gun position being unloaded and set up, and even some of the drivers brewing up, they left the ditch and started to move forward over the open country which sloped upwards to the Periers ridge. This was a commanding feature, overlooking the beaches, and was defended by two concrete strong-points code-named 'Morris' and 'Hillman'. At the same time King's Shropshire Light Infantry (KSLI), the leading battalion of the brigade, passed the cross-roads on their long road to Caen. They had been supposed to go forward mounted on the tanks of the North Staffordshire Yeomanry, but the tanks, although they had landed before us, were still north of Hermanville – so the Brigadier ordered the KSLI to go on without them, hoping that they would catch up.

It was now midday and I went to join the infantry battalion we were supporting, 1st Royal Norfolks with whom we had trained for over a year and whom we knew well. I found their CO, Hugh Bellamy, with his HQ in a small orchard on the southern outskirts of Colleville. With him was the CO of the Suffolks, one of our assault battalions, who told us that they had just captured sixty very demoralised Germans in Morris, and that the attack on Hillman was just going in. There was heavy firing from in front for about half an hour, when the Suffolk CO told us that, although his assaulting company had blown their way through the minefield protecting Hillman with Bangalore torpedoes (long snake-like objects containing an explosive charge which were pushed manually through the mines and then detonated making a pathway), they were held up by small arms fire from a deep concrete earthwork which was strongly defended. His bombardment liaison officer had been wounded, so that he had no communication with the battleship whose 16" guns firing armour-piercing shells provided the most effective fire against such strong-points. The capture of Hillman was crucial to the Norfolks, since it was sited across a track which led to our forward assembly area.

At this moment K. P. Smith appeared at the HQ. His first words filled me with horror. He said that the KSLI were in Bieville and had captured a POW of 21st Panzer

Division. Consequently he was going to pass the Royal Warwickshires round the left flank behind the Norfolks, as he was afraid of a tank threat in the more open country on the right. I thought, 'Oh God! This is Exercise Leapyear [our final dress rehearsal] over again.' I thought that K.P. must have failed to appreciate that by now the KSLI would have an armoured regiment with them protecting their right flank, and that soon the remaining armoured regiment would be landing whose task was to move fast across the open country on our brigade's right flank, thus affording further protection. The total strength in tanks of 27th Armoured Brigade was approximately the same as that of a German Panzer division; moreover a quarter of their tanks mounted the 17-pounder anti-tank gun which was superior to any gun in the German tanks, except the Tigers and Panthers which we did not believe were with 21st Panzer. So why be frightened of a tank battle?

K.P.'s next remark was even worse. He said that the General had said that the Norfolks must secure the high ground overlooking Beuville (code name Rover) by last light at all costs. Rover was the forward assembly area for the Norfolks for their attack on Caen. Now it was to be our final objective, although there were still eight hours of daylight left. I wondered why our plan had been so suddenly changed.

Hugh Bellamy said that he was going to by-pass Hillman on the left and asked if the village of St. Aubin about twelve hundred yards to our left was clear of the enemy. If it was he would keep well away from Hillman, but if not he would have to pass between the two of them. K.P. did not know, but said that the Norfolks must get out of Colleville as soon as possible.

We found a track leading out of the eastern side of the village which led to Rover and the companies deployed on either side of the track and moved forward in open order through the standing cornfields. I went on foot with Hugh and a portable wireless set and told my FOO John Handford in his tank to join the Norfolk carriers and anti-tank guns until I called him forward. After about four hundred yards we came under machine-gun fire from Hillman. We had about one and a half miles to go to Rover, most of which we covered on hands and knees through the corn, with the machine-guns firing amongst us like angry hornets. Soon after we started I was astonished to see John Handford's tank and my carrier, which was following him, emerge from St. Aubin and drive straight towards us. He had taken the wrong turning in Colleville and driven straight through St. Aubin without seeing any enemy. This news would have been most valuable half an hour earlier, but now the battalion was committed, pinned by the machine-gun fire and suffering casualties. I sent John back to the Norfolk carriers and saw his tank twice hit by a small anti-tank gun firing from Hillman, fortunately with no damage apart from smashing a portable wireless set lashed to the turret. We did not reach Rover until about 5 pm and it was not until 7 pm that we were firmly established with anti-tank guns, and John Handford in an OP with good communications.

A dramatic incident now occurred. The Airlanding Brigade of 6th Airborne Division started landing in gliders in the Orne Valley to our left. The big transport aircraft flew in slowly, released their gliders and turned away. The gliders landed at speed, several of them coming to a halt with their noses on the ground and their tails in the air. Soon they were parked so closely together that we could not understand how they could avoid one another. It was an impressive demonstration of power precision and planning which lifted our morale.

News came through of events elsewhere (see map page 57). The Warwicks, inevitably, had been held up in the Orne Valley, and had only reached Blainville well short of their objective. The KSLI had done well. They had dealt with a battery of guns firing from Periers Sur Le Dans, and had been joined by a squadron of the North Staffordshire Yeomanry at Bieville. South of Bieville ran a stream crossed by a road bridge, and beyond was Lebisey Wood on the forward slope of rising ground which overlooked Caen about two miles beyond. At least to capture the Lebisey feature on 'D' Day was vital to the divisional plan. The Yeomanry squadron remained on the Bieville side of the stream, while a company of the KSLI and some carriers went on alone and reached the cross-roads in the middle of Lebisey Wood where the rising ground levelled off. There they were attacked by the Panzer Grenadiers of 21st Panzer Division. The Warwicks and Norfolks should by then have been close behind the KSLI ready to support them, but were strung out on their wild goose chase round the left flank. So Jack Morris, CO of the KSLI who was killed a few days later, decided to withdraw the company at Lebisey to Bieville behind the obstacle provided by the stream. He was already short of one company, mopping up the gun position at Periers, which should have been done by the Warwicks, leaving the KSLI the strength to push boldly forward.

At about 5 pm, as K. P. Smith had predicted, German tanks attacked the right flank of the KSLI in Bieville. They were seen off by the Yeomanry squadron and SP 17-pounder anti-tank guns with the KSLI, with casualties on both sides. The German tanks then drove due north straight for the beaches. As they breasted the Periers ridge they were met by the fire of a squadron which Bill Eadie, the experienced Yeomanry CO, had placed there hull down in expectation of that very event. In a few minutes thirteen German tanks were knocked out with no loss to the Yeomanry, and the remainder broke off the battle and retreated south. I read after the war that the German retreat had been due to their dismay at seeing the Airlanding Brigade apparently landing behind them. I do not believe that a German Panzer division would have reacted in that way to airborne troops. They would have known that such troops would not have tanks or sufficient heavy anti-tank weapons to compete with tanks in open country. We were told at the time that the Germans had been surprised at the speed with which our Sherman tanks with 17-pounders had moved inland, and had not expected such heavy casualties. This seems to me the more likely explanation. But whatever the reason, the fears of K. P. Smith of a tank attack on our right flank were shown to have been groundless. It had been stopped and forced back by two squadrons of Yeomen and a few 17-pounder anti-tank guns. The third squadron, which should also have been on that flank, was diverted to support the assault on Hillman, an extraordinary use of Sherman tanks against concrete fortifications.

We also heard that our reserve brigade, the 9th, instead of racing down the right flank led by their armoured regiment, the East Riding Yeomanry, had been moved to the left flank about St. Aubin. The reason for this was said to be that the Airborne Division east of the Orne were being attacked by tanks, and that the vital bridge at Benouville was threatened. I found this incredible. The country east of the Orne was wooded and unsuitable for tanks. In any event a battery of our divisional 17-pounder anti-tank guns had crossed the Orne bridge to reinforce the Airborne, whose own anti-tank guns had landed in gliders with the Air Landing Brigade. It seemed to be another example of the British practice, so evident in the desert in 1942, of reacting to every threat, real or imagined, instead of concentrating our strength against vital ground which would force the enemy to react to our moves. This was all the more surprising because, in all our briefings, we had been urged to 'bash on regardless', by-passing opposition until we reached Caen and even 'staking claims' beyond. Indeed our objectives were ambitious. Not only were we to seize Caen, but also the Orne bridges south of the town so that 27th Armoured Brigade could pass through the infantry and operate in the open country to the south. That plan now lay in ruins. 9th Brigade and the East Riding Yeomanry hardly fired a shot all day and took no part in the advance towards Caen. The Airborne held the tank attack, and the Benouville bridge remained open, so that the supposed 'threat' never materialised.

At the time I assumed that the decision to change the role of 9th Brigade had been made by Tom Rennie, our divisional commander, and put it down to his inexperience of handling armour. But after the war I learnt that it had been made in consultation with the corps commander, John Crocker. This made it all the more extraordinary since Crocker had spent his service in the Tank Corps, and was reputed to be an expert in armoured warfare.

The immediate result of this decision was the existence of a wide gap, which should have been filled by 9th Brigade, between us and the 3rd Canadian Division who had landed on our right. The gap contained a number of villages which were assaulted in the ensuing days and weeks by our 8th and 9th Brigades in battles reminiscent of the Great War, with commensurate casualties. But the longer term effects were even more serious. Our failure to capture Caen, which was a vital road junction, affected the whole future conduct of the operations of the British 2nd Army and even Monty's conduct of the battle came under criticism, especially from the Americans. There were calls for his removal from the command of the invasion forces.

I have always been convinced that if our divisional plan had been executed with vigour, and 185th Brigade kept concentrated as had been intended, we could have seized the high ground at Lebisey on the evening of 'D' Day, with 9th Brigade protecting our right flank. The two brigades between them disposed of over one hundred tanks available to deal with any counter-attack in the open country towards the Carpiquet airfield, while two strong infantry brigades would have been available for the assault on Caen, which would have lain before and below us like a plum ripe for the picking.

Although we were disappointed and frustrated at sitting on Rover on the evening of 'D' Day instead of fighting in the outskirts of Caen, I remember my feelings being predominantly those of relief. Not so much at my personal survival, as strangely I never considered the possibility of being killed. That no doubt would happen and had happened to others. But I always had the basic feeling that it would never happen to me. It was just impossible to imagine death as affecting oneself. On the other hand I was intensely relieved that we had survived the assault over the beaches with remarkably few casualties. For over a year our whole minds and energies had been directed towards this one stupendous event: the storming of the West Wall. Now that we had achieved it, mental readjustment was required to brace ourselves for what we all knew was to be hard fighting ahead.

185th Brigade lay spread-eagled across the divisional front with the KSLI in Bieville, the Norfolks on Rover above Beuville, and the Warwicks in Blainville. Hillman had not fallen until the morning of the 7th, and there were still snipers in the woods and villages. We were told on that first morning in France that the Warwicks were to attack Lebisey Wood from the direction of Blainville, and by mid-day it was clear that the attack was held up. In fact it was a disaster. 'H' hour had been postponed for an hour, but the message did not get through to the assaulting companies, who crossed the start line without artillery support, and the battalion was pinned down in front of the wood by heavy fire. To make matters worse the battalion's carriers and anti-tank guns, thinking that the rifle companies were on their objective, drove straight up the road from Bieville into the German defences, where they were virtually wiped out. The bodies of the many killed were not recovered until we captured Lebisey Wood a month later.

At about 2 pm K. P. Smith arrived at Rover, walked up to Hugh Bellamy and said, 'Hugh, I've got a bloody awful job for you; you've got to go through the Warwicks and get Stout [code name for the Lebisey feature].' Hugh asked if the Warwicks had cleared Lebisey Wood, and K.P. replied, 'I don't know for sure, but we must get on. How soon can you do it?' It was arranged that there should be a Brigade Order Group in the northern edge of Lebisey Wood at 4 pm and that the battalion was to assemble in Bieville. We went in our carriers via Colleville and up the road through Beuville. On the way we passed the guns and half-tracks of the regiment moving to new positions near Beuville.

On arrival at Bieville we discovered that the 'O' Group was to be held there at the HQ of the KSLI. The Warwicks had still not got into Lebisey Wood, and K.P. ordered the Norfolks to make contact with them, and to make a plan for the two battalions to clear the wood. There was to be no artillery support as the positions of the Warwicks were not known, and K.P. did not want to risk hitting them with our own shells. The 'O' Group was actively sniped by riflemen still in Bieville, and John

Handford, who was there in his Sherman tank, did good work with his Browning machine-gun against the church tower and the windows of houses from where the fire was coming.

Eventually the Norfolks debouched from Bieville with their carriers and anti-tank guns, to be met by heavy shelling from the German artillery which caused considerable casualties. When they reached the edge of the wood they met the Warwicks who were pinned down by fire and unable to move. At 10 pm K.P. ordered both battalions to withdraw covered by fire from all available guns, which included two field regiments, a medium regiment which had just landed, and a cruiser controlled by the BLO. I stood with Hugh near the Bieville bridge as the infantry marched back under this heavy protective fire, and was relieved to see my other FOO, Jack Talbot, who had been with the Warwicks, walking back down the road, a portable wireless set on his back. He had spent the day in the German anti-tank ditch which ran along the northern edge of Lebisey Wood, and was quite unshaken by his first experience of fire.

The events of this disastrous day confirmed the lesson which should have been learnt in 1915 at Gallipoli – you can do with a platoon on 'D' Day, what you cannot do with a battalion on 'D' + 1 or a division on 'D' + 3. Within a few days K. P. Smith had been sent back to England and replaced as Brigade Commander by Denis Boles, an active young brigadier who later commanded 6th Airborne Division. But Tom Rennie remained with the division until he was appointed to command his old 51st Highland Division. He was a gallant soldier and was killed later in the war while on the start line characteristically encouraging his Highlanders forward to an attack. But I have always thought that he was in fact more to blame even than K P. Smith for the blunders of 'D' Day and 'D + 1'. When the KSLI failed to hold Lebisey Wood on the evening of 'D' Day, he should surely have insisted on an immediate and properly co-ordinated brigade attack by the whole of 185th Brigade, supported by all available artillery and the bombarding squadron, instead of allowing K.P. to commit his battalions piecemeal without proper support twelve hours later. After all Rennie was in command of the division and responsible for control of the battle.

Fortunately for us 185th Brigade was not involved in the desperate battles for the villages, such as Cambes, La Londe and Epron which were written in blood in the annals of the 3rd Division. We sat glaring at the Germans in Lebisey Wood and they glared back at us. The infantry patrolled the wood by night, and each side shelled the other intermittently. I divided my time between HQ 1st Norfolks on Rover and the gun position near Beuville, which had been the HQ of the German regiment defending our sector of the beaches. On arriving on the position BSM Lacey had taken a posse of our gunners armed with rifles, bren guns, and tommy guns into Beuville, and had captured the entire HQ staff of the German regiment, an exploit for which he was awarded the Croix de Guerre.

The SP guns of the battery stood in a line along a gentle slope rising in front of them. Behind the guns was a vertical bank about 8 to 10 feet high into which we dug shelters for the gun detachments. Behind the bank we dug deep dugouts for the command post's cookhouse and officers' mess. We lived well off local chicken, Camembert cheese and local cider, with a glass of Calvados as a digestive to supplement our rather monotonous 'compo' rations. The position was regularly shelled, but most of the shells either exploded on the crest two hundred yards or so in front of the guns, or went over into the stream which ran behind the position. So we had few casualties, although at dinner one evening, during some heavy shelling, one of our subalterns decided to get under the table for added protection.

Our wagon lines, near Periers, were heavily shelled and my battery captain John Hearn was unlucky enough to have the whole of his lower jaw removed by a shell splinter. John was a regular, senior to me, who had unfortunately fallen out with his previous Colonel, so was sent to us as a captain instead of commanding a battery. He was a very serviceable officer and I handed over the whole administration of the battery to him. He was a sad loss.

On about 10th June I was told to report to the CRA in Colleville. He said that 51st Highland Division, which had just landed, was to break out of the Airborne bridgehead east of the Orne, supported by 4th Armoured Brigade and strike south towards Troarn. All three field regiments and a medium regiment of 3rd Division were to support the attack, and I was to report to HQ 51st Division as CRA's representative with all four regiments at my disposal. 51st Highland Division had earned a high reputation with 8th Army, and I was excited at the prospect of working with them as I crossed the newly constructed Bailey bridge, known as Pegasus bridge, at Benouville. I had been given the map reference of the HQ but the further I went the fewer people I saw, until I reached a deserted village and was stopped by a Parachute sergeant who said, 'I shouldn't go any further if I were you, sir. The Jerries are just round the corner.' The map reference proved to be wrong.

I eventually found HQ 51st Division and reported to the CRA Gerry Shiel, who had been Second-in-Command of the HAC before we left for the Middle East. Gerry was to be killed in Germany a few days before the end of the war. With him was Len Livingstone Learmouth commanding 4th RHA who were with 4th Armoured Brigade, and whom I had not seen since Knightsbridge. Everyone was very cheerful, and Gerry had to rebuke Len for making light-hearted interruptions while he was trying to give out his orders for the fire plan.

I arranged over the wireless for 3rd Divisional Artillery to fire 'stonks', as we called concentrations, on various selected targets at stated times and in due course the attack went in. The Germans at once opened up with very heavy mortar fire on our infantry start line, and they were unable to move forward through the fire. The attack was called off – a sad disappointment. One day, one of the new VI rockets passed overhead on its way to England. Soon after it crossed our lines something must have gone wrong with its controls, because it turned through 180° and flew back whence it had come. Our troops were delighted, and shouted and cheered at the sight.

Just as it seemed that the war had reached a state of stalemate in our sector, we were told that there was to be a Corps attack on the Lebisey feature leading on to the capture of Caen. A freshly landed division, the 59th with an Army Tank Brigade was to attack on our right. The Norfolks were to be one of the assaulting battalions, and 'H' hour was to be 4.15 am on 8th July. I decided to shave the evening before, and while doing so cracked my shaving mirror. I have never been superstitious, but for some reason felt worried and that night said our family prayer with even more attention than usual. The prayer was from the 4th Psalm:

> I will lay me down in peace
> And take my rest
> For it is Thou Lord only
> That makest me dwell in safety.

My father had said the prayer every night during the Great War. He told me that when he was in the Ypres salient in the winter of 1914/15 he could never complete the prayer without hearing a gun of one side or the other firing. It was the same in the Normandy beachhead, although the desert nights had been quiet. My grandfather had said the prayer during the Burma War, and my great grandfather in the Peninsula. The prayer must have been efficacious because we all survived.

Soon after I arrived at the Norfolk HQ and as dusk was falling we saw an awe-inspiring sight. Over one thousand bombers from Bomber Command started to bomb Caen, just three miles ahead. This was a surprise to us as we watched them come in quite low and directly overhead, not in any formation, but flying in a loose column which stretched back as far as the eye could see. Having heard so much about the big Bomber Command raids on Germany, it was fascinating to see a raid from near the target. At first there was heavy anti-aircraft fire from the city, and several of the leading planes were shot down, some in flames. But gradually an immense pall of smoke and dust rose high above the city, and we could see no sign of opposition. The noise was terrific, the throbbing engines of the bombers overhead mingled with the crash and explosions of the bombs. The heavy four-engined bombers each released their bombs and turned slowly away, climbing as they went. The effect on our troops was electric. They stood on the parapets of their trenches cheering wildly as they realised what was happening. The raid lasted nearly an hour before the last bomber dropped its bombs and turned home for England. Certainly the raid lifted our morale, but its military value was doubtful. Caen was reduced to rubble and bulldozers had to be used to clear tracks sufficient even for our infantry to enter next day. There were few German troops in the city itself, and the civilian casualties were unacceptable. But we did not know all that at the time, and went to bed in good heart.

Next morning I went forward on foot with Hugh Bellamy under the barrage, one signaller carrying a portable wireless set and another reeling out a land line to keep communication to the guns. We passed Eric Cooper-Key with his company in a quarry on the edge of Lebisey Wood. Eric was one of the best company commanders in Normandy who enjoyed the good things of life. As we passed he shouted to me above the noise, 'God, Robin. Don't you wish we were in the Berkeley Buttery?' A few dazed looking German prisoners were coming down the slope as we walked up, and we soon established HQ on the edge of the wood. We heard that the forward companies were making good progress against light opposition.

As we were digging in we were shelled from behind. A first we thought it was our own guns, and I sent an indignant message over the wireless to our Regimental HQ. But we soon discovered that our assailants were a German battery east of the Orne near the coast, to whom Lebisey Wood, lying on the forward slope, must have presented an inviting target. The shelling was heavy and accurate; I remember an explosion very close and falling to the ground. I found I could not speak, although I could think, and wrote a fire order on a message pad for transmission to the guns. I felt no pain. Hugh Bellamy ordered up the stretcher bearers, and I was carried back through the shellfire to the Regimental Aid Post. I have always been grateful for the calm courage of those two men, who walked slowly back under heavy fire, talking quietly and telling one another to be careful not to jolt me unnecessarily. My steel helmet was on my chest, and I noticed it had a large hole in one side.

I remember very little of the next few hours. Our stretchers were loaded from the beach on to an empty tank landing ship, whose engines broke down in mid Channel, so the journey took longer than it should have.

My next clear memory is of lying face downwards on an operating table in the Park Prewet Hospital at Basingstoke, my head shaved, with a surgeon chipping at my skull. He said that as I had a head wound I could not be given a general anaesthetic, so he was using a local anaesthetic to remove the shell splinters. I next remember being in bed in the General Hospital at Stratford-on-Avon which had been made available for casualties from Normandy.

I still could not speak. A doctor told me that my skull had not been fractured, and that my loss of speech was probably due to shell shock, which would clear up in due course. To my surprise and delight the day after I arrived my mother's cousin Cara Brocklebank arrived in the ward wearing a smart Red Cross uniform. She was working there as a volunteer. I wrote out a telegram to send to Judy and also wrote down what the doctor had told me, saying that I did not believe it.

As soon as Judy received the telegram she telephoned my father, who had an administrative job commanding the Gloucestershire District and told him he must 'do something'. Fortunately my father knew Professor Hugh Cairns, consultant neuro-surgeon to the army, who was in charge of a special hospital for head injuries which had been opened at St. Hughes College, Oxford. He telephoned Cairns and within a very few days I was taken by ambulance to St. Hughes.

Next morning the great man came into my room with a group of young doctors and examined me. I felt rather like a specimen under glass. He never addressed me personally, but turned to the group and said, 'This is a very interesting case. The

Germans have a new shell which explodes into thousands of tiny high velocity fragments. These fragments do little external damage, but because of their speed the internal damage is severe. In this case the impact has caused a haemorrhage of that part of the brain which controls the speech. I shall carry out a series of lumber punctures which will remove the blood and fluid down the spine and relieve the pressure on the brain. Then he will have to be taught to speak again.' Without a word to me they then left.

As soon as she heard that I was in St. Hughes, Judy caught the first train for Oxford. She arrived in the late afternoon to find that all the hotels were fully booked. So she started to call on houses in the Banbury Road to find lodgings. Just as she was becoming exhausted carrying her suitcase – she was by then six months pregnant – she met quite by chance a woman she knew slightly who, when she heard her predicament, offered her a bed for the night and helped her find lodgings. The following day Judy came to St. Hughes. As she was about to walk upstairs she was met by two orderlies carrying down a coffin draped in a Union Jack, which did not improve her spirits. However she seemed very happy and cheerful when she walked into my room.

The lumber punctures were unpleasant but not painful and I soon started a course of speech therapy, so that I now talk rather more distinctly than before.

I have often wondered what would have happened if I had not been rescued from Stratford through Judy's efforts or if my condition had not been properly diagnosed and treated. I think it probable that I should have been left with a speech impediment for the rest of my life. So I am grateful to Cairns and all involved in my recovery.

I recently watched a much publicised television programme about a young officer of the Scots Guards who had suffered serious head injuries in the Falklands. The programme, which was supposed to be factual, portrayed the young man in an orgy of self-pity, railing against his fate and blaming the army medical services for inadequate treatment, and his regiment for not looking after him properly during his convalescence. I found the whole programme not only distasteful but also not true to life. During my two spells in hospital I met many badly wounded and disabled people. None behaved like the young man in the film. I remember one young man in hospital at Tel El Kebir who was bitter at having been deprived by the war of the best years of his youth, and the opportunity to enjoy himself. But he blamed Hitler. Everyone else was cheerful, thankful for survival and for what was being done for them, and looking forward to rebuilding their lives. I am sure that there cannot be all that much difference in the attitude of the present generation to misfortune. Perhaps a film portraying the odd exceptional case is more likely to be a commercial success than one showing the reactions to war of the majority of ordinary courageous young men, who were proud to have had the opportunity of serving their country. Why I wonder have we so far not had such a film about the Falklands or the Gulf War?

In what seemed a remarkably short time I was passed fit after some sick leave at

Lynch, and posted to a field battery in the 61st Division in Kent, which was being trained and equipped for the projected assault against the Japanese in Malaya. After three months I would lose my temporary rank of major, and was told that there was no prospect of my commanding a battery as there was a large pool of regulars, all senior to me, who would have priority. I knew that I had already been replaced in command of 16th Battery by a senior major from the staff, although I wrote to Nigel Tapp saying that I was fit. I also wrote to my old friend John Gibbon, Staff Officer to the Major General Royal Artillery at HQ 21st Army Group telling him of my circumstances. Meanwhile I was sent on indefinite leave to Lynch, the Colonel saying with a grin that he did not suppose I would be with them for long.

On 7th October Judy's baby arrived, to our delight a boy whom we called Allan John Keith. In those days fathers were discouraged from being present at the birth, on the ground that they caused more trouble than the mother, and I first saw Allan lying in his cot dressed in a blue and white striped jersey and looking like a professional footballer. Judy and I were thrilled to have a son and a brother for Jennifer.

Very soon after Allan's birth I received a posting order to 7th Field Regiment in 21st Army Group. I had very mixed feelings about this. I was glad to be returning to my battery, but sad at having to leave Judy on her own with the baby once again. However, we all expected the war with Germany to be over by Christmas and I had at least avoided being sent to the Far East.

CHAPTER X

The Maas and the Reichswald, 1944–45

3rd Division was holding the line of the River Maas north of Venlo in Holland. They had just had some hard fighting in the battle for Venraij, and the Norfolks had had heavy casualties. Shortly before I arrived Nigel Tapp had told my predecessor that he was to be posted to the pool of majors at the base, which did not please him. Nigel could be quite ruthless in his quiet way. When my predecessor heard that I had arrived at RHQ he at once left the battery saying, 'I don't want to meet Robin Dunn.' I felt sorry for him, but glad to be back with the battery.

Soon after I arrived 16th Battery was detached in support of the Household Cavalry armoured cars, holding a sector of the river to the north of the division. The regiment was commanded by Henry Abel-Smith. His adjutant was Arthur Collins, a solicitor and partner in the well-known family firm of Withers & Co. After the war Arthur acted for most of the dukes and many big landowners and became a good friend and client of mine when I went to the Bar. He received a KCVO from the Queen. As well as 16th Battery there were anti-tank guns, medium machine-guns, mortars and anti-tank guns supporting the Household Cavalry. Every evening we had a meeting in the estaminet used as regimental HQ. A large map was spread out on the table illuminated by an electric light on a long flex which Arthur would hold over the map while Henry discussed what we were to do next day. It was all very grand. I suggested that all the supporting weapons should fire what had become known as a 'pepper pot' on selected German positions to keep them on their toes. Henry thought this a splendid idea. Although the fire was not very accurate, we hoped it would keep the Germans' heads down. The Household Cavalry were over-subscribed in officers and there were more subalterns than troops for them to command. Arthur ordered that each subaltern should drive in an armoured scout-car, or Dingo, along the road which ran beside the river in full view of the enemy. When I said that this might be rather wasteful in lives he replied, 'Not at all. Teach them to be steady under fire.'

I had been awarded the MC after Normandy and went with others to Divisional HQ to be presented with my medal by Monty. He stopped in front of me, looked at my Africa Star, and asked, 'Whereabouts in the Middle East did you serve?' Now this was a sore point. The Africa Star was awarded to anyone who had served in the Middle East or North Africa, including people who had spent the war in Cairo or Khartoum and had never seen a shot fired. Anyone who had served in 8th Army after Monty took command in August 1942 was entitled to the 8th Army clasp, a silver 8 on the medal. 8th Army had been formed in June 1941, so that anyone like myself who had left 8th Army before Monty joined was not entitled to wear the clasp and this caused hard feelings, as we felt we had not done so badly at Sidi Rezegh and other battles. So in reply to his question I said, 'The Western Desert and Libya, sir, before they became fashionable.' Monty's eyebrows shot up and at first I thought he was going to hit me. Then he scowled and with a gesture of irritation pinned on my MC. At that moment a photographer snapped us and I received a print of the photograph autographed by Monty, which stood in a place of honour at Lynch. The children used to say, 'Why is that man angry with daddy?'

At about Christmas time Nigel Tapp left the regiment on promotion as CRA to one of the divisions earmarked for the assault on Malaya. I was sad to see him go as he had been a good friend – we had asked him to be godfather to Allan. After he left, as senior major, I was temporarily in command of the regiment as the second-in-command was on leave. The only order I remember giving was on New Year's Eve, when I ordered all guns to fire five rounds gunfire at midnight on the German positions as a taste for them of things to come in 1945. Nigel was succeeded by Charles Bazley who had been one of the pioneers of the Air OP in North Africa.

We were allowed forty-eight hours leave in Brussels that winter, which was very cold with ice and snow on the ground, and I spent mine with Bobbie Erskine, at that time head of the SHAEF mission in Belgium. Although Bobbie was ten years younger than my father, he was his uncle. My father's Erskine grandfather, having come home a widower from his labours in Oudh, had married a lady much younger than himself who we called 'Grannie Erskine', and who lived at Worthing where I often used to visit her from St. Aubyns, and Bobbie was their son. Bobbie had commanded 7th Armoured Division in 8th Army, and taken it to Normandy, where he had been sacked by Monty after the division had had a bloody nose at Villers Bocage. Bobbie told my father that he had so many friends in the division that he was not going to ask them to do something today, which he knew they could do tomorrow with far fewer casualties. 'You may say,' said my father, 'that such a man is not fit to command an armoured division in wartime. But I admire him.' In spite of this set-back to his career, Bobbie achieved high command, becoming a full general in command in Kenya during the Mau Mau rebellion and receiving a knighthood. He was a most charming and cheerful man and I thoroughly enjoyed my short leave. The mess where I stayed, in the Avenue Louise, had been the HQ of the Gestapo.

At about the same time Hugh Bellamy had spent his forty-eight hours leave with Monty at his tactical HQ. Monty had commandeered a group of small houses in a suburb near Brussels, where 'the Chief' as he was then called lived with his military family consisting of a few staff officers, mostly intelligence, liaison officers and ADCs. There he was free of the hurly-burly of his main HQ and had time for what he called quiet thought and reflection. One of the houses was earmarked for visitors, and there Hugh stayed with two or three other infantry battalion commanders. Hugh said the house was warm and comfortable. Monty himself was out all day visiting various HQs, but they all met for dinner punctually at 7 pm. The conversation was light-hearted and Hugh said even puerile. Monty would leave by 9 pm for his caravan where he always slept. Although Monty did not drink alcohol himself, Hugh said there was plenty available, but no smoking was allowed in the dining room. Everyone had to be out of the dining room by 8 am each morning so that Monty could breakfast alone. Hugh was summoned one day to Monty's office caravan and asked about his battalion, the quality of his officers and reinforcements, and whether he had any problems. Otherwise 'shop' was never mentioned. This was just after the battle of the Ardennes when the Germans broke through the thinly held American front in that sector and advanced rapidly towards Brussels. Monty was called in to restore the situation and took command of the US armies involved, as well as moving 30th Corps from 21st Army Group to the line of the River Meuse as a long stop. The Germans were eventually stopped and forced back to their start line. The joke in the army was, 'When does a bulge become a pocket?' Answer, 'When Monty takes over.' At dinner one evening Hugh, rather provocatively, asked Monty, 'What were the Americans doing, Chief, to get caught napping like that in the Ardennes?' Monty gave a self-satisfied smile and said, 'My dear Hugh, you should never play a game before you learn the rules.' No wonder he was so disliked by the Americans.

Soon thereafter Hugh was promoted Brigadier in command of the Airlanding Brigade of 6th Airborne Division, to be replaced by Peter Barclay. Unlike Hugh, Peter was a Royal Norfolk, and had been commanding a battalion of another regiment in 49th Division. He was a real fighting soldier and very popular in the battalion. He was a keen shot and one day soon after he arrived said to me, 'Why don't we go duck flighting on the Maas tomorrow morning, Robin?' I said I had no suitable gun, and anyway what about the Germans just across the river? Peter said he had a pair of 12-bore shot guns and that the Germans opposite were too sleepy to take any notice. So next morning we set off just before dawn, walked down to the river bank and had some good sport with the duck, both bagging some good birds. There was no reaction from the Germans, which I thought sporting of them as we were in full view throughout. We walked back over the water meadows with a glorious red Dutch winter sky high above us, and enjoyed an enormous breakfast of ham and eggs in the large solid Dutch farmhouse which Peter was using as his HQ.

At this time we had an OP in a fine stone windmill not far from the river bank, from which we had a superb view deep behind the German lines. We were rationed for routine shooting to five rounds per gun per day. I decided to do no shooting, except in emergency, for a week during which time we hoped the Germans would become careless and disclose their positions, which we could then pin-point with accuracy. We would then fire the whole week's ration of ammunition on the exposed positions. The evening before we were due to do this shoot we were told that the Corps Commander, Bubbles Barker, would be visiting the windmill at 10 am. As all arrangements had been made for the shoot, I decided very unwisely to go ahead. Exactly as we had hoped, after two or three days the Germans had started to become careless, standing up and walking about round their positions, and even queueing up at their cookhouse for their meals. We carefully marked all these places on the map. On the day of the shoot I went to the windmill just before first light, and when I saw the Germans queueing up for breakfast brought down the first stonk right on top of them. I then switched to the other targets we had recorded, and went on firing until all the ammunition was expended. It was a great success and the fire was very accurate. Punctually at 10 am Bubbles Barker arrived with some staff officers and a large map, and spent about an hour in the windmill. He was delighted by the view, which extended to the Reichswald in the distance. He said, 'People talk of passing a corps through the Reichswald. How could you possibly send troops through a thick forest like that?' I had never considered the possibility, but now realised that our next battle would be in the Reichswald, and that Bubbles had made a clumsy attempt at deception having come to reconnoitre the forest. After Bubbles left I sent George Haigh to the OP and returned to the guns. Just as I was starting lunch George rang up to say that two German SP 88 mm anti-tank guns were driving fast towards the Maas and could he have the whole regiment to engage them? Very soon our shells were landing over the river, but not before the guns had halted and drilled six holes like waistcoat buttons down the front of the windmill. The first round went through the aperture at the top through which George was looking and hit the rafter above his head. Fortunately as it was armour-piercing shot it did not explode. Thank goodness the Germans did not react more quickly and send up their SPs while the corps commander was still in the windmill. It was a lucky escape, and I blamed myself for not having postponed the shoot until after the corps commander's visit. Fortunately no damage was done, except to the windmill, but I felt the incident might have ended in disaster and marked the end of a promising career.

Shortly after this event the Germans sent a patrol in rubber boats across the Maas one night and established themselves in some strength on our bank. One of our infantry battalions was sent to turn them out, and I was ordered to send an FOO to support them. I chose a replacement captain, who had just arrived from the base, because I thought it would be a good experience for him before we became engaged in more serious things. In fact it turned out to be a nasty tough little battle, in the course of which a mortar bomb landed on his OP, killing one man and wounding the others. The officer was unscathed and apparently comparatively unshaken, although naturally upset by the loss of his men. He had spent the war as an instructor at the School of Artillery at Larkhill and had very good technical knowledge of gunnery. I thought he had survived his baptism of fire well.

By this time the Reichswald battle had started and we were warned that the division was to move north to take part in the battle, which was becoming bogged down. We were taken out of the line for a few days' reorganisation before moving. A day or two before we were to move this new captain came to my battery office, in a Dutch café, where I was doing some paper work and asked to see me. He sat down in front of me and said, 'I'm sorry, Major, I can't go into the line with the battery.' I was taken aback and said, 'How do you mean you can't go? The battery are going and you will go with us.' He said, 'I just can't bring myself to do it.' I said, 'We none of us like going into the line and I can tell you it gets worse every time you do it. You did well on the Maas and you will have to make up your mind to do well again. We all get frightened in a battle and you will have to learn to control yourself.' He said, 'I was not frightened on the Maas and I am not frightened now. It is just my nerves. I cannot sleep at night and I feel a wreck all day. I just cannot go.' By this time I was beginning to feel angry and I said, 'If I ordered you to go would you refuse?' He said, 'Yes, if I had to.' I said, 'Do you realise that in the last war you would have been shot if you had refused to go into the line?' He said, 'Yes. But things are different now. People like me are taken from the fighting units and get medical help.' By then I realised that there was nothing more that I could do, so I said, 'You will have to explain this to the Colonel. I shall send you to RHQ.' He asked if he could go back to his troop to collect his kit. I said, 'No. I am not going to have you contaminating your troop. I will have your kit sent to RHQ.' I arranged for another captain to take him to RHQ and rang up the Colonel to tell him what had happened. I heard later that there had been a very similar interview with the Colonel and later with the Brigadier. The captain was sent back to the base and then to hospital suffering from what was called Anxiety and Depression.

This was the only time in the whole war that I actually saw a man refuse to do his duty. On 'D' Day my signal sergeant had demurred when I had told him to go and mend a broken field telephone line, saying that there were German snipers near the line. But when I pointed out the dire consequences of disobeying an order in battle, he went off and mended the break. Thereafter he worked like a Trojan keeping the vital communications open to the guns, and I recommended him for the MM which he was awarded. This time, however, I was angry because I felt that the captain was getting away with a soft option, when everyone else in the battery was yet again going into what, by all accounts, was an unpleasant battle. I did not believe that there was anything the matter with him which could not be remedied by determination and self-control. It could be said that if he had come with us he would have let us down, perhaps causing danger to his men and that it was better that he should be allowed to go back to the base. On the other hand the pressure of battle is such that if people have the feeling, even at the back of their minds, that they have an option whether to take part or not, they may opt out. If there is no option, except perhaps severe penal sanctions, people are more likely to exercise self-discipline and do their duty.

I put it in terms of duty because I believe that this is the fundamental requirement for the soldier on the battlefield. It was not always easy to do one's duty when one was wet, hungry, tired and frightened. I found shortage of sleep the worst handicap. On an average of about four hours' sleep a night over a long period I found that I could just about do my job, but that it was difficult to find much in the way of initiative. I also found that one's resolution was not constant, rather like an electric battery which needed re-charging by periods of rest. Each time one went into action, however, the level was a little lower than it had been before. Eric Cooper-Key told me that after Normandy, when the rifle companies of the Norfolks had had over 100% casualties in the two months of fighting, he was content in an attack if he, his platoon commanders and sergeants and perhaps half a dozen men of his company reached the objective. The rest would appear over a period of perhaps twenty minutes after the worst of the fire was over. I found his remark fascinating because it stressed the importance of leaders.

The task of the infantry was by far the most onerous and dangerous of any arm of the service, and the rifle companies suffered the highest casualties in the army. Yet in the wartime selection procedure the lowest category was allotted to the infantry. Higher standards of intelligence and physique were required for the armoured corps, gunners and especially signals than for the infantry, who had the most exacting role. In addition thousands of men who would have made first-class infantry NCOs became air gunners and navigators in Bomber Command, thus reducing the pool from which infantry junior leaders could be drawn. I have always thought that it was for lack of these vital junior leaders that the infantry did not perform in our war as they had in the Great War. Our infantry would simply not have gone over the top and walked across no man's land in the face of withering machine-gun fire, as their fathers did on the Somme and at Passchendaele. It is easier for the leader to do his duty because he knows that his men are watching him and will take their cue from him, and that he is there to set an example. The whole of his training and the traditions of his regiment are there behind him to help him do the right thing. If he fails he knows that not only will be let himself down, but also his men and his regiment.

I am not here discussing individual acts of heroism, which are often performed on the spur of the moment, and sometimes out of character. Eric Cooper-Key told me that at Sordeval in Normandy his company had borne the brunt of a last desperate German counter-attack designed to cut off the Americans, who were beginning to strike south down the Cherbourg peninsula. A lance-corporal from his forward platoon had appeared at his company HQ in a state of distress and high excitement and said, 'Our forward section has been overrun, and the Jerries are swarming all over the position. I can't take any more, sir. I must go back to the RAP.' Eric had said, 'No. You go back to your platoon.' The man went back, picked up a bren gun, and walked forward firing from his hip into the masses of German infantry who were moving on to the position. Many fell, the rest stopped, hesitated, turned round and went back. The lance-corporal was mortally wounded and awarded a

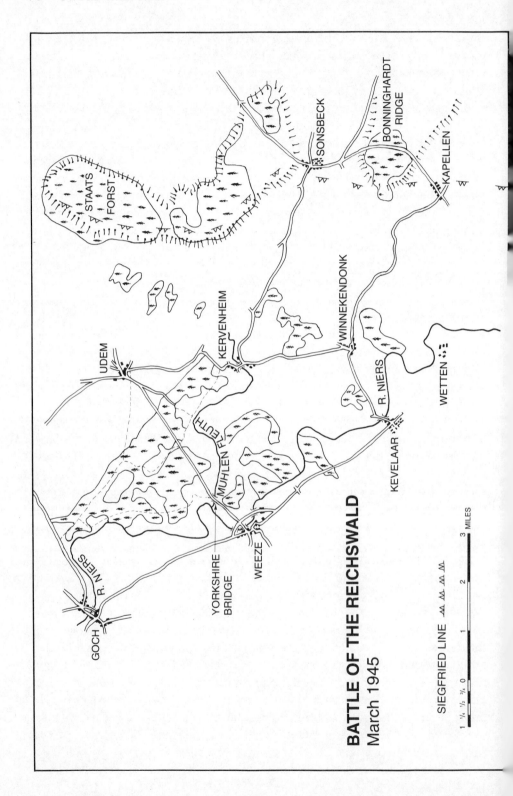

BATTLE OF THE REICHSWALD
March 1945

SIEGFRIED LINE ⋏⋏ ⋏⋏ ⋀⋀

1 ¼ ½ ¾ 0   1   2   3 MILES

posthumous VC. What I am discussing is the reaction of ordinary, not particularly courageous, men who over long periods of discomfort, often under heavy shell and mortar fire, managed to do their duty sustained by the example and support of their comrades and their innate self-respect.

But in 1945 there was no time for such philosophising. On 24th February the division joined the Reichswald battle at Goch. This was for me the worst battle of the war, partly because of the appalling weather. The thaw had started, and the continuous rain caused the tanks and heavy vehicles to churn the sandy tracks through the forest (there were no metal roads) into rivers of liquid mud. I watched the Warwicks, small men from Birmingham, moving up to the attack. Their new pattern steel helmets appeared top heavy, and they were weighed down by haversack, water bottle, entrenching tool, bandoliers of ammunition, and their rifles and bayonets so that they trudged slowly knee deep through the mud. 'Poor buggers', said my driver as we watched them from the side of the track. As in all Monty's big battles the noise of artillery fire was incessant, as the massed guns of the whole corps switched from one target to another. And, as well as the weather, we were faced by a German parachute division who fought like tigers in defence of their frontier. I remember seeing one of their prisoners, a sergeant, tough, unyielding and disdainful of us.

The division was attacking on a narrow front in a south-easterly direction, and it was a dogged battle with every village fortified and desperately defended by the Germans. On 1st March the Norfolks and the KSLI attacked the village of Kervenheim. We were supported by a battalion of the Scots Guards in Churchill tanks, part of 6th Guards Tank Brigade. This was the battalion in which both William Whitelaw and Robert Runcie, the future Archbishop of Canterbury, were serving. I did not meet either of them at the time, but many years later the Archbishop and I were sworn in as Privy Councillors on the same day. While we were waiting at Buckingham Palace to fall on our knees and kiss the hands of the Sovereign, we discussed the battle of Kervenheim.

Although we attacked early in the morning it was not until late at night that the Norfolks finally cleared the village. The German paratroopers fought suicidally, and I entered a house from which a machine-gun had been firing all day to find hundreds of spent cartridges strewn over the floor, with the German gunners dead by their guns. It was not until the Crocodile flame-throwers were brought up that the Germans were literally burnt out of the buildings. The Norfolks suffered terribly.

I spent the battle with Peter Barclay at his Battalion HQ. The noise was deafening, the characteristic sound of the German Spandau machine-gun, rather like a sewing machine, mingling with the regular tap-tap-tapping of our bren guns and the crump of mortar bombs. The Germans were making great use of their Nebelwerfer, a multi-barrelled mortar which made a loud whirring sound as it was fired, soon followed by the crash as its six or eight bombs fell together.

All the officers of 'A' Company had either been killed or wounded; so our FOO George Haigh took over and commanded the company for the rest of the battle, for which he was awarded the MC which he had already earned several times over since landing in Normandy.

The second-in-command of the Norfolks was Humphrey Wilson who had been a Ghurka. He was absolutely calm even under the heaviest fire, and seemed positively to enjoy danger. His favourite adjective was 'grand'. During the battle Peter sent Humphrey forward to one of the companies who seemed in trouble. As Humphrey left Battalion HQ to walk across a field leading to the company, a stick of Nebelwerfer bombs landed all round him. He had thrown himself on the ground when he heard the Nebel firing and after the bombs landed stood up and shouted back to us, 'Everything grand.'

I always felt more refreshed in the morning if I had been able to sleep in pyjamas rather than in my dirty and often wet uniform. So after we had captured Kervenheim I changed as usual into my pyjamas and climbed into my warm jaeger flea bag in the cellar which was Battalion HQ. During the night I was woken up by Peter Barclay, in full uniform including his equipment, who wanted some fire to break up a counter-attack. This was duly arranged and I returned to my flea bag. I thought no more about the incident and Peter did not mention it. After the war Peter used to shoot with my cousin Prudence and her husband Colin Balfour at their beautiful house at Wintershill in Hampshire. One night at dinner Peter said to Prudence, 'Do you know that during the war that bloody cousin of yours, Robin Dunn, once made a fire plan at my HQ wearing a pair of pyjamas? Bloody man.'

After Kervenheim 185th Brigade pushed on through the forest to capture Kapellen which was in the Siegfried Line and heavily defended with wire and mines. Peter said to me, 'I am not going to have another Kervenheim at Kapellen. We will go round the place in the dark without any artillery support and take them by surprise by infiltrating through the Siegfried Line. Send an FOO with me on foot. You stay with the carriers and mortars and bring them on as soon as it is light.' So, early next morning, I led my little column forward along one of the forest tracks which led through the Siegfried Line. We came across a group of German soldiers, who at once surrendered, pointing at the track and shouting, 'Achtung, Minen.' I asked one of them, a corporal, if he knew the way through the mines which he said he did. I asked if he would lead us through them, 'Jawohl,' he said, so I put him in the leading carrier which I was following and we drove slowly on. Before we had gone very far there was an explosion under the front of the leading carrier and the German corporal, who was standing up beside the driver, was thrown out of the carrier and landed on the ground. We all stopped and I walked forward to find the leading carrier had struck a mine, blowing off its tracks. The German was dead and both the driver's legs were broken. I walked back to my carrier and my driver said, 'Look at that, sir.' Our carrier had passed over a mine, which had been planted just too far below the surface so that although all the soil above it had been removed it had failed to detonate, even though two carriers had passed over it. This incident shook me more than any of the narrow escapes I had had in the war. Whether it was the sight of the unfortunate German being thrown out of the carrier or the realisation of how nearly we had suffered a similar fate I do not know. The leading carrier must also have crossed that mine and it was a miracle that it did not explode when we crossed it. After that incident I sent for a mine detector and arranged for the track to be cleared before moving the column forward. I had been reluctant to do this originally as there were still Germans in the woods and I wished to reach the comparative safety of Battalion HQ as soon as possible. However, no Germans appeared and we eventually arrived intact.

We found Peter and his HQ installed in the keeper's cottage of a large country house called 'Haus Winkel'. The keeper, a big man in his fifties wearing a green velveteen coat and Homburg hat with a badger-hair shaving-brush at the back, told us that the forest was full of deer and wild boar, and a great place for sport. The owner was 'Die Baronin' who had left when the battle had started. The cottage was comfortable and well furnished, with many sporting trophies and photographs on the walls. When our infantry had cleared the woods I walked up to Haus Winkel itself, which was deserted except for a pair of ancient servants. The house was full of family photographs, some of young officers in the uniform of the Panzer Grenadiers. One had been killed in Russia in 1942. I liked the look of them, and wondered how they would react to the inevitable German defeat and the dismemberment of their country, and how many would return to what had clearly been an idyllic country life at Haus Winkel.

By this time the Guards Armoured Division had passed through us on its way to the Rhine, and the battle was over. A most unexpected event then occurred. A signal arrived from 21st Army Group ordering me to leave 7th Field Regiment and take command of 'C' Battery in 4th Regiment Royal Horse Artillery. It was sad to leave the battery which I had trained and commanded in battle, especially at the end of the war. But I was naturally pleased to be given command of a horse artillery battery.

CHAPTER XI

Beyond the Rhine, 1945

I was naturally proud to have been given command of an RHA battery, especially 'C' Battery which was one of the senior batteries of the regiment. The battery had fought at Corunna and in the Peninsula and had supported the successful charge of the Heavy Brigade as well as the charge of the Light Brigade at Balaclava. Immediately before the war the battery had been serving in India, but in 1938 was mechanised and moved to Egypt to join the newly formed 4th Regiment RHA. At that time it was commanded by Jock Campbell, and during the war was unofficially known as 'Campbell's Battery'. When Jock was promoted to command of 4th RHA the battery was commanded by Geoffrey Goschen, who before he was taken prisoner was awarded the DSO, an unusual honour for a battery commander. The battery had acquired a very high reputation in the desert, especially during the early campaigns against the Italians and at Sidi Rezegh, and I felt somewhat daunted at the prospect of keeping up these traditions following my distinguished predecessors.

Many of the soldiers had served with the battery in India and, apart from a few months before the invasion, when they had been brought home, had been abroad for many years. By the time I took command their attitude to life can best be described by the Arabic word 'maleesh', which can be loosely translated as meaning 'nothing is worth worrying about because the fates will decide'. They had adopted the desert approach to informality of dress and showed a bored disregard of military discipline and administration. But they were superb in battle, and the response to calls for fire was quicker and more accurate than anything we had been able to achieve in 16th Battery. They were also contemptuous of anyone, including officers, who had not shared their experiences.

The Colonel was Len Livingstone-Learmouth who had served as a subaltern in my father's 'D' Battery at Aldershot. Len had had a long war, during which he had won the DSO and MC and Bar. He was tall and good looking, with an infectious grin and curly hair. He was also a born leader and the only officer I knew whom the troops would cross the road especially to salute. During the early part of the war he had commanded a battery in 2nd RHA. When he was told in the desert that he was to leave the battery on promotion, he collected all ranks round his jeep, stood up on the bonnet and said, 'You and I have been through a lot together. We were evacuated from Dunkirk and Greece and now we have been up and down this f—ing desert together too many times – and I still think you are a lot of bastards.' The troops loved it and cheered him to the echo. By the time I joined Len was very tired, his wife had run off with another man and he was fed up with the war. But he gave me a charming welcome and all his old dash and fire appeared as soon as we went into battle.

My battery captain was John Weller-Poley who had served in the battery throughout the war, winning the MC in the desert, and by rights should have been given command. But he was not a regular, and as the war drew to its close the policy was to appoint regulars to command regular batteries. From the outset John was utterly loyal to me, full of wise advice, and never showed the disappointment he must have felt when I arrived. We became great friends and after the war Judy and I visited him at his beautiful estate at Boxted in Suffolk where he lived with his wife Nancy and his family. Sadly he died comparatively young.

Just before the regiment crossed the Rhine I was felled with a sharp bout of influenza, and the MO said that I was to remain with the transport echelon and on no account to go into action with the regiment. This was a bad blow and could not have happened at a worse time. The battery were naturally suspicious that this was not a genuine illness, and my chances of being accepted by them received an immediate set-back. So I watched from the west bank of the Rhine when one fine morning the aircraft carrying 6th Airborne Division flew over to drop the paratroops across the river. Fortunately my temperature soon dropped and within a few days I crossed the new Bailey Bridge over the Rhine at Wesel and rejoined the battery.

4th RHA was part of 4th Armoured Brigade, which was an independent brigade and consisted of three armoured regiments and a motor battalion, as well as our regiment. It was commanded by Mike Carver, later to become Chief of the Defence Staff and a peer. At that time he was aged about thirty and had had a brilliant war both on the staff and commanding an armoured regiment. He was very unpopular with the officers of the brigade because of what they saw as his ruthless methods of command. He had even tried to replace Len, but the gunner establishment had intervened and refused to allow one of their most distinguished commanding officers to be sacked by a young brigadier from another arm of the service. I felt that Mike's unpopularity was largely due to military snobbery. He had served in the Tank Corps, whose officers were then regarded by some of the cavalrymen and riflemen as their social inferiors, though this was certainly not true of Mike. This attitude persisted even though the Tank Corps had been amalgamated with the armoured cavalry regiments into the Royal Armoured Corps and re-named the Royal Tank Regiment. In fact I thought up to that time that the Tank Regiments on the whole performed rather better in battle than the armoured cavalry regiments. I personally admired Mike. He would arrive at my OP driving his own Dingo, hatless and relaxed, and would ask in a friendly way how things were going and whether there was anything he could do to help. He was also a decisive and aggressive commander in battle.

'C' Battery was in support of the Royal Scots Greys who had been in Palestine with my father's 1st Cavalry Division. They had not been mechanised until 1941, and had been at El Alamein and all the North African battles thereafter before being brought home for the invasion with the rest of the brigade. They were reputed to be one of the richest regiments in the army, and not to be friendly to strangers in their mess. But from the moment I arrived they were kindness itself and I was made to feel completely at home by all of them, especially by their doyen Hugh Brassey, the second-in-command, whom I had known before the war and who became Lord Lieutenant of Wiltshire.

When I joined the Greys they were assembled in a large wood just east of the Rhine waiting for the order to break out through the assaulting infantry who had crossed the river. The CO Frank Bowlby, having been sacked by Mike Carver, was waiting to be relieved by Duggie Stewart who had been brought out to command in the middle of his staff college course at Camberley. A light rain was falling and I found the officers sitting under a tarpaulin attached to the side of the adjutant's tank, drinking champagne in farewell to their colonel. The adjutant, Adrian Sprot, suddenly said, 'We have just had a message from the 60th (our Motor Battalion) to say that there is a Tiger tank at a map reference which I make a few hundred yards from where we are sitting.' Frank Bowlby at once drank down his champagne, stood up and said, 'This is a job for me.' He called his soldier servant to collect a bazooka and they went off together, Frank wearing a gas cape against the rain, to stalk the Tiger. Soon after they had left the wireless started crackling again and Adrian produced another message which said, 'Reference our last message. Map reference in error. Should be 10,000 yards to the east.' So poor Frank Bowlby never bagged his Tiger, and Duggie arrived soon afterwards.

While the armoured divisions were swanning due east towards Hanover and the Elbe, we were in support of infantry divisions thrusting north-east towards Bremen and Hamburg, and covering much country against sporadic resistance. Peter Hankey was second-in-command of 4th RHA and his principal function was to find a suitable house for Len and his HQ. In the early afternoon Peter would appear among the leading tanks and would place the regimental sign at the gate of the most comfortable looking house he could see, even though it might still be under fire. At 9 pm after a good dinner Len would hold an 'Order Group' for all battery commanders, which was not strictly necessary as we all knew what to do next day. However Len enjoyed a party, and after a glass or two of brandy we would do our best to find our way back to our batteries along the narrow German country lanes. Such was Len's charm that no-one objected to this, although we had to be on the move before first light each morning. Len, on the other hand, never got up before a more civilised hour, when he would come roaring up the column demanding to

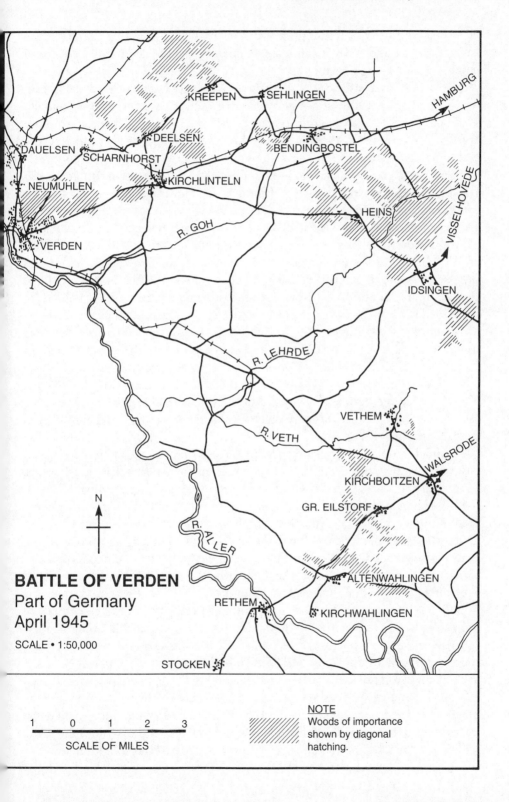

BATTLE OF VERDEN
Part of Germany
April 1945

SCALE • 1:50,000

N

1   0   1   2   3

SCALE OF MILES

NOTE
Woods of importance
shown by diagonal
hatching.

know why we were not pushing on. Even in the desert, when his battery broke leaguer, Len's camp bed would remain alone in its same position until Len judged it appropriate to join the battle.

Our first serious resistance occurred on the River Aller south of Verden. On 14th April 53rd (Welsh) Division had secured a bridgehead over the river at Rethem. Their subsequent task was to turn north, up the east bank of the river, and capture Verden. 4th Armoured Brigade was to break out of the bridgehead, capture Walsrode, then turn north and north-west through the enemy gun areas and invest Verden from the north and east to prevent the escape of the garrison. 7th Armoured Division was to pass through us at Walsrode, headed for Hamburg and the Elbe.

Although we were due to cross the Rethem bridge at 9 am, the infantry had met stubborn resistance from a German marine division which was holding that part of the river, so that it was not until 6 pm that the Greys were ordered to cross the bridge and concentrate at Kirchwahlingen. As darkness drew in Mike Carver gave out his orders in the blazing hamlet of Altenwahlingen. The Corps Commander had said that Kirchboitzen must be captured at all costs early next morning to allow 7th Armoured Division through. 44th Tanks were to go on through the night and open the main road to Greilstorf. The Greys would go across country through the thick woods to the east of the road, establish themselves on the high ground south of Kirchboitzen and capture the village as soon thereafter as possible.

With the Greys was a battalion of my grandfather's regiment, the Royal Welch Fusiliers, mounted in Kangaroos – turretless Sherman tanks which each carried a section of infantry. The woods were said to be full of bazooka men and infantry who were holding up the 60th, and it was plain that an elaborate wood clearing operation by the infantry would take too long if we were to reach Kirchboitzen by morning. So it was decided that the tanks would advance along a single track through the woods, firing their machine-guns with incendiary bullets to either side and setting the woods on fire. The plan worked well, the leading squadron started a good fire, the flames crackling down to the edge of the track like the tide and the bazooka men and snipers could be seen running before the flames. In spite of bad going and broken-down Kangaroos we found ourselves, just before first light, on a bare hilltop a thousand yards south of Kirchboitzen. It was cold and windy on the hill and everyone looked grey and unshaven after our sleepless night.

At 8 am the attack on Kirchboitzen went in. At once a delay was caused by the Kangaroos halting some three hundred yards from the village and dismounting their infantry. This manoeuvre was greeted by considerable Spandau and mortar fire, and there developed a rather slow and sticky little battle, with the tanks helping the infantry forward until they reached the edge of the village, where prisoners started to come in. It was a slow business – every house had to be cleared against, in some places, considerable resistance. A battery of German 105 mm guns shelled the approaches to the village and defied all our rough and ready means of locating them, and they did not cease firing until the village was captured shortly after midday. By this time most of the houses were on fire and about a hundred and fifty prisoners had come in, some terribly wounded. They said that the village had been held by the reserve battalion of the marine division on the Aller, so it looked as if we might be through.

Mike Carver evidently thought so, because he ordered the Greys to push on to Idsingen without delay. At this point the infantry CO, looking gaunt and unshaven, came up to Duggie Stewart and said that his men had eaten nothing but a haversack ration for 24 hours and that he could not go on until their cooks' lorries had arrived and they had fed. The tanks had the advantage of carrying three days rations which were cooked by the individual crews, but the Kangaroos had no such arrangements and depended on centralised cooking. 'Very well,' said Duggie, 'we will go on without you, and you must catch us up as soon as you can.'

As soon as we were replenished with petrol, Duggie sent his reconnaissance troop with its Honey tanks under James Hanbury to see if Vethem was held. James was a keen fox-hunter and later became master of the Cottesmore hounds. The troop reported coming under fire from four guns which were sited along the edge of a wood commanding the open country in front of Vethem. Duggie's reaction was very quick. Leaving the Honeys in observation, he sent his leading squadron to work round the woods and attack the guns from the rear. The FOO with the leading squadron brought the whole of 4th RHA down on the guns. It was all over in twenty minutes. The leading squadron using the ground very cleverly crept round behind the guns, past some burning buildings, up a valley and soon the rattle of Browning machine-guns and the boom of their 75 mms told that they were engaged, and shortly afterwards all the guns were silenced.

By this time we could see enemy infantry in their trenches in Vethem, which lay on the only road to Idsingen and consequently had to be captured to enable the supply echelon to get through. The infantry having fed were arriving in their Kangaroos, and it was decided to attack with a company and a squadron straight into Vethem from the south. Almost immediately six enemy field guns sited only a thousand yards away began to snipe the tanks over open sights. The FOO with the squadron at once ranged on them with 'C' Battery, a round hit some ammunition and set it off, and the Germans shortly thereafter abandoned their guns. Meanwhile the infantry had got into Vethem, where they found about three hundred Germans dug in in an orchard in the middle of the village, and were met with heavy Spandau fire. Casualties began to trickle back. It became clear that Vethem was going to prove troublesome.

Duggie was by now becoming impatient. Idsingen was still five miles off and it was late in the afternoon, so he handed over the Vethem battle to the infantry CO and, taking one of his own squadrons and two infantry companies in Kangaroos, set off across country to Idsingen. It was a pleasant drive across rolling country on a fine spring evening, with no enemy in sight except a super-heavy gun firing in support of the Germans holding Verden, whose detachment were astonished to find themselves suddenly surrounded by tanks. At 8 pm we closed in on Idsingen, our guns which were still back beyond Vethem firing at extreme range. However, there was in the event no opposition, although we captured about seventy bewildered Germans retreating from Verden. Idsingen proved to be a collection of farms and large houses and, having established posts at various road junctions, we settled down at about 11 pm in a large and comfortable farmhouse in the centre of the village and slept for the first time for thirty-six hours. We were across one of the enemy's main lines of retreat from Verden, and rather isolated we felt with our little force and Vethem still holding out behind us.

We stood to at 5 am on 16th April. We heard that Vethem had not been finally cleared until 1 am, but that the road was now open and the remainder of the group and the echelon were on their way to join us. During the night a German horse-drawn battery retreating down the road had bumped into one of our posts, and when Duggie and I visited the post in the early morning the road presented a heart-rending scene of devastation. The detachments had put up a fight, and there were dead gunners lying in the road. The horses, still harnessed and some badly wounded, stood patiently in the road, the dead horses lying in their traces. I thanked God that in our army, at least, no horses were taking part in the war. The unfortunate wounded horses were shot, and the road cleared, while James Hanbury's reconnaissance troop rounded up the gun detachments who were hiding in the woods. We took about a hundred prisoners, who proved some embarrassment as we had no food for them and very few men to spare as guards. However they were quite happy when we told them they could take any food they could find in the farms.

We just had time for an excellent breakfast and a shave when Mike Carver arrived with the rest of the group, including 'C' Battery which came into action near the village. Mike said that we must push on without delay to Bendingbostel. Once again the infantry were a problem, having not eaten since mid-day the previous day, so they were left to come on when they had fed and the Greys, led by James Hanbury's troop, pushed straight up the Bendingbostel road which, a mile from Idsingen, crossed a stream. The bridge was blown, and the banks of the stream were too boggy to be fordable by tanks. The opposite bank was held by infantry. Word was at once sent back for a scissors bridge, a portable bridge carried on a tank, which arrived very quickly and was laid, covered by concentrations of fire from 'C' Battery. A troop of tanks followed by a platoon of Welch Fusiliers was soon across and the advance continued. Progress was slow as thick woods flanked either side of the road and the tanks were sniped by bazookas, fortunately inaccurately, as they moved forward. So it was mid-day before we reached the main Verden to Hamburg road half a mile south of Bendingbostel. It was not until 3.15 pm that the attack on Bendingbostel started. Most of the opposition, which included 88 mm guns as well as infantry, came from two woods astride the road into the village, on which 4th RHA fired concentrations, and eventually the woods were cleared by the infantry supported by the Greys' tanks, which succeeded in knocking out the 88 mms. We took over a hundred prisoners, including some Hitlerjugend aged only fifteen or sixteen. Concentrations were then fired on the village itself, which was soon burning and was taken without opposition. The guns were then moved up from Idsingen to Heins, which made communication easier. A squadron of Greys and a company of Welch Fusiliers was sent north-west to secure the bridges over the River Goh. They soon ran into trouble from bazookas, infantry and well-sited 88 mms causing some casualties, and night fell on a confused little battle some four hundred yards from the village. Just as Duggie and I with the Greys' HQ were moving into the burning village, the Germans greeted us with some fairly heavy shelling which did not please us, especially as one very large gun continued to fire throughout the night on the main cross-roads, near which RHQ had been established. The Greys group moved out of Bendingbostel at 5 am on 17th and advanced to Kreepen which had been captured by 44th Tanks. The guns moved to near Kirchlinteln. On debouching from Kreepen we left the road and struck across country to avoid the woods reputed to be full of bazooka men. After about a mile we spotted a battery of guns sited on the edge of the woods, which the Greys supported by 4th RHA immediately engaged. A later count revealed three 150-mm guns and two 75 mm guns knocked out, together with a mass of abandoned transport and about fifteen dead Germans. By mid-day, after what seemed like a good hunt over galloping grass country, we were on our final objective, the high ground about four hundred yards south of Scharnhorst, where we had a late breakfast and shaved. The afternoon was spent mopping up Kirchlinteln, Scharnhorst, Neumuhlen and the woods around. At 6 pm we were relieved by infantry of 53rd Division and drove back in the fading light, sitting on the turrets of our tanks, to a large and comfortable farmhouse where we found brew fires going, mail up and plenty of hot water.

I was very pleased to have taken part in this 'cavalry action' as I called it in an account I wrote shortly after the war from which the above is taken. For the first time I had seen armour handled as it should be. It is true that by that time the German army was crumbling and there were no enemy tanks, but the villages were almost all strongly, and at times fanatically, defended by desperate men fighting in their own country for their fatherland. Mike Carver had pressed on relentlessly to his objective and I had unbounded admiration for the leadership of Duggie Stewart. His decision on 15th April to leave the infantry to take Vethem, while pressing on with a small force to Idsingen, was just the kind of calculated risk and initiative which had so often seemed lacking in the past. And the response of the Greys was superb. The speed with which they executed orders could only have been achieved by a most highly trained and experienced regiment. They manoeuvred like a well-oiled machine.

Duggie retired from the army soon after the war and become an Olympic rider, before moving to farm on the Scottish Borders, where Judy and I occasionally went fishing with him on the Tweed. He was slight in appearance with a quiet almost diffident manner. But he had the heart of a lion and an ice cold brain which worked with great rapidity and decision. He died in 1990. He was a very fine fighting soldier.

This effectively marked the end of my war. On the day the Germans surrendered, 8th May, 4th Armoured Brigade drove into Hamburg, to be met with a scene of devastation such as I had never witnessed. The whole city lay in ruins from the Allied bombing. Whole districts were reduced to rubble, with only a few buildings still standing. The population were confined to their houses, and we could see them nervously watching us through the windows as the tanks rumbled through the streets.

Meanwhile the Greys had joined 6th Airborne Division who had been pushed rapidly forward to Wismar on the Baltic, which was east of the line agreed as the boundary between us and the Russians. Duggie had asked that 'C' Battery should accompany the Greys, but this had been refused and they were supported by a battery from the corps SP regiment. The ostensible reason for this forward move was to destroy the German army facing the Russians, but the real reason was to prevent the Russians from overrunning the Schleswig-Holstein peninsula.

Duggie later gave me a fascinating account of this operation. They overran the German army from the rear, first capturing hospitals, dumps and HQ and later fighting troops withdrawing towards them. The Germans were told to keep marching to the west, while their arms were collected. At one level-crossing the Greys met a train heading west carrying about a hundred tanks on railway flats. The leading tank put a round of armour-piercing shot through the boiler of the engine bringing it to a stop. Eventually at about mid-day they drove into the main square of Wismar. After about two hours a dilapidated US half-track containing six Russian men and one woman drove in from the east. They looked like brigands, wearing an assortment of uniforms, all very shabby and dirty, and slung about with Tommy guns and bandoliers of ammunition. They said they were from a reconnaissance unit which had left Berlin (seventy miles away) that morning, and that there were no Russian troops between Wismar and Berlin. Duggie told me, 'There we were, full of petrol and ammunition. We had only to motor on and we would have been in Berlin that evening.' When I repeated the story to Judy's father after the war he said, 'If that's what the young army thought I think it's disgraceful.' But it might have saved a great deal of trouble in the future if all the allied armour had adopted Duggie's suggestion.

During the afternoon more Russian half-tracks drove into Wismar and a party ensued in the square, the Greys exchanging their rum ration for the vodka with which the Russians were plentifully supplied. Towards evening a column of lorries carrying supplies for the Russians approached Wismar. At this moment a squadron of our Typhoons appeared overhead and, thinking the lorries were Germans, went screaming in with their rockets causing havoc to the column. Promptly all fraternisation stopped and next morning a barrier had been erected blocking any movement to the east of the town. A day or two later a workmanlike looking Russian tank unit arrived, and the officers of the Greys were invited to dinner. They arrived, dressed in their battledress tops and corduroy trousers, to find the Russians in parade dress, with high collars and red stripes on their trousers. They were mostly very young and said that they were having the time of their lives in Germany. Never had they seen such affluence and plenty. They were mostly of quite humble origin and did not know what they would do after the war. They were not looking forward to returning to their factories and collective farms. The Greys were billeted in a large farm and eventually were ordered to move west of the agreed boundary with the Russians so that the Russians could move in. The farmer and his family, including two pretty daughters, had been very friendly and gave the Greys a sad farewell. When the regiment was lined up preparatory to moving Duggie heard gun shots from the farm. He quickly returned to the house to find the whole family lying dead in the kitchen, with a shot gun beside the farmer.

4th RHA were now settled near Kiel. Our task was to screen the SS who had been moved into the Schleswig-Holstein peninsula, other German troops being allowed to return home to help with the harvest. 'C' Battery was put in charge of the local prison, which was used as a transit camp for SS officers en route for an island in the Baltic where they were to be held. Rather unwisely I put a subaltern in charge of the prison, who had escaped from a POW camp in Italy where he claimed to have been badly treated. One evening after dinner I went to make an unheralded inspection of the prison, and was told by the sergeant of the guard that the subaltern was in one of the cells. When I went in I found the occupant, a senior SS colonel, standing stark naked rigidly to attention with the subaltern sitting on the bed in front of him. I asked what was happening to which the subaltern replied, 'A routine search.' I turned to the Colonel and asked if he had any complaint. 'Nein, Herr Kommandant,' he replied crisply, 'Alles in ordnung.' All the same I felt uneasy, even when the subaltern explained later that such searches were common at all hours in the Italian POW camp. I was uneasy because many of our troops seemed to enjoy humiliating the Germans. It is true that we were just beginning to learn of the atrocities which the Germans had committed against the Jews and others, but I began to realise that even the best disciplined troops with ordinary decent standards of humanity, even British troops, may actually enjoy ill-treating their enemies if they have been convinced that such treatment is justified because of the misconduct of those subjected to it. I was shocked to discover that in that respect we were not perhaps so different from the Germans themselves, although I do not suggest that we would ever have indulged in the kind of organised terror meted out by the latter.

After the surrender no 'fraternisation' was allowed with the German population. They were to be ignored, and communication with civilians was limited to the minimum essentials for administrative arrangements. There was a curfew after dark. For their part the Germans seemed unconcerned by our presence. I was amazed by their smart and prosperous appearance, and by the smartly-dressed women who would emerge from bunkers and damaged houses looking as if they had come from comfortable well-equipped homes. There were practically no men of military age to be seen, and the most usual reply of a woman to the question, 'Where is your husband?' was, 'Gefangener im Ostland.' The country districts which had escaped the bombing showed a life of considerable prosperity. There were many more consumer goods in the shops than in England, and the German economy did not seem to have been geared to war production in the same way as the British.

There were, however, very many displaced persons – Poles, Czechs, French and Belgians from all over Europe. These unfortunate people had been working in the factories and on the farms and were living in squalid conditions in DP camps. Some only wished to go home, others, whose homes were now occupied by the Russians, preferred to stay or move west. Many wished to have the opportunity to retaliate against the Germans for their treatment. 4th RHA had responsibility for some of the camps containing this human flotsam, and they caused far more trouble than any of the Germans. Some had distilled a particularly noxious spirit which caused blindness, and which a few of our troops were unwise enough to drink.

My letters to Judy show the hatred and contempt which we felt for the Germans at the time. The houses were full of books and pictures glorifying the Nazi régime and the achievements of the German Army. Frederick the Great, 'Der alte Fritz', was a particularly popular figure, and when the German army invaded a country the men were obviously expected to put up their hands, and the women their skirts. It amazed me that this intelligent and industrious people should have this streak of militaristic madness. I had the feeling that Germany was a pagan country. In England then the Christian ethic prevailed, and one could sense it. But Germany, with its dark forests full of giants and goblins, and its Wagnerian heroes had a completely different atmosphere to any I had previously experienced. I have never returned and do not wish to.

One day I visited Charles Armitage who had been a contemporary at the Shop, and who had had a most distinguished career in the desert winning the MC and two Bars. He was now Brigade Major to Frizz Fowler who was CRA 11th Armoured Division. During one of the battles the artillery of 11th Armoured had been supporting 3rd Division, and I had had to visit their HQ. Charles was on the wireless in their armoured command vehicle with Frizz pacing up and down outside and continually interrupting Charles. Eventually Charles took off his earphones and said to his Brigadier, 'Why don't you shut up Frizz? Can't you see I'm fighting a battle?' Frizz turned on his heel and said no more, although his eyes were blazing with anger. I thought the incident spoke volumes for their relations. I found Charles in a fine modern house with a marvellous view over the Baltic, which had been built for the Gauleiter of Schleswig-Holstein. On a coffee-table was a beautifully produced art book which I idly picked up. It contained black-and-white drawings of Poles, mostly emaciated, brilliantly executed so as to make them appear degraded and almost sub-human. I thought it cast a revealing light on the character of the Gauleiter.

One afternoon we were having tea on the verandah of the house we had requisitioned as a mess, when a jeep with 21st Army Group signs pulled up, and out stepped John Sharpe. John had served with the regiment in the desert where he had won the MC, and was now a major and one of Monty's liaison officers. He told us that he had come back to the regiment as a captain and explained the circumstances. A few days before Monty had been invited to dine with Marshal Zhukov commanding the Group of Russian armies beyond the Elbe. John had gone with him to act as ADC. It was a large party, with many senior Russian officers present. At dinner many toasts were drunk in vodka and John's glass was repeatedly filled. Eventually he slid under the table, and had to be helped into Monty's staff car when they left. As they drove away a salute was fired by a regiment of Russian tanks drawn up beside the road. As soon as the guns started firing John had stood up in the front of the car, drawn his revolver which was loaded, and fired into the air shouting 'To hell with all Russians; God bless the Royal Horse Artillery.' Next morning he was woken by an ADC and told that the Chief wished to see him. He entered the caravan with a terrible hangover and Monty said: 'Can't have my staff officers behaving like that, John. You will have to go back to your regiment and lose your rank. Won't affect your career. Good-bye and thank you.' Nor did it, for John was to take over 'C' Battery from me and in due course became a full general commanding the Northern Group of NATO armies.

John gave me a fascinating account of life as an LO at Monty's HQ. The LOs were used as the gallopers had been by Wellington in the Napoleonic wars. They were all young men with battle experience, and their task was to visit the divisions actually engaged in operations and report back to Monty personally. They had direct access to the divisional commander. John said that he would arrive at a divisional HQ in the afternoon, when the General would be making plans for next day. He would go first to the main HQ to find out how many casualties the division had suffered in the previous twenty-four hours, especially the names of any senior officers who had been killed or wounded, and also find out if they had any supply problems. He would then go to the tactical HQ where he would see the General personally. The General would brief him off the map as to the locations of his troops and talk generally about the battle. John said Monty was particularly interested in the frame of mind of the General, whether he seemed tired or depressed, or whether he was cheerful and confident. Armed with all this information John would then return to Monty's HQ by 9 pm and go straight to the office caravan, where he would brief Monty, who saw each LO separately. Monty would listen attentively, occasionally asking a question about the morale of the division and its commander. If he disapproved of the proposed plan he would act most correctly. He would never communicate direct with the divisional commander, but would at once telephone the army commander or corps commander saying, 'The – division propose to do this tomorrow. It's just not war. He must do so and so.' It seemed to me a marvellous way of exercising high command in battle. In the Great War the armies in France had become bogged down largely by lack of communication. Even when the infantry had broken through, communications, in the absence of wireless, were so bad that reserves could not be switched to the decisive point before the enemy had had time to recover, and perhaps counter-attack. The higher commanders could not influence the battle, because they were out of touch, and had devised no means of receiving information quickly and transmitting orders in time to be effective. They were also out of touch with the feelings and problems of those on the spot who were actually fighting the battle. Monty's use of LOs enabled him to control the battle in the same way as the great captains of the past.

We were beginning to return to peacetime soldiering in Germany. We had requisitioned a number of horses and I organised early morning rides, gymkhanas, showjumping and other events to keep us fit and occupied, and as an alternative to our rather grim duties of guarding camps. Then suddenly I received an order that I was to return to England to join the next course at the Staff College. I cannot say that I was sorry. I would be with Judy and our two small children and I was not enjoying life in Germany, even commanding 'C' Battery. So I drove to the coast without any regret. En route I stopped by the road to eat my sandwiches when a young German with one arm walked up in a friendly fashion and said how lucky we were to have so much transport. He said he had been in the infantry, 'Nach Stalingrad und zurück, immer zu fuss.' Although he must have travelled most of the way by train, his remark seemed to me to typify the spirit of the German army.

CHAPTER XII

Post-War Soldier, 1945–48

The best thing for me about my time at the staff college was that, after three years of marriage, Judy and I for the first time lived in our own house with our children. She had managed to rent 'Drumrash', a decent-sized Edwardian house with a garden, in Farnborough for the six months of the staff college course, and very happy we were. Although the German war was over, there were still many shortages, including fuel. There was no central heating, few power plugs and it was difficult to get coal or wood so the house was bitterly cold that winter and Judy had problems in keeping the children warm.

My sister Barbara and her husband John Pelly were also living in Farnborough. He was in the Coldstream Guards stationed at Pirbright and they thought it would be fun to be close to us, as John was one of my oldest friends through the friendship of our parents and Barbara was very fond of Judy. John had been taken prisoner at Tobruk and had been much affected by his experiences in a POW camp. Barbara was very young and pretty and full of life, and was quite unable to cope with the situation. Within another three years they divorced, but there was a happy ending. Both remarried, both their second spouses died and over forty years later when John had succeeded to the baronetcy they married for a second time and lived in a comfortable modern house which John had built on his estate at Preshaw in Hampshire, where they were blissfully happy until he sadly died in 1993.

I found life at the staff college a relief after commanding troops during six years of war. We had no responsibility except to arrive in time for the various lectures and discussions. Everyone on the course had spent the war with their regiments, so that there was a great deal of diverse battle experience among the students.

During the course Judy's father asked me how I saw my future in the army. He was what my father called 'soldier bred', his father having been a general in the Great War, so that he knew a good deal about the army, although he was himself what he called 'a-military'. At that time the army was almost entirely stationed abroad. We had large armies in the Middle and Far East and Germany was regarded as a home station. There were very few troops in England, so that we faced the prospect either of Judy and the children following the drum or of long periods of separation. Judy's father said, 'I expect you joined the army, like my brother (who was killed in the Great War) primarily for the opportunities for sport and to be with horses. But all that seems to be changed now. Do you think you will enjoy the peacetime army?' I said perhaps not, but that I did not think I had any option as the only trade I knew was soldiering. He said, 'Why don't you read for the Bar? Lots of soldiers have. There is no need for you to commit yourself, but you can pass your examinations and become qualified, so that at least you will have a label round your neck even if you don't practise.' I thought a great deal about this and discussed it with Judy. She was very attached to Lynch and the life on Exmoor, but had decided to marry a soldier and said, 'I don't believe you would be happy out of the army.' In any event regular officers were not at that time allowed to resign their commissions, so we agreed to leave my decision for the time being until the staff college course was over.

Before the course ended the atomic bombs were dropped on Hiroshima and Nagasaki and the Japanese surrendered. How different was our reaction at the time to the modern attitude of censure of that decision. It was not surprising that we at the staff college were delighted. There would be no invasion of Malaya and no fierce battles in the jungles against the Japanese, in which we were anticipating heavy casualties. Those on the course who had been in Burma said that, whereas all armies preached the doctrine of fighting to the last man and the last round, the Japanese was the only army that actually practised the doctrine. The Japanese had fought the war with great brutality and inhumanity. Those who had been prisoners of war returned with horrific stories of the callous brutality of the Japanese in the POW camps, of near-starvation rations, relentless work in terrible conditions on the Siam railway and of prisoners being beaten and bayoneted to death for trivial offences. These events had received wide publicity and the whole country felt that the Japanese had received their just deserts, that many Allied lives would be saved by the bombs and that Japanese military power must be destroyed for all time. There was no heart searching. No moral doubts of the justice of what had been done. Just joy and relief. Judy and I went to London to celebrate on the night of the surrender. We walked down Piccadilly, which was blocked by a large crowd of pedestrians all cheering and singing at the news. I was wearing my Blue Patrol uniform and was kissed on both cheeks by a pretty girl in the crowd who said, 'Oh! You do look nice. I'm so glad you're not going to have to fight those horrid Japanese.'

At the end of the course I was told that I was to be posted to India. This was a bad blow. Judy and I had spent so much of the war apart and had hoped for a home posting, so that I could get to know the children. Although it was possible for families to go to India, the political situation was uncertain and there was the possibility of an armed uprising against British rule, so that India would not be safe for women and children. However, we decided to wait and see what the situation was when I arrived there. Meanwhile I would read for the Bar as a second string in case I decided to leave the army when I could. So I enrolled for a correspondence course for part

I of the Bar examinations at Gibson & Weldons, the law tutors in Chancery Lane, and arranged for the papers to be sent to me in India.

While on leave after leaving the staff college I went to Cardiff as marshal to Judy's father, who was sitting there as one of the judges of assize. This was my first experience of the law in action. I sat on the Bench in my uniform and was responsible for swearing the witnesses and acting as ADC to the judge. I found the cases difficult to follow. We lived in great comfort in the judges' lodgings with the two other judges, 'Owlie' Stable and Stephen Henn-Collins, and played billiards in the evenings. They were both very kind to me. 'Owlie', who was a keen shooting man and had his spaniel with him, said to me one day, 'I can't think, marshal, why you want to go to the Bar. Why don't you go into the Church? With reasonable intelligence and a slightly defective conscience you would be bound to become a bishop.' 'Owlie' became known as a character. His favourite breakfast was a brace of snipe washed down by half a bottle of hock, which he was given on his 80th birthday when he was sitting at Birmingham. He had won the MC in the Great War, as had Judy's father. Like me he was addicted to the works of Surtees. I always found that generation easy to get on with, as in their youth they had shared so many of my own experiences. Those who had grown up between the wars and were too old to take an active part in our war seemed to me to have a different attitude to life. Little did I think, when I left Cardiff, that I would be back in those same lodgings twenty-two years later as a judge of assize.

I was more upset at leaving Judy and the children for India than at any time during the war. Perhaps I was beginning to get used to family life, but the principal reason was that I felt that this separation was unnecessary. When en route for the Middle East, the Normandy beaches and Holland I had felt a sense of high excitement at being able to play a small part in great historical events. But now that the war was over I felt there was no real purpose in my absence from those I loved. On the other hand I felt a strong affinity with India. My mother had been born there. Both my grandfathers had spent much of their service there, and twenty-five of my Colvin relations had made their lives there and contributed much to the country. I had been brought up on stories of life in India. Now I was to see it for myself – so I determined to make the best of it.

On arrival by air in Delhi I was interviewed at GHQ by a charming elderly civilian in a white suit, who told me that I was to be posted as Gunner Instructor at the Tactical Training Centre at Clement Town, near Dehra Dun. He said it would be an interesting job as we would be training potential battalion and regimental commanders, most of whom were now Indian since the Indianisation of the Indian army. He also said, more importantly, that Dehra Dun was a good station. It was about four thousand feet up in the foothills of the Himalayas and was classed as a semi-hill station and never became unbearably hot. He said that the best shooting and fishing in India were available.

I was then summoned before the Major-General Royal Artillery, Mead Dennis, an old friend of my father's. In the Great War they had travelled together in a very slow troop train from Calais all across France and Italy to Brindisi where they had embarked for Palestine. There was a great shortage of water and all had been troubled by lice. After that war Mead had become a leading amateur steeplechase jockey, and had won the Foxhunters' Cup at Aintree. He had been commander of the 30th Corps RA at El Alamein and in North Africa and had been brought home for the invasion by Monty as Major-General RA 21st Army Group. Mead greeted me with great affability and invited me to lunch the following day. He said I must do three things in India: learn the local language, Urdu; study the Indian problem and get to know Indians; and learn to fly. He had enthusiastically taken up flying himself and was hoping to start an RA Flying Club. In the course of our conversation he said that the most noticeable change, since he had been in India before the war, was the emancipation of women. He said they were very much leading their menfolk by the nose in the field of Indian nationalism. Many of them had been educated in Europe and were very intelligent, as well as being most attractive and sophisticated. 'In fact,' he said, 'it is extremely difficult when having a mixed British/Indian party to find English women who are fit to be invited if British prestige is not to be lowered.' He went on to say that I would miss a lot of the advantage of being in India if I did not meet educated Indian women. Unfortunately at Dehra Dun I was unable to take his advice. I naturally asked him about bringing Judy out, since this was uppermost in our minds. His reply was, 'Quite apart from the political situation, I would not insult my wife by asking her to live in the sort of accommodation available. People are living in what would, before the war, have been considered servants' quarters.' I did not, in my mind, accept that advice, nor did I tell him that I was considering leaving the army and going to the Bar. Finally he said, 'I don't suppose you want to stay on the Staff for more than a year. Then you must go back to the regiment.' He said that a lot of old duds were being sent out by the War Office to command regiments, just at the time when we could not afford to have failures. The whole interview lasted over half an hour and I felt encouraged and stimulated by what he had said – except about wives.

Next day I left on the night train for Dehra Dun. It was my first experience of the famous, or infamous, Indian railways of which I had heard so much. There were two Indians in the carriage, one a holy man who was visiting the Ganges, a Gurkha colonel wearing a DSO and MC who had not been home for twelve years, and myself. I was impressed by the great courtesy and even respect with which the Colonel treated the Indians, especially the holy man. We stopped and waited endlessly at every station so that we did not sleep much. The third-class carriages were filled to overflowing with Indians, some travelling on the roof or sitting astride the buffers. Early in the morning we stopped at Hardwar on the Ganges, the holy river where the halt and the maimed came to wash in the healing waters. Old people came to drink the water before they died, although it was the main sewer of northern India. When we arrived the people swarmed out of the train like lemmings, carrying their pathetic bundles of clothes and making their way to the river. Just before 8 am we arrived at Dehra Dun, relieved at the cool air after the oppressive heat of Delhi.

Clement Town was a disappointment. It was a wartime hutted camp built in a jungle clearing for training in jungle warfare. On one side the jungle, with its incessant croaking of crickets, came right to the edge of the camp and in the evenings buck, cheetah and monkeys were to be seen. On the other a flat plain with nullahs and a tea plantation ran down to Dehra Dun, about three miles away. In the mornings the village women went to the narrow stream running down the nullah to do their washing, while the bullock carts drove slowly along the bank, clouds of dust engulfing them. The Dun valley, as it was called, ran between the Himalayas and the Silkha hills (said to be the origin of the Seeonee hills in *The Jungle Books*) and in Hindu mythology was known as 'the playground of the gods', as it was here that they were supposed to come from the mountain tops to enjoy themselves. Certainly it was a pleasant place. Beyond the Silkhas the plains lay sweltering in the heat and the line of the Himalayas, a misty gold in the distance, provided a superb backcloth to the north.

Dehra Dun was an established military station, the home of the Indian Military Academy, with well-built bungalows, long tree-lined avenues and playing-fields and open spaces not unlike Sandhurst.

Clement Town itself had long been a centre for Anglo-Indians, or Eurasians as they were called, and was a shabby run-down place. These unfortunate people, the progeny mostly of British fathers and Indian mothers and their descendants, were not accepted by either community. They were not eligible for British clubs and not welcomed by the Indians. I often wondered what happened to them after Independence. Jobs were reserved for them on the Indian railways, which were effectively operated by Anglo-Indians. The men were the only people in India who appeared habitually to wear sun helmets, or 'Bombay bowlers'. Many of the girls were divinely pretty when young, but the older women had a tendency to run to fat. Some wore the colourful and very becoming sari, but most wore European clothes and all referred to England as 'home', although they had never been there and probably never would. They talked in a lilting sing-song voice called 'chi-chi' and, not surprisingly, were inclined to be excitable and unsure of themselves.

On arrival I was allotted a bearer, Akbar Khan, who, although a willing enough young man with quiet manners, was not really up to the job, so I soon engaged Mohammed Afsar. Like so many bearers he was a Kashmiri Mussulman, an experienced bearer, highly intelligent and an excellent cook. We always had tea in our bungalows but, as time passed, I increasingly often dined in my bungalow off delicious vegetable curries and other Indian delicacies cooked by Afsar, instead of in the mess.

Following Mead Dennis's advice I engaged a Munshi who came for an hour every evening to teach me Urdu, for which I paid him 30 rupees, or £2 a month, about

1s 6d an hour in those days. He was a bearded Sikh from the Punjab called Khenis Singh and very talkative.

There were, at the centre, half a dozen horses, none under the age of thirteen, and I used to ride one of them every morning before breakfast. The horses were in the charge of Naur Mohammed, who had served as an NCO in one of the Indian cavalry regiments. He treated me in a fatherly way and persuaded me to take on the running of the stables. He called me 'Husoor' (Lord) or 'Bahadur' (Hero) and always wore an immaculately cut pair of jodhpurs. I used to get up at 6 am and ride out before breakfast. This was the best time of day in India. I rode through the villages, with the yellow pie-dogs barking and snapping at my pony's heels. Half a dozen women in single file with chattis (brass circular jars) on their heads, would be swaying gracefully down to the nullah for water. An Indian on a pony, its head held high in the air, would pass me at a curious gait, half trot half canter. At that time of day all was very quiet, the only sounds being the smack of wet clothes onto flat boards as the dhobi men beat out their washing, and the call of the kites circling in the clear sky overhead. The vultures sat round menacingly waiting for death, or devouring a carcass. There were herds of sheep and goats, white and black, moving into the shade for the day, water buffaloes standing lazily in the nullahs, and hobbled ponies hopping across the plain. The people in the villages were as friendly as those in the English countryside, calling out 'Salaam Sahib' as I rode through.

About thirty miles from Dehra Dun stood the hill station of Mussoorie where most people went at weekends. But I preferred fishing and went most weekends with 'Wilkie' Wilkinson, another instructor at the centre, to fish the Jumna and its tributaries.

The two of us would hire a 15-cwt truck from the centre, load our camp kit and cooking utensils on board, and drive to the river with our bearers squatting in the back on top of the assorted equipment and thoroughly enjoying our change of scene. We would camp in the jungle, beside the river and fish from dawn until about 10 am, when we would have tiffin, a kind of brunch, usually freshly caught fish and eggs, and fish again in the late afternoon and evening until it was dark.

The fish were mostly trout and mahseer, the latter the leading game fish of India which, when hooked, races off downstream with a tremendous rush and surge; but thereafter, unless it sulks behind a boulder, allows itself to be reeled in without fighting. Mahseer varied in weight from two up to over forty pounds and we fished with a spoon, standing in sandshoes up to our waists in the fast running water, which at that time of the year was tepid except when a flood of snow water came down from the Himalayas, taking our breath away.

This was the way to see the sights and sounds of India. We drove through the cultivation near Dehra Dun, where the farming was of the most primitive and uneconomical kind. There was no mechanical equipment, and the bullock cart, the yoked oxen in the plough and the water wheel still reigned supreme. The rivers all ran through jungles, where there was a surprisingly large number of people, who appeared as if from nowhere as soon as we arrived. They were charming and friendly and always enquired whether we had had good sport. Wilkie carried a medical chest, and in the evenings a string of prospective patients would arrive at our camp to be given remedies from his modest stock, mostly quinine and antiseptics. One man arrived with a badly poisoned swollen finger, over which he had placed a raw egg which he insisted was an infallible cure. Once we camped near a ferry, which carried bullock carts and pilgrims across the river, and had an ingenious method of operation. It would swing out at right angles to the current, swirl round and finish up in the correct position on the opposite bank. It must have needed a good deal of skill to achieve this feat time after time.

Once we were lucky enough to obtain a forest rest house for the weekend. This belonged to the Forestry Commission, and was typical of hundreds scattered all over India, belonging to various government departments, for the use of officials on tour. When not in use they could be rented by people shooting and fishing in the jungles, and were naturally much in demand and usually bespoken by the powerful retired community of Dehra Dun. However, this particular weekend we were lucky and drove up to the Kansrao Forest Rest House amid subdued cries of 'bahut achha' or 'very good' from our bearers. And indeed the bungalow and its setting in a jungle clearing were charming. The bungalow itself, built in 1891, was a square white solid-looking building with a thatched roof and low eaves. It consisted of a large living room, with two bedrooms and bathrooms, a scullery and a small bungalow for the servants. It was very well built with good solid fittings, comfortable arm chairs, well framed pictures from Christmas numbers of the *Illustrated London News*, and two copies of *Blackwoods* for the year 1919. A feature of the bungalow was the punkah, a large screen with a skirt attached, which was suspended from the ceiling (at least 15 feet high) by ropes. While the sahibs sat beneath, the punkah was moved backwards and forwards by another rope pulled from the ground by the punkah wallah, a venerable old gentleman with a white beard who sat cross-legged on the verandah with the rope attached to his big toe, moving his leg so as to operate the punkah, which disturbed the air in the room and was much more effective than the electric fans which had replaced it in most Indian houses.

The jungle round the rest house was full of game, cheetah, black partridge, jungle fowl, barking deer, snipe and most remarkable of all a lizard the size of a small crocodile, six feet long, which we found sleeping in a wallow. Soon after we arrived at the rest house a group of locals appeared in our clearing to apply for the various jobs available, sweeper, punkah wallah and so on. The jobs were by tradition in the gift of our bearers and there followed a long period of bargaining and chatter before the various posts were allotted. Wilkie said that the jobs went to those who were prepared to return most of their wages to the bearers. Before we left our temporary servants lined up to receive their money, each in turn placing his hands together before his face as if in prayer saying, 'I shall pray for the sahib's long life and happiness.'

Many of Judy and my letters at this time contained discussions of if and when she should come out, and whether she should bring the children. I had applied for a passage for her when I was at GHQ in Delhi, and she had done the same in London. We both agreed that she should not come until October when the weather would be cooler. But our main worry was the political situation.

In May, at the height of the hot weather, we drove down to Agra to take part in a HQ Signals exercise to practise all headquarters in our role in the event of an emergency.

I visited the tomb of my forebear John Russell Colvin who was Governor of the North West Province and was murdered in Agra during the Indian Mutiny in 1857. His tomb is still very prominent in the centre of the city and was recently visited by our daughter Janie and her husband. I also visited the Red Fort and the Taj Mahal. I was so moved by the latter that, for the first and only time in my life, I expressed my feelings in verse:

> Standing there, fierce Moghul warrior,
> Revelling in war like a modern Hun,
> Your foul mouthed soldiery clustered round you
> Stinking, cursing, in the terrible sun,
> You look along the river Jumna,
> Limp and static at your feet,
> Lust and lechery in every line of your
> Squat hard body, sweating in the heat.
> Gracious and poised she sits by the river,
> Her perfect proportions so chaste and rare;
> The wonder of her charm, her magical presence,
> With a cool white body passing fair.
> She sits and laughs, innocent and friendly,
> But with hint of passion in her sparkling eye,
> Tempting, inviting, repelling, gently
> Twining round the heart of a passer-by.
>
> The sun goes down o'er the River Jumna
> The turtles feed along the banks,
> The crickets croak and the jackals snarl,
> And the Red Fort gazes at the Taj Mahal.

Amongst my papers is a document headed 'Ten rules for a young man in India.' I do not remember its origin, but one rule states, 'Treat the educated Indians as equals, don't patronise them and remember they hate your guts.' There were many educated Indians at the centre in Clement Town and we would often talk far into the night. They all acknowledged the benefits of British rule. For the first time in history the warring races and religions of the sub-continent had been welded into a united India. This has been achieved through relatively uncorrupt government and the even-handed administration of justice, ensuring the hitherto unknown boon of security of life and property. That British rule was accepted by the overwhelming majority of the disparate peoples was plain from the small numbers of British administrators and British troops which in peacetime formed the garrison. But they could not bear our superiority and arrogance, which they said would oblige us to quit India sooner rather than later, since we had lost much of our relative power in the war, although we had been victorious.

Every Indian with whom I spoke would eventually produce some story of an unforgivable insult or humiliation which he had suffered at the hands of the British. The most horrific was that of Yaqqub Khan. He was the nephew of the Rajah of Rampur, a small north Indian state, and his family had a long tradition of service to the Imperial Crown. So, after Harrow, he went to Sandhurst and received a King's (as opposed to a Viceroy's) commission in an Indian cavalry regiment, where he was the first Indian King's commissioned officer. He had made many friends in England and had stayed in some great houses. He had been a POW in Italy with John Pelly and Geoffrey Goschen, who had told me about him when they heard that I was going to India.

Yaqqub said that it was a shock to return to India and find himself treated as a second-class citizen in his own country by people, especially women, whom he knew were second-class citizens in their country and would never be invited to the houses of his English friends. Soon after the outbreak of war Yaqqub's regiment was ordered to the Middle East and duly arrived at one of the camps by the Suez Canal. One day the Colonel, who was an old-fashioned Indian army officer, called a conference of all officers, except Yaqqub. After the conference Yaqqub asked his tent mate, with whom he had been at Sandhurst, what the conference was about and why he had been excluded. The young man, looking extremely embarrassed said, 'I should not tell you this, because the Colonel said you were not to be told. But of course I shall. The fact is that we are moving up to the desert shortly, but the Colonel did not want you to know because he regarded you as a security risk.' Yaqqub said that he felt as though he had been slapped on the face. 'After all,' he said, 'this was not my war. It was a British war. But I had sworn allegiance to the King Emperor, partly because of my family tradition and partly because I felt the British had done so much for India. It had never entered my head to break that oath, or that anyone should suppose that I would.' He went on to make excuses for the Colonel, saying that he came from a generation which had never trusted Indians since the Mutiny and that the younger British Indian army officers were quite different. All the same it was a shaming story for me to hear and explained a great deal of what was happening in India. Yaqqub later became a general in the Pakistani army. I last saw him in the Cavalry Club in London, where he seemed more at ease than he had at Clement Town. Like so many of my wartime contemporaries he has now died.

In July the monsoon broke and the rain poured straight down out of the sky and off the roofs and gutters, filling the nullahs and greening the grass. Judy and I were becoming frustrated because there was no news of her passage and we were both unhappy at our enforced separation. She had suggested a compassionate posting home, but I had said that unfortunately there was no ground for that. One day I was summoned to the office of the commandant, a nice old Indian army brigadier waiting to go home on pension. He said, 'I am so sorry to hear about your wife.' I asked what he meant. He said, 'Nothing critical I understand, but I fear she is not at all well and I have had a signal from GHQ that you are to be posted forthwith to England.'

Eighteen days after leaving Bombay we docked at Southampton.

Judy met me at Taunton station dressed in riding boots and breeches, having come straight from the Exford horse show where she had won the Hunter class. Once in the car I said, 'How on earth did you manage this? Do tell me what happened.' 'Well,' she said, 'I thought something drastic had to be done. So I went to the War Office where I explained our family situation to a most charming young man. He said, "Leave it all to me. You don't have to tell any lies. I will tell the lies and have your husband home in a jiffy."' I knew Judy was most attractive and charming, but I had never imagined that she could use her feminine wiles so effectively. I wondered who the young officer at the War Office had been, and would like to have heard what reason he had given for the compassionate posting.

My last years in the army were spent as military secretary to the Commander-in-Chief Anti-Aircraft Command. HQ AA Command was at Stanmore, next door to HQ Fighter Command RAF with whom they had worked closely in the war. The C-in-C was Lieutenant-General Sir Otto Lund, who had been in the same term as my father at the Shop. He had been a protégé of Alan Brooke's and, when the latter was succeeded as CIGS by Monty, Otto felt somewhat out of sympathy with the higher direction of the army. He once said to me, sadly, 'Orthodoxy is a question of timing. One year you may be ultra-orthodox, the next unorthodox and regarded as an outsider.' Like many senior soldiers he was disappointed when told he would not be promoted, as he had looked forward to a seat on the Army Council. On a personal level I could not have had a better or more considerate chief. He was fun to work with, very decisive and full of charm. He enjoyed the good life and had a most beautiful wife, Peggy, and they were both very kind to Judy and me.

We had bought a modern house with a large garden on Stanmore Hill, a good place for the children, although the shortages were even worse than in wartime and Judy spent long hours queueing for food. In the bitterly cold winter of 1947 we once again ran out of fuel for our solid-fuel boiler since the coal trucks were frozen at the pits, and Judy used to make the children jump up and down to keep warm. But it was marvellous at last to be together as a family and entertain our friends.

In 1947 my father was remarried to Joan De Lisle Bush, whose husband had died in 1942. She lived at Eastington Park in Gloucestershire, where she was struggling to keep up the farm for the benefit of her young son Michael. A few years after they married Eastington was sold and my father bought Bencombe at Uley near Dursley. This was a charming Queen Anne house with an orchard, paddocks and stabling for half-a-dozen horses. Joan was, if possible, more passionately fond of fox-hunting than my father. They hunted for many years regularly with the Berkeley and occasionally with the Beaufort and with common interests their marriage was a very happy one until my father died in 1985. From the outset of the marriage Joan identified herself completely with our family and was known by our children and grandchildren as 'Grandma Joan'.

In 1948 it was announced that regular officers could resign their commissions. By that time I had passed part I of my Bar exam through my correspondence course, and had decided to go to the Bar as soon as I could. I did not relish the idea of staying in the army, with constant movements between stations at home and abroad, nor of possibly returning to command a battery in peacetime having done the real thing in war. The Inns of Court made things easy for those who had served in the forces. We were excused eating our dinners, a process which would normally have taken three years. The only requirement was to pass the Bar final exam. So I retired with a gratuity of £1000 after ten years service and enrolled for a three-month intensive course of cramming at Gibson & Weldon's in Chancery Lane.

This involved going to London every day for two hours of lectures. The method of instruction was simple but effective. There were only a limited number of questions that could be asked for each paper. Gibson's were experts at spotting the questions that were likely to be asked for the next examination and provided us with a printed sheet giving the answers. Having a reasonably good visual memory I simply learnt the answers by heart and was astonished when the results were published to find that I had got a 2nd Class. No 1st Class was awarded. So in October 1948 I was called to the Bar by the Inner Temple.

For thirty years thereafter I had no connection with the army, except through my many soldier friends. Indeed, I deliberately put the army behind me and tried to absorb the ethos of the Bar. Then in 1980 when I was appointed to the Court of Appeal, I was asked to become an Honorary Colonel Commandant Royal Artillery. This surprised and delighted me. It was a unique honour, since all Colonels Commandant were either generals or senior territorial officers who had done good work for the regiment. My duties were not demanding and I felt that I was coming home. Sitting in the Woolwich mess at our annual Colonel Commandants' dinner, with my grizzled contemporaries round me listening to the superb rendering of the Post Horse Gallop by our trumpeters, I can re-live the scenes of my youth.

Exmoor Interlude

From the time of my marriage to Judy her home, Lynch, became my home and her family became my family. Although my practice at the Bar obliged us to live in London for most of the year, Lynch was our base and the place where our children were brought up. We spent all the holidays there and most week-ends. Our youngest daughter, Janie, like our other two children, was born there in 1950. We lived a real country life, centred on the stables. We rode every day and hunted as much as our horse power would allow, especially with the staghounds. I became increasingly involved in local affairs: the National Trust which owned much of the local countryside; and the hunt committee. Although engrossed in the law, and with many friends in London, I always kept one foot firmly on Exmoor. So it was natural that, when I had completed fifteen years on the Bench, I should retire to devote myself to the life there. And once I had retired I did not feel any compulsion to continue to sit part-time in the Court of Appeal. I put the law behind me, although I retained contact with my old friends and contemporaries. So, throughout my time at the Bar and on the Bench, I was strongly influenced by country life as lived at Lynch. Leigh Holman, an old friend of Judy's father, once said, "Robin's principal interest will always be his work." In a way this was true, but the family and the life at Lynch was my background and were the true realities of my life.

PART II

THE LAW

CHAPTER XIII

Fountain Court, 1948–57

Judy's father had arranged for me to go as a pupil to Jim Hale, who had worked with him in MI5 early in the war and for whose ability he had a high regard. Jim had a fine mind and I often wonder to what heights he would have risen had he not died from a brain tumour while still in his forties. He had won a scholarship to Charterhouse and an exhibition to Balliol, where he had thrown himself into social life and got a disappointing degree. But he had had a meteoric start at the Bar and after the interruption of the war started to re-build his practice. He modelled himself on F. E. Smith, to whom he had a certain physical resemblance.

Jim was in chambers in Fountain Court, a rabbit warren of a building in the Middle Temple which resembled a public lavatory, with stone staircases and white-glazed tiled walls. The whole building was occupied by one set, about a dozen barristers which was large for those days. Although Blanco White KC, who sat regularly as a divorce commissioner, was nominally head of chambers, they were in fact run by the head clerk Arthur Smith. Arthur appeared in manner as a cross between a bishop and the butler to a duke, although he would do anything to obtain a brief. He was one of the first clerks to realise that a large set of chambers was better for the clerk than the previous small sets. So, over the years he had extended his empire from the ground floor, where he had started with a single barrister, until he was clerk to the whole building. He also realised that, from the point of view of the clerk, a large number of small cases was more remunerative than a smaller number of big cases. This was because of the system of clerk's fees. The clerk was paid by the client a standard fee for every case whatever its size and, in addition, the barrister paid the shillings on the guineas in which he was always paid. 'The charm of the job,' said Arthur once to me, 'is the shillings on the guineas.' It gave Arthur more satisfaction to get a young man into good practice than to clerk an established practitioner. 'There are two hurdles,' he would say. 'The first is to earn £1500 a year. If you can earn £1500 you can earn £2000. The second hurdle is £3000 – that means a High Court practice.' He believed in encouraging the young men and if one returned to chambers having lost a case he would say, wiping a tear from his weeping eye with a cambric pocket handkerchief, 'Ah – but no doubt justice was done.'

Because of Arthur's influence the chambers, when I joined, were 'small work' chambers. There were many chambers clients, mostly suburban solicitors, who would send briefs to 'one of Smith's men' without too much regard as to who held the brief. Arthur discouraged the taking of silk and, until the appointment of Edward Pearce shortly before my arrival, chambers had never produced a High Court judge. Arthur was a Master Mason when that arcane movement was strong in the law, especially among solicitors and managing clerks, and many of our solicitor clients were Masons. Arthur was said to be the only person, except judges and law officers, for whom the policeman stopped the traffic outside the Law Courts, so that he could cross the Strand in safety. Rumour suggested that this service was rendered in consideration of a small payment, but I prefer to believe that it was due to Arthur's distinction of bearing and his acknowledged position as the doyen of the Temple clerks.

There were two other clerks, Clement Mulhern and Fred who wrote out the fee notes in a fine copper plate hand. Clement succeeded Arthur as head clerk and was one of the best in the Temple. Although Irish by origin he was a real cockney, with a quick mind and an extraordinary memory. He was also a hard taskmaster, pressing us to do our papers and discouraging us from taking too much of the vacations. Although papers were sent down to be done at Lynch, Clement would always ring up in the middle of September to say, 'When are you coming back? I've got some cons [conferences] I've been putting off and there are a few jobs in court.' He was also very good with solicitors, building up good-will and never overcharging although, as Arthur would say, 'The labourer is worthy of his hire.' The amazing success of chambers over the years was due in large measure to Clement, whom I was proud to count as a friend. There was one part-time typist and most of our pleadings and opinions were written in longhand and sent out in manuscript.

Other members of chambers were Frank Laskey, who at the age of 25 had commanded a tank battalion in the Great War, Malcolm Wright who sadly died shortly after becoming a much-loved County Court judge, and Christopher Besley who became a metropolitan magistrate. These three all practised principally on the Western Circuit, which I joined, and where Malcolm especially had a large practice in Devon and Cornwall. Then there was Donald McIntyre, who had been a prisoner of war of the Japanese, and Roger Ormrod who became an outstanding Lord Justice and made a unique contribution to family law. At that time Roger already had a large divorce practice and was a most stimulating and entertaining companion. Dougal Meston had little practice, but published a series of notes and commentaries on various more or less esoteric acts of parliament, and went every day to sit in the House of Lords, where he supported the Liberal Party.

My own immediate contemporaries were James Comyn, from a distinguished Irish legal family, one of the leading advocates of my generation (he was almost unbeatable before a jury), and later a High Court judge until ill-health obliged him to retire; David Moylan who became a Circuit judge; and Roger Gray who became a

QC and was for many years head of chambers. All these had done well at Oxford. James had been president of the union, David had got a first in Greats and was the best lawyer in chambers and Roger had also been president of the union with a first in jurisprudence and just missed a cricket blue. At first I felt at a disadvantage, since they all had a fluency and felicity of expression which I could not match. However, we all became lifelong friends and there was no jealousy or competitiveness between us. Indeed we often used to do one another's cases – Clement would rush in with an undefended divorce brief and say, 'You're on in ten minutes in Court III. JC (or JDFM or RG) is tied up and can't make it. Read the papers as you go over.' The fee was invariably paid to the one whose name had originally been on the brief.

As a pupil I paid Jim 100 guineas for the privilege of sitting for a year in his room, reading his papers, attending conferences and sitting with him in court. Inevitably I soon asked, 'How can you appear for someone who you know to be in the wrong?' Jim characteristically replied, 'See what Johnson says about it' – he was a Johnsonian. So I looked up Boswell's *Life* and found the relevant passage, 'If lawyers were to undertake no causes till they were sure they were just, a man might be precluded altogether from a trial of his claim, though, were it judicially examined, it might be found a very just claim.' This satisfied my conscience and I began to learn to approach a case, not on the basis of what I thought of its merits but on what I thought the reaction of a judge or jury was likely to be. I also learnt that the result of cases depends on how the evidence comes out in court on the day, and apparently weak cases sometimes become stronger in court and vice-versa.

One day, while having coffee between cases in the crypt of the Law Courts, Jim and I were joined by Quintin Hogg (now Lord Hailsham) who had been with Jim at Oxford. In the course of conversation Quintin said, 'My father could have been either Prime Minister or Lord Chancellor. I could never understand why he chose the latter.' Jim replied, 'I always knew there was a strong streak of vulgarity in you, Quintin.'

In the middle of pupillage Jim was obliged to go to hospital and never returned to chambers. Harry Phillimore then offered to take me for the remainder of my pupillage and, if we suited one another, suggested that I should stay on as his 'devil', researching the law and doing a first draft of his pleadings and opinions, in return for a rent-free seat in a small cubby hole of a room next door to his room on the ground floor of Fountain Court. This was a marvellous opportunity. In those days there was no legal aid and the best way to get into practice was to climb on someone else's shoulders. A devil gained much experience of paperwork, came to know his master's solicitor clients and would hope to get some smaller work from them and eventually to inherit his master's practice when he took silk.

Harry taught me my business in the law. After Eton and Christ Church he had started in practice a few years before the war. He had served in the disastrous Norwegian campaign in 1940 and then gone into the POW department of the War Office as a staff officer. In that capacity he had attended the Yalta conference and was present at the plenary sessions. He said that Stalin was terrifyingly able with a phenomenal memory, who had run rings round both Roosevelt, who was dying, and Churchill, who was exhausted. After the war Harry had gone with David Maxwell-Fife, then Attorney-General, as part of the British prosecuting team to the Nuremberg War Crimes trial. He said that Goering was by far the most able of the defendants, never giving anything away in cross-examination and treating the whole proceedings with an amused contempt. Now Harry was busy rebuilding his practice.

I told Harry that I felt handicapped as, having been crammed through the Bar exams, I knew practically no law. 'That does not matter,' he said. 'You can always look it up once you know where to find it. The only branch of the law which you must have at your fingertips is the law of evidence. Take Phipson (the leading textbook on evidence) home for the long vacation and master it.' It was good advice, which I followed.

Harry said, 'You cannot start to be a barrister until you have seen a High Court case through its various preliminary stages and learnt to plead. Keep a precedent book and any pleading you think useful copy into the book. The best way to learn to plead is to copy out good pleadings in long hand, so that you absorb the style.' I later followed the same practice with my own pupils.

I also sat in on all Harry's conferences and watched his technique. 'Never pontificate or play the great man,' he said. 'The purpose of a conference is to find out what the client wants and decide how far you can deliver. Most clients simply want to know what to do next. And always support your instructing solicitor if you can. Never never make him look a fool in front of a lay client.'

Harry was a master tactician and many cases were won, or favourable settlements reached, by carefully drafted letters, or well-judged preliminary moves before the masters or registrars.

Harry was a relaxed and charming advocate. 'I do not,' he said 'admire the man who wins a good case with style and panache. If the case goes wrong it will be a disaster. I admire the man who can save something from the wreck of a hopeless case, even a few costs.' 'Open the case low,' he would say, 'and let it grow. If you open high your client may go into the witness-box and make your opening look foolish.' He was a great believer in careful preparation before he went into court. We would spend hours working out a cross-examination. 'Cross-examination,' Harry said 'is like ferreting [he was himself a countryman]. 'You must block every hole and then put in the ferret. And never ask a question to which you do not know the answer. One loose question in cross-examination can lose a case.' But he always maintained that examination-in-chief was more important than cross-examination. 'You must get out your client's evidence in an orderly and logical sequence so that it comes across convincingly. Otherwise you will never get the case off the ground.' He seldom re-examined. 'If the witness has been discredited in cross-examination there is not much you can do about it. If not, leave well alone.'

Our days were those of a busy common law junior. Harry was in court almost every day and often had a 1.30 summons dealing with one of the preliminary or interlocutory stages of a High Court action. After a quick lunch in the Crypt below the Law Courts we would go to the Bear Garden, a large room which lived up to its name. Here was assembled a crowd of counsel and solicitors, all talking at once. The masters' chambers led out of this room, and each master had three or four summonses to deal with before 2 pm. Naturally speed and brevity were at a premium. One master once said in an unguarded moment in the bar of the Garrick Club, 'I look at the names of the parties and solicitors on the pleadings, see who are the counsel, make up my mind which side is the more respectable and make the order accordingly. If they don't like it they can go to the judge.' He was seldom reversed on appeal. Harry regarded it as important to gain the confidence of the masters, never to make an application unless he was sure it would succeed, never to take a bad point and never to mislead them.

After court and a quick cup of tea there would be a conference at 4.30 and probably another at 5.15. Then there were pleadings and opinions to be checked and signed before we went home. Some members of the Bar used to go to chambers early and do their paperwork before they went to court. But I preferred to work at home after dinner, especially if I had a brief to digest and note up for next day. I hardly ever stopped work before midnight.

For each of my first three years at the Bar I never earned more than £1000, but it paid handsomely in the long run. I spent most of my time doing Harry's papers and researching the law, so I learnt to plead and to find my way about the textbooks and law reports. I also got to know Harry's solicitors and learnt how to take a note of the evidence while sitting with Harry in court. And I saw a wide range of cases and watched the leading advocates of the day. Gradually I began to get some work of my own. My first case was before the registrar of the Bow County court. The solicitor was one of our best chambers' clients. Jas. H. Fellowes, who had been a railway porter at Stratford station, qualified as a solicitor and built up a large practice in the East End of London. His managing clerk had marked the brief 10/6, until Clement pointed out that the minimum fee was one guinea, which he paid in cash. The case was of such little importance that Jimmy Fellowes did not even send the young man who usually accompanied counsel to the County Court. So I had to interview the client myself, take his proof of evidence and do the best I could before the registrar. Fellowes afterwards became a good client and I did a lot of small work for him.

There was an organisation called the Services Divorce Department which was publicly funded and paid one guinea for an undefended divorce case in the High Court. I was on their list and they would send six cases at a time, which was the equivalent of one paid undefended divorce.

I also once had the temerity to move 'in forma pauperis' in a wardship case in the Chancery Division for a distraught mother whose husband had removed her little boy when she had taken him to live with her lover. 'But Mr. Dunn,' said the judge, 'your client is living in open adultery. I cannot possibly allow this child to be in such moral danger.' This in spite of evidence that she was an admirable mother who had brought up the child from birth. Greatly daring I went to the Court of Appeal who, though sympathetic, did not feel they could interfere with the discretion of the learned judge.

There was a good deal of divorce work in Fountain Court, mostly undefended cases, which were all heard in the High Court before County Court judges sitting as Special Divorce Commissioners, who used each to deal with over twenty cases in the day. We all inevitably became involved in this work, although most of my work at first was in the County Courts scattered round London. The cases were predominantly possession cases and small claims for the supply of goods and services for which we were paid two or three guineas. A fee of seven guineas in the County Court was what Clement called 'a well marked brief'. These cases involved mastering the intricacies of the Rent Acts and the Sale of Goods Act. But the cases almost invariably turned on the facts and we were essentially dealing with all sorts and conditions of people with problems, all under the stress of unfamiliar court proceedings and some distraught. It now seems to be fashionable, especially in the press and media, to assert that judges are out of touch with 'ordinary people' whatever that may mean. This is nonsense and ignorant nonsense at that. I soon learnt how extraordinary are the lives of most people and how their characters differ. All judges have been barristers and most have started out as I did knocking round the County Courts and magistrates courts of the big towns and cities. That involved meeting hundreds of different people of all kinds and hearing their case histories. It is one of the great strengths of the English judicial system that, unlike some continental countries, we do not have a career judiciary who start as junior judges as soon as they have qualified and climb up the judicial ladder. An English judge will probably, from his experience as a barrister, know as much about human nature as any provincial newspaper reporter, and a great deal more than the highly paid columnists and commentators who enjoy criticising the judiciary. Of course there are wide differences of speech and outward behaviour between people of different classes, and from different parts of the country, and they all live very different lives. But I soon learnt that there are rogues and honest men and women from all the different walks of life. Kipling was right when he said:

> The Colonel's lady
> And Betty O'Grady
> Are sisters under the skin.

There are some high born sluts and many humbly born gentlewomen. We met and discussed their problems with the woman struggling to bring up a family in a tower block on a council estate with a drunken, unemployed, violent husband. We wrestled with the difficulties of the young couple living in two rooms in a terraced house and sharing a kitchen with a bitter harpy who longed to be rid of them, although they had nowhere to go. And we tried to obtain justice for the old widowed lady who had been persuaded by some cowboy to have her roof repaired and been presented with an excessive bill for shoddy work. To say that we did not know how these people lived and that that knowledge was not ingrained in our minds and hearts throughout our lives would be an insult if it were not so absurd.

In my early days I hardly ever met a solicitor, much less a partner. We were instructed in those small cases by managing clerks, unqualified men, many of them with great knowledge and experience of litigation. We would travel with them, lunch with them in the bar of the local pub or at a cafeteria and discuss their families, their lives and their interests. One said, 'I spend my week biting my tongue trying to be polite to clients. But on Saturday afternoons I go to White Hart Lane and scream my heart out in support of Spurs.' Kenneth Brown Baker Baker, who had an immense litigation practice and were good clients of Harry's and later of mine, had a particularly strong team of managing clerks. Each was in charge of a department which had to show a profit. Indeed it was said that the senior, Henry Merkle, occupied the best room in the building and took a share of the profits. His son, also Henry, was an outstandingly able solicitor, and became senior partner. I learnt a great deal from these men and have always been grateful to them. Many managing clerks loved what they called 'a fighter', and were not so concerned by the result of a case as 'putting up a show for the client'.

One big contrast with the army was that nobody criticised one's handling of a case. In the army, after an exercise or even a battle, the result would be analysed, one's performance criticised and suggestions made for improvement. If Harry Phillimore did not approve of my draft of a pleading, he would simply throw it in the waste paper basket and draft his own. But nobody told one where one had gone wrong in court or suggested a different approach. The only criterion was whether the solicitor instructed one again, 'the accolade' as Arthur described it, or not. So it was a question of self-examination to see how one could have done the case better. We learnt mostly by example and most barristers are much influenced by their pupil masters. There was, however, a danger of copying the form, the mannerisms and tone of voice, rather than the substance. I could often tell what chambers an opponent came from by his style in court.

Most of the practitioners in the County Court were, like myself, beginners. But there were some old hacks who had been going round the County Courts for years and would never leave them. These were sad figures, who never learnt from their mistakes. Experience is essential at the Bar, but quality is more important than quantity. It is no good having experience if you do not benefit from it.

One day Harry said to me, 'Tom Denning has asked me to take his step-daughter Hazel Stuart as a pupil. I don't know what to do. She is very good. She got a double first at Oxford. But we have never had a woman in chambers before and I don't know what Arthur will say.' Fortunately Arthur agreed and Hazel joined us. After her pupillage Hazel stayed on as Harry's devil, as I became busier with my own work, and joined me in my cubby-hole which was just large enough for two knee-hole desks facing one another, while another pupil went into Harry's room. After some years, to the chagrin of chambers, Hazel married Michael Fox, of the Chancery Bar, who became a Lord Justice. She brought up four children as well as finding time to teach law at Oxford, be a magistrate, chairman of Rent and Valuation Tribunals and appear in the occasional international case. She is now editor of the respected *International and Comparative Law Quarterly*. I became and remain devoted to her. If she had stayed with us on a regular basis I am sure she would now be in the Court of Appeal – if not the first woman Law Lord or Lady.

Harry had two other able pupils. Donald Hawley came from the Sudan civil service to qualify for the Sudan judiciary. After independence in Sudan he joined the diplomatic service, where he had a distinguished career and was knighted. Philip Shelbourne left after his pupillage to acquire an enormous practice at the tax Bar. He was one of the few barristers who understood money and enjoyed dealing with it. Balance sheets and accounts, which I always found difficult, were meat and drink to him. He also had the engaging quality of enjoying laughing at himself. After some years he left the Bar and joined the Rothschild merchant bank, later having a distinguished career in the City. Over thirty years later after I retired, Philip, who was then chairman of Britoil, arranged for me to visit an oil rig off Shetland as an act of friendship.

In the early fifties Harry took silk. This was too soon for me and almost all his better clients moved elsewhere. However, one leading city firm, Wilde Sapte, remained faithful, probably because Clement kept my fees low. The firm had three important clients: the Head Office of the then National Provincial bank; the Portman estate which owned much of the Metropolitan Borough of Marylebone; and St. Bartholomew's Hospital. This involved three quite different branches of the law; banking law, landlord and tenant, and medical negligence. But Wilde Sapte liked to use a single junior for all their common law work. They also employed a venerable conveyancer to draft the bank standard forms of mortgages, guarantees and so on, whom I once had occasion to meet in his dusty Dickensian chambers in Lincoln's Inn. The disorderliness of his person and surroundings contrasted with the acuteness of his brain.

I soon discovered that, although the bank would be indulgent to well secured customers, once they decided that the security did not meet their debt, they would force a customer into bankruptcy and take the shirt off his back. So I became involved in the difficult law of bankruptcy and came up against Muir Hunter, the leading practitioner in that field. The senior partner, who looked after the banking work, was Francis Sapte, who lived with his wife and family in a comfortable Victorian house with a large garden in Watford. He had an encyclopaedic knowledge of banking law. When the bank wished to appoint a receiver, Sapte would use an accountant to whom I always referred (but never to his face) as Uncle Basil. Like Sapte Uncle Basil was short in stature and once on a case they were like two terriers hunting a rat and would never let go. Sapte had one extravagance – fast cars. He drove a car called a Railton, in which I once travelled, followed and sometimes passed by Uncle Basil in an SS Jaguar, to the bankruptcy court at Norwich. It was a hair-raising drive. The debtor, a Norfolk landowner who had succeeded in obtaining large sums of money from the bank by inviting the local manager to shoot, had particularly enraged Sapte by buying several pairs of handmade shoes from Lobbs in St. James's Street. 'I'll have him behind bars,' said Sapte. 'Spending the Bank's money at Lobbs. I can't afford to buy my shoes at Lobbs.' Sapte, I should say, was very proud of his feet which were small and well shaped. So, eventually, behind bars the debtor went.

The Portman Estate work was looked after by Harry Litchfield, who became senior partner after poor Sapte died before his time. Litchfield was also a very able solicitor. Although the firm never briefed me in silk, they did not believe in the extra expense of leading counsel; Litchfield would come to my chambers in the evenings after my consultations and discuss the difficulties of the practice and with his clients. Both were at that time contemplating mergers. Although he never directly asked me for any advice I believe it helped him to clear his mind to discuss his problems with an independent outsider. Clement never charged for these meetings, but Litchfield would always send me an expensive card at Christmas, usually a view of 18th-century London from the river. Although I was closely associated with them both for over ten years we never addressed one another by our Christian names.

For the medical negligence work I was instructed by an articled clerk. Sapte once complained to me of the difficulty of finding a good managing clerk. I said I believed that such men were paid £1500 a year. 'I'd see them damned first,' said Sapte. Although the work involved a great deal of advising and drafting, most cases were settled; only about once a year did we go to court. But the firm formed the foundation of my practice.

Soon after he took silk Harry asked me to take Clive Wigram, son-in-law of David Maxwell-Fife, by then Lord Kilmuir the Lord Chancellor, as a pupil. I said I did not think my practice warranted a pupil, but Harry said Clive had done brilliantly at Oxford and he would like to have him in the team. So Clive joined us but sadly after a few months became terminally ill and died soon afterwards. Judy's father then asked me to take John Lawrence, son of Lord Oaksey an old friend of Judy's family, as a pupil. John had done well at Oxford and won a scholarship to the Harvard law school. He arrived at Whitsun and at the end of July I asked him how he was going to spend the long vacation. 'I am going on the Western Circuit,' he said. I pointed out that the Western Circuit did not sit during the long vacation. 'Oh I don't mean that Western Circuit,' he replied. 'I mean the early National Hunt meetings at Haldon, Newton Abbot and Buckfastleigh.' During the vacation John wrote to say he would not be returning to chambers, as he had been offered a job as racing correspondent to the *Daily Telegraph*, which would enable him to ride regularly. When I told Clement he said, 'A pity. I could have made something of Mr. Lawrence. He would have been a clever little advocate, like his father.' In fact Lord Oaksey was a distinguished judge, having presided at the Nuremberg trials, which of course Clement knew.

At about this time Judy and I decided to sell our house at Stanmore and move to central London. I was finding the journey to the Temple increasingly irksome and the journeys to some of the County Courts were even more tedious. So we found a large flat on the top and attic floors of one of the big Victorian houses in Queen's Gate. We took a ten year lease, with no premium, at a rent of £520 a year.

Until then my practice, such as it was, and my prospects had been typical of those who had joined the Bar in the immediate post-war years. But two events occurred, both fortuitous, which immediately widened my practice and introduced me to fields quite outside those of the normal common lawyer, as well as bringing me into contact with some of the leaders of the Bar at a time when they were also national figures. However, I must first digress and turn to horses and point-to-point racing.

CHAPTER XIV

The Pegasus Club

The Pegasus Club was formed in 1896 for judges, barristers and students of the four Inns of Court with the object of running a point-to-point meeting. Its badge was a winged horse, the crest of the Inner Temple, ridden by a barrister in wig and robes. The first meeting was at Northhaw in Hertfordshire and, from the first, the club was well supported by members of the Bench and Bar who were interested in hunting and racing. *Bench and Bar in the Saddle* by C. P. Hawkes, a divorce registrar, well describes the history of the club down to the second world war.

Judy's father had been secretary before the war and had ridden many winners on his own and other people's horses.Both the then Duke of Gloucester and Prince Aly Khan had ridden winners, although the latter had been successfully objected to by Lord Wright, the owner of the second horse ridden by Judy's father, on the ground that the Prince's horse had come from a public racing stable and was therefore ineligible. When told of this and that he could object, Wright, who was a Law Lord, had said, 'I'll object to anything.'

The first post-war meeting was at Friar's Wash near Luton in 1947 when I was still in the army, though a Bar student. There was one Bar race and Judy's father, who was fifty-seven at the time, bought a horse called Dalesman from Harry Ivens, a well known Northamptonshire dealer, to run in the heavyweight section. He paid £200 for the horse and Ivens said he would take the horse back for the same money after the race if Judy's father did not want to keep him. I rode a little horse from Lynch called Marigold in the lightweight section. Dalesman proved difficult to steer and as we were going round Judy's father said, 'Keep close outside me round the bends, I can't steer the animal.' However, he went on to win the heavyweight section, and Marigold, who was favourite, blew up. The lightweight section was won by Gerald Ponsonby, now Lord Morley, riding a horse belonging to Geoffrey Oaksey. After the race Tom Elder-Jones, who was secretary of the club, brought a man into the changing tent and said to Judy's father that his friend would like to buy Dalesman. Judy's father said he could have the horse for £300 and the deal was done. Soon afterwards Ivens came into the tent, full of smiles, and said, 'Well done, sir. I expect you'd like me to take the horse back for what you gave me.' 'I'm sorry Harry,' said Judy's father, 'I've just sold the horse for £300.' Ivens's face was a picture and the incident gave great pleasure to Judy's father who enjoyed nothing more than a horse deal. He was only the second High Court judge to have ridden a winner in the Bar race, Willy Grantham (not a good judge) having won the race before the Great War.

At the meeting I was introduced to Mick McElligott who had just started at the Bar having been a regular officer in the RAF. I told him I was thinking of going to the Bar myself, but was afraid I would not get any work. 'I am making a living,' said Mick, 'and I am sure if I can make a living you can.'

Soon after I was called to the Bar Mick and I became joint secretaries of the Pegasus Club and remained together for nearly ten years. Mick was one of the great characters of my generation at the Bar. He was an Irishman, his father having been a County Court judge in Ireland, and was a good horseman who also knew a great deal about horses. But his principal characteristic, apart from his mercurial temperament, was that he did not overestimate his ability (which was considerable), and knew exactly what he wanted from life. This was to hunt and ride whenever he could, to have sufficient practice to enable him to live in comfort and eventually to become a metropolitan magistrate, all of which he achieved.

He was a good advocate, specialising in criminal work, and became the unofficial attorney-general in Hertfordshire. David Moylan once went to the Quarter Sessions there and asked the clerk if his case (which was a plea of guilty) could come on early as he was engaged elsewhere in the afternoon. 'I'll do my best,' said the clerk, 'but Mr. McElligott is prosecuting in that case, and he always rides out before court, so we keep his cases back till 11 am.'

Soon after the war the venue of the Bar point-to-point was changed back to Kimble near Aylesbury, where the meeting had been held since 1931. The course was owned partly by John Robarts and partly by a dear old boy called Harry Rose, who had been a great friend of Judy's father. Mick and I soon made friends with both of them and spent many happy times at Kimble.

There were only a comparatively few members of the club who actually rode in the races. Apart from Mick and myself there was Kenneth Diplock, who became a Law Lord and was an enthusiastic though not very proficient horseman. Once I remember approaching the open ditch second time round to find Kenneth lying in front of the ditch with his leg trapped under the guard-rail. 'Keep down,' roared Mick, and we all sailed over the future Law Lord. A great stalwart was Sandy Temple, who became Recorder of Liverpool and practised on the Northern Circuit. He would box two horses down after court in Manchester, breakfast with John Robarts, ride in the two Bar races, go to London for the club dinner which at that time was held after the races and drive north next day. Then there was John Syms who lived in Surrey and provided birch for the racecourses at Sandown and Kempton, and was known ironically as 'the comrade' because of his extreme right wing views. Harold Sebag-Montefiore and Anthony Goodall who became a Circuit judge and, with his wife

Anne, a close friend of ours, were also regular jockeys.

The club was lucky to have two loyal supporters who ran their own horses for members to ride. Jack Weir Johnston lived in Hertfordshire and always had two good thoroughbred horses to run in the Bar races. Jack was an Irish KC who was chairman of Tote Investors, a great character and very kind. He had what he called 'linen interests' in Northern Ireland. Judy and I would occasionally hunt his horses with the Old Berkeley, whose master was Lionel Cecil, a connection of the Pilchers. Once he said to us, 'I can't think why you come out with my dreadful hounds. If you want to hunt from London why not go to Leicestershire.' I arranged for John Lawrence to ride one of Weir-Johnston's horses, Next of Kin, one year at Kimble. When he mounted in the paddock she stood up on end and went over backwards, which she had done before with Judy out hunting. However, John remounted and won the race – his first winner. He always said afterwards that it was the excitement engendered by riding Next of Kin, who was a good fast jumper, which determined him to leave the Bar and devote his life to racing.

Our other loyal supporter was Geoff Shaw who was master of the North Norfolk Harriers and always ran two horses at Kimble. Judy's father had ridden for him before the war and I took over the rides in the fifties. Although I had my share of falls, I rode several winners at Kimble, once winning both Bar races in the afternoon, but never on my own horse. The nearest I got was on Well Caught on which I won the maiden race at the Tiverton point-to-point at 16 to 1. Judy's father, who loved a bet, left the course with his pockets stuffed with fivers. So we went with high hopes to Kimble. Unfortunately Well Caught, who started favourite, dropped his hind legs in the water jump and injured his back, so that I had to pull him up.

The meeting at Kimble in those days was very well supported by the Bench and Bar, and a great social occasion. So the club prospered, and bought two horses for members to hunt and ride in the Bar races. They were bought by Mick and kept at livery under his eagle eye near his home in Hertfordshire. Judy and I used to go up every year to hunt them with the Puckeridge, which was hunted by Charlie Barclay, one of the great amateur huntsmen in a bad scenting country. He used sometimes to walk a fox to death. We always stayed with Mick and his wife Suzanne, both of whom were splendid company, and our many convivial evenings together formed the basis of a lifelong friendship. Mick in due course became magistrate at Old Street in the East End of London, where he was much respected by what he called the honest villains. He was not so happy at Marlborough Street dealing with rich shoplifters, many of them ladies from the Middle East, and took early retirement. Sadly he was knocked down and killed by a motor-cycle when exercising his dogs near his home in Northamptonshire.

The Pegasus dinner, held in London after the races, was always a great occasion. Those who had them wore hunt coats and there were many masters of hounds and other guests. The speeches were always of a high standard, with many legal and sporting anecdotes. A. J. Munnings the great artist once spoke, but unfortunately for too long. At the dinner we met the more senior members of the club: Theo Turner KC a great friend of Judy's father, whose son Michael succeeded me as secretary and is now a High Court judge; and Cyril Harvey who was another friend of Judy's father and a brilliant and witty speaker. When he won the lightweight race on a good grey horse he compared his view from the saddle with the famous picture by Snaffles, *The finest view in Europe*. Cyril wrote a most amusing book called *The Advocates' Devil* in which he poked fun at the traditional style of advocacy, especially as practised by Norman Birkett the leading advocate of his day. This so outraged the establishment that his election as a Bencher of the Inner Temple was postponed for several years and was only allowed when Judy's father persuaded Lord Goddard not to blackball Cyril. 'I won't blackball him, but I'm damned if I'll vote for him. For your sake Toby I shall abstain,' said the Lord Chief Justice. Tom Elder-Jones was another Pegasus character. He had lost an arm while serving in the Gloucestershire Hussars at Bir Gubi. He became a County Court judge in Gloucestershire, where he was well known for his forthright approach to litigation. Finally there was John Marnan, an Irishman like Mick who, after a checkered matrimonial career, became a judge at the Old Bailey.

As well as the dinner the club organised a ball which was held in the summer at one of the Inns of Court. It was run by Norman Richards who, although he did not ride, was a keen supporter. He became an official referee.

Edward Cazalet and Michael Connell, who joined my chambers, were both enthusiastic supporters of the club and with Michael Turner kept it going for another generation. Now, due to lack of support, the meeting has been abandoned but a Bar race is run at one of the hunt meetings. I find this sad. We were the only point-to-point club to survive the war, and the Pegasus Club provided me and many of my generation with much fun and many friends. Many members of the Bar still hunt, but point-to-pointing has become so much more professional that few now have the time or inclination to take part. In my day the Pegasus Club provided a forum where judges, silks, junior barristers and students with a common interest all met on easy informal terms. Long may it continue.

CHAPTER XV

Communists and Oil, 1950–60

One Saturday morning, soon after I was called, I appeared before the Bow Street magistrate to defend a ship's master who had been charged with some technical offence in the London docks. I was instructed by Constant & Constant, a well known city firm who had been clients of Judy's father, and whom Arthur had persuaded to send me a brief 'for old time's sake'. Although it meant giving up a day's hunting on Exmoor, it was worth it.

Soon afterwards I was briefed by Constants as second junior in the case of Boguslawski *v* Gydnia Amerika Line. D. N. Pritt was the leader, with Arthur Hodgson, an experienced Admiralty junior. My task was to take a note of the evidence and submissions. The case arose out of the nationalisation of the company after the war by the Polish communist government. When this happened most of the officers left their ships and sued for arrears of wages. The nationalised company, for whom we appeared, refused to pay, alleging that they were not liable for debts incurred before nationalisation. The case turned on whether the nationalisation decree had retrospective effect, to a date before the Polish communist government was recognised de facto by the British government, and also upon various questions of Polish law. We ended up in the House of Lords, by which time Hodgson had become a County Court judge and I was the only junior. We lost all the way up.

Pritt had long been one of the leading advocates of the day, especially in the appellate courts. He had been an MP, but had been expelled from the Labour Party for his extreme left wing views. He had a brilliant mind, having been a scholar at Winchester, but his judgment was clouded by his political views. Although extremely kind to me, he was arrogant and short-tempered in court. He once told me that he found it impossible to behave himself in court unless he was appearing before a tribunal as least as intelligent as himself. At first instance he once called his opponent Linton Thorpe a 'stuck pig', which caused that rather pompous figure to leave court in a huff. Pritt said, 'You never know what point will attract your tribunal. So open all your points, and watch to see which one attracts them. In opening an appeal it is essential to get your opponent on to his feet. So I make the appeal sound as difficult as possible, saying as little as I can about my best point, hoping that my opponent will not deal with it. Then, in Reply, I concentrate on my best point making the argument as clear and persuasive as possible.' These questionable tactics nearly succeeded in our case in the court of Appeal, Richard Elwes who then led for the plaintiffs having been taken by surprise when Pritt made his submissions in Reply. But in the House of Lords Richard's junior, Niall MacDermot, foreseeing Pritt's tactics followed Richard and dealt comprehensively with Pritt's point. It was characteristic of Pritt that he was amused and delighted by Niall's intervention and afterwards gave him a red bag, a unique compliment by an opposing leader.

Niall was one of the most able of my generation at the Bar. He became a Labour MP in 1957 and a Minister in 1964. However, he became disenchanted with the Labour Party, resigned his seat and became involved in the human rights movement on the Continent. If he had returned to the Bar he would undoubtedly have achieved high judicial office.

Pritt's political philosophy was well summed up in a conversation we had one day at lunch in the House of Lords. We were discussing the opponents of the communist regime in Poland. Pritt said, 'They are all determined to work for the new Poland. I recently visited a coal mine where doctors and lawyers were willingly working at the coal face for the good of Poland.' He appeared to believe it.

At about the time I was first briefed for the Gydnia Amerika Line I was approached by John Proudfoot, our neighbour at Stanmore and a partner in Bischoff & Co. He said, 'We act for Iraq Petroleum Company (IPC). We have always employed a standing junior counsel for the company work. Hitherto we have had a senior junior, but Hubert Parker was made a judge and his successor Brian McKenna has just taken silk. So we have decided to look for a younger man to provide continuity, since the company's affairs are complicated and take time to absorb. Would you be interested? Of course we would expect you to give us priority over your other work.' Judy was hanging out of an upstairs window during this conversation, which took place in the Proudfoot's garden, anticipating something important afoot. We had arranged that I would scratch the back of my neck if I was offered a brief, which with three children to support (Janie had been born in 1950) we badly needed. This was an amazing stroke of luck, especially as I had practically no other work. Naturally I at once agreed and began an association which led to some fascinating work and introduced me to fields not usually entered by members of the Bar.

IPC had been formed soon after the Great War to take over and secure for the Allies the oil resources of the Ottoman Empire in the Middle East. Four international oil groups – BP, Shell, Compagnie Française des Petroles and an American Group – each owned 22.5% of the equity. The remaining 5% was owned by the Armenian Nubar Gulbenkian. The management of IPC was wholly British and head office was at Oxford Circus. Over the years IPC had acquired oil concessions in Iraq, and down what was then known as the Trucial Coast on the west side of the Persian Gulf as far as Muscat and Oman, but had refused a concession from Saudi Arabia, which had been granted to the American company Aramco. In 1950 the only oil fields operated by the company were in Iraq and there were those who said that the real purpose of IPC was not to exploit Middle East oil, but rather to freeze it in the ground so that supplies from Persia and Kuwait (both British owned) could be fully tapped and the price kept up.

The various IPC concessions were expressed to cover 'the whole territory of the grantor' who, on the Trucial Coast, were the rulers of the small sheikhdoms, and in Oman the Sultan. Thus, for the first time in history, the frontiers of the various desert sheikhdoms became of international importance. In 1945 President Truman had made a formal declaration declaring that the continental shelf contiguous to the coasts of the USA was under American sovereignty. Similar declarations were made by each of the Trucial sheikhs on the advice of the British government, which was charged with the conduct of their foreign relations. Each sheikh then purported to grant offshore oil concessions to companies other than IPC. The latter claimed that the continental shelf formed part of the territory of the sheikh and was thus included in the original IPC concession. This issue was accordingly referred to arbitration. The first arbitration was between IPC and Qatar, Lord Radcliffe being the arbitrator – IPC lost. The second was between IPC and Abu Dhabi, with Lord Asquith as arbitrator, and was held in Paris during the long vacation of 1951. It was the first case in which I appeared for IPC.

The case raised difficult questions about the construction of the concession and of international law. We agreed to apply the 'law common to all civilised states', which turned out to be English law with all its technicalities. IPC was represented by a team led by Walter Monckton, consisting of Hersch Lauterpacht, professor of international law at Cambridge, with Gwynn Morris and myself as juniors. The opposition, although nominally the sheikh, was in fact the grantee of the continental shelf concession, Superior Oil, an independent oil company from California. It was also represented by a team of English lawyers consisting of Roy Fox-Andrews, Humphrey Waldock, professor of international law at Oxford, and Stephen Chapman and Jo Stephenson, both of whom later became High Court judges.

Monckton had a greater influence on my approach to advocacy and work at the Bar than anyone, except Harry Phillimore. This was his last case at the Bar before he joined the government as Minister of Labour in the autumn of 1951. He told me later that Churchill had told him, 'Give the unions all they want, so long as they keep the wheels of industry turning.' I stayed a week alone with Monckton and his wife at their house near Worcester working on the case, and was made to feel absolutely at home and at ease. Monckton's famous charm was not synthetic. He genuinely liked and was interested in people and would talk freely of his life and ambitions. At that time he hoped to be Attorney-General if the Conservatives won the general election, with a view to becoming Lord Chief Justice in succession to Rayner Goddard. He recognised that he could not be Lord Chancellor since he had been divorced and the Lord Chancellor was keeper of the King's conscience.

Monckton's preparation of the case was meticulous. He insisted on having all the facts at his fingertips. 'Nothing is more amateurish,' he said, 'when the judge asks you a question, than to say, "Forgive me, my Lord, I must take instructions." It is your job to know the answer.' He also said, 'If I am asked in which branch of the law I specialise I say advocacy. It is a true specialisation. It is your job to persuade that old man sitting up there that you are right. And you don't do that by thumping the table and being rude to him.' He was, I believe, the founder of the conversational style of advocacy. His appeal was to reasonableness and he was a master of attractive presentation, flexible in argument, following the line of thought of the tribunal, dropping the points which did not appeal and concentrating on those which did. 'I don't win my cases by cross-examination,' he would say.

Our team stayed at the Hotel Royale Monceau in Paris and the case lasted a fortnight. Monckton, who had been gassed in the Great War, slept badly. He kept a writing pad beside his bed on which he would make notes if he woke during the night. He was nervous before going to the arbitration, walking up and down his room rehearsing parts of his submission. 'What do you think of this?' he would say. 'How will Asquith take it?' He said that unless one was keyed up in court one could not do full justice to the case. 'I keep a box of matches, which I break during the case to keep me from fidgeting,' he said. 'Nothing is worse than an advocate who is moving about all the time.'

The Sheikh of Abu Dhabi with his retinue attended the arbitration every day in their picturesque head-dresses and robes. When the sheikh first saw the Eiffel Tower he is alleged to have said, 'What an enormous oil rig.' I made friends with the sheikh's brother Zaid, who succeeded him as ruler. Zaid was an enthusiastic horseman who enjoyed hawking in the desert. I invited him to Exmoor for a day's stag-hunting, which he accepted saying, 'But I have never ridden with stirrups.' I pointed out that he might find it difficult to gallop over our combes and bogs without stirrups, so sadly he never came. He was like a mediaeval baron.

In spite of Monckton's superb advocacy and judgment in the conduct of the case and the presentation of our arguments, the arbitration award went against IPC. But Superior Oil never operated the concession, because IPC denied them all base and port facilities for their rigs and installations and eventually Superior sold their concession to Shell. This was typical of IPC policy: always to fight on all fronts. In this case they lost the legal battle and won the business war. After the case Walter Monckton gave me my red bag and there is no-one from whom I would rather have had it.

At the end of the case Judy came to Paris. As well as, for me, an enormous fee, I had been paid a generous expense allowance which we decided to spend on a week in Paris.

At that time there were just five five-star restaurants in Paris listed in the Guide Michelin. So Judy and I decided to go to a different one each night. The experience has spoilt my taste for English food ever since. It certainly had a disastrous effect on our livers. On the last day we lunched at the airport restaurant at Le Bourget, which was very good. Indeed we enjoyed our lunch so much that we missed our flight back to London.

Soon after the Abu Dhabi Arbitration Ibn Saud made claim to an eastern frontier which left Abu Dhabi only a narrow strip of coastline on the Persian Gulf. He also claimed the Buraimi Oasis, an important collection of villages lying between Abu Dhabi and Muscat and Oman. The British government was responsible for the foreign affairs of Abu Dhabi and of the Sultan of Muscat and Oman, who laid claim to part of the Buraimi Oasis. IPC were of course vitally interested and I was lent to the Foreign Office with all the documents in the possession of IPC to help them prepare their case. Thus began my connection with the Foreign Office and their legal advisers.

The idea of fixed frontiers had hitherto been unknown in the deserts of Arabia. Groups of herdsmen from different tribes moved according to the availability of grazing and the location of wells. Most owed a loose tribal allegiance to a particular ruler who from time to time collected 'Zakat', a religious tax based on numbers of camels.

In 1953 negotiations began at Dhahran and I flew out to Bahrain with Vincent Evans, one of the Foreign Office legal advisers. En route our aircraft was held for the night at Cairo airport because of anti-British riots in Cairo. The Turf Club had been burnt down that day and those members in the club had been murdered. It was an unpleasant night, as we were all obliged to stay in the aircraft with a mob milling round and shouting slogans. Vincent Evans rather optimistically said that he would be all right because he had a diplomatic passport. I felt more uneasy than at the worst times of the war, since there was nothing we could do and no way of defending ourselves if we were attacked. In the morning we were allowed into the airport building for breakfast, harangued by a fat and sweating Egyptian brigadier, and then took off with the mob chasing us down the runway, in spite of the presence of a company of Egyptian infantry drawn up ostensibly for our protection.

On our first night I dined with our political resident at Bahrain. He asked, 'How much is the oil company prepared to give up?' I said, 'Nothing.' In fact we had a strong case, since the inhabitants of the disputed areas all belonged to the Beni Yas tribe of which the ruler of Abu Dhabi was the chief, and the Saudis had never exercised any power in Buraimi where Sheikh Zaid ruled as Viceroy. But the Foreign Office were interested in the realities of power. British power in the Middle East was waning and they wished to encourage the Americans to take over more of our commitments, in return for a larger stake in Middle East oil.

The negotiations came to nothing. Eventually the Prime Minister, Winston Churchill, who was himself in charge of the Foreign Office in the absence of Anthony Eden, persuaded Ibn Saud to refer the dispute to arbitration. In the meantime a joint British/Saudi force was to be stationed at Buraimi to keep the peace and maintain the status quo.

We then began busily to prepare our case for arbitration. The claim of Abu Dhabi was comparatively straightforward, but the claim of the Sultan of Muscat to part of Buraimi was much more nebulous. Accordingly I was sent out to visit the Sultan and to try to collect some evidence to support his case. This was at the suggestion of Edward Henderson, who at that time was on the staff of IPC in Bahrain and with whom I made friends during the negotiations. Edward was a highly intelligent man, an Arabist who had served in the Arab Legion after the war. He was in the same mould as the great explorer Wilfred Thesiger, who had crossed the Empty Quarter by camel and who also helped us collect evidence. Thesiger always called Henderson 'Bin Hender'. Edward afterwards joined the diplomatic service and served with distinction in the Middle East. He was typical of those who worked for IPC in the field in those days – they were on easy friendly terms with the sheikhs and Arab merchants and they had vast knowledge of the history and politics of the region. Their job, as they saw it, was to keep the 'brown gold' flowing and they had great sympathy for the Arabs and their aspirations, while at the same time recognising their foibles. One day, returning from a visit to the refinery at Bahrain, Edward and I noticed that the flag flying over the Sheikh's palace was at half mast. 'I expect they have just not bothered to pull it up,' said Edward. But it was a mark of respect for the death of King George VI, news of which had arrived while we were at the refinery.

I flew to Cairo where I stayed the night in an uncomfortable bungalow near the airport. Next morning I flew on in a Dakota, stopping first at Jiddah, where I was relieved that the Saudi customs did not seek to open my brief-case, which was full of documents relating to the dispute. Next stop was Asmara in what had been Italian Somaliland and we arrived at Aden in the evening. I was relieved to find British trained police in starched shorts and to be taken through the customs to the only air-conditioned room in the Crescent Hotel. It was June 1954 and very hot. A day or two later I flew on in a very ancient Dakota to the Sultan's summer palace in Salalah. We flew over southern Arabia and touched down in the Wadi Hadhramaut, a lush green valley with fortress-like houses in the middle of an otherwise lunar landscape. Many rich Arabs who had made fortunes in Indonesia retired to this El Dorado.

The Sultan's summer palace was built on the beach and we had long discussions every morning in a room facing the sea, with wide open windows and furniture by Maples. The Sultan was an engaging despot of great dignity and subtlety. He was a baffling client and the highwater mark of our discussions occurred one morning when, after the usual exchange of compliments, he said, 'You asked yesterday for evidence that our writ runs in Buraimi. Observe that photograph.' He then handed me a photograph of a man's head on the sand with two villainous-looking tribesmen with rifles standing by. 'That man,' he said with a glint in his eye, 'committed a murder in Buraimi. He was executed on our instructions and the head sent here to us.' I was speechless.

After ten days in uncomfortable conditions in a tent at the RAF staging camp near the Sultan's fort I was not sorry to leave, but not before I had explored some of the desert around Salalah and bathed in the salty Indian ocean. The Sultan in retrospect was a sad figure; educated at Victoria College, Alexandria, completely oriental in outlook and depending for his survival on the rapidly waning power of the British. He was later deposed by his son and died in exile. They tell a story on the Trucial Coast of the occasion when Curzon visited the sheikhs when he was Viceroy. He landed in full uniform and addressed the sheikhs in these terms: 'I am the representative of the great white King, whom you will never see, but who is watching your every movement.'

In 1955 reports came from Buraimi that the Saudi contingent, instead of maintaining the status quo, were smuggling arms into the oasis and distributing them to the tribes with a view to a rising by the Imam against the Sultan. It was therefore decided to apply to the tribunal, which was to sit in Geneva, for an order equivalent to an injunction restraining the Saudis from pursuing this activity. Our team consisted of Hartley Shawcross, Humphrey Waldock and myself, as well as the Foreign Office representative. Shawcross was by then the leading advocate of the day, having been Attorney-General in the Labour government, and had taken over much of Monckton's practice. He was immensely thorough and hard-working and was a powerful advocate. Although he worked even harder than Monckton, he was completely relaxed and would lie on the couch in his sitting room waiting to go to court, reading a detective novel instead of walking up and down. He was more of a politician than Monckton and took a great deal of trouble to brief the press and to keep them in the picture. He was a good companion and I enjoyed working with him.

The atmosphere at Geneva was full of suspicion and secrecy. Our hotel rooms were found to have been bugged. One evening, on our return to the hotel after dinner in a restaurant, our car pulled away as soon as we had got out, and a large limousine drove up beside us, out of which stepped Sheikh Yusuf Yasin, the Saudi representative on the tribunal and head of the Saudi Foreign Office. He said to Shawcross, 'If you will come to my room for an hour, Sir Hartley, I am sure we can settle this stupid misunderstanding between old friends.' The young man from the Eastern Department of the Foreign Office at once stepped forward and said, 'I'm sorry, Your Excellency, Sir Hartley has no authority to settle anything. He appears here only as an advocate. That can only be done by a Minister and there is none available.' I was much impressed by this example of diplomatic presence of mind.

After the hearing started we learned that the Saudis had offered a bribe to a member of the tribunal and it was decided to break off the arbitration. Hartley announced this decision in a dramatic voice to the tribunal and he and I then stalked out of the hall in which the tribunal were sitting. Shortly after this British troops moved into Buraimi and captured quantities of arms, ammunition and incriminating documents. It was expected that the Saudis would raise the matter at the United Nations and I was given the task of going through the captured documents and of briefing our UN representative in case he had to defend our action. In the event the

Saudis never did complain to the UN, no doubt because they knew their conduct had been indefensible. But diplomatic relations between the two countries were severed until 1963.

After the Suez operation in 1956 the IPC pumping stations in Syria were blown up as a protest by the Arabs against 'imperialist aggression'. With the Suez canal closed, all Middle East oil had to be transported round the Cape until the canal was reopened and the pumping stations rebuilt, so that oil could flow through the pipeline to the Mediterranean terminals. The pumping stations were insured in London, practically the whole market being involved, by tariff companies and syndicates at Lloyds. The leading underwriters were the Royal Exchange. The claim was the largest insurance claim made until that time and liability was repudiated by the insurers in reliance on a 'riot' clause. This was a standard riot clause such as is usually included in industrial fire policies. Its inclusion had been agreed between a manager of the Royal Exchange and the insurance manager of IPC, during, it was said, a luncheon at the Savoy. No legal advice had been obtained by either of them and the clause was quite inappropriate to the subject matter of the insurance and the risks to be covered.

The IPC team consisted of Gerald Gardiner, Sam Cooke, who held a retainer from Shell and afterwards became a judge, and myself. Gerald was by that time the acknowledged leader of the Common Law Bar. He was an extraordinarily lucid advocate and I never heard him repeat himself in court. He had a very distinctive, direct and concise way of expressing himself. He also retained his political and social principles in a way which inhibited him in his practice. For example, Monckton, although a Conservative, often appeared for trade unions against their employers. Gardiner generally appeared for the unions, and some large commercial enterprises, though not IPC, refused to employ him on account of his politics. He once said to me that he had been reading a political testament which he had written while an undergraduate and that most of his ideas had appeared in the Conservative Manifesto for the 1959 General Election.

Gardiner said that the case must be settled at the highest level. He made the characteristic remark that the majority of men in positions of real power in this country had either been to Eton or belonged to the same clubs, and that they therefore spoke the same language. He was not amused when I asked, 'What about Harrow, Magdalene Oxford and the Coldstream Guards?' – which was his own background. However, as a result of Gerald's advice, Monckton, then Chairman of IPC and a Harrovian, met Kindersley, chairman of the Royal Exchange and an Etonian, and they settled the case over lunch on the basis that the insurers should pay £1 million to IPC. This was the approximate sum paid by IPC over the previous thirty years by way of premiums. A gentle hint was dropped by Monckton that it would be most unfortunate if IPC should decide thereafter to insure their installations outside London.

As will have been seen, most of my work for IPC had a political background. It was vital to the economy to keep the oil flowing, so as to maintain sterling sales of oil which contributed so much to our balance of payments. At the same time the British position in the Middle East was in decline. The Americans wanted a larger share of Middle East oil, while showing reluctance to take over our military commitments in the area. So in the various disputes and arbitrations our opponents were American. At that time they had little knowledge of the area and few of them spoke Arabic. I once lunched with Superior Oil in Bahrain, their Lebanese interpreter being present throughout. When I reported this to IPC I was told, 'We know all about him. He's been in our pay for years and we have already had a report of your lunch.' In spite of this lack of local knowledge the Americans were determined to increase their influence in the area, using the power of the dollar. One American delegate at the Buraimi negotiations said, 'I'm not interested in any proposition which is not 100% American.' Faced with this attitude the British could do no more than fight a skillful rearguard action.

CHAPTER XVI

Queen Elizabeth Building, 1957–62

In the mid-fifties Blanco White retired and Harry Phillimore became head of chambers. He was determined to improve the standing of chambers and the quality of the work and applied for a whole floor of the new Queen Elizabeth Building, which was being built on the site of the bombed Middle Temple library on the Embankment. After a brilliant negotiation with Kenneth Carpmael, then treasurer of the Middle Temple of which Harry was a member, we moved in August 1957 into the second floor of this splendid new building, where there were four other sets: a libel set and Kenneth Carpmael's Admiralty set on the ground floor; Victor Durand's busy criminal set and Lionel Heald's patent chambers on the first floor. Our set was on the second (which was much the best as the ceilings were higher) and the Lord Chief Justice and his son-in-law Eric Sachs had the two residential flats on the third floor. Tom Roche (head of the libel set) said, 'We should put a notice outside the door: Every branch of the law catered for at maximum cost.'

Arthur Smith also retired when we moved and Clement became Head Clerk. Harry, while accepting the vital role of the clerks, made it plain that all major decisions should be made by him after consultation with the members of chambers (there were no chambers meetings in those days). Clement loyally accepted this new régime. As well as Blanco, Frank Laskey retired, Christopher Besley became a metropolitan magistrate, Donald McIntyre and Harris Walker moved elsewhere and Hazel married. Harry laid down that each of us should have our own room and that there should be no sharing. Even so there was room to spare, so Kenneth Willcock joined us from his chambers in Truro to keep up the Western Circuit connection. Peter Bruce also came from other chambers in the Temple. Peter was an outstanding lawyer. He specialised in trade union and hire purchase law and spent much time drafting hire purchase agreements. He took over the National Provincial Bank work when I took silk. He was a charming companion, a great sportsman (his father had been factor to the Duke of Sunderland and Peter had been brought up in the Highlands) and it was a tragedy when he died of leukaemia. Edward Pearce's son Bruce came as a pupil to James Comyn and stayed on in chambers. He became a

Circuit judge and also died before his time. After a year in Queen Elizabeth Building I had doubled my practice. I put this down entirely to having my own room, which had a balcony looking out over Middle Temple gardens, and to the lift, which enabled solicitors' clerks to deliver briefs and papers, without having to walk up two flights of stairs. By 1958 I had a High Court practice and gave up going to County Courts.

As soon as we moved into Queen Elizabeth Building Robert Johnson joined me as a pupil and stayed on in chambers, later becoming chairman of the Bar Council and a High Court judge. Thereafter Edward Cazalet, son of Peter Cazalet the trainer, joined me at the suggestion of Walter Monckton and also stayed on in chambers to become a High Court judge. My other pupils were Michael Fitzgerald, who left to go into planning chambers where he became a leading silk, and Gilbert Rodway who went to Hong Kong where he acquired a large practice in family work. Finally I agreed to take Michael Connell as a pupil, but took silk before he joined so he went to Peter Bruce. Michael too stayed on with us and became a High Court judge. I was devoted to all my pupils and very proud of their ultimate success.

Soon after we moved into Queen Elizabeth Building Harry became a High Court judge and Roger Ormrod became head of chambers, Malcolm Wright having by then become a County Court judge. But Roger himself became a High Court judge in 1961 and James Comyn succeeded him as head of chambers. These were happy times. We all got on well together, there was much laughter and camaraderie and a great deal of work of all kinds. Everyone had stories of their cases and of the foibles of the judges before whom they had been appearing. The success of chambers was due to Harry's foresight in moving from Fountain Court and choosing the right people to stay in chambers.

We robed in the west robing room at the Law Courts, presided over by two uniformed attendants Charlie and Tom, both ex-regular army NCOs. Together they would have made a wonderful music hall turn. They were keen followers of forensic form, knew exactly what was happening in every court and their humour was well informed and topical. During the Boguslawski *v* Gydnia Amerika Line case Charlie said, 'Come on Tom. Help Mr. Dunn get ready for the bogus law.'

When not in court I lunched in Inner Temple Hall, always sitting at the same table whose waiter was Steed, who gave fast service to the regulars but neglected those who only lunched there occasionally. Apart from opponents whom I met in court, and of course my own chambers, most of my friends at the Bar were made from those who sat at that table. Fred Lawton, who became a Lord Justice, Harry Fisher of whom more hereafter and John Willmers were all regulars. I was often against John in court, and there was no-one who could open a case at such a sustained level of indignation on behalf of his client. But he was a kind friend and a brave man, having served with paratroops in the war. Then there was Alan Campbell who became a life peer and with whom I used to play squash. Alan had escaped three times from Colditz where he was a prisoner-of-war, always being recaptured, and the intransigence which had fired him then made him a formidable opponent in court. The conversation at lunch was almost entirely legal shop, but always amusing. Dick Nicholas, who was a County Court judge and sat at our table when he was sitting in the Divorce Court, said in reference to a well publicised libel action which was proceeding in the Law Courts, 'That is just the kind of case which should be tried by a High Court judge. The plaintiff is a rich actress, the defendant is a newspaper, and the result is of no importance to anybody. There are only two things which matter in life: where and with whom you live. Both are decided by County Court judges.'

There was a marked contrast between the attitude of members of the Bar to their colleagues and that of soldiers. Although close friendships were formed within regiments and amongst junior officers, many staff and senior officers were suspicious of one another, and the more ambitious did not hesitate to steal a march on those they saw as rivals for promotion. I found the Bar much more helpful and considerate. While the interests of the client were paramount, there was a strict code of conduct, mostly unwritten, which required absolute integrity in dealing with one's opponent. The partner of a well-known firm of city solicitors once said to me, 'I heave a sigh of relief when I send a set of papers down to counsel, because I know that the case will go out of the jungle and be dealt with according to the rules.' A barrister had only to break the rules once to become a marked man throughout the profession, which was so small (less than two thousand practising barristers in England and Wales at that time), and divided into even smaller compartments dealing with different kinds of work, that everyone knew his opponent personally or by repute. I have often wondered at the difference between the approaches of soldiers and barristers to their colleagues. One reason may be that until comparatively recently the army had not been a competitive profession. Most soldiers were content to enjoy life serving in their regiments, only a small minority being sufficiently ambitious to go to the staff college and seek promotion. The Bar, on the other hand, had for six hundred years been a highly competitive profession, perhaps the most competitive in the country since there were no partnerships, and over that long period its members had learnt to live in a competitive environment and had evolved a civilised code of behaviour within the profession. No such code had yet evolved in the army.

A good example of the helpfulness of the Bar occurred when I applied to Malcolm Hilbery to stand a case of Wild Sapte's out of the list. I had taken the papers down to Lynch before Christmas to write the advice on evidence and had fallen on my head and concussed myself out hunting. So I could not complete the advice until my return to London. Wild Sapte said they could not possibly do all the work I had advised in time for the case, which had been fixed early in the new term. My opponent was Rodger Winn, at that time Treasury devil (junior counsel to the Treasury who acted for all government departments) who later became a Lord Justice. I explained the situation to Rodger who said, 'Don't worry. I will support you.' When I made the application on the basis that the solicitors had not had time for the work advised in my advice on evidence, Hilbery said in his sarcastic way, 'Was this because you did not do the papers with your usual despatch, or because you did not receive them in time?' Rodger at once jumped to his feet and said, 'My Learned Friend has explained the full circumstances to me, which I accept, and support his application.' Hilbery gave him a long bored look and said, 'Very well. The case will stand out to a date to be fixed.' I never forgot Rodger's kindness.

The Bar was recruited from people of all walks of life and backgrounds, although when I joined most had been to Oxford or Cambridge and all had brains. But after a few years almost all assimilated the common ethos, whatever their political and social views. It was not until the late sixties that 'the alternative Bar' emerged, mostly practising in the criminal courts, which did not accept the standards adopted over generations by their predecessors. I believe that it was the emergence of this 'alternative Bar' which was a prime factor in the government decision to grant solicitors the right of audience in the Crown Court and by extension in the High Court. If a monopoly is abused it is right that it should be lost. It remains to be seen how far this reform will improve standards at the Bar.

There can be few more agreeable places in London in which to work than the Temple, a quiet oasis between the bustle and traffic of Fleet Street and the Embankment., Originally a transit camp, convenient to the river, for the Knights Templar en route to the Crusades (there is an identical church at Acre in the Holy Land to the round-towered Temple church), the Temple was bought by the lawyers in the fourteenth century. It had been heavily bombed in the war and the rebuilding proceeded all through the fifties. Wisely the previous courts and buildings were rebuilt in the same eighteenth-century style and a rather haphazard layout, with the Jacobean Middle Temple Hall, its magnificent screen carefully restored at the centre, and the graceful line of King's Bench Walk saved from the bombing. Here one felt the ghosts of Johnson and Goldsmith and the great advocates of the past as they hurried from their chambers to Westminster Hall, or later the Law Courts. Only Inner Temple Hall was a disappointment, since the acoustics were deplorable and no amount of remedial work could improve them. On a fine evening I enjoyed walking home along the Embankment Gardens, via Whitehall to St. James's Park, where I would stand on the bridge admiring the view back over the lake to the Horse Guards, with the towers of Whitehall Court rising like a fairy-tale castle behind, and the pelicans and ducks in the foreground. The finest view in London.

Soon after we moved to Queen Elizabeth Building I was briefed by the Foreign Office to appear before the Commission of Human Rights at Strasbourg.

The Greek government had made a complaint to the Commission of Human Rights alleging acts of torture on Greek Cypriots by the British army and certain officers of Special Branch. The Foreign Office briefed Hylton Foster, the Solicitor General, John Foster and myself to represent the government before the Commission, with Francis Vallat the legal adviser. Robert Johnson, while still my pupil, was sent to Cyprus to help in the collection and preparation of evidence. The Commission consisted of seven members, all representatives of signatory governments of the treaty. The British representative was Humphrey Waldock. The proceedings were translated simultaneously into English, French and German and the skill of the translators was incredible. The Greeks were represented by a distinguished Belgian international lawyer. The British case was opened by Hylton Foster, later Speaker of the House of Commons. He had arrived in Strasbourg the evening before, and he sat up till 3 am preparing his speech. He was a man of tremendous charm of manner who had practised largely on the North-eastern Circuit, and his opening was a model of its kind. After his opening he left for London and John Foster and I continued the case.

John Foster was a brilliant man, a Fellow of All Souls. He lived four extremely active lives – as MP, as a leading silk, as a business man and as a socialite. He had a great zest for life and was the only man I know who, when in France, ate an English breakfast and a large French lunch and dinner. He neither drank nor smoked. He needed very little sleep and told me that he would rather wear himself out and die young than linger into old age. He was a bachelor who had a number of close friends of the opposite sex, one of whom he brought to Strasbourg as his secretary. With all his talents his brain worked too fast for him to express his thoughts in words. The words poured out and he scarcely ever completed one point in his argument before darting on to another. I always noticed that the most successful advocates were those who tempered their performances to the rate of mental intake of the tribunal. John went much too fast. He was most excellent company and I enjoyed being with him.

The Greeks made eighteen separate cases against us. We succeeded in having half of them dismissed on technical grounds and before the other half could be heard, the Treaty of London intervened, whereby the British agreed to give independence to Cyprus with safeguards for the Turkish minority. It was a term of the treaty that the Strasbourg proceedings should be withdrawn.

The situation in Cyprus, not unlike that at present in Northern Ireland, showed how dependent is the administration of justice upon the good will and cooperation of the populace. Martial law had not been declared and the judges were manfully trying to apply English notions of the strict burden of proof and the application of the judges' rules. All these concepts were quite incompatible with a situation in which a British NCO in uniform could be shot in the back in broad daylight in the main shopping street of Nicosia, when it was crowded with shoppers. Although the street was cordoned off within two minutes not a single person came forward with evidence and the pistol was passed from hand to hand and concealed behind a carefully loosened brick in a wall. Under this kind of provocation it is not surprising that British troops were rough with Eoka suspects. But there was no evidence of the kind of organised brutality in which any other army would have indulged.

This was the last case in which I appeared before an international tribunal. But, fortunately, I developed a surprisingly varied practice. There had always been a great deal of divorce work in chambers and Harry, Roger Ormrod and James Comyn all had large divorce practices although they all did other work as well. As a junior about one third of my work was divorce, but in 1959 I became junior counsel to the Registrar of Restrictive Trading Agreements which, until I took silk in 1962, took up much of my time. and, as well as Wilde Sapte's work, there was other work covering different branches of the law.

One case in particular was unusual even for me. I was briefed in a 'passing-off' case in the Chancery Division (Clement never refused a brief). The only reason I can think that I was sent the brief was that Edward Pearce and Dougal Meston had once written a textbook on 'passing-off'. Malcolm Wright, who had just taken silk, was brought in to lead me. Our client was a manufacturer of kitchen equipment who had produced a food mixing machine, said to be a copy of a similar machine manufactured in France and on sale in this country. Cyril Salmon, who became a Law Lord and was one of the leading advocates of his day, appeared for the plaintiffs and persuaded our client to admit in the witness box that he had copied the French machine and also to admit in terms that that was 'dishonest trading'. The judge, Roxburgh, obviously disliked our client and gave judgment against us. After some argument he announced the terms of his order. When he had finished speaking a tall scholarly looking young man, wearing thick spectacles, who was the pupil of Cyril's junior, stood up and said, 'But your Lordship cannot make that order. It is beyond your powers,' – and proceeded to explain why. Cyril, and indeed all of us, sat in astonishment listening to this remarkably courageous intervention, as Roxburgh was a formidable judge. However, he was also a good lawyer and after listening to the young man and asking Cyril and Malcolm if they agreed, he said, 'I shall now rescind my previous order and make a fresh order' – which he did. It was a unique incident.

We appealed to the Court of Appeal and lost. So we went to the House of Lords where Lionel Heald, later Attorney-General replaced Malcolm who had become a County Court judge. Lionel was a specialist in patents, trade marks and passing-off. The Lords were initially hostile in view of the finding of 'dishonest trading'. But Lionel opened the appeal with great confidence and authority saying, 'There is no evidence that the French manufacturer ever acquired a reputation for his machine in this country. This is an essential prerequisite to an action for passing-off. Since the plaintiffs have failed to prove it the action must fail in limine.' So we won in the Lords and I was most impressed by Lionel Heald. Perhaps it would have been wise for the clients to have briefed a specialist earlier.

I appeared quite regularly before the official referees, since Blanco White had had a large practice in building work and some of his clients had remained loyal to chambers. This was the most expensive form of litigation, since both parties had to employ experts who charged higher fees even than the lawyers, and most of the cases were settled either before trial or during the hearing. The cases involved the production of a 'Scott schedule', in which all the alleged defects in the building work were set out and there were columns in which each party recorded its comments. The drafting of those schedules was time-consuming and detailed. The official referees sat in their own corridor at the top of the labyrinth of the Law Courts, and ranked below High Court judges and above County Court judges. Cases involving detail were referred to them from the Queen's Bench Division. It must have been hard and unrewarding work for them and, not surprisingly, some had a reputation for impatience. One, Brett Cloutman, had won the VC in the Great War, it was said, in a fit of bad temper.

Occasionally I became involved in libel actions, a highly technical branch of the law. The facts of one such case were so unusual that it is worth a reference here. In the late fifties I was sent a set of papers by Wilde Sapte on behalf of a client called Fay. Mr. Fay was a garage proprietor at Eastleigh near Southampton, who had wished to erect some new petrol pumps. He had been told by a knowledgeable friend that if he wanted to obtain planning permission he would have to provide the chairman of the local planning committee, a Mr. Curtis, with a motor-car free of charge. Fay was so outraged by this suggestion that he determined to stand for election to the council, so that he could expose Curtis. Having been duly elected he was present at the first council meeting when the members of the various committees were appointed. Curtis was duly proposed as chairman of the planning committee, a position he had held for many years. Fay then stood up and said, 'I oppose the election of Councillor Curtis as chairman of the planning committee, since he has used his position for personal gain.' This statement appeared under banner headlines on the front page of the local paper, which later published a retraction and apology at the request of Curtis's solicitors. Fay, however, refused to withdraw and Curtis eventually, and apparently with some reluctance, issued a writ.

When I saw Fay I told him that his only defence was justification, that is that the words were true and pointed out that there was no chance of proving this unless the friend was called as a witness and even then it was problematical. But I said that as a councillor he would have access to the minutes of the planning committee and that if he wanted to contest the action he should go the council offices and find some evidence to support his allegation. Eventually Fay returned with particulars of six planning applications, all of which on the face of them showed some irregularities of procedure, so I pleaded them all in the defence by way of justification. A seventh application related to a fish-and-chip shop which, though there was no real evidence of irregularity, I decided to plead as a make-weight.

The case came on at Winchester Assizes in 1960 before Fred Lawton and a jury. I was led by Hugh Park, who had been brought into the case at the last moment as my original leader had returned the brief. Hugh had only just taken silk, had received the papers on a Friday and spent the whole weekend working on the case which opened on the Monday. He knew all about the case and did it beautifully. Curtis was represented by Joe Molony, the Leader of the Western Circuit, who opened his case on the top line. 'Members of the Jury,' he declaimed, 'Councillor Curtis has devoted his life to the public service in Eastleigh.' The case lasted over a week and Fred very sensibly left just one question for the jury: 'Are the words complained of true in substance and in fact?' After being out for most of the afternoon the jury returned, and in answer to the question the foreman said, 'We find the words true in respect of the application for planning permission for the fish-and-chip shop.' It was enough. The libel was justified. Pritt's advice to plead everything was vindicated.

By that time I had about a hundred Queen's Bench actions on the stocks at various stages in their progress through the courts, as well as about half that number of divorce suits, many of which involved drafting long affidavits of means and affidavits in custody proceedings, which took much time. I felt like a juggler keeping too many balls in the air at once. So in most cases of any substance which came to court I insisted on a Leader. But one case I had to do myself. An old friend from my County Court days, James Hyde, an experienced managing clerk with Evan Davies, good clients of chambers, had briefed me to appear for Dr. Barbara Moore in a libel action. 'I shall want Mr. Dunn to do the case himself,' he told Clement. 'We can't afford a leader.' There was of course no legal aid for libel actions. Dr. Moore was a vegetarian who had walked from John O'Groats to Land's End on a diet of fruit and vegetables to prove that it could be done. The walk had attracted wide publicity and the day after its completion the *Daily Mail* had published a double-page spread of advertisements congratulating Dr. Moore. The advertisements were from firms such as Dunlop, whose shoes she wore, Calor Gas which she used on the walk and other suppliers of camping equipment. Dr. Moore was furious, alleging that the only inference to be drawn from the advertisements was that she had been sponsored by those companies, whereas she had always asserted, as was the fact, that she had no financial backing for the walk, which was purely a scientific experiment with no commercial element.

The *Daily Mail* was represented by Neville Faulks, the leading silk at the libel Bar, and at that time at the height of his fame as an advocate. He also sat at our table in Hall and was a great friend of mine, a charming companion and a considerable wit. I deliberately opened the case low, because I was not sure what effect Dr. Moore, who was a flamboyant figure, would have on the jury. While I was opening Neville turned to his junior David Hirst, also an old friend of mine and now a Lord Justice, and said in a voice audible to the jury, 'I cannot imagine how they think they can win this case.' But Barbara Moore, dressed at my suggestion in a demure black dress instead of the usual anorak and trousers, made a good impression on the jury, but not on the judge who was Willy McNair, a specialist in shipping law. Despite a hostile summing-up the foreman of the jury, in answer to the question, 'What damages do you award?' said, '£1000 and costs.' 'No,' said McNair. 'Costs are for me.' Although I pointed out that the jury obviously intended that the plaintiff should have £1000 clear, McNair only gave us half our costs, because I had been obliged to amend my pleadings during the trial. I have always thought that it was an unjust decision since the defendants were in no way taken by surprise. It certainly had a disastrous effect on poor Barbara Moore. She became quite unbalanced and conceived a strong sense of grievance against the law and the courts. Thereafter she was continually in the courts, representing herself, in disputes with her neighbours and other people and was eventually declared a vexatious litigant.

Shortly before I took silk I was briefed to appear in the Election Court on behalf of the Attorney-General. In fact I had nothing to do, but there was a requirement that the Attorney-General should be represented on all petitions to the court, so I was able to spend several days watching a fascinating case. Following the death of Lord Stansgate his son and heir Anthony Wedgwood Benn had won a by-election in 1961, having purported to disclaim his peerage. His unsuccessful Conservative opponent had petitioned the court on the ground that Lord Stansgate (as he then was) was ineligible to be a member of the House of Commons. The court consisted of Willy McNair and Bill Gorman. The petitioner was represented by Andrew Clarke, the acknowledged leader of the Chancery Bar and a formidable advocate. After he had opened the case for the best part of a day he sat down and Stansgate, who was representing himself, stood up to address the court. For the hour or so that remained he varied his submissions with jokes and witticisms, which amused everyone in court, except the judges. English judges as a rule only appreciate their own jokes in court. Overnight, however, Stansgate must have received some good advice because next morning his speech was a model. There had obviously been a great deal of research behind it and he took the judges unerringly through the history of the peerage from mediaeval times, contrasting the position of hereditary peers and peers of parliament. It was an outstandingly able performance and Andrew Clarke was obliged to put his best foot forward when he came to Reply. However, the petition was granted and Stansgate was declared ineligible for the House of Commons. It was ironic that he was later able to disclaim his peerage and become Tony Benn, as the result of legislation passed, it was said, to enable Quintin Hailsham to disclaim his peerage and stand for election as Prime Minister,

It was received wisdom in the early sixties that no junior should apply for silk unless and until he had earned at least £4000 a year for three years. By 1961 I had reached this target, but James Comyn applied that year and it was thought that two applications from the same chambers would not be granted. So I waited until 1962. Reggie Manningham-Buller, who was then Attorney-General, said to Judy's mother, who was an old friend, 'I see Robin has applied for silk. Of course he won't get it first time. He will have to wait a year.' But my name appeared in the list, much to my relief, because I was exhausted by the work and had had enough of the drudgery of drafting endless pleadings and opinions. The best reason for taking silk is to protect oneself by reducing the burden of work. Silk opened fresh fields and new pastures, but before entering them I shall describe two important aspects of my junior practice, so far unmentioned.

CHAPTER XVII

The Divorce Court, 1948–62

No branch of the law in my time saw such changes as the law of divorce. Until after I became a judge, when the reforms of the early seventies were introduced, it was impossible for parties to agree to divorce, although it was the one thing that they both wanted. Collusion, as it was called, was an absolute bar. So if, for example, a husband had found another woman and the wife, understandably, refused to divorce him unless she was properly financially provided for, no agreement could be made on that basis. And if the husband in that situation, as many did, charged the wife with a weak case of cruelty, and the wife agreed not to defend in return for a financial settlement, that also was prohibited. Consequently many semantic approaches were adopted, the most usual being that the husband would make the wife an offer 'win, lose or draw'. I remember one experienced divorce practitioner making such an offer to my client in open court. When I turned it down, saying that my client did not want a divorce and would fight, my opponent lost his temper and retorted, 'Well then, the offer is withdrawn.' This was an unsatisfactory state of affairs for all concerned, especially the judges. Judy's father, who had practised at the Admiralty Bar, became a judge of the Probate Divorce and Admiralty Division (PDA) and spent most of his time trying divorce. Indeed Charles Hodson, who became a Law Lord, was the first divorce practitioner to become a judge of the division. Hitherto they had all been Admiralty specialists (there were only three judges in the division before the war), except the President, who was often an ex-law officer. Judy's father referred to himself in the Divorce Court as a 'hoodwinkee' saying it was obvious that the law of collusion was constantly being broken, but that the judges were not told the true situation. After ten years he persuaded his friend Rayner Goddard to ask for him in the Queen's Bench Division, so becoming the first judge to be transferred from the PDA. Thereafter the practice became common, the PDA being referred to as 'the OCTU' for judges.

In order to obtain a divorce in those days it was necessary to prove a matrimonial offence. The most common were adultery and cruelty. The great majority of adultery cases were undefended, many involving the evidence of a chambermaid at a hotel to say that she had taken early morning tea to a particular room, to find the husband in bed with a lady other than his wife. These cases were confined to people with money and there were firms of solicitors who provided a service including the booking of the room, the presence of the lady and no doubt careful briefing of the chambermaid. Usually there was another lady in the background. The whole procedure was artificial and unreal and everyone concerned knew it. Each case took ten to fifteen minutes and the judge was expected to sit quiet, ask no questions and grant a decree. The only one who persistently broke the rules was Harry Leon, who usually sat in Willesden County Court. Harry became widely known as Henry Cecil, the author of several legal books including the best-selling *Brothers in Law*. He took seriously his duty under the Matrimonial Causes Act to inquire into the cases, sometimes opening up a Pandora's Box which made it impossible for either party to get a decree. Many a young barrister had an awkward time before Leon and our clerks were skillful in keeping our cases out of his list.

Damages were sometimes awarded against the co-respondent if he had been found to have seduced the wife and the marriage had been happy until his appearance. The sums awarded were not large and were thought by many to be an insult to women, especially as they were reduced if she had been an unsatisfactory wife.

Sometimes the charge of adultery was contested, but the judges were sceptical of denials of adultery, if there was evidence of what was called inclination and opportunity. It was said that there was an irrebuttable presumption of sexual intercourse if two persons of the opposite sex spent an hour together after dark in the same room, unless they were married. Daylight meetings were for some reason not so suspect. The stock questions in cross-examination of the parties in such cases were, 'Did you like him (or her)?' and 'What did you both find to talk about all that time?'

But the meat and drink of the Divorce Bar were the defended cruelty cases. If the parties were socially or financially prominent (as they often were), these developed into the most popular free show in London, with the court crowded with onlookers. A cruelty petition would consist essentially of 'particulars of cruelty' running to perhaps twenty paragraphs of alleged incidents, which the petitioner had been able to dredge up from the ruins of an unhappy marriage. The petitioner, followed by the respondent, would be examined and cross-examined about each incident and witnesses to some of them called. Although many would be acts of violence, examples of nagging by wives and selfishness and unkindness by husbands were common, as were all manner of sexual perversions. The reality of the latter cases were usually that the acts had occurred and that the wife had consented, at any rate until she became bored with her husband or fell in love with someone else. But many husbands could not bring themselves to admit the facts in public, so they denied everything. The judges did not believe them, thought they were liars and granted decrees to the wife, albeit on a false basis. However, in one such case a newly appointed judge, who had no experience of the Divorce Court and was a rather unworldly man, dismissed the petition saying, 'I cannot believe that an apparently decent man, like the husband, could have been guilty of such filthy practices or that any decent woman would have allowed them.' Harry Phillimore, who was leading me, said after the case, 'Of course he did it and she loved every minute of it, until she met the co-respondent.' In one case involving well-known people, a chariot stood for days outside the court, in which it was alleged the husband had harnessed his wife and driven her naked round the garden, whipping her with a special ivory whip from Swaine and Adeney in Piccadilly. The press were only allowed to report the judgments, not the evidence in these cases. But the London evening papers usually featured at least one judgment, by-lining the more lurid details.

All concerned learnt a great deal about human nature. Indeed some said that all judges should sit in the Divorce Division for a spell to learn how people really behaved. One thing that I learnt was how many apparently happy marriages were in fact deeply unhappy. Friends would be called by the respondent to say how good the marriage was and would be astonished to be told of some incident, admittedly true, which showed the opposite. 'No-one except the parties,' said one judge, 'knows what goes on behind the door of the marriage bedroom.' Very often each party charged the other with cruelty, so that the whole humiliating process would have to be gone through twice, once on the petition and once on the cross-petition. In such cases the first question in cross-examination was often, 'Have you done anything during the marriage with which to reproach yourself?' If the answer was 'No' the strongest allegation would be put. If 'Yes' then the cross-examiner would build on the admission.

It surprised me how well the parties stood up to this ordeal. Many seemed positively to enjoy the disclosure of their most intimate and private matrimonial secrets. The only thing to be said for this system was that it enabled the parties to unburden themselves of their rage and hostility against one another, instead of having their grievances bottled up inside them, causing them frustration and a feeling that they had been denied justice, as frequently happened when the law was reformed. To that extent it may have been a kind of therapy and few complained about the loss of a case.

The leaders of the Common Law Bar often appeared in these cases. The most prominent was Gilbert Beyfus, the complete advocate, as effective in cross-examination as in making submissions of law to an appellate court, and very shrewd. He enjoyed hunting and had ridden in the Bar point-to-point. He had once been kicked by a horse on the side of the head, severing a nerve which operated his eyelid. This left him with a kind of twitch, which could be alarming to a witness he was cross-examining. For some reason he was not well regarded by the establishment and was never made a judge. Consequently he continued in practice for much longer than most leading silks and seemed to attract colourful clients and sensational cases. Once, during the long vacation, when Judy's father was sitting at the Old Bailey,

Gilbert appeared before him. When asked why he was working instead of enjoying himself in the South of France, Gilbert replied, 'I would rather do this than anything.'

He was often opposed in the Divorce Court by Melford Stevenson, who could be a dangerous opponent but lacked flexibility, making up his mind how he was going to run the case and refusing to be deflected. Harry once said, 'Melford is a tramline advocate. If you stay on the track he will knock you down. But if you step off he will go puffing past and miss you altogether.' Some said that Melford was one of the great wits of his generation, and certainly some of his remarks were very funny. But they were always directed against someone else, often unkind and sometimes cruel. Typical was his comment when Eric Sachs, son-in-law of the Lord Chief Justice, was appointed to the Bench. When asked whether it was not time he became a judge, Melford replied, 'Not me. The Lord Chief Justice has another son-in-law who is a dentist.' In fact Eric was a good judge and made a considerable contribution to the Court of Appeal. Melford, on the other hand, was I suppose about the worst judge who sat after the war. Not so much because of his savage sentences, but because he simply did not know how to behave himself and could not resist the admittedly often witty but unjudicial intervention.

I was once led by Geoffrey Lawrence in a nullity case. He successfully defended Dr. Bodkin Adams, who was charged with the murder of one of his elderly patients by prescribing overdoses of drugs. Geoffrey often appeared in the Divorce Court, where his style was quite different from that of Gilbert Beyfus, though in its way just as effective. Where Gilbert was tall Geoffrey was short; where Gilbert raised his voice, Geoffrey was quietly spoken; where Gilbert would mock a witness Geoffrey was always polite. Geoffrey became a High Court judge, but sadly died soon after his appointment.

The law of nullity had developed in the Ecclesiastical Courts which exercised jurisdiction until 1873 in Doctors Commons, where the great exponent of the law was Dr. Lushington, whose judgments were still cited when I practised. 'I worship Lushington,' David Moylan once said and certainly his judgments were models of clarity. When referring to the details of sexual intercourse the doctor always used Latin. One learned but inexperienced young counsel once asked his client in the witness box, 'Was there *vera copula?*' 'I don't know,' was the reply. 'I never met the woman.' The facts of our case were unusual, even in that court. Our client, an attractive young woman married to a rich husband, alleged that the marriage had never been consummated, although she admitted to regular sexual intercourse before the marriage. The medical examination, to which both parties were obliged to submit, disclosed that physically she was a virgin, but the doctors agreed that though unusual this did not necessarily mean that she had not had sexual intercourse. In the course of the trial Neville Faulks, who appeared for the husband, craftily persuaded the judge, Seymour Karminski, to suggest that the lady should undergo a further medical examination. This we could not refuse without damaging her credibility and the examination showed that she was no longer a virgin. She then admitted to us that she had committed adultery after she had left her husband, but nobly refused to name the man as he was married. Although strictly not relevant to the issue of nullity, this was damaging to her credit which had already been shaken by a most able cross-examination by Neville, supported by her private diaries which had been disclosed. It is very dangerous to keep a diary of your married life. In the result we abandoned the nullity petition and the husband was granted a decree on the ground of adultery with a man unknown. But the case had a happy ending for her. After the decree the husband changed his will, leaving her penniless. But before he could sign the new will he died of a heart attack, so that under the previous will she inherited the whole of his estate.

The most effective, as well as the fairest, leader at the specialist Divorce Bar at that time was Rawden Temple, who it was said would have become a judge had he not fallen out with the President, Jack Simon. However, he became a highly respected Social Security Commissioner and received a well-earned knighthood. He once led me appearing for a beautiful French lady married to a well-known tycoon, who had offered her £250,000 not to defend a charge of adultery. When we saw her in consultation she said, 'It's not enough.' 'How much do you want?' asked Rawden. '£300,000,' replied the lady. When asked to justify the figure she said, 'For three reasons. First because of the way he treated a young hostess in a night club. Second because he charged me with adultery in Italy, where it is a criminal offence. And third because I hate him. Each of those is worth £100,000.' She got her £300,000 on a 'win, lose or draw' basis.

The main suit, as the trial of the divorce was called, was vital to the parties, since the custody of the children and financial provision for the wife depended largely upon it. Although the judges paid lip service to the statutory provision that the interest of children was paramount, in practice the 'guilty' party usually lost the children. Great weight was given to the wishes of an 'unimpeachable' spouse. If the divorced wife was living with another man it was considered that the children would be in moral danger, at least until she remarried. Custody cases were dealt with relatively perfunctorily by judges other than those who had heard the main suit, usually on affidavit evidence. Witnesses were seldom called. When appearing for an adulterous wife, it was common practice at the Divorce Bar for the children to be made wards of court, which effectively removed the custody issue to the Chancery Division, whose judges were less interested in the rights and wrongs of the marriage and more interested in the welfare of the children. Indeed it was a Chancery judge, Harry Vaizey, who coined the phrase: 'It takes three to commit adultery.'

Financially women were very badly treated under the then current divorce laws. There was no power to transfer property or to make a lump sum payment. The only financial provision available to a successful petitioner was maintenance or periodical payments as they were called. A 'guilty' wife could expect nothing for herself except a 'compassionate' allowance, a derisory sum which barely put her on a subsistence level. Even maintenance was usually expressed to be payable *dum casta et sola*, so that a single act of sexual intercourse if discovered would stop her maintenance. If the guilty wife was lucky enough to be awarded custody of her children, she would receive maintenance for them, but the amounts awarded were usually wholly inadequate for their needs. 'Ancillaries' as they were called were dealt with by the registrars, all ex-members of the Bar, at Somerset House. The senior was Bertie Long who, like his predecessor Charlie Hawkes, was a keen supporter of the Pegasus Club and gave some style to those arid proceedings. The so-called 'one-third rule', which fixed the wife's maintenance at one-third of the husband's gross income, was applied more or less rigorously by the registrars, although they were always at pains to say that the rule did not exist.

In the late fifties I appeared in a wardship case in the Court of Appeal, the opposing solicitor being Derek Clogg of Theodore Goddard, who had a great deal of divorce work at that time. I was naturally delighted when, soon afterwards, I received a set of papers from Derek. Thus began a most enjoyable association which lasted until I took silk. Derek almost always acted for the wife and was a brilliant negotiator. He and his assistant Willy Roxburgh, who became a partner in Herbert Smith the city solicitors, were also fun to work with. Derek liked to negotiate from strength and would often employ inquiry agents to follow the husbands. He enjoyed meeting his opponent and, in the course of a discussion about finance, calmly producing the inquiry agents' report showing that the husband had committed adultery. He preferred to have all financial details settled before the petition was filed, leaving it to counsel to explain to the judge that there had been no collusion. A great deal of expertise was involved in getting these cases through without breaking the law. Derek once said to me, 'I simply could not do your job. I like to operate behind the scenes and could not bring myself to stand up and risk making a fool of myself in public.' I thought of this remark when I heard that solicitors were to have rights of audience in the higher courts – the temperamental requirements of the two branches of the profession are so different. Derek was ahead of his time, always insisting on the provision of a house for the wife and also a lump sum payment as well as maintenance. He treated collusion lightly, rightly regarding it as a bad and outdated law. Indeed by that time the judges were beginning to take a more relaxed view of collusion, granting decrees provided that any bargain was fully disclosed and was not contrary to the justice of the case. This view was later enshrined in a statute which preceded the major reforms of the early seventies. No wonder the ladies all flocked to him: we appeared for a duchess, peeresses and the wives of the landed gentry and business tycoons, as well as actresses.

In those days, if the petitioner had committed adultery it was necessary to file a 'discretion statement' setting out particulars of the adultery, as the court had a discretion in those circumstances to refuse a decree. The judges were supposed to uphold the sanctity of marriage, a phrase frequently used but which I never wholly understood, and would occasionally refuse to exercise their discretion if the adultery disclosed was not only of long standing, but also with several different people. 'I do not think it safe,' said one judge, 'to allow this petitioner to become available on the marriage market. She is promiscuous and a danger to men.' This difficulty appeared when Derek and I appeared for a famous actress, who was asking for the discretion of the court in respect of a single incident of adultery some years earlier. When I saw her the night before the hearing and had gone through her proof of evidence with her, I said, 'And then I shall put your discretion statement to you and ask if it discloses all the adultery you have committed during the marriage.' 'If you ask me that Mr. Dunn,' she replied, 'the answer will be no.' I looked at Derek, whose duty it was to obtain particulars of all adultery from her, but he wisely said nothing. So I said, 'I shall leave you with Mr. Clogg. You must disclose all your adultery to him and we shall have to file a supplemental discretion statement.' Next morning, when she was in the witness box and both discretion statements had been put to her (the second involving several men), she turned to the judge with a gesture of abasement and said, 'I am deeply sorry, My Lord. When my husband left me for a younger woman I regarded the marriage as at an end. So when Mr. Clogg told me I must disclose all the adultery committed during my marriage, I did not include what had happened after he left. It was a grievous error, for which I apologise.' It was a brilliant performance and the judge was happy to exercise his discretion.

This was the state of the law thirty years ago. The whole procedure was undignified and humiliating to the parties, especially the women. Divorce was made so difficult and the social consequences to the parties were so unpleasant that people tended to make the most of their marriages and stay together. After the reforms of the law the divorce rate increased dramatically and society embarked on a régime of serial polygamy. I do not know which option was worse.

Inevitably, since we were recognised PDA chambers, I appeared in the Probate Court. These cases brought out the worst in human nature. I suppose it was the prospect of getting something for nothing. The usual allegations were of undue influence or that the testator was not of sound mind. The evidence of the two sides was irreconcilable and the pictures drawn of the testator by each so different as to be unrecognisable as the same person. Those supporting the will, often a housekeeper or friendly neighbour, would describe him as an alert old man, taking a close interest in his affairs; those in opposition, usually disappointed relatives, would describe a senile geriatric. The judges tended to uphold the last will. 'I always find for the last will if I can,' said Harry Barnard, a most experienced judge. 'Why shouldn't the old lady leave her money to the dustman, if he has been kind to her, instead of a pack of grasping relatives who ignored her for twenty years?' The doyen of the Probate Bar was the father of my friend John Mortimer QC, the creator of the Rumpole stories. Mortimer Père was a tall impressive figure, totally blind. I can see him now, standing in counsel's row, with his wife in the gangway beside him helping him with his books and papers. He had written the best textbook on Probate Law and had a photographic memory. Having referred the judge to a case in the law reports he would say, 'If your Lordship looks at page 83, the last paragraph, your Lordship will see the passage on which I rely.' It was an awe-inspiring performance.

CHAPTER XVIII

Restrictive Practices, 1959–68

In 1959 I was appointed junior counsel to the Registrar in the Restrictive Practices Court. This was the Court set up under the Restrictive Trade Practices Act 1956, which was designed to do away with 'horizontal' agreements between companies, or members of trade associations, intended to restrict the terms of trade of parties to the agreements, particularly, but not exclusively, 'price fixing' terms. Roualeyn Cumming-Bruce had been the first junior counsel to the Registrar and it was on his appointment as Treasury junior that I was appointed. Arthur Bagnall from the Chancery Division was the other junior counsel.

I appeared in ten contested cases in the court, which was more than any other member of the Bar, of course always for the Registrar. Of those ten, one went to the Court of Appeal and another to the House of Lords. Of the ten, eight were full-scale references of agreements and in three of these the agreement was upheld on the ground that it was in the public interest; in the remaining five the agreement was declared void.

The first of my cases was re Phenol Producers' Agreement. Phenol, or carbolic acid, is an important raw material in the chemical industry used particularly in the manufacture of plastics, paints and dyestuffs. The agreement was one of the last of the old-fashioned 'price fixing' agreements to come before the court. After a twelve-day hearing the agreement was condemned as all other price fixing agreements had been. I was led by Tom Roche who, in his final speech, pointed out that the price was not fixed by reference to any costings (which varied widely between different producers) but was based on opportunism tempered by caution.

Tom appeared in many cases in the court, latterly usually for the trade. He was head and shoulders above any other advocate who appeared there during my time. He moved among the mass of uncorrelated statistics which formed the bulk of the evidence as if it was his natural element. He was a most effective cross-examiner of expert witnesses; I once saw an eminent accountant collapse in the witness box during his cross-examination. He was also amazingly adept at doing mental arithmetic on his feet and his calculations on a scrap of paper made during the trial were often conclusive in his final speech. He always managed to go to the root of the most complicated cases and he was always out to win. On his merits Tom should certainly have been made a judge; unfortunately he was not always tactful with the judges, especially those whose mental equipment was inferior to his own. This was sad because he was basically one of the kindest men that I ever knew.

There followed an interesting point on the law of contempt in the Retail Newsagents case. One of the members of the National Federation considered that the agreement was harmful to the public and at the hearing gave evidence for the Registrar. As a result he was deprived of his offices as branch delegate and treasurer. The Attorney-General moved to commit the members of the branch for contempt of court. The Court refused the motion, holding that since the expulsion had occurred after the termination of the proceedings and was accordingly not calculated to prejudice the trial, it could not amount to a contempt of court. The Court of Appeal reversed this decision, holding that contempt of court was not confined to pending cases and that victimisation of a witness was contempt, whether it was done while the proceedings were pending or after they had finished. The case was called A-G v Butterworth and is now a leading case on the law of contempt.

The next case arose out of an agreement between certain newspaper proprietors fixing a common retail selling price for their newspapers. The agreement was then terminated and thereafter the Registrar referred it to the court. The proprietors applied to have the reference set aside on the ground that the agreement had already been terminated. The point depended on the construction of one of the sections of the 1956 Act and the Registrar asked for the opinion of the law officers. I was commissioned to write the first draft, which I did and circulated copies to Reggie Manningham-Buller and Jack Simon, then the Solicitor-General. I expressed the view that the proprietors were right and the Registrar should not have referred the agreement. Jack Simon agreed with me. Reggie said my opinion was a lot of nonsense and proceeded to attack my reasoning. After about a quarter of an hour Jack agreed with him, so he turned to me and said, 'Well, Robin, I suppose you will dissent.' I said if both the law officers agreed I would go along with them, although I thought the point was difficult. In the event we won in the court and in the Court of Appeal (Kenneth Diplock dissenting) and also in the Lords. Ever after that Reggie always said I was a bad lawyer.

Reggie Manningham-Buller was one of the most criticised figures in my time at the Bar and there is no doubt that he was tactless and tough and had had very little practice before becoming a law officer. But he was much underestimated both as a lawyer and, especially latterly, as an advocate. He was hard working, very quick on to a point with a sound knowledge of principle and his parliamentary experience stood him in good stead in construing statutes. As Attorney-General he carried great weight in court. He eventually became Lord Chancellor and thereafter a Law Lord and greatly increased his stature in the House of Lords. After his death he was attacked by Patrick Devlin, a former Law Lord, in his book *Easing the Passing* describing the trial of Dr. Bodkin Adams for murder. Devlin had been the trial judge and Reggie as Attorney-General had led for the prosecution. Devlin in his book made fun of Reggie, saying that he had no judicial sense. I took up the cudgels in the press, writing a letter saying that the criticism was unfair and hurtful to Reggie's family, and that in the House of Lords Reggie had made a great contribution to the development of the law. Leslie Scarman and Nigel Bridge, who had both sat with Reggie in the Lords, wrote at my suggestion in similar terms.

By the time the Newspaper Proprietors case got to the House of Lords Reggie had become Lord Chancellor taking the title of Lord Dilhorne and the new Attorney, John Hobson, came in to lead. He was one of the nicest men I ever met, but even then he was beginning to show signs of the disease from which he died.

Standard Metal Windows was one of the few cases in which the agreement (a minimum price agreement) was upheld. I was led by Arthur Bagnall and Tom Roche appeared for the trade. It was a dull case and I remember nothing of note about it, except that I passed a note to Arthur during his cross-examination of the leading witness for the trade saying, 'For God's sake take a wicket.' Arthur was a keen cricketer and the best advocate of the day in the Chancery Division.

Net Books, however, was the most interesting case in which I appeared in the court. Arthur Bagnall who led for the Publishers' Association, coined the phrase 'Books are different' and so it proved, because the agreement was upheld. The basis of the agreement was that if a book was designated a 'net book' (as nine out of ten of all new books were) then it could not be sold below the 'net' price. The publishers won by satisfying the court that if the agreement was abrogated many stock-holding booksellers would be forced out of business and there would be no market for many books of literary or scholastic merit. The case was brilliantly presented by the Association; their main witnesses were impressive and their bookselling witnesses carefully chosen and admirable. The judge, Denys Buckley, had a great deal of sympathy for the case. Harry Fisher led me. Harry was one of the leading advocates of my generation and became a close friend.

There followed the Tyre Trade case. Shortly after this case ended I was invited to a private luncheon at Buckingham Palace and after lunch Prince Philip said to me, 'You do a lot of restrictive practices work, don't you?' He then mentioned the Tyre Trade case, saying that he was a friend of the chairman of Dunlop and had heard a good deal about the case. It was an example of how well briefed the Royal Family are on those occasions. I suggested that he should sit on the court for one of the references, which he jumped at, but nothing came of it.

Paper and Board and Waste Paper, which were heard together, were the first two cases in which I appeared as leader for the Registrar, having by then taken silk. My opponent was John Arnold, then a leading silk at the Chancery Bar.

The Building Trades Employers case was the longest case which up till then had taken place in the court. It lasted thirty-three working days. The restrictions which were attacked related to the use of the RIBA standard forms of contract in all building work and also to the compulsory use of bills of quantities and fixed rates for 'day work'. As a result of the case I learnt a great deal about the building industry and the activities of architects and quantity surveyors.

The last case in which I appeared in the court was the Distant Water Vessels Development scheme. This was a scheme whereby owners of vessels fishing in distant water, i.e. the Barents Sea and around Norway, Spitzbergen, Bear Island, Iceland, Greenland, Newfoundland and Labrador, agreed not to sell their catches at auctions at Hull, Grimsby and Fleetwood below the minimum reserve prices. I led for the Registrar and Harry Fisher led for the industry. He opened the case by saying that the only fish concerned in previous cases were red herrings and Roche (sic). The case lasted forty-three days and the agreement was upheld on the ground that the removal of the reserve prices would lead to a fall in the overall price of fish sold at auction which could not be compensated for by increased sales, and which would result in the scrapping of trawlers and consequently in the long run reduction in the catch with an eventual increase in prices.

This was another case in which the trade witnesses – the trawler owners – were impressive and demonstrated that trawling was only marginally profitable because of the very large sums of capital locked up in the ships, so that if large-scale trawling was to continue the industry did require support. I believe the industry has now virtually collapsed due to international quotas.

After the case I was asked by the Trawlers Association to attend their annual dinner in the Fishmongers Hall, when 'King Cod' in full regalia was brought in with due ceremony on a silver salver. The trawler captain with the largest catch for the year was also presented with the traditional 'silver cod'.

These were the heydays of the court and by the late sixties it had practically worked itself out. Most of the price fixing agreements, which dated back to the 'slump' years of the thirties, when manufacturers required price protection, had been abrogated. The Registrar's basic submission in most of the cases was: 'The efficient can produce at below the fixed price which is only to support high cost producers. Let them go to the wall unless they can reduce their costs and so increase their efficiency.' The logical outcome of this argument was monopoly and so it proved. In industry after industry there were mergers and takeovers and 'nationalisations', largely I believe due to the policy of the Restrictive Trade Practices Act. By the seventies industry was dominated by large corporations, with a virtual monopoly of their product, and all kinds of labour difficulties.

The court was given a new lease of life by the Re-sale Price Maintenance Act 1964, which prohibited the fixing of retail prices by manufacturers. But after the first case (Confectionery) it became apparent that it would be even more difficult to justify an agreement under that act than under the Restrictive Trade Practices Act, and agreement after agreement was abandoned by the parties.

I was instructed by the gramophone industry to lead in their reference. I always thought that the industry had a good chance of success, as books had been expressly exempted from the act after the Net Book case. Indeed Ted Heath, who had introduced the 1964 act, when asked what industries he thought should be excluded from the act, had said, 'Books and gramophone records.' But shortly before I was made a judge the industry abandoned their defence on the ground that 50% of the records sold in this country were imported from the USA and were not subject to any re-sale price agreement. The main English companies – EMI and Decca – decided that in that situation their re-sale price agreements would put them at a commercial disadvantage with the US companies.

The restrictive practices cases were more difficult and involved harder work than any other class of case in which I appeared at the Bar. One of the main difficulties was to define the issues out of the mass of evidence and it was often not possible to do this until the conclusion of all the evidence enabled one to take a long look at the case. It was easy to lose sight of the wood for the trees. The techniques of advocacy were also different, because the proofs of evidence of witnesses were exchanged before the hearing and delivered with the brief. Appearing for the Registrar the principal tasks were the preparation of the cross-examination of the main witness or witnesses for the trade and of the final speech. Some of the cases had already been referred to the Monopolies Commission, whose findings were not always supportable after the more detailed examination of the Restrictive Practices Court. The Commission adopts an inquisitorial procedure, whereas the court followed the traditional adversarial system. My experience in the Restrictive Practices Court confirmed my view that the best way of forming a judgment is to allow each side to put its case forward in the strongest possible way and allow the tribunal to decide on the evidence. The inquisitorial system has the serious disadvantage that the inquisitor may proceed on a 'hunch' and miss the main point in the case.

CHAPTER XIX

Queen's Counsel, 1962–68

In 1961 the lease of our flat in Queen's Gate expired and Judy and I decided to buy our own house. She found a charming house, with room for the family, which had just been built in Roland Way, a quiet mews in South Kensington. Jennifer, who by then had left school, was living with us.

In 1962 Jennifer became engaged to marry Bill Montgomery, whose family owned a beautiful eighteenth-century house and estate in Northern Ireland, which of course we visited. The family had gone there from Scotland in the early seventeenth century and had lived there ever since. The descendants of some of the original tenants who had gone over with them still lived in the same cottages. We were happy for Jennifer, as she would be living in the country, able to do the things she enjoyed. They lived in a pretty house on the Strangford Loch, which we helped them furnish. They were married in the Temple in July 1963, as it would have been difficult for Bill's family and friends to go to Lynch. Eight months later Jennifer was killed in a motor accident. Bill was driving the car and was injured but survived. This was a terrible blow to the whole family. The Greeks were right to say that the worst thing that can happen to parents is to lose a child. Nothing was ever quite the same, but we still had our two other children and our lives had to go on.

When I took silk in 1962 Harry Phillimore said, 'Never suggest that a case should be settled. Nothing is more demoralising for clients than to be brought to meet leading counsel and to be advised to settle the case. Leaders are taken in to fight cases. Of course, if you are asked to settle a case, do so. But remember that the lay client, the solicitors and junior counsel will all have tried and failed to settle the case and have decided to fight. What they expect from you is to fight it for them.' He also said that I would find that most of my junior clients would desert me and that I would have to build up a fresh clientèle. Both warnings proved correct.

Taking silk in those days was a gamble. Many successful juniors failed, as Walter Monckton once put it, to get out of the ruck. Although for the first year I was entitled to be briefed in all my junior cases, leading briefs were few and far between. So Clement fixed me up with some criminal legal aid defences on the Western Circuit

My great-grandfather Major-General William Dunn, wearing his Peninsula medal while commanding the Chestnut Troop RHA; my father, Brigadier Keith Dunn CBE (below left) who commanded 'D' Battery RHA; and myself while commanding 'C' Battery RHA (below right).

LEFT: *Brigadier-General Robin Dunn inspecting a wartime camp with Lloyd George, 1915. "My grandfather knew Lloyd George."*

BELOW: *On my first pony "Joey" at Daventry, 1925, before cub-hunting with the Pytchley.*

LEFT: *Judy with the cup on Manana, 1939.*

RIGHT: *Judy at Lynch when we first met in 1940.*

RIGHT: *Judy's brother John with Ruby on the terrace at Lynch. He was killed by a stray bomb on the RMC Sandhurst in 1941.*

BELOW: *Judy and her father Toby Pilcher arriving at Selworthy Church, 23 August 1941, one month before I sailed for the Middle East.*

LEFT: *Quentin Drage (killed in Italy 1945), self and Slogger Armitage (killed in the desert 1942) on board* SS Samaria *approaching Cape Town, 1941.*

RIGHT: *'D' troop – 'A' Battery H.A.C., Libya 1942. BSM Eldridge, self and George Buchanan just after escaping from the Afrika Korps.*

LEFT: *My Honey O.P. tank and crew, Libya 1942. Left to right: Gnr Cobb (Radio Operator), Dvr Finneron (both wounded), self, my O.P.A. L/Bdr Tinsley (killed at Knightsbridge), and my soldier servant Gnr Cook (POW).*

ABOVE: *Honey O.P. tank in the desert, 1942.*

RIGHT: *Four generations at Lynch, 1942. Judy with her mother and grandmother, and Jennifer on my return from the Middle East.*

ABOVE: *My father inspecting the Gloucestershire Home Guard in 1943, followed by Brigadier John Campbell (also mounted) who won the VC in 1916 rallying his troops with a hunting horn.*

LEFT: *With Joyce Collings (VAD) while convalescing after being wounded in the head in Normandy, 1944.*

RIGHT: *Field-Marshal Montgomery pinning on my MC in Holland, 1944. "Why is that man so angry with daddy?"*

BELOW: *'C' Battery RHA firing a salute on Kiel harbour to mark the end of the war in Europe.*

ABOVE: *Lynch, Judy's home on Exmoor where we brought up our family.*

ABOVE: *My discussion with the Sultan of Muscat at Salalah in 1954 when he produced evidence of his exercise of jurisdiction at Buraimi (see left). The political agent (Chauncey) looks less surprised than me.*

RIGHT: *Just back from international tribunal at Geneva 1955, at Lynch with Judy and the children on their ponies.*

ABOVE: *Bar point to point at Kimble 1956. Jumping the first fence (left to right): John Syms, self on Black Venus, Mick McElligott. Michael Turner in background.*

LEFT: *Arriving at the church with Jennifer for her wedding in 1963. She died following a motor accident 8 months later.*

BELOW: *Allan winning on Judy's horse Hisrita at Nottingham 1965.*

RIGHT: *Leaving church after the assize service, Bristol 1970, followed by Sebag Shaw and Jo Stephenson. The judges carry posies to ward off the plague.*

LEFT: *Being interviewed by the press outside our house in Roland Way, 1972.*

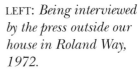

LEFT: *The Colonel Commandant RA inspects a passing out parade of recruits at Woolwich, 1981.*

BELOW: *Walking over to lunch through the Temple with John May and Christopher French, 1981.*

Princess Diana's first state opening of Parliament, 1981. Front row on the woolsack left to right: self, Tom Denning, Geoffrey Lane, Desmond Ackner. Tasker Watkins VC faces the camera. Quintin Hailsham backs down the steps to the throne with difficulty.

ABOVE: *The last Denning Court of Appeal, 1982. From left to right: back row – Kerr, self, O'Connor, Ackner, Donaldson, Griffiths, May, Watkins, Slade, Oliver, Templeman, Fox; front row – Cumming-Bruce, Waller, Stephenson, Denning, Lawton, Ormrod, Eveleigh.*

BELOW: *Hunting on Exmoor with the Devon & Somerset Staghounds, 1993, with Judy (on foot), Janie (second from right mounted), and our grandchildren Sarah, Anna, Jessica and (on foot) Peter Clifford.*

and at the Old Bailey. This was fresh ground for me. I had hardly ever gone circuit as a junior or appeared in a criminal court before a jury. So I had to learn the rules of criminal cricket, what one could or could not do, which were mostly locked in the chests of the regular criminal practitioners, and learn the technique of addressing a jury, which did not come easily to me.

My first such case, in which I was coincidentally briefed by my old friend Jimmy Fellowes from Stratford, was to defend a client of theirs charged with a wages snatch, or more accurately an armed robbery, near Southampton. The client, whose first name was Eric, belonged to one of those close-knit East End families, which might have been the original of one of the Rumpole stories. Our defence was an alibi, the robbery having been committed on Eric's birthday, which the family said had been celebrated by a large party at a local public house at which all of them, including Eric, had been present. The difficulty was to find a witness without 'form', which would have let in cross-examination of his criminal record. Eventually we found two young female cousins who fulfilled the necessary criterion. Unfortunately the publican could not help as, although he remembered the party, he could not swear that Eric was there. In due course Eric was convicted of the robbery, despite the evidence of the two girls. I did not call Eric, because, after the robbery, he had disappeared with his wife. They had in fact gone to Manchester, where Eric had enjoyed a profitable eighteen months, before being stopped on the motorway by the police with a car full of stolen goods. There had been a chase down the motorway, in the course of which various objects, such as iron bars, panes of glass and other impedimenta, had been thrown out of the window of Eric's car to obstruct the progress of the police car. The move to Manchester gave too many hostages to fortune to risk calling Eric. The trial took place at Winchester Assizes and for some reason was held in No. 2 court in the Castle, from which there was no direct access from the dock to the cells. Eric was duly found guilty and after the judge, Cecil Havers, had sentenced him to a long term of imprisonment, he broke away from two warders in the passage between the court and the cells, ran through a door at the back of the building and climbed a wall behind which his loyal and faithful wife was waiting in a car to drive him to freedom. When he was on top of the wall one of the pursuing warders seized his ankle and I last saw my client being frog-marched down the steps to the cells. I had certainly been introduced to crime at the top level, since armed robbers of Eric's type were regarded by other prisoners as the élite of the prison population.

The young woman from Jimmy Fellowes's firm, who came to Winchester, told me an amusing story of the difficulties of organising a general practice in the East End of London. An old lady, who wished to make her will, said to the solicitor, 'I would like to leave all my money to the charming young man I have just met in your waiting room.' The 'charming young man' had in fact been charged with numerous offences of fraud, for which he had a long record of convictions, and was waiting to discuss his case with another partner. So Jimmy thereafter arranged two waiting rooms, one for the criminal clients and one for the others.

In another case on the Western Circuit I defended a local councillor charged with defrauding the revenue. 'No Somerset jury will ever convict me of fraud,' he told me before the case. But our jury at Wells did and I had difficulty in persuading Fred Lawton not to send him to prison.

But most of my criminal work was at the Old Bailey. Patrick Hastings in his memoirs described the Old Bailey as a human conveyor belt, where a succession of accused persons passed unemotionally through the system to prison or freedom. I too found it a gloomy soulless place. I lunched every day in the Bar mess, where the Treasury counsel, who did all the prosecutions, sat at one end of the long table, and the defenders below the salt at the other, although I was personally welcomed by Mervyn Griffiths-Jones, the senior Treasury counsel, and invited to sit next to him. Another of the Treasury counsel was Sam Morton, Mervyn's brother-in-law. When, after an interval, Mick McElligott appeared at the Bailey he wrote:

> Oh! It's nice to be back at the Bailey
> Where its done on a wink and a nod
> Where Sammy speaks only to Mervyn
> And Mervyn speaks only to God.

I have never understood why the system of Treasury counsel continues. It is not followed on the circuits, where a barrister may prosecute one day and defend the next and the cases are done just as well if not better. The physical division of prosecutors and defenders at the Old Bailey Bar mess in those days (I do not know whether it still continues) exemplifies the difference in attitude between them. The prosecutors tend to become prosecution-minded and the defenders defence-minded; this has undesirable consequences for the administration of justice. The essence of an independent Bar is that barristers should be prepared to take on any case, prosecution or defence, without any preconceived idea of their rôle. For this reason to allow members of the Crown Prosecution Service rights of audience in the Crown Court would be a further erosion of this principle.

Occasionally, while at the Old Bailey, I was invited by the judge to the Sheriffs' lunch, which is held every day for all the judges and their guests. It was a lavish affair, with wine (although few of the lawyers drank alcohol at lunch) and port for those who wanted it. I believe that, soon after he became Lord Chief Justice, Geoffrey Lane suggested to the Lord Mayor that the judges would prefer a more modest lunch in their own mess, as they have in other large Crown Courts, but was told that the Sheriffs (who paid for the lunch) would not want to give it up, as it was a unique opportunity for them to entertain their friends and business acquaintances. It must cost them a fortune.

Most of the cases I did at the Old Bailey were fraud cases. In one I was instructed (not on legal aid) by Withers & Co whose partners Arthur Collins, George Doughty, his nephew Charles and Andrew Rollo had been good clients of mine as a junior.

Withers were one of the leading firms of family solicitors in London, acting for most of the dukes and other big landowners. Although they had a large divorce practice, they never briefed me in a divorce case, regarding me as a common lawyer, to which I did not object. Our client was senior partner of a firm of stockbrokers charged with fraudulently pledging their clients' share certificates, which they held in safe custody as security for the firm's overdraft at the bank. When the firm failed the bank predictably foreclosed on their security. Our client came from an old county family and should never have been a stockbroker, let alone senior partner. When I first saw him he said, 'You would not understand this. It is all very technical.' When I pointed out that, technical or not, his clients had suffered heavy losses he replied, 'Well, all firms of stockbrokers do it.' We pleaded guilty to some of the more recent counts at the close of the prosecution case, having seen the judge, and my client was sentenced to six months' imprisonment, which he spent in an open prison working in the garden. I was told that he was relieved not to have the responsibility of working in the city and quite happy as the authorities did not object to him visiting the local public house in the evenings. In those days 'plea bargaining' was acceptable until it was effectively prohibited by the Court of Appeal in a case in 1971, on the ground that innocent defendants might be put under pressure to plead guilty by the inducement of a lighter sentence. I have never agreed with that decision. No-one in his senses would plead guilty to an offence which he had not committed and the result has been long and expensive trials of hopeless cases. Even the guilty defendant has certain cards that he can play: the prospect of a long drawn out trial with the possibility that in the end the jury might acquit, with large sums of public money wasted. So why not settle for a plea of guilty to minor charges and a reduced sentence? Such an approach might have avoided the fiascos of some of the well-publicised fraud trials of recent years. One partner in our case, who insisted on brazening out his defence to the bitter end, was quite rightly sentenced to a long term of imprisonment on being found guilty. Another partner was represented by Jeremy Hutchison, who managed to secure a verdict of 'not guilty', having made a submission that there was no case to answer at the close of the prosecution case. Jeremy was one of the best, if not the very best, of the regular criminal advocates at that time. He had an apparently bored and rather languid manner in court, but he kept his eye firmly on the main point of the case, asked the minimum of questions and could be very firm in dealing with disputed questions of law. He was very persuasive with a jury. Jeremy was a member of the Labour Party, and later became a 'working' life peer in the House of Lords, where I am told his advocacy is still as effective as ever. He once said to me, 'Defending in a criminal trial is like a horse dragging a loaded wagon up a hill. You are always on the collar.'

My last case at the Old Bailey became known as 'the Dairy Murder'. One Saturday morning, when all the cash had been collected by the roundsmen, a gang of men burst into the office on the first floor of a dairy in East London, where a young woman was sorting the money. With great presence of mind she pressed the panic button, which set off the alarm in the manager's house. The manager immediately ran to the office and met the gang coming down the stairs with the cash. The leader of the gang shot him in the chest with a sawn-off shot gun, killing him. I appeared for the driver of the getaway car, who was an expert minicab driver. Such people I was told are employed as independent contractors by the gangs of armed robbers for a particular job and are not privy to the planning of the raid. They are simply told the time and place and where the car is to be driven afterwards, usually to another car to which the money is transferred. The cars used in the raids are usually stolen by the drivers and abandoned thereafter. Our defence was an alibi. At the material time the driver was sitting in the minicab office watching television, while waiting for a call. I was also told that minicab offices are popular places for alibis, since other drivers are prepared to testify that the accused was present at the time, and to add verisimilitude by describing the television programme that they were all watching. The whole gang was convicted of murder and my client of aggravated burglary and stealing the car. I stressed to the jury that, even if they concluded that he was the driver (he had been identified by a sharp-eyed young woman with whose car he had collided in the hectic drive after the raid, and who was an impressive witness), there was no evidence that he was party to any joint venture involving the use of serious violence. The gun was in the car, but covered with sacking.

One of the other accused was represented by Sebag Shaw, a leading silk at the criminal bar at that time. Sebag had great charm, and an attractive light-hearted manner which appealed to juries. Some said that he was the nicest man at the Bar, where he was very popular, and after we both became judges we made great friends. Although most of his practice had been in crime, he was a successful Lord Justice, having a firm grasp of the principles of the common law. He was not appointed a judge until he was in his sixties and sadly died soon after his retirement.

My first break as a silk came in 1963, although I welcomed my short experience of First Division crime, which stood me in good stead later when I became a judge. In that year Peter Richardson, a partner in the city firm of Simmons & Simmons (who had occasionally consulted me as a junior), briefed me for the *Sunday Telegraph* at the Vassall Inquiry. Vassall had been convicted of spying for the Russians and sentenced to a long term of imprisonment. He had been employed as a technician by the Admiralty and was seconded to the Foreign Office working at the embassy in Moscow, where the offences were committed. Vassall was homosexual and after his conviction an extensive press campaign was launched against the government. It was said that it was obvious from Vassall's appearance and behaviour that he was homosexual, consequently that he was a security risk and should never have been sent to Moscow. It was further alleged that he associated in Moscow with Russian homosexuals and that this was or should have been known to those in charge of security at the embassy, but no steps were taken to restrain him or send him back to London. There were also allegations that he was on friendly terms, beyond the call of duty, with Tam Galbraith, a junior minister at the Admiralty who was in fact happily married. The press called for a public inquiry into these allegations and the government eventually appointed a tribunal of inquiry under the chairmanship of Cyril Radcliffe, a Law Lord, who had been in the Ministry of Information in the war and had extensive knowledge of security, as well as possessing one of the keenest legal brains of his generation. Most of the national press were represented by leading members of the Bar, including John Foster and Bill Mars-Jones.

The Attorney-General, John Hobson, was counsel to the tribunal and it became clear from the outset that this was to be a trial, not of the government, but of the press. Two journalists from the *Daily Mail* and *Daily Sketch* refused to disclose their sources for a story they had written, were referred by the tribunal to the High Court, charged with contempt of court and duly sentenced to terms of imprisonment. This outraged the press and there was an angry meeting of the proprietors and editors of all the newspapers involved in the tribunal, with their leading counsel, to discuss strategy. The *Sunday Telegraph* had published a piece by a freelance journalist, who must have been the original 'Lunchtime O'Booze' of *Private Eye*. O'Booze reported that inquiries into the Portland spy case (which had taken place at about the same time as the trial of Vassall, and which also involved the Admiralty) had not been closed, as it was suspected that there was a link between Vassall and the Portland spies involving other people not yet charged. O'Booze was to be called as a witness by the tribunal and asked me what he should say if he was asked for his sources. 'You must tell the truth,' I replied. So, when he went into the witness box, O'Booze told the tribunal that it was his custom at lunchtime to visit a public house near Scotland Yard, which he knew was frequented by Special Branch officers. One day he saw an officer, whom he knew had been involved in the Portland spy case, deep in conversation with two sinister-looking characters, one with a beard who looked like an Eastern European. The officer was making notes in his notebook. The newspapers at the time were full of Vassall and O'Booze deduced that the bearded man was connected with the Portland case and was being asked about Vassall. 'So you made it all up?' asked Cyril Radcliffe. 'Yes, my Lord,' replied O'Booze. 'Thank you, Mr. O'Booze. You may leave the witness box,' said Radcliffe, which he thankfully did, a free man.

The piece by O'Booze was picked up by various other newspapers and enlarged upon, different aspects of the link between Vassall and the Portland spies being advanced and commented upon. For the first time I realised how much of the news is created by the press itself. One newspaper will publish a story, which will be accepted by others as if it were true and the others will go on to advance different angles on the story and comment upon them.

Many lawyers who, like myself, knew nothing of how the press worked were shocked by the disclosures at the Vassall tribunal, since we were trained to say in court only that which we believed could be proved by evidence, and relations between the Bar and the press became strained. One senior journalist said to me, 'You must realise that the position of a journalist is quite different from that of a barrister. You receive factual instructions from a client, which form the basis of the case you are putting forward. We, especially in the political and foreign fields, seldom receive a comprehensive statement of facts. We are given a fact here and a fact there and we have to use intelligent deduction to fill in the gaps and produce a readable story consonant with the policy of the paper.' This was the dilemma and, of course, unless the story was apparently based on fact, the newspaper would not sell. The reservations and equivocations of the lawyer have no place in journalism.

The Vassall inquiry, because of the imprisonment of the two journalists, also marked a serious breach in the relations between the government and the press. Until then there had been a convention that the press did not, as a rule, publish details of the private lives of public figures. But after Vassall the press decided to ignore the convention and the Profumo scandal broke. The facts of that are too well known to require repetition here, but it was a major factor in the defeat of the Conservative government at the General Election the following year. Until Profumo the great mass of people did not believe that members of the Establishment, as it was beginning to be called, became involved with prostitutes. Profumo changed all that and people began to question whether the Conservative Party, which was linked in the public mind with the Establishment, was fit to govern.

An amusing incident occurred during the hearings before the Vassall tribunal. One day Judy and Jennifer came to the hearing. Roger Hollis, Director-General of MI5 and a wartime friend of Judy's father, who with his wife had stayed at Lynch, was called as a witness. The identity of the Director-General of Security Services, as he was called, was not supposed to be publicly known (although of course it was) and before he gave evidence Cyril Radcliffe announced that he was not to be referred to by name, but by his title of 'Director'. When Hollis stepped into the witness box I heard Jennifer's clear voice, from some rows behind me, say, 'Mummy! I never knew Sir Roger Hollis was director of the Security Services.'

It was in 1964 that there was a real breakthrough in my practice. Just before the long vacation in 1964 I was approached by a firm of solicitors who acted for a Greek shipowner called Alachouzos. A case had been going on all that term in which Alachouzos was suing an insurance company. Gerald Gardiner was leading for Alachouzos and had said he might not be available after the General Election to be held in October. He had suggested my name as a replacement. Although Bob McCrindle was second leader, Alachouzos wanted a common law leader outside the 'commercial establishment'. Would I take the case? Of course I said I would and spent most of the vacation reading the transcripts of the evidence and a mass of documents.

At that time the commercial work was concentrated in two or three sets of chambers, including the largest in Essex Court. Alachouzos said that the specialist commercial Bar was too close to the shipping community of insurers, brokers and agents in the city and he did not trust them to take on the vested interests, while acknowledging their ability. So he wanted someone to lead the team who was prepared to 'take on the city' as he put it. Bob McCrindle had had a meteoric career at the commercial Bar, having taken silk the previous year while still in his thirties, although he looked even younger. He was of outstanding ability. He later left the English Bar to practise commercial law in Paris.

For the first fortnight of the new term I sat between Gerald Gardiner and Bob. Gerald was busy electioneering every night and appeared in court every day. We lunched together every day. Gerald told me that Harold Wilson had the best memory of any man he knew, with a brain like a computer. I said, 'What about his judgment?' He said, 'Ah! That's a different matter.' Gerald hated the City of London and all it stood for. He said one of the first objectives of a Labour government would be to destroy the power of the city. After Gerald became Lord Chancellor, Bernard Waley-Cohen, as a senior city alderman, went to see him to persuade him not to appoint magistrates to sit with the aldermen in the Mansion House, where for centuries they had acted as sole magistrates. 'Why don't you want them?' said Gerald. 'Is it because you don't like sitting with people who are not as rich as you?' Bernard was taken aback and most upset. 'What did he think he would gain by insulting me?' he said to me afterwards.

The day after polling day the overnight results showed that it would be a very close run thing. Gerald told me he had advised Wilson not to form a government without an overall majority in the House of Commons. At 4 pm he came into court and said they had got their overall majority, and he was to be Lord Chancellor in the new government. The court rose at 4.15 pm and Gerald's last words at the Bar were, 'And will your Lordship be sitting at 10.30 on Monday as usual?' They were typical of him.

The case concerned an ex-Liberty ship belonging to Alachouzos called *The Medina Princess*. She was carrying a cargo of grain to China. By the time she reached Port Said there was severe trouble with her engines, which were found to be full of salt. This was because, for some unexplained reason, two of her fresh-water tanks had been emptied in the Bay of Biscay, and refilled with salt water. She continued after voyage repairs at Port Said, but in the Red Sea her engines seized up completely and she put in to Djibouti. While there it was said that she touched the bottom and damaged her hull. Alachouzos claimed as a constructive total loss the full amount for which she was insured – £350,000. The insurers denied liability and alleged that she was unseaworthy at the start of the voyage. What was more serious was that the shipowners protection and indemnity society (the Club) refused to support Alachouzos in his claim, so that he had to finance it himself.

The background to these events lay in the personality and career of Alachouzos himself. He had come to England soon after the war as a young Greek with plenty of money and a flair for running ships and had fallen foul of the city because of his reluctance to pay his bills and dues. He always said that the charges were too high because too many people were entitled to commissions, so why should he not hold onto his money until the last moment. The allegation in the case was in effect (though the insurers denied this) that he had scuttled the ship. Alachouzos agreed that the ship had been scuttled, but maintained that this had been done by the crew, who had been bribed by the insurance brokers. He said there was a conspiracy to ensure that the cargo never reached China, that the underwriters should pay the insurance on the cargo, that the insurance money should be divided between the consignors of the cargo and various agents and brokers, including the managers of the Club and that the blame should be put on Alachouzos.

These allegations in fact never saw the light of day, much to the annoyance and frustration of Alachouzos. He was a colourful character and a professional gambler, who had regularly attended the private parties of John Aspinall. He had a good deal of charm and an extremely tortuous and suspicious mind. His main purpose in fighting the action was to clear his name and to be reinstated in the 'Club' and in the city.

The case lasted seventy-six days, the longest case at that time to have been fought in the Commercial Court. One of the difficulties was that neither party would allow the ship to be dry docked, so that her hull might be examined. So divers were sent down and a plan of the berth at Djibouti was produced which was linked to the damage to her hull, as it appeared from examination inside the holds. There was also a detailed examination of her machinery. So the case was a combination of a Board of Trade Inquiry, a 'bad berth' case and a fraud case, with some very difficult questions of marine insurance law thrown in for good measure.

I gave each member of the legal team a separate part of the case to deal with. Bob McCrindle dealt with most of the expert evidence relating to the condition of the hull and engines, one junior, John Hobhouse, dealt with the survey of the berth and the other, Stephen Terrell, tried to keep Alachouzos happy, which was a full-time job in itself. My final speech lasted a week: I dealt myself with the fraud issue and relied largely on notes provided by Bob and John on the other issues. John Hobhouse later became a Lord Justice. Alachouzos, who had unrivalled experience of the commercial bar, since he was so litigious, used to say, 'I like John. He never yields.'

Half-way through the trial Henry Brandon, on behalf of the underwriters, withdrew the allegation that the ship was unseaworthy from the start. This delighted Alachouzos, but annoyed the underwriters. In the end Eustace Roskill, the judge, found no Constructive Total Loss, but awarded us £150,000 as the cost of repairing the ship and half our legal costs. This was a great triumph, but Alachouzos did not regard it as such. He claimed against the Club to recover the balance of his legal costs. The Club paid £50,000, but Alachouzos was not satisfied. There were long negotiations and some court appearances. Alachouzos went to other leaders, Mark Littman (who was I suppose the best advocate of my generation) and Sebag Shaw, but always came back to me. We spent hours together, often lunching at the Mirabele restaurant, and the case was still rumbling along when I was made a judge at the end of 1968. As a result of the case Henry Brandon and I became firm friends. He was at the Admiralty Bar and Judy's father, when he was Admiralty judge, said to me, 'You watch Henry Brandon. He will end up in the House of Lords.' Which in due course he did. Henry's junior was Tony Lloyd, now a Law Lord.

There were two other results of the *Medina Princess* as far as I was concerned. One was that I gave Judy a mink jacket – she had had to put up with weeks of being a 'court widow'. The other was that I got a good deal of commercial work thereafter. The first case concerned Cyprus carrots, for which there was a very large English trade in May. One of the consignments arrived at Liverpool in a putrified condition. The consignors blamed the ship, for which I appeared. The ship claimed that the carrots suffered from some inherent disease. This was one of those 'commodity test cases' which from time to time come into the Commercial Court. Judy's father was in a case which settled the correct way of carrying apples from Australia. Shortly before the carrot case there had been a case about the carriage of cocoa from West Africa, which the ship had won.

In the carrot case, Robert Goff, then a young and very able silk, appeared for the Cypriots. He is now a Law Lord. They traced the history of the whole consignment from the picking fields to the hold. The ship was a refrigerated ship, normally employed in carrying meat in the Baltic. Carrots, like fruit, do not die when they are lifted or picked. Unlike meat they continue to breathe and give off oxygen at a high temperature. Therefore great skill is required to regulate the temperature after the cargo has been stowed, at a high temperature, to bring it down to a safe temperature without damage from freezing. As the case went on it became clear that the First Officer had no idea of how to deal with these problems and it was also doubtful whether the refrigeration system was capable of dealing with such a large cargo of living matter. So we settled the case, much to the delight of the Cypriots, whose whole trade was at risk.

In addition to these cases in the Commercial Court I was employed as a silk in the Admiralty Court. The first case was 'the *Kazimah*' which concerned a 'pile up' of a convoy in the Suez Canal.

Another Admiralty case in which I appeared was the *World Beauty* which had collided with the *Andros Springs*, for which I appeared, in the Gulf of Suez. Liability was admitted and the only issue was damages. The principal dispute was as to the loss of profit suffered by the owners of the *Andros Springs*, the Goulandris family. Their ships were managed by a very competent American firm, who had substituted another ship to complete the charter of *Andros Springs*. This meant that the latter was available, after her repairs, to start a profitable charter with Mobil Oil earlier than if she had completed her existing charter. The insurers of *World Beauty* alleged that Goulandris had suffered no loss because the profitable Mobil charter had been brought forward.

John Naisby, an experienced Admiralty silk, had advised damages on a basis I will call A. I persuaded the Admiralty Registrar to award the *Andros Springs* much higher damages on basis B which had been put forward by the managers. *World Beauty* appealed to the Admiralty judge, Gordon Willmer, who awarded damages on basis

C, higher than A but much lower than B. Both sides appealed to the Court of Appeal, two of whom awarded damages on basis D, higher than C but lower than B. Rodger Winn, the third Lord Justice, found a fifth basis E, between B and D. I came away from court wondering how any member of the Bar could be expected to advise confidently on damages in a complicated case.

Sam Cooke was against me in that case and we renewed a friendship which had begun when we were both acting as juniors for IPC.

But my practice was not all ships. I was briefed by the Performing Rights Society to appear before the Performing Rights Tribunal to determine the rates at which the BBC should pay for music still in copyright. All composers assigned their performing rights to the society which negotiated the rates payable by users of music, the largest of which was the BBC. The case was not unlike a case in the Restrictive Practices Court, involving much detailed financial evidence and the cross-examination of accountants, which is perhaps why I was taken in. The chairman of the tribunal was Walter Raeburn and my opponent Desmond Ackner, whom I had not been against since our County Court days. By that time Desmond had the largest general practice at the Common Law Bar and was a formidable opponent. In the end we obtained a 16% increase in rates for the composers, but they were disappointed having hoped for much more.

Another unusual case in which I appeared was for Hoffman-La Roche, the Swiss pharmaceutical firm, before the Patent Appeal Tribunal. It was an application for a compulsory licence to manufacture the drug Librium, one of the first tranquilizers, for which Roche held the patent. Roche were the most realistic clients I ever had. They were engaged in defending the patents for their various products all over the world. A high-powered team came to London to brief me, whose attitude was: 'This is just one battle, which we may lose. But we shall win the war.' They produced a large volume of evidence, showing the immense sums they spent on research and how only a tiny proportion of the products were commercially successful. So the prices of these had to be maintained during their patent life to finance the unsuccessful research. In the result the licence was granted at a much reduced price, but the licencees were prevented from using the name Librium, being obliged to use the generic name of the drug, and also prohibited from using the get-up of Librium, a green and black capsule. This meant that the licencees had little commercial advantage, since most users of the drug knew it by the name of Librium, with a green and black capsule. So Roche were happy and went on to develop Valium, an even more popular tranquilizer.

In all these cases I usually had specialist juniors, who could brief me as to the law and the technicalities of the facts and point me on to the target. One junior said to me, at the conclusion of my final speech in one case, 'You did not do justice to my note.' I replied, 'Your note quite rightly covered all the points. My job as leader is to sort the wheat from the chaff and concentrate on the good points.' I found it a relief, when in silk, to have time to prepare each case properly instead of as a junior, being burdened with a mass of papers, which had to be done at the same time for other cases, although to Clement every day not spent in court was wasted. Judy's father had said, when I took silk, 'You will find that being in the front row is like the difference between travelling first and third class on the railway.' He was right.

One of my cases was of no interest, except that my client was Robert Maxwell, then chairman of Pergamon Press, which published specialised medical and scientific books. Maxwell had refused to pay the full royalties due to one of his authors, a distinguished Austrian scientist, and had insisted on going to arbitration. There was only a few thousand pounds in issue, which I told Maxwell were due under the terms of his agreement with the author. Maxwell said, 'I am not going to have my authors telling me how much to pay them. It will do them all good to know that I am prepared to fight.' The arbitration, before Desmond Ackner, lasted two full days, during which Maxwell was present throughout and gave evidence. Desmond did not believe his evidence and awarded the author the full amount claimed with costs. I was not surprised, some years later, when Board of Trade inspectors held that Maxwell was not fit to be a director of a public company, but astonished when I heard of his reestablishment in the city and of his takeovers of large public companies and could not understand how the various financial institutions could have given him credit.

In the early sixties Mrs. Florence Nagle came to see me to say that she wished to bring an action against the Jockey Club for an order that they should grant her a licence to train racehorses. Mrs. Nagle was a wealthy middle-aged lady, who had in fact trained racehorses for many years. But, because the Jockey Club never granted a licence to a woman, the licence had to be in the name of the head lad, although she, of course, owned the stables and took the whole financial responsibility. In spite of this I had to tell her that such an action was hopeless. In case after case over the years the courts had refused to interfere with the discretion of domestic tribunals, such as the Jockey Club and the Council of the Stock Exchange, to run their own affairs, provided they did so honestly and bona fide. Mrs. Nagle said she had expected this answer, but that even if she lost the case the publicity would be sure that the Jockey Club would have to give way and grant trainers' licences to women. The difficulty was to get the necessary publicity because, as soon as the writ was issued, the Jockey Club successfully applied in chambers to have it struck out as disclosing no cause of action. So we appealed to the Court of Appeal. Fortunately Tom Denning, Cyril Salmon and Danckwerts composed the court. They were all sympathetic to Mrs. Nagle and I was able to show that there was at least an arguable case. So the writ was reinstated and, as Mrs. Nagle had predicted, the Jockey Club agreed to grant a licence, provided that the action was withdrawn. My only regret was that there was never a trial, as I was longing to ask the stewards, who included the Duke of Norfolk and Sir Randle Feilden, what was their objection to women trainers. The only one that I ever heard was that it would be embarrassing for women to go into the jockeys' changing room, see them *déshabillés* and hear their language. I somehow do not think that this prospect worried Mrs. Nagle. Desmond Ackner appeared for the Jockey Club, but even his silver tongue could not move the Court of Appeal.

The case caused a good deal of feeling among the racing establishment. One member of the Jockey Club was heard to say in his club, 'Robin Dunn, I'd like to see the bugger dead!' As a result of the case, I became a champion of women's causes and was shortly after responsible for the election of the first woman to the Birmingham Stock Exchange. But that did not even require an action – just a gentle threat.

Almost my last case at the Bar was a banking case in the Chancery Division called Selangor Estates v Burden, which lasted a whole term with a number of parties involved. It was remarkable that four of the counsel engaged, Arthur Bagnall, John Arnold, John Balcombe and myself, all became judges of the Family Division. A far cry from the law of banking.

CHAPTER XX

The Bar

In 1965 I was appointed a member of the Bar Council, one of six members representing the Common Law Bar in London. I had already served for four years on the Council from 1959 under the chairmanship of Gerald Gardiner, who was a brilliant trade union leader and had persuaded the government to increase substantially the fees for criminal legal aid. In 1966 Harry Fisher became chairman, Desmond Ackner deputy chairman and I was treasurer, my principal contribution being to effect a change in the constitution of the Council, so that its funds could be invested in equities. It was remarkable that this had never been done before. I also persuaded Hartley Shawcross and Philip Shelbourne, both of whom were then in the city, to join our finance committee.

In those days, as I suspect today, there were those on the Council who favoured reform of the profession and those who did not. I was in favour of moderate reform, especially of the rule which prohibited a silk from appearing in court without a junior, and of the 'two-thirds' rule, whereby the junior was entitled to two-thirds of his leader's fee. Both of these I felt were unjustifiable restrictive practices which were damaging the public image of the profession, which was beginning to come under attack from the press. For the first time in 1966 we set up a public relations committee, of which I was a member, occasionally inviting members of the press to our meetings. I felt that defending the Bar publicly was rather like defending hunting. Both were generally unpopular, especially with liberal reformers, both were regarded as the prerogative of an élite, not true in the case of hunting, and the attacks on both were carried on with a good deal of prejudice and ignorance.

At that time the Bar Council was dominated by the circuits, who ensured, by the size of their membership, that their nomineees would be elected. So Peter Webster, then a leading junior and now a High Court judge, suggested that we should form an association to represent the London Bar on the Council and to sponsor our own candidates for election. So the London Common Law Bar Association was formed and I was invited to be the first chairman. We at once espoused the policy of reform in the Council, which was carried on by my successor, Hugh Griffiths, after I became a judge.

So, for the first time, I was obliged to think seriously about the profession, its practices and procedures and its future. The disciplinary arrangements of the profession were very unsatisfactory. Discipline was in the hands of the benchers of the four Inns of Court, who exercised their jurisdiction in an informal and casual fashion. The charge was brought by the Inn and heard by as many benchers as wished to attend a disciplinary hearing. So they were judges in their own cause and procedure was flexible. Judges, as benchers, often sat at the hearings and those same judges sitting in court would not have hesitated to condemn the disciplinary procedures of their own Inns. Later the system was changed and cases were heard by a small number of benchers, mostly practising barristers, sitting as a disciplinary committee. The charge was laid by the disciplinary committee of the newly-formed Senate.

Just before I had taken silk I appeared, with Buster Milmo, later a High Court judge, to defend Victor Durand who had been charged by the Inner Temple with professional misconduct. Victor had appeared for the defendant before Geoffrey Streatfield and a jury in a case called Meek v Fleming. Fleming was a policeman sued for wrongful arrest by Meek, who was a press photographer. At the time of the arrest, which arose out of a demonstration in Trafalgar Square, Fleming was an inspector. but between that time and the trial he had been demoted to sergeant. Victor never told the court this or his opponents. He referred to the defendant as 'Mr. Fleming' and in his final speech to the jury he invited them to rely on the evidence of a 'senior and experienced police officer'. The jury found for the defendant. The plaintiff then discovered the demotion and applied to the Court of Appeal for a retrial, alleging that Fleming had been demoted for misleading a court and that this would, if known, have affected the jury's view of his veracity. The Court of Appeal granted a retrial and reported Victor to his benchers.

At the time Walter Monckton was Treasurer of the Inner Temple and for this case a selected number of benchers were invited to sit. They included Lord Goddard, then Lord Chief Justice, Lord Hodson, Reggie Dilhorne, then Attorney-General, and others. The atmosphere was like that of a Court of Honour in Potsdam in about 1912. There were only two members of the Bar sitting and neither of those was present on the second evening of the hearing.

Victor was suspended from practice for three years. We appealed to the judges sitting as Visitors to the Inns, with Lord Parker then Chief Justice presiding and four other judges, including Denys Buckley and Harry Phillimore. The suspension was reduced to twelve months, largely because we were able to put before the judges evidence that Fleming had been demoted for the comparatively venal offence of getting another officer to stand in for him to give evidence of an arrest. Technically this was 'misleading a court', but the evidence was merely formal and the arresting officer had other duties elsewhere. It was, rightly or wrongly, common practice in the police at that time.

There is no doubt that Victor misled the court and was guilty of *suggestio falsi*. But he was by training a specialist criminal advocate in a sphere where the defence are not expected to bring out any facts detrimental to their client. I do not believe that he ever realised the difference between the duty to the court of defending counsel in a criminal case and the duty of counsel for the defence in a civil case. But he paid dearly for his error. As a result of his suspension he was debarred from any judicial appointment and for many years from the Bench of his Inn.

My other experience of defending a barrister for professional misconduct was before the benchers of Lincoln's Inn, when I defended a barrister charged with accepting a fee direct from a client. As the offence took place in West Africa where there is a fused profession it was of a somewhat technical nature, although the barrister was instructed by solicitors in England. However, there were a large number of distinguished benchers present, including Denning, Pearson, Pearce, Harman and Buckley. When we took our seats the treasurer said to me, 'There is no dispute about the facts is there, Mr. Dunn?', to which I replied that there was a great deal of dispute. 'What do you say happened?' asked the treasurer. I pointed out, with some heat, that this was a serious charge of professional misconduct and it was for the Inn as prosecuting authority to call their evidence and then we should see if my client had a case to answer. This was greeted with amused approval by the benchers and the trial continued. In the course of it Harman asked my client, 'Have you ever accepted a fee direct from a client?' I objected to the question on the ground that it was irrelevant. The objection was upheld, again with amused approval, as if we were engaged in an after-dinner moot. At the conclusion of the evidence we were asked to withdraw while the Bench considered their decision. I pointed out that I had had no opportunity of addressing them. This caused some consternation, as it was nearly time for the benchers' dinner, but Denys Buckley came to my rescue, suggesting that the Bench should confer and call upon me if they wished to hear me. Accordingly we withdrew and were called back in a few minutes to be told that the Bench did not find the case proved – a rather ungracious way of saying 'not guilty'.

In 1967 I was asked by the Bar Council to represent a barrister, Michael Worsley, in the House of Lords in the case of Rondel *v* Worsley. Worsley had unsuccessfully defended Rondel in a case at the Old Bailey. Years later, just before the expiration of the limitation period, Rondel sued Worsley for negligence in the conduct of his case. The writ had been struck out in chambers on the ground that it disclosed no cause of action, since barristers were considered not liable for negligence. The Court of Appeal upheld that decision. Patrick O'Connor and Graham Swanwick had both appeared for Worsley in the lower courts, but both had become judges. Both had greater experience than me of negligence actions, but Raymond Kidwell, a very able junior in Patrick's chambers, had produced a note of the law which I adopted as my argument and a very good note it was. Louis Blom-Cooper, then a junior, was against me. He complained to me at lunch one day that he was not taken seriously as an advocate, as he did so much writing and broadcasting. I told him he need not worry, as I took him very seriously indeed. He did the case beautifully and was a flexible and charming advocate, who later acquired a large practice as a silk. Between us we cited over one hundred and twenty reported cases and investigated the history and status of the Bar since the formation of the Inns of Court in the 14th century. I urged the Lords to uphold the traditional immunity from all claims for professional negligence by barristers, however arising, and there was certainly a strong legal case to support that view. Louis claimed that the law as previously understood was anachronistic and that there should be no immunity. In the result the Lords reached a compromise, holding that no action lay against a barrister in respect of his conduct of a case in court (which was the position in Worsley's case), but going on to hold by *obiter dicta* that the immunity did not extend to advisory work or the drafting of documents, although Edward Pearce dissented on this issue, upholding my argument in its entirety. I believe that the compromise decision of the Lords was influenced by the climate of opinion at the time and the possibility of legislation if the blanket immunity was upheld. In a later case in 1978 the Lords extended the immunity to cover the drafting of documents preparatory to an action in court.

The Durand case and the Worsley case both helped to clarify my mind as to the position of the Bar. One starts, inevitably, with the fact that like all common law countries, such as the USA and the Commonwealth countries, and in contrast with most continental countries, we adopt the adversarial as opposed to the inquisitorial system of both civil and criminal trials. My experience in the Restrictive Practices Court had, as has been mentioned, taught me that the adversarial system was more likely to produce a just result than the inquisitorial system, as practised by the Monopolies Commission. The only other courts in England which practise the inquisitorial system are the Coroner's Courts and my occasional appearances as counsel in those courts did not instill any particular confidence in their procedure. A junior judicial officer is empowered to call only those witnesses he selects to support his theory as to the cause of death. The objections to the adversarial system in civil courts are the length of time taken to resolve the cases and the consequent expense. These are serious objections, and there is a case for judges taking a more robust line in the County Court and small claims courts. But in a case of any substance or difficulty, if justice is to be done, I remain convinced that the adversarial system is superior.

In the criminal courts the same primary objection to the inquisitorial system exists as in the civil courts, namely that the examining magistrate, or *juge d'instruction*, may proceed on 'hunch' and overlook the reality of the case. I believe that in the inquisitorial system there is more chance of the judge being subjected to external pressures, even the acceptance of a bribe, than in the adversarial system. Despite recent attacks on the judiciary the possibility of an English judge being offered a bribe is so remote as to be laughable. But such is not the case in other jurisdictions, where junior judges, with little standing in the community, may be tempted, by a bribe, to exercise their considerable powers in favour of an accused. Moreover the adversarial system in a criminal trial provides the accused with built-in safeguards, such as the right of silence, the non-disclosure of his criminal record and strict rules of evidence which are not available in the inquisitorial system and it is difficult to see how they could be incorporated. Some might say that too many people are acquitted under the present system and that the introduction of the inquisitorial system would be a salutary measure. I do not take that view although, as I shall show later, some of the safeguards are outdated and should be modified or abolished. But those who advocate the inquisitorial system should understand the consequences in terms of a fair trial for the accused which, added to the other disadvantages already mentioned, cause me to continue to support the adversarial system in criminal trials.

All this is self-evident to many, but those who oppose the adversarial system tend to misunderstand or ignore the disadvantages of the inquisitorial system. If the former system is to work properly the cases must be presented by competent advocates on each side, each of whom must bring out the facts and law relevant to his case. As Tony Benn showed in the Election Court, any educated man with a knowledge of the relevant law can do a case well. The true professional never does a case badly and constant practice is necessary. As this narrative has shown I followed Walter Monckton's advice to become a specialist advocate and appeared at one time or other before every type of court in the land, as well as numerous tribunals and inquiries, including planning inquiries. The necessary techniques vary – addressing a jury requires a very different technique from arguing a point of law before the House of Lords or addressing an inspector at a planning appeal. But the essential principles are the same; persuasion of the particular tribunal concerned. It was not until I became a judge that I realised how dependent is the Bench upon the Bar. The English judge is not required to inquire into the facts or law of the case. He comes to it with an open mind and acts throughout the trial as a referee or umpire, before giving his decision, or summing up to the jury, solely on the evidence and legal arguments he has heard. Unlike the judiciary in the United States, he has no help in research into the law, except what he receives from the Bar, who are responsible not only for calling evidence of all relevant facts, but of making their submissions on the law. Indeed it is unwise for a judge to advance a point of law unless he has heard argument upon it from counsel. The rule that counsel should cite all relevant cases to the judge, even those against them, is an example of the vital rôle played by counsel in the administration of justice under the system.

Now solicitors are to be given rights of audience in the higher courts. I have serious doubts about the wisdom of this, not because I believe that the Bar will suffer from increased competition, but because few solicitors are likely to have the inclination or time to become specialists in advocacy and the system may suffer from those who attempt to do so. In the course of my time at the Bar I met many exceptionally able solicitors, excellent lawyers at the top of their profession, who admitted, like Derek Clogg, that they were not interested in advocacy. If a solicitor wishes to be an advocate he should follow the example of John Widgery, transfer to the Bar (which is comparatively simple), and become Lord Chief Justice. Even the largest firms are not likely to have sufficient work to justify the formation of a specialist advocacy department, covering the whole field of the law embraced by the specialist advocates at the Bar. I once took the son of neighbours of ours on circuit as marshal. He was very clever, having won a first in jurisprudence at Oxford, and his mother wished him to be a barrister. At the end of the assize I asked him, 'Well. Which is it to be, the Bar or a solicitor?' He replied at once, 'A solicitor. I could not spend my life arguing about the value of a workman's eye or making speeches to a jury.' So he joined a leading city firm, soon became their youngest partner and spent his time drafting documents for company mergers and new issues. Every man to his last.

Because of the vital rôle of the advocate in the adversarial system a very strict code of conduct is necessary. Although his primary duty is to his client, he also has duties to the court and to the public. Victor Durand's case was an illustration of the former. The advocate must not mislead the court, either by what he says or by what he does not say, if by his silence he suggests a falsehood. This rule does not apply so strictly in a criminal case where the barrister is not required to disclose facts detrimental to his client. But even there he must not suggest facts which he knows not to be true. And the prosecuting advocate has no duty to secure a conviction. His duty to the public requires him only to put the relevant facts fairly before the jury and to disclose to the defence all facts favourable to the accused.

An essential rule of the Bar is the so-called 'cab rank' rule, whereby a barrister is bound to accept any brief before a court in which he practises, irrespective of the nature of the case or the personality of the client. The Law Society has suggested that this rule is honoured by the Bar more in its breach than its observance. This is not so. I never remember refusing a brief or hearing of my colleagues refusing a brief because they did not like the case or approve of the client. The rule was well stated by the great advocate Thomas Erskine (a forebear of mine) in 1792 in these words: 'From the moment that any advocate can be permitted to say that he will or will not stand between the Crown and the subject arraigned in the court where he daily sits to practice, from that moment the liberties of England are at an end.' This rule does not apply to solicitors, who may pick and choose their clients. So a solicitor may, and many do, refuse to act for a rapist or a child-abuser or, in a civil court, for someone advancing a cause of which the solicitor does not approve. Solicitors should not be given rights of audience in the higher courts unless they are prepared to accept the 'cab-rank' rule, otherwise there will be two classes of representation: solicitors on the side of the angels and the Bar on the side of the dragons.

The 'cab-rank' rule formed an important part of my submissions to the House of Lords in Rondel *v* Worsley. If the barrister is, unlike any other profession, to be required to act for rogues and villains, he should be protected against claims, even frivolous claims which can be damaging and expensive, made against him by such people. In the United States litigation against doctors has given rise to 'defensive medicine' where the doctor prescribes treatment, not in the interests of his patient, but in order to provide a defence to a possible claim of negligence. 'Defensive medicine' is beginning to appear in this country for the same reason. The introduction of 'defensive advocacy' would be a disaster for the administration of justice. For example, to take a common complaint against barristers, witnesses would be called, damaging to the case, simply because the client wished them to be called, against the advice of counsel, in order to prevent a claim for negligence.

But I believed at the time of Rondel *v* Worsley, and still believe, that the principal argument in favour of the immunity of the advocate from actions for negligence was the practical one: that there must be an end to litigation. Proof of damage is an essential element in the tort of negligence. It must be proved not only that the defendant was negligent, but that his negligence caused damage. So the client would have to prove that it was the negligence of his advocate which caused him to lose the original case. This would require a retrial of that case including, where other parties were involved, those parties being joined in the negligence proceedings. And suppose they refused to take part? And, if the original trial was by jury, how would the judge in the subsequent negligence action know on what ground the jury had found against the client, since they would have given no reasons? And suppose there was a claim for negligence against the advocate in the second negligence action? Then that action would have to be retried as well as the first action, and so on ad infinitum. These examples are not fanciful. They simply demonstrate the practical difficulties of proving causation in an action for negligence against an advocate.

The concept of 'gross negligence' has no place in the common law. But I have long thought that it should be applied to actions for professional negligence. Momentary inattention or lack of concentration, which may amount to negligence by the driver of a motor car, should not render the surgeon liable to a claim for damages. Gross incompetence is another matter. But the advocate stands in a class by himself.

I have one further thought about the Bar in my time. None of the leaders of the Bar of my generation entered Parliament. There was no Monckton or Shawcross, much less a Simon or F. E. Smith. In those days, after a man took silk, he might go into Parliament. But in my time no-one with a quality practice did so. Peter Rawlinson acquired a quality practice after he had been Attorney-General, but had a predominantly criminal practice before he became an MP. This was because, I am sure, the work of the House of Commons became so much more demanding and time-consuming after the war, when parliamentary committees were held in the mornings, so that it was impossible to combine Parliament with a busy practice at the Bar. Moreover people tended to regard politics as a profession and enter Parliament much younger, instead of making their way in the law or in business before becoming an MP. The result was that MPs who were barristers could not give up the time required for a heavy practice involving much paper-work and confined themselves to criminal work. I mention this because I believe that it has affected the general quality of the law officers and candidates for the woolsack, although there have been notable exceptions such as Peter himself. Mick McElligott, seeing a newly-appointed law officer walking through the Temple, was heard to remark, 'Look. There goes the lightweight champion.' We need heavyweights as law officers.

CHAPTER XXI

Quarter Sessions and Bookmakers, 1964–68

In 1965 I was appointed deputy chairman of Somerset Quarter Sessions, 'the lowest form of judicial life' as Clement politely put it. Quarter Sessions was an ancient magistrates' court which had, until towards the end of the last century when elected local government was founded, exercised such administrative functions as existed in the counties, as well as a criminal jurisdiction covering appeals from the magistrates at Petty Sessions and less serious indictable offences; burglary, housebreaking, theft and motoring offences, including being drunk in charge of a motor-car. This was before the days of the breathaliser, when public opinion was not so strong against drunken driving and Somerset juries were reluctant to convict on the basis: 'There, but for the grace of God go I.' In order to exercise the full jurisdiction it was necessary for each court to have a legally qualified chairman and the arrangements in Somerset were typical of most County Sessions. The chairman was Harold Paton, the local County Court judge, who had won the DSC in the war commanding a motor-torpedo boat in the Channel. There was a local landowner, who had practised for a few years at the Bar before inheriting his estate, two or three practising members of the Bar such as myself and a retired High Court judge, Geoffrey Streatfield, who lived in the county. We were none of us paid, except for a modest petrol allowance, and all were obliged to be sworn in as magistrates before we could sit.

All magistrates were entitled to sit at Quarter Sessions, but in practice there was a rota, and we usually sat with two or three magistrates, although the chairman and deputy chairmen were responsible for the conduct of the trial and for summing up. We always retired to discuss the sentence. The Sessions sat for a week every quarter, alternately at Taunton and Wells the two Somerset Assize towns, and I arranged always to sit at Taunton where two or three courts sat during the week. So I sat for two weeks in every year. Any cases left over were dealt with by Geoffrey Streatfield the following week. The administration of Quarter Sessions, like that of the Assizes, was the responsibility of the County Council and the clerk to the Council (now the chief executive) was clerk of the peace and sat as associate in one of the courts throughout the week. The system had worked well and cheaply for centuries, but by the time I was appointed was becoming unable to cope with the increase in crime, especially in the larger towns and cities. There the jurisdiction was exercised by a recorder, who sat alone without magistrates, and was always a practising member of the Bar. Many Borough Sessions, as they were called, were obliged to sit for most of the year, the recorder often nominating a deputy or deputies to sit in his absence. Following the Beeching reforms in 1971 Quarter Sessions were abolished and their jurisdiction merged in the Crown Court, with the jurisdiction of Assizes, which were held three times a year in each county.

County Sessions had a strong social element. The night before Sessions opened there was a dinner in the Shire Hall attended by the chairman and deputy chairmen and any magistrates who wished to be present. Every day there was a lunch for any magistrates who were sitting and also the Bar. I enjoyed these occasions, which added style to the proceedings, and came to know many of the magistrates from the other side of the county. They also gave the magistrates an opportunity of meeting the Bar and we all learnt from one another. Now I understand the local Circuit judge, or recorder, contents himself with sandwiches in his room and the magistrates make their own arrangements.

Somerset Quarter Sessions was supported largely by the local Bar from Bristol, in those days consisting of just two sets of chambers, with a total of about a dozen barristers. It had been the only local Bar on the Western Circuit, though a small local Bar had just been formed at Exeter. I had at first been attracted by the idea of localising at Bristol. It would have meant that Judy and I could have lived in the country, but it would also have meant putting a ceiling on my career at the Bar. No member of the Bristol Bar had at that time ever taken silk and we decided that if I was going to the Bar I had better practise in London and try for the 'glittering prizes'. I got to know the Bristol Bar well and made many friends among them. The acknowledged leader was Cyril Williams, a high-class advocate by any standards and particularly effective with a Somerset jury. He had no ambition and was happy to live quietly in the West Country, where he had a large practice at Assizes and Quarter Sessions. But there were also some able performers among the younger generation, especially Peter Fallon and Hazel Counsell, both of whom became Circuit judges and eventually married.

One set of chambers from London regularly attended Somerset Sessions. Its most faithful member was Herrick Collins, who always came down with a few briefs and who was a fund of knowledge about the history of the Circuit and the Sessions. He would stay with us in the judges' lodgings in the Shire Hall and regale us with stories of the characters of the past. He had joined the Sessions in the twenties. At that time Somerset were 'closed Sessions' and counsel who was not a member of Sessions was obliged to charge a 'special fee', which he paid to the wine committee, enabling them to accumulate a fine cellar at the County Hotel, where the Sessions mess would dine. By my time Somerset Sessions were 'open' to all members of the Western

Circuit, but any counsel from another circuit, who appeared at Somerset Assizes or Sessions, was obliged to charge a 'special' fee, the proceeds of which went to the circuit wine committee and was used for the same purpose. Another young man from Herrick Collins's chambers who regularly attended Sessions was David (now Sir David) Calcutt, now Master of Magdalene College, Cambridge, and frequently used by the government as a 'wise man' to chair committees of inquiry into such controversial subjects as the law of privacy. In those days he specialised in securing the acquittal of persons charged with drunken driving.

Any silk or senior junior with a criminal practice was, so long as he was regarded as trustworthy, considered eligible for appointment as deputy chairman of Quarter Sessions. There was no training of any kind although, soon after I was appointed, I attended the first day-long sentencing conference organised by the Lord Chief Justice, Hubert Parker. These conferences were so successful that they have flourished over the years, are now institutionalised under the Board of Judicial Studies and have become much more elaborate. At that first conference Fred Lawton gave us a useful pro-forma of a summing-up which I always used thereafter and the rest of the day was spent on 'sentencing exercises' involving a series of imaginary cases to be considered by syndicates.

I found sentencing at Quarter Sessions far more difficult than subsequently, when trying crime as a High Court judge. At Assizes the cases were usually so serious that the only option was prison. The only question was for how long. But at Quarter Sessions few of the accused were real criminals; most were inadequate youths who were a nuisance in the community. Many had appeared before the magistrates at Petty Sessions and had been dealt with by way of conditional discharge, probation or a fine – often all three. The question then was, after conviction for a not particularly serious offence, whether the accused should for the first time receive a custodial sentence, either prison, borstal or a detention centre depending on his age. Nobody suggested that prison had any significant reformatory effect, except for the very few who decided after a taste of it that the game was not worth the candle. For most it represented a school for further crime and if a young man could be kept out of prison until he was in his mid-twenties there was a chance that he would settle down and live a respectable life. On the other hand many of them had been such a nuisance that their activities had to be stopped, if only for a short time. There were no sentencing guidelines, such as were laid down by Geoffrey Lane when he was Lord Chief Justice, although an excellent book called *The Principles of Sentencing* had just been published which attempted to rationalise the decisions of the Court of Criminal Appeal, and to lay down some general principles. The magistrates were a great help, many of them having long experience of sentencing at that level, but all looked to the chairman to take the lead and in the end it was he who took the final responsibility for the decision.

98% of all crime in this country is tried by lay magistrates, who are unpaid and in those days virtually untrained in the law, upon which they are advised by their clerks.

There are fewer professional judges in England than in any continental country of comparable size or in many of the states of the USA. I was greatly impressed by the quality of the magistrates I met at Quarter Sessions, especially their common sense and their knowledge of local conditions and of human nature. The strength of the system in magistrates' courts is that the question of guilt is decided in effect by a mini-jury of three from the local community and sentencing is dealt with by experienced people, advised on the law by their clerks, and with knowledge of local opinion and of the pressures on young people in the locality. It is a pity that Parliament has consistently refused to increase the powers of magistrates so as to include more serious offences, giving as their reason 'the inalienable right of an Englishman to trial by jury'. The lay magistrates are just as capable of doing justice as a jury of twelve and in deciding the question of guilt they in effect act as a jury. Some statistics show that a higher proportion of accused are acquitted by magistrates than by juries. Even twenty-five years ago the magistrates at County Sessions were beginning to complain about the statutory constraints put by Parliament on their sentencing powers. Now sentencing has become so technical that I am told that clerks are called in in almost every case to advise the magistrates as to their powers. This is putting too great a burden on people who are public-spirited enough to do this important voluntary work.

In 1964 I had been appointed first chairman of the Betting Levy Appeal Tribunal, set up under the Betting and Lotteries Act 1961 to enable bookmakers to appeal against the levy fixed by the Betting Levy Board. In fact the provisions of the Act were such that there was no effective appeal, except to a very limited extent in individual cases, so the work was not demanding. But I learnt a good deal about the practice and economics of bookmaking. The principal effects of the Act were two-fold: gambling casinos appeared in all the large industrial towns, in contrast to France where casinos were only permitted at seaside holiday resorts; and betting shops were legalised, in order to stop street betting which was and is unlawful. John Aspinall once said to me, 'This Act, brought in by Rab Butler of all people, was intended to legalise lotteries at church fêtes. Instead it has turned London into the Las Vegas of Europe.' The amount of the betting levy was derisory and the large firms of bookmakers, who soon took over the great majority of the betting shops, made enormous profits. Instead of going into racing, which provided the basis upon which the money was made, the profits were used by the large firms to diversify by building hotels and for other capital expenditure in the 'leisure' industry.

I could not understand why, with the introduction of betting shops, the successful French system of a tote monopoly, or at least the Australian system of a tote monopoly for off-course betting with on-course bookmakers, could not have been introduced here. The government could have taken the same amount by way of tax as under the present system, but the profits would have gone into racing to improve facilities and increase prize-money instead of into hotels and casinos. The on-course bookmaker is a popular part of the racing scene in England, but he could have been preserved if the Australian system had been adopted and the big money is laid in the betting shops. Some said that the English punter favoured sophisticated bets such as 'Yankees' and 'Double Yankees' which could not be struck on the tote, so that betting turnover would decrease with a tote monopoly off-course. Others blamed the strength of the bookmakers' lobby both in and out of Parliament and suggested that in those days too many senior figures in racing were 'in hock to the ring', and so unable or unwilling to confront the bookmakers. Unfortunately now that this is not the case if it ever was, it seems that it is too late to effect this much-needed reform. The system is too deeply entrenched. Meanwhile English racing continues to decline through lack of prize money and deplorable facilities at most racecourses, while our competitors on the Continent and elsewhere flourish with their tote monopolies. A good opportunity was missed.

Soon after I became a judge and gave up the Appeal Tribunal, I was invited to lunch by the Levy Board, where I sat next to the chairman Lord Wigg. He had been in Wilson's government and was an entertaining and well-informed companion. During lunch he said, 'The trouble with this government is that we have a Lord Chancellor [Gerald Gardiner] who knows nothing about politics, and an Attorney-General [Elwyn Jones who later became Lord Chancellor] who knows no law.' This, although containing a grain of truth, was unfair to both of them. I had once been against Elwyn in a long inquiry about trade union representation in the banks and he was a charming and persuasive advocate who knew as much law as most of us. And Gerald was certainly successful in piloting many reforms of the law through Parliament.

CHAPTER XXII

High Court Judge, 1969–74

In no profession, other than the law, are those who reach the top expected to change their whole style of life immediately on their appointment. Judges of the Queen's Bench and PDA Divisions were (and still are) expected to spend at least half their working lives on circuit, at one or other of the numerous assize towns throughout the length and breadth of England and Wales. Unlike a general or ambassador, who is *en poste* for several years and takes his family with him, a judge spends only a few weeks on circuit before returning to London. He cannot take his children with him, and his wife is no more than a guest if she chooses to accompany him.

So Judy and I agreed that I should retire as soon as I had completed fifteen years and qualified for my pension, although the compulsory retiring age for judges was then seventy-five.

Gerald Gardiner had sent for me shortly before Christmas 1968 and said, 'There is a vacancy in the PDA Division which Jack [Simon, President of the Division] and I would like you to take. The Division is no longer regarded as an OCTU and you would be expected to stay there.'

Early on a dark winter's morning on 13th January 1969, with all the family present, including Judy's mother and my father, I was sworn in by Gerald at the House of Lords, and in the afternoon motored down to Cardiff for my first assize. I had asked Clement to come with me as clerk but was not surprised when he said that, although he would love to come, he felt his loyalty to chambers came first. Until then a barrister's clerk had usually gone with his master to the Bench. Judy's father had taken his clerk, Albert Harris, when he was appointed in 1942. Arthur Smith once said, 'Poor Albert. Such a nice man. But just a lackey.' By 1969 barristers' clerks were anything but lackeys. They were running increasingly large sets of chambers and their skills would have been wasted looking after one judge. After a short time with a venerable retired clerk, Ernest Harvey, who had been clerk to Marshall Hall and looked after newly appointed judges, I engaged Frank McGrath. Frank had served for twenty years in the Metropolitan Police, after war service as an officer pilot in

Coastal Command. He was an excellent clerk and we became great friends. He was a keen golfer and persuaded me to take up the game, which I had hardly played since I was a child at St. Andrews. When on circuit in the summer we would go out after court and play nine or ten holes before dinner. He was one of several ex-policemen who at that time, with retired NCOs and petty officers from the services, were becoming judges' clerks. They did the job admirably.

Three other judges, all old friends, were with me at Cardiff; Brian McKenna, Patrick O'Connor and Sam Cooke. Brian had been in Walter Monckton's chambers, and had often acted as junior in his big cases, especially the long negotiations on behalf of the Nizam with the government of India after independence, about the future of his state Hyderabad. Some said that Walter provided the charm and Brian the brains of the partnership. Brian had had a high quality practice and when a junior I had borrowed many of his best pleadings and copied them into my precedent book. By 1969 Brian should have been in the Court of Appeal, but was regarded as a little eccentric by the Establishment. He was a 'keep fit' fanatic and when we were together at Sheffield would walk the two miles along the pavements from the judges' lodgings to court, instead of travelling in the judicial car. He said to me in Cardiff, 'We are men without hope.' He believed strongly in the various safeguards for defendants and would not hesitate to rule out police evidence if he suspected it had been obtained contrary to the rules.

Life on circuit was rather like returning to St. Aubyns. Our lives were ruled by the clock and we were kept sufficiently occupied throughout the day. I found this a relief, after working an average of sixteen hours a day for twenty years. Judy's father once said to me, 'If you ever become a judge, you will find that your brethren, almost without exception, improve on acquaintance.' He was right. I was impressed from the outset by the very high standard of manners and consideration shown by the judges for one another in the lodgings. Perhaps this was not so surprising. Life would have been intolerable otherwise for men in late middle age, who did not know one another intimately, obliged to live together cheek by jowel. A curmudgeon would have been impossible.

On that first morning at Cardiff we all assembled at 10 am in the drawing room wearing our robes and big wigs. A few minutes later the butler announced 'The High Sheriff, my Lords', and in walked Sue Williams accompanied by the Under Sheriff and her chaplain. She looked very smart in a black velvet coat and skirt, with lace at her neck and wrists, and a cocked hat like an admiral's. The High Sheriff was nominally responsible for our accommodation, although that was in fact arranged by the County Council. She was also responsible for executing our judgments and the Under Sheriff, who was a solicitor, still executed all civil judgments. In the days of capital punishment the High Sheriff was obliged to be present at all executions, and to certify death. The High Sheriff of the county is the most ancient office under the Crown, going back to Saxon times. By 1969, when capital punishment had been abolished, the functions of the office were almost entirely ceremonial, and the High

Sheriffs acted as hosts to the judges when we were in their counties. They held office for a year, and were mostly local landowners. Their presence certainly made life more agreeable for us, as they entertained us at their houses, introduced us to their friends and looked after us at weekends if we stayed in the county. Soon after I was appointed Owlie Stable said to me, 'You are a lucky young man. You can look forward to at least fifteen years' free sport at the expense of the High Sheriffs of England.'

Sue Williams was an excellent High Sheriff, one of the first women to be appointed. She is now Lord Lieutenant of South Glamorgan and a keen supporter of National Hunt racing. When we dined with her she wore a scarlet dress, saying, 'I am bored with wearing black all day, with you dressed up like peacocks. So I thought I would reverse the rôles.' At the end of the assizes she gave a lunch for the judges' clerks. 'I always like to know what really goes on in the lodgings,' she said.

After some conversation we drove in large limousines, preceded by police outriders, to the assize service at Llandaff cathedral, where the congregation consisted mostly of schoolchildren, who sang at the tops of their voices. Then we drove to the Law Courts, part of the fine city centre at Cardiff, built in Edwardian imperial style for the reading of the Commission. The Commission appointed us judges of assize for the county, not just as representatives of the crown, but in some strange way part of the crown itself – not unlike the doctrine of the Trinity. This dated back to the reign of Henry II, when the King's Justices of Oyer and Terminer and General Gaol Delivery first travelled the country to empty the gaols and sentence felons to hanging, drawing and quartering. As a result we took precedence over everyone in the county, and were always invited to lead the way into dinner. One judge, Reggie Croom Johnson, father of my friend and contemporary in the Court of Appeal, David, but of very different character, always stood on his dignity in such matters. Once, when at Somerset assizes, he was dining with the High Sheriff the night before the Commission was read. His hostess said before dinner, 'It is a large rambling house, so shall I lead the way into dinner?' 'No,' said Reggie. 'As his Majesty's judge of assize I precede you.' 'Oh no you don't, Reggie,' said the Bishop of Bath and Wells, who was also dining. 'The Commission has not been read yet and, until it is, I take precedence as the Lord Bishop of Bath and Wells.'

In those days the Queen's Bench judges spent practically the whole of their time on circuit trying crime. The new offence of 'causing death by dangerous driving' had to be tried at assizes, and Maurice Lyell, with whom I was at Gloucester, later that year told me that he had just tried ten of those cases in succession. So the PDA judges were in charge of the 'general civil list'. As all undefended divorce cases were by then tried in the County Court, and almost all the defended cases on circuit 'went short', this meant in effect that we tried the civil list, which consisted almost entirely of personal injuries cases, either factory accidents or road accidents. At the Bar I had done very few of these cases, as chambers had no trade union or insurance company as clients, who were the main sources of that work. What knowledge I had been had gleaned from Marven Everett, whom I had by chance been against, or who had led me, in most of such cases in which I had appeared. Marven was a large formidable figure and an expert in the techniques of personal injuries litigation, although like Beyfus he was not well regarded by the Establishment. He had led me for Madame Mendoza, wife of the Mexican Ambassador in London, after she had broken her ankle when her taxi had been involved in a collision in Bond Street. Withers had started their Instructions with the striking words, 'Madame Mendoza is the most beautiful woman in the world.' Certainly she had very shapely feet and ankles, and was paid by Charles Clore, who was a friend of hers, to wear shoes from his Dolcis shoe shops at the smart diplomatic receptions in London. Now her ankle was disfigured and this formed an important part of our claim, although the cynics were prepared to bet that she would still be paid by Clore. The judge was Bill Gorman a bachelor who, as the case progressed, could be seen gradually falling in love with our client. He awarded her £3000, which was a large sum in those days for a broken ankle. I was against Marven when I appeared for Lady Fisher, wife of the MP Nigel Fisher, who had been sent a bottle of jewellery cleaner from Harrods as a present by Alan Campbell. The bottle had burst in her face, affecting the sight of one eye. When I met Marven in the corridor outside court I asked him, 'How much are you going to pay me, Marven?' 'Nothing, not a shilling,' he replied. 'This is a blackmailing claim. Just because your client is the wife of an MP you think you can hold Harrods to ransom.' But we won, although there were legal difficulties as we could not sue the manufacturers, who were bankrupt, and the Sale of Goods Act did not apply as Lady Fisher was not the purchaser. Harrods were furious at the result, which had wide publicity, and both the buyer who had bought the cleaner and the insurance manager who had fought the claim were sacked. Withers were delighted, and as usual George Doughty wrote me a charming grateful letter after the case.

The first thing a judge trying personal injuries cases has to know is the 'tariff' for damages. Claims for loss of earnings were computed by taking the annual loss of earnings and multiplying it by a number of years purchase, based on the age of the plaintiff and his expectation of life. The use of actuarial tables was not encouraged but in every case there was in addition an element of the damages for 'pain and suffering and loss of amenity'. This was a conventional figure, depending on the gravity of the injury and its probable consequences, so as to achieve uniformity of awards. I had little experience of all this, but fortunately Patrick O'Connor had specialised in personal injuries work at the Bar, usually appearing for insurance companies. I picked his brains while we were together at Cardiff and gradually learnt the 'value' of the loss of a limb or chronic pain in the back, as well as the method of computing loss of earnings. Patrick was also most helpful with the form of my judgments. At first I found it difficult to give an *ex-tempore* judgment in a logical and reasonably well expressed way. Patrick said, 'I am like a gramophone record. I start by summarising the plaintiff's case. Then I describe the place where the accident occurred, how the machine worked or the layout of the road, then I summarise the pleadings and make my findings of fact which I link to the issues on the pleadings.

It is a good tip to ask counsel at the end of the evidence what are the live issues on the pleadings, so as to cut out any irrelevancies.' By the time I left Cardiff I was giving judgment in fifteen to twenty minutes, at least to my own satisfaction, thanks to Patrick. He was a good decisive judge who joined us in the Court of Appeal shortly after I was appointed. He was also a good companion.

From the very outset I never found any difficulty in controlling my court, and never found it necessary to assert myself or raise my voice. I put this down entirely to the English method of appointing judges. I believe that in France the great *maîtres* or leading *avocats* treat the junior judges with contempt and only behave themselves in the Cour de Cassation in Paris. In England the Bar know that the judge has spent his working life 'in the ring' in court and has had a better practice than the barrister is ever likely to have. So the Bar 'take it' from the judges in a way they would not do if we had a career judiciary. I also tried to create a relaxed atmosphere in my court and to put the witnesses at their ease, so that they could do themselves justice. I always kept a large silk pocket handkerchief on the Bench for the use of any lady who broke down in the witness box, as I found that women seldom had a pocket handkerchief with them. Although, unlike some judges, I did not have a notice in front of me with the words 'shut up' on it, I tried not to interrupt the evidence, especially in cross-examination, except to elicit a point I did not think was clear. But I found it useful at the Bar to know how the judge's mind was working, so I used to intervene a good deal during counsel's final speeches, putting points to them, often in a light-hearted way, and trying to get to the heart of the case. This once got me into trouble. I was trying a divorce case in which 'unreasonable behaviour' was alleged. In the course of counsel's speech I said, 'What is unreasonable to one person may not be unreasonable to another. Going round the circuits I notice that in the north of England women don't mind being beaten up, but if their husbands commit adultery they go straight back to mother. In the south women think nothing of adultery, but if their husbands raise a finger to them, they are off.' That evening I was telephoned by the news editor of the *Daily Mirror* to ask if I had made that remark. I said I had, but pointed out that it had not been said in the course of a judgment, so that the press were precluded by statute from reporting it. 'I'm sorry, my Lord,' he said, 'but it makes such a good story that we shall risk being charged with contempt.' So next morning the story broke in all the newspapers, with appropriate remarks from the feminist lobby about male chauvinist judges, and a cartoon of Mrs Andy Capp saying to her husband, 'I don't mind you beating me, but don't you go off with the neighbour.' Shortly afterwards I was addressing the magistrates at Birmingham and during the subsequent discussion a lady stood up and said, 'I am sure you were right about the difference between northern and southern women. But here we are midlanders, and we don't like either violence or adultery.' So I was more careful in future.

This experience caused me to reflect that the judicial decision-making process is the only one that takes place in public. The politician, the civil servant, the captain of industry, all make their decisions in the privacy of their offices, where they can freely discuss the problem with their colleagues or try out their ideas upon them. But the judge sits in open court in the full glare of publicity, while he is still making up his mind not only what to do but how to express his decision. The English judge is required, unlike almost all judges elsewhere in the world, to deliver an *ex-tempore* judgment in most civil cases, and a summing-up of the facts in all criminal cases, immediately following counsel's speeches. I hardly ever delivered a reserved judgment, unless there was a point of law, when I always did.

During my three weeks at Cardiff I tried nineteen civil actions, and only found for one-third of the plaintiffs. Brian McKenna said, 'You will become known as a defendants' judge.' I mentioned this to Roger Ormrod when I returned to London. He said, 'My striking rate in civil actions is one successful plaintiff in five. You must remember that the cases you try are a very untypical sample of all civil actions. Over 80% of them will have been settled before they ever come to court. You are dealing with the hard core, where the insurance companies have refused to pay and the lawyers have advised them to fight. So no wonder there is a small proportion of successful plaintiffs.'

We had a typical circuit social life at Cardiff. As well as dining with the High Sheriff, we dined with the Bar in their circuit mess. After dinner, in true Welsh tradition, they sang some rousing Welsh songs conducted by Tasker Watkins. I realised then why he had won the VC leading Welsh troops in Holland, as he was obviously a born leader. He joined us later in the Court of Appeal and became Deputy Chief Justice. He was a great figure in Wales, especially with the TA and in rugger circles. This was the first time I had met him and I later became very fond of him. We dined with the local Law Society, with about five hundred people present. These dinners were always held during an assize so that the solicitors could entertain their best clients, local bank managers, accountants and estate agents, and hear a judge speak. It has always surprised me that, whereas the English like their judges to sit quietly in court, they expect them to behave like comedians when speaking after dinner. I never achieved the art of after-dinner speaking, but many of my brethren were most accomplished. One of the best was Ted Eveleigh, who was much in demand. One of his favourite stories at that time was that, when treasurer of the Bar Council, I had rung up Roy Jenkins, then Chancellor of the Exchequer. In the budget the tax concession on barristers' outstanding fees, which had formerly been untaxed on a barrister's retirement or appointment to the Bench, had been abolished. Ted was one of the first judges to be affected by this change in the law. According to him I had said to the Chancellor on the telephone, 'It's Robin Dunn here.' 'Yes,' Jenkins had replied, 'and there's a lot of robbin' done here too.' 'Why,' I asked Ted, when I was told how well received this story had been, 'do they they think it so funny?' 'I think it must be the pathos,' said Ted in his lugubrious way. I was and am devoted to Ted. I was appointed a judge immediately after him, and we always sat next to one another at the annual legal service in Westminster Abbey. Later we were together in the Court of Appeal. He never failed to see the funny side of any situation and like me he retired long before he need have done.

Shortly after Cardiff I went with George Waller to the Law Society dinner at Newcastle, which was also attended by the president of the Law Society from London. George spoke first, followed by the president, who launched an attack on the judiciary. George was furious and said to me afterwards, 'I don't mind being attacked, but I do expect a right of reply.' As well as dining with the local magistrates we also entertained at the lodgings. We gave a dinner for the Lord Mayor and the bishop and two dinners for the local Bar and their wives. I did not much enjoy the big public dinners – civic dignitaries can be very grand and the food was often moderate – but then and thereafter I never failed to enjoy my evenings with the High Sheriff and the Bar, and the easy relaxed atmosphere of our own dinners in the lodgings.

Shortly after I returned to London from Cardiff, having replied to over three hundred letters of congratulation I had received on my appointment, I went to Buckingham Palace to be knighted. Judges and ambassadors do not attend investitures and are knighted at a private audience with the Queen. Judy drove to the palace saying, 'I can't come in. I'm not wearing a hat.' However, I insisted, so we both went up to a sitting room in the royal apartments. I was then taken by a naval equerry to a waiting room where I was briefed for about ten minutes. It has always amused me that courtiers bow by inclining their necks forwards, whereas the Bar bow deeply from the waist when the judge comes into court. The equerry led me to another large room, opened the door, and said, 'Sir Robin Dunn, Your Majesty.' I bowed, walked across the room to where the Queen was standing, knelt down with one knee on a stool, bowed my head and she touched me lightly on one shoulder with a dress sword. When I stood up she spoke for the first time, saying, 'I'm so glad to be able to do that for you.' She then took me over to the fireplace and we sat down on two French chairs, with a small table with daffodils on it between us. As when I had sat next to her at a private luncheon at the palace a few years before, I was impressed by her memory and her knowledge of affairs. She had met the leading figures from all walks of life and remembered what they had said. After exactly twenty minutes of conversation she pressed a bell beside her and the audience was over. She shook me by the hand and said, 'I have enjoyed our talk. I think you will have a difficult time as a judge, but I hope you will enjoy it.' I then walked to the door, turned round and bowed. She was still standing where I had left her and smiled as I turned away.

In London I of course sat in the PDA Division, where the work was not so demanding as on circuit. We spent most of our time trying defended divorce cases, which saddened me. The contrast between the high hopes with which almost everyone, especially women, embarked on marriage and the ultimate disillusion and despair was depressing to the onlooker. The more of these cases that I tried, the more I came to realise that in almost all of them there were faults on both sides. We were still in the days of the 'matrimonial offence', but usually there were two offenders. There was not often deliberate unkindness; thoughtlessness and selfishness were more common causes of the failure of the marriages. Fortunately the law of collusion had been relaxed and judges were able to approve 'collusive agreements', so that sensible financial arrangements could be made and one or other or both parties could obtain an undefended decree. I did my best to help the parties make these arrangements, rather than wash their dirty linen in public, with possibly disastrous effects on the children. The following year at the end of the assizes at Winchester, the Bar presented me with a stone 'to sharpen your knife for carving up divorce cases'. Jack Simon also asked me to help Henry Brandon with the Admiralty work, which added variety to what would otherwise have been a dull and unrewarding jurisdiction. Even so I spent much time sitting in my room, while counsel negotiated in the corridor, so I volunteered to try Queen's Bench cases while I was waiting.

There were at that time about eighteen PDA judges, many of them like Roger Ormrod and Neville Faulks, old friends. Stanley Rees, whom I had once been against in a long public inquiry about an airfield in Hampshire and who sat at our table in Hall, was another. He was a true professional. Roualeyn Cumming-Bruce had refused an appointment to the QBD having been Treasury Devil, since he had married late in life and had a young family whom he did not wish to leave during long periods on circuit. Roualeyn had been my predecessor as junior counsel to the Registrar in the Restrictive Practices Court, and was already in the Court of Appeal when I joined it. Roualeyn had a keen sense of humour. His identical twin brother was in the Foreign Office and once, when they were both young, they changed places: Roualeyn spent the day in Whitehall, and his brother in chambers (but not in court). Nobody noticed. John Latey was the only one who had specialised in divorce at the Bar, and a very good judge he was too.

About a year after I was appointed I suggested to Jack Simon that we should hold a 'custody conference' on the same lines as the sentencing conferences which had been so successfully introduced by the Lord Chief Justice. All custody cases in undefended divorce suits were by then being tried by County Court judges up and down the country. The High Court judges only dealt with custody cases in defended divorce suits, and wardship. So it seemed to me a good idea to have some forum at which problems could be discussed and a common approach arrived at. At first some of my more senior brethren were opposed to the idea, saying that each case depended on its own facts, which were so infinitely various that no common approach could be achieved. However Jack agreed saying, 'All right, Robin, but you must run it.' So I arranged for nearly one hundred County Court judges, and any High Court judges who wished to attend, to meet in the Inner Temple for a one day conference. I asked Gerard Vaughan, a child psychiatrist and later an MP, to speak, together with the senior welfare officer attached to the Divorce Court in London, and we had 'custody exercises' similar to the 'sentencing exercises' at the Lord Chief

Justice's conferences. The conference was a success and was well received by the press, to which Jack allowed me to make a statement and speak on the radio. The conference was the forerunner of the residential 'President's conferences', which are now held regularly at Cumberland Lodge in Windsor Great Park.

Life for a judge in London was very different to life on circuit. Allan, who had embarked on a career in racing, was then in Australia with Bart Cumming, the leading trainer there, having spent three years with Tim Forster, the National Hunt trainer, near Wantage. Janie had gone out to stay in the Embassy in Tokyo with Delia and John Pilcher, who was ambassador there. However she had found life working in the embassy as 'social secretary' somewhat constricting, and had set out on her travels which included Japan, Korea, Bali, Malaya, Siam and Laos – although the Vietnam war was still raging. She was away for eighteen months, an anxious time for Judy and me. So we were alone together at Roland Way. There was no pomp and circumstance in our lives as on circuit, and like all judges in London I travelled to and from court by car or public transport. On my appointment as a judge I had automatically been elected a bencher of the Inner Temple, where I used to lunch every day, either at the high table in Hall or in the 'cold' room behind. The Inner Temple became in effect my club in London, and a very agreeable club too. The benchers were all either judges or senior silks and several of them had sat at our table in Hall before going on the Bench. But the Inner Temple, like the other Inns of Court, was not just a luncheon club. It owned half the Temple, which was let either as professional or residential chambers to its members. And it was responsible for their education, admission and discipline. These functions were exercised by the 'Bench table', which all benchers were expected to attend, and which conducted the affairs of the Inn through a number of committees. Maurice Lyell, who was master of the Aldenham Harriers and who, like me, had been a member of the Bar Council and was interested in the administration of the profession, told me that he was so shocked after attending his first Bench table that he had written to the treasurer to say that he would never attend another. I very nearly did the same after my first Bench table. The principal question under discussion was whether or not we should wear dinner jackets, instead of white ties and tails, at Grand Nights. One very senior bencher stood up two or three times to address the Bench, in a quite incoherent fashion. The first time I passed a note on my agenda paper to Jo Stephenson, who was sitting next to me, saying, 'Is he tight?' Jo wrote one word on the paper, 'yes', and passed it back. At the next intervention Jo took my agenda paper and wrote the word 'very' after the word 'yes'. After one or two more rambling speeches, knowing smiles appeared even on the faces of the more venerable benchers and the younger benchers were frankly laughing. The risibility of the scene was enhanced by the grandeur of our surroundings, the eminence of some of those present, the triviality of the subject of debate, and the gravity not to say pomposity of tone of the speakers. It was as if a bishop had been drunk at the Convocation of Canterbury.

Thereafter I took little part in the affairs of the Inn. The treasurers were elected on seniority as benchers, and most of them were too old to take on what became an increasingly arduous commitment. After I became a Lord Justice I sponsored a motion at the Bench table to introduce a maximum age of seventy for the appointment of treasurers, with the strong support of Fred Lawton, Jo Stephenson and Roger Ormrod, all of whom were affected by the proposal and would have made excellent treasurers. But they readily agreed that in the interests of the Inn younger treasurers were essential, and the motion was passed. It was not until Peter Rawlinson became treasurer in 1984 that the administration of the Inner Temple was rationalised. He swept away many of the old time-consuming committees, replacing them by individual benchers in charge of particular aspects of the running of the Inn, and introduced other much needed reforms. But badly as the affairs of the Inn were conducted in my time, I passed some of the happiest hours of my life there in the company of my friends and contemporaries.

The best advice I was given as a judge was by Edward Pearce, whose stature had increased with each step he had taken up the judicial ladder to the House of Lords. He said, 'Just because you are a judge you must not forget your skills as an advocate. In the Divorce Court especially you must sell your judgment to the loser. The winner does not matter; he has your judgment in his favour. But you must deal with all the points made by the loser, however bad they may be, so that he may know that you have understood them.' This good advice once nearly got me into trouble with the Court of Appeal. A Lord Justice said to me at lunch one day, 'We nearly had to overturn you the other day. Your judgment seemed all in favour of the appellant, until at the end you found for the respondent.' I explained that in the Divorce Division, unlike the Queen's Bench, the parties had to live with the judgment and hopefully co-operate in the upbringing of the children. A one-sided judgment which slated the losing party, although probably unappealable, could cause havoc in the family with disastrous effects on the children.

At the beginning I thought I should never be able to decide where the truth lay. My first few cases seemed at the outset so difficult and complicated. But I soon discovered that the system worked and that the cases often decided themselves if given enough time. Sooner or later something would happen – a witness would be called, or a document put in evidence – and the whole case would fall into place. But I never could be sure whether a witness was telling the truth. Juries are always told 'to watch the demeanour of the witnesses', but I soon discovered that demeanour can be very misleading. The most accomplished liars give their evidence with great conviction and apparent sincerity. I learnt this soon after I was appointed. I had been trying a defended divorce case in which the husband charged his wife with adultery with a named co-respondent. The wife did not defend, but the co-respondent did. The principal witness was an inquiry agent, who had seen wife and co-respondent sitting in the dark in a motor-car in a lay-by on a remote country road. Beside the car was a used contraceptive. The co-respondent strongly denied adultery.

He said that he had met the wife at work and taken her for a drive in his car. He knew nothing about the contraceptive and said that he would not have dreamed of committing adultery as she was so unattractive and that he had no romantic feelings for her. He was an impressive and convincing witness and I believed him and dismissed the charge of adultery. The case was widely reported in the popular press, which the wife read with indignation. She then sent to the Queen's Proctor a passionate love letter she had received from the co-respondent which, if I had seen it, would have left no doubt in my mind that they had committed adultery. The Court of Appeal, however, dismissed the husband's appeal, saying that the judge had seen and heard the co-respondent, had formed a favourable view of his evidence and that the letter would have made no difference. The husband appealed to the House of Lords who, quite rightly, having read the letter said that its terms were only consistent with adultery having been committed. After that I was very cautious of accepting uncorroborated oral evidence unless it was supported by some contemporary document or was consistent with the inherent probabilities or surrounding circumstances of the case. I could never tell, just by watching a witness, however closely, whether he or she was speaking the truth. Women especially I found difficult to assess, especially if they were attractive and charming. People can control their eyes but not their mouths, and I found that a mouth gave a good guide to character, but not to veracity.

At the Bar counsel is always looking ahead during a case in court. He is thinking of the next question, or the next witness, or points for his final speech. But there will be periods of time when he will know that nothing important is likely to happen, and can 'switch off' mentally. The judge, on the other hand, does not know what is going to happen next, and it is unwise for him to look ahead during the trial. He must not allow his concentration to wander for a moment from the immediate present, or he may miss the vital piece of evidence which may decide the case. This total concentration is a parlour trick, but difficult unless one is accustomed to it. I found that juries were unable to concentrate for a whole two-and-a-half-hour session in court, so in long cases with a jury I used to sit early and rise late, so that we could have a mid-morning and mid-afternoon break, when the jury could refresh themselves and keep their concentration for an hour or so.

For the first five years on the Bench, when I was not in London, I travelled the circuits and visited most of the great industrial towns in the north and midlands, usually trying personal injuries cases, though occasionally crime when the list was too heavy for the Queen's Bench judges. I found, especially trying crime, that my wig and red robes gave me a confidence which I had not had sitting in a suit and no robes as deputy chairman of Quarter Sessions. One defendant, whom I had sentenced to a long term of imprisonment, said to the warder as he went down the steps from the dock to the cells, 'At least the bastard looked like a judge.' I have no doubt at all that judges should continue to wear wigs and robes when trying crime. Civil cases are different. Most of the work in the Family Division was heard in chambers, when we sat without robes trying important custody cases and financial cases often involving large sums of money. And robes are not worn at commercial and other arbitrations when immense sums of money are often involved. In all those cases, especially in the Family Division, a certain informality is desirable, and the judge should not be seen as a remote and alarming figure. When in chambers in the PDA Division we sat at the Associates' table on the same level as the parties, since witnesses were not involved. But if there are witnesses the judge should sit, as he now does, at a higher level than the witness or the rest of the court. Not only does he have a much better view of the witness, but also all round his court. I always found it helpful to be able to watch the reaction of the parties and waiting witnesses to the evidence being given, and this is much easier if the judge sits at a higher level than others in his court. But in the criminal courts, trying serious crime, the judge should not be indistinguishable from others in court. A certain awe and majesty is appropriate. And if the judge is to be robed so should counsel, if only out of courtesy to him.

CHAPTER XXIII

On Circuit, 1969–80

During my first years as a judge I was always responsible for the civil list on circuit, while the senior Queen's Bench judge ran the criminal list. My clerk, Frank McGrath, would meet the Bar clerks at noon and fix the list for the following day. Birmingham, which I first visited in May 1969, had a particularly long civil list, mostly accidents in the numerous factories in the district. I was often obliged to sit until 6 pm, giving two, and once three, judgments in the day. There was so much work that the Bar did not waste time on their cases and we got through a great deal of work. Mostly the plaintiffs were operators on an assembly line, who had become bored with the soul-destroying work and inadvertently become entangled in the machine. At that time the great motor industry in Birmingham was bedevilled by strikes, led by a shop steward called 'Red Robbo'. The result of these strikes was that the financial institutions would not invest in the motor industry, which was in decline. The managing-director of one motor company, who dined with us in the lodgings, said, 'I would rather compete with the whole Japanese car industry than have one Red Robbo.' But, despite our efforts, I left much unfinished work behind and the following November went to Shrewsbury for a special civil assize to try and reduce the backlog of Birmingham work. I went there alone with Judy and it was a very happy time. The lodgings were in a large 18th-century town house overlooking the River Severn and facing the school which, with its classical tradition, had produced more High Court judges than any other, as well as some of the satirists who helped to bring down the Conservative government in 1964, through such TV programmes as *That was the Week that Was* and the publication *Private Eye*. In the ten days that we were there I disposed of twenty-five Queen's Bench actions, as well as six defended divorce cases. Even so I had one or two early days and Judy and I motored out into the beautiful countryside on the Welsh borders. When we dined with the High Sheriff, who was quite young, I demurred when his wife asked me to lead the way into dinner. This threw the whole party into confusion, as all had been briefed as to the protocol. Thereafter I always did what I was told, or what was expected of me, on official occasions. After the very senior bishop had dined with us in the lodgings he wrote saying, 'I have met many hanging judges, but never before a swinging judge.' I did not know whether to take this as a compliment.

A few days after leaving Shrewsbury I went to Newcastle where, as at Cardiff, the lodgings were in the Mansion House, which the Lord Mayor vacated during the assize. There was an ancient custom at Newcastle whereby the judges were each presented with a golden noble as 'dagger money'. Until the advent of railways and the separation of the North East from the Northern Circuit the judges had travelled along the border from Newcastle to Carlisle, escorted by the High Sheriff and a posse of 'dagger men' as far as the boundary with Cumberland, where the High Sheriff of Cumberland took over. This was wild dangerous country, with the Moss Troopers swooping over the border to rustle cattle and attack wayfarers, but the 'dagger men' were expensive and were found by the Newcastle Corporation. So a deal was done with the judges whereby they provided their own escort in return for payment of a golden noble. While Judy's father had been a judge all judges received the noble whenever they went to Newcastle, but in my time it was only presented to a judge on his first visit. I was lucky, because I was the last judge to receive a golden noble; thereafter, on grounds of expense, a silver coin was presented. The presentation took place at a dinner given by the Lord Mayor in the lodgings. I had my noble made into a brooch for Judy, suspended from a silver dagger with a diamond-studded hilt. Unfortunately it was stolen in one of the three burglaries which have occurred during our married life, so I bought another noble from Spinks, had it mounted in the same way at Tessiers and gave it to her for a Golden Wedding present.

The other judge at Newcastle was George Waller and Rudolf Lyons, Recorder of Leeds, was with us as Commissioner of Assize to help George with the crime. Judy came up for a few days from Leicestershire, where she had been staying with our old friends Dheidre and Humpo Philips. There was thick snow all the way and only one lane open on the roads, but she has always been an intrepid driver. In those days it was the custom for the senior judge to invite the junior judge's wife to stay in the lodgings and some of the senior judges did not always do so. This caused some ill-feeling amongst the judiciary, so the Lord Chief Justice persuaded the judges to agree (some were reluctant to do so) that wives had a right to accompany their husbands on circuit. George Waller, of course, wrote as soon as he learnt I was coming, saying that he hoped that Judy would come whenever and for as long as she liked. Even so she was a guest in the lodgings. The housekeeping was done by the senior judge, although when I became senior judge I always consulted Judy about the menus. But some of the cooks in the lodgings did not like what they called 'interference from the ladies', so I usually saw the cook myself after breakfast, unless we knew her well, and she was happy to take orders from Judy. When we had dinner parties the judges always acted as hosts, although as I became more senior, and especially when I was Presiding judge of the Western Circuit, Judy and I behaved as if we were in our own house, since she was very good at creating a relaxed family atmosphere in the lodgings.

We went to Newcastle again the following May, but Judy went straight on to Jedburgh to stay with Brenda and Stevie Johnson to fish on the Tweed. I went up there for the weekend and we returned with a fine basket of trout, which fed the lodgings for several days. George Waller was there again with his wife Pegg (he had been a 'local' at the Newcastle Bar before becoming a judge); also Ray Hinchcliffe, former leader of the North Eastern Circuit, with his wife Poppy and Jack Willis, and a very happy party we were. I was out again shortly afterwards with Ray at Winchester and George at Stafford and I learnt a great deal from both of them.

Ray was a proper, old-fashioned judge, very decisive and a tough sentencer. George, in spite of being really too old to fly, had been a pilot in RAF Coastal Command in the war. He was in 1970 vice-chairman of the Parole Board and was interested in criminology, being a member of the Home Office Advisory Council on the penal system. He was a first-class judge and was already in the Court of Appeal when I joined in 1980. He used to say, 'When you sentence a man always ask yourself, 'What am I doing to him?'' His views on sentencing were very different from those of Ray, who said when we parted, 'There has been more heresy talked about sentencing during this assize than I have ever heard in my life.'

Ray told me, 'Before summing up always write down your directions on the law, and read them out to the jury. Never repeat them and never try to paraphrase them.' Good, simple advice, but how often disregarded. Sitting later in the Court of Appeal (Criminal Division) I was struck by how often we had to allow appeals because the judge had either misstated the law or, having stated it correctly, gave a further direction on the same point in different or muddled terms which nullified the first direction. The worst offenders were the regular judges at the Old Bailey who, I suppose, become so bored continually summing up to juries that they forget the most elementary rules. Or perhaps they think that they can explain the law better in their own words than in the words of the statute or of the Court of Appeal.

I tried my first criminal case as a High Court judge at Newcastle, sitting in the ancient Guildhall by the River Tyne, near to the house from which Lord Eldon had eloped with his bride while still a struggling barrister. I had attended a four day sentencing course the previous September, during which we had visited two conventional prisons, an open prison, a borstal, and a detention centre. I had been profoundly depressed by the experience. If they had been soldiers I would have said that the men in the open prison were on the verge of mutiny. When I asked the reason the governor replied, 'They are all cockneys and they hate having to work outside in this cold place [the Isle of Sheppey]. What they like is to be crowded into a nice warm place like the Scrubs or Wandsworth, where they are with their pals and near their families.' Canterbury was a remand and short term prison, where the maximum sentence being served was three years. The men were three to a cell and did not work except stitching mail bags. There was no attempt at reformation or rehabilitation. I was taken round Maidstone by an assistant governor, a retired infantry major in his thirties, who treated the prisoners with the robust heartiness of a company commander. It was a medium term prison for those serving three- to ten-year sentences and there was a great variety of work – amongst other things all the motorway signs were made there. I asked what were the chances of a man 'going straight' after being there. The assistant governor said, 'A few who are in for the first time may decide they don't like prison and the game is not worth the candle. As for the rest, there is practically no chance of a man in his twenties giving up crime once he is here. They will never admit they are in the wrong. They always blame everyone else – their parents, their environment, the police, their counsel, for being here. Never themselves. But once a man is in his late thirties and knows that if he is caught again he will get a long sentence, there is just a chance that he may decide to chuck it.' He went on to say that there was a strict hierarchy amongst the prisoners. The 'aristocrats' were the bank robbers, the lowest category being those found guilty of sexual offences, especially against children. These had to be kept in solitary confinement for their own protection. At the borstal I asked the 'housemaster' who showed me round how much good he thought they did. 'Very little,' he said. 'Sometimes they come in at the age of fifteen or sixteen. We only keep them for about a year, when they return to the same environment and the same coffee bars. If we did not have them until they were at least seventeen, kept them for three years and then sent them for two years into the armed forces, where they married a decent girl away from their own home town, there might be some hope for them.' I remembered that my BSM in 'C' Battery RHA had been an ex-borstal boy, so perhaps he was one of the lucky ones. He was certainly a good smart BSM. The detention centre gave me the best 'feel' of all. The boys looked very fit and were obviously kept busy and made to work hard. But I did not ask how many reoffended. At the end of the course I came to the conclusion that the reformatory aspect of prison was negligible, that prison was simply a punishment and that the whole punishment was the deprivation of liberty.

With that limited knowledge, my experience of sitting at Somerset Quarter Sessions and the help and advice of my brethren in the lodgings, I had to deal with the Geordies of Newcastle. I had found, trying civil cases, that they were the most honest witnesses I had yet seen. Sooner or later a plaintiff would admit that the accident had happened differently to the way he had originally described and that he had been 'put up to it' by his union. It was the same in crime: there were many pleas of guilty and many admissions of 'a fair cop'. Looking closely at the young men in the dock, I saw broad shoulders, fair hair and wide-apart blue eyes. The fathers of these boys had fought with the Durham Light Infantry at El Alamein and been welcomed home as heroes. Most of the cases were woundings, often with knives, following a brawl outside a public house. The English are by nature a violent and rumbustious race. For two hundred years they had worked off their energies in wars against the French, conquering one fifth of the surface of the globe or beating the Germans in two world wars. Now they had no-one to fight but one another. But they had to go to prison, although I tried to make the sentences as short as possible.

I visited Leeds in the winter during the miners' strike, which brought down the Heath government in 1974. There were constant power cuts, due to shortages of fuel at the power stations. The butler at Leeds had been butler to Lord Halifax and was a keen fox-hunter. He used to bring me the meets of the local packs of hounds and news if any of them had had a good day. He called me one morning during a power cut saying, 'That Scargill, 'e's like a little 'Itler.' I was determined not to allow the power cuts to interfere with the administration of justice, so I sat in court by lantern light until the usual time. I was trying crime in the imposing Victorian Crown Court and it was a mediaeval scene in the late afternoon in that vast room, so dimly lit that one could barely see people's faces. I told the usher to hold up the lantern so that the jury could see the face of the witness.

The lodgings at Leeds were at Carr Manor near Chapel Allerton, which by then was a sprawling suburb. My great-great-grandfather, William Williams Brown the banker, had lived there when it was in the country and had ridden into his counting house in the city every day on horseback. I had an old map showing the position of the house and determined to find it. One day after court I found a large early Victorian house, used as an old people's home, which was in the middle of a housing estate and in the exact position shown on my map. Beside it was a block of stabling, approached through an imposing stone arch, on which was carved the Brown crest which was on some of our silver. So I had found one of my roots.

But my favourite place was Liverpool, and I returned there whenever I could after my first visit. Although much of it was derelict and surrounded by unsightly tower blocks, Liverpool had style. We sat in the magnificent St. George's Hall, surrounded by the other fine buildings of the city centre and the beautiful Anglican cathedral. Then there was the water front, with the Liver building and other wonderful buildings looking across the River Mersey and the docks. Inland there were the spacious public parks, where I used to walk after court. The lodgings were in one of these, Newsham Park in Anfield, within walking distance of the famous Liverpool football ground and also of Everton. It was a comfortable early Victorian house, with a beautiful circular study overlooking the garden where we could work in peace and comfort. And, on an early day, there were the glorious golf courses nearby at Formby and Hoylake.

I also loved the Liverpudlians with their quick friendly wit, and their 'scouse' accents. Above all they were realists. They knew what life really meant and what went on. I found the Liverpool juries the best in the country. The more genteel the jury the more likely they are to bring in a perverse verdict because they simply cannot believe it possible that people behave in the way alleged. Hampshire juries were the worst in this respect. But Liverpool juries knew exactly how people behaved and were surprised at nothing. I tried my first murder case at Liverpool, in which the defendant had been working on an oil rig in the North Sea. He came home on leave one evening, drunk, and continued drinking all that evening and the following morning as soon as the public houses opened, returning home for lunch at about

2 pm. As he walked into the house he heard his wife speaking on the telephone in terms which suggested to him that she was having an affair with the caller. So he picked up a carving knife from the kitchen table, and thrust it into the back of her skull. She ran out of the house, screaming, with the knife stuck out of the back of her head, and fell dead in the road. The defence was provocation, which would reduce the verdict of murder to manslaughter, and it was apparent from the evidence that she had in fact been having an affair in his absence. I had some sympathy with the defendant, but following Ray Hinchcliffe's advice, I read out my direction on the law of provocation (never easy) and summed up the facts impartially to the jury. I had already learnt at Quarter Sessions that the surest way of producing a perverse verdict was to show any bias in summing up the facts, either in favour of the prosecution or the defence. After less than an hour the jury, which included several women, returned with a unanimous verdict of guilty of murder. I suppose they may have felt that if a man was entitled to kill his wife because she had been unfaithful in his absence, many Liverpudlian women would be at risk. Whatever the reason, it was the right verdict and a good decision by the Liverpool jury.

I much admired the local Bar at Liverpool. They had a long tradition and there were in my time several good judges, such as Joe Cantley, Robby Crichton, Danny Brabin and George Bean from the Northern Circuit. There was a great deal of work and in civil actions they would agree everything they could before coming into court. 'We've agreed the dummages, me Lord,' they would say in their flat Lancastrian voices. 'We've agreed the expert evidence. We've agreed the medical reports. There's just one issue we want your Lordship to decide, and it is this.' I revelled in this approach and we would deal in half a day with a case which in London or sadly on my own Western Circuit would have taken over twice as long. Danny Brabin told me that when on the Northern Circuit, trying a straightforward case which depended solely on the facts, he would ask counsel whether they wanted a verdict or a judgment. Often they opted for the former, which then became unappealable. But I never dared to do this, even at Liverpool.

One day after court I walked down from St. George's Hall to the docks, wearing a dark suit and bowler hat and carrying an umbrella, as I loved to see the ocean terminal, no longer in use, where the great Cunarders would dock and the film stars and tycoons in their furs and smart clothes would walk along the jetty to the dining car in the waiting boat train, which would take them to London. When I reached the dock gates I was stopped by the uniformed security guard who said, 'If you go in there dressed like that, sir, someone will shout 'Everybody out' and you will stop all work for the rest of the day.' At that time the Liverpool Docks were plagued by strikes and the port was rapidly losing trade, so I walked away, thanking him for his advice. Shortly afterwards I attended a reception given for the assize judges on board a ship belonging to the Holt Line, one of the great Liverpool shipping companies, and told the story of my experience at the docks to the chairman of the company. 'You can hardly blame them,' he said. 'The introduction of cargo containers has destroyed the work of the stevedores. Previously they were the aristocrats of the docks, since the safety of the ship depended on their skill in stowing the cargo. Suddenly those skills have become unnecessary. It is no consolation to them to be told that they can be retrained as dockers or car workers, any more than it would be to suggest to a barrister, if the Bar became redundant, that he could be retrained as a solicitor or accountant. They were proud of being stevedores, and that is what they want to be.' Coming from a shipowner I thought this an interesting comment on labour relations.

Sometimes, on circuit, I would take a marshal, a recently qualified barrister who lived in the lodgings and acted as ADC to the judge, sitting with him in court and swearing the witnesses. I always chose my marshals carefully, trying to find people who would find us and our interests congenial and they became a kind of legal family. When I retired Judy and I gave a dinner for all of them and their spouses at my club in London. I hope and believe they all benefitted from the experience and certainly Judy and I enjoyed having young people about us. I was able to help some of them get started in the Temple, several became pupils in Queen Elizabeth Building and one, Andrew Tidbury, stayed on as a tenant. Before one of my first visits to Liverpool Suzannah Fitzgerald, who had been at school with Janie and had just graduated from Bristol University, asked if she might come with me as marshal. Female marshals were virtually unheard of in those days and I suggested she should approach Elizabeth Lane, the first woman High Court judge. Elizabeth was an extremely nice woman and a good judge, but she believed in keeping up standards on circuit and Suzannah's face fell at my suggestion. So I said I would ask the senior judge Joe Cantley who said, 'I don't mind who you bring as marshal, so long as he does not wear a beard. I cannot stand young men with beards.' I replied that I was sure my marshal would not have a beard, so Suzannah came with me to Liverpool, where she was a great success. Before we left for Liverpool I asked Elizabeth, who had had several female marshals, if there was anything special I should know about them. 'Make her wear a hat in court,' said Elizabeth, 'and don't let her wear jeans in the lodgings.' I told Suzannah about the hat, but said that if she wanted to wear jeans after court she could certainly do so. I am glad she did because she looked extremely decorative in them.

Whenever I went on circuit I took with me McKinnon's book *On Circuit*, a beautifully written and erudite account of the assize towns he visited before he became a Lord Justice. For the first time I realised how many beautiful and interesting places there are to see in England and Wales, not just in the towns but also in the surrounding countryside, especially in the north. Judy and I would often spend the weekend at a pub, or with friends, near the assize town and explore the Lake District, the Yorkshire Dales, the Peak District and the Welsh mountains. In the summer we would combine this with fishing on the rivers. It was a marvellous opportunity to see some of these places and we took full advantage of it. The last place we visited in 1979 was Swansea and at the weekend we drove round the Gower Peninsula and along the lovely South Pembroke coast to Pembroke Dock where my grandfather, Robin Dunn, had been stationed towards the end of the last century. There he had met and married a lady from one of the very English Pembroke families, who had settled there hundreds of years ago, but never regarded themselves as Welsh. She sadly died in childbirth and Robin married my grandmother. His only son by his first marriage died in his teens.

I never hunted while on circuit, as I did not like the idea of riding strange horses in strange countries. The only judge in my time who did was Kenneth Diplock, who took his horse round with him, stabling it either with the mounted police or at livery locally, riding out before breakfast and hunting on Saturdays. He called the horse 'Circuit' and his clerk, if asked the whereabouts of the judge, would say, 'On Circuit'.

During 1979 I visited two of the nicest places where I had never been before. During the bitter winter of 1978/79, 'the winter of discontent', I went to Lincoln and was fascinated by the cathedral, in a superb position overlooking the old mediaeval town. The lodgings were in an 18th-century house just west of the cathedral, from where we used to drive in an ancient Rolls Royce to court in the castle. There was a box seat facing us in the Rolls for the High Sheriff, on which was an ancient horse rug which still smelt of horses. Judy did not come, but I was happy to be with my old friend Tudor Evans and his wife Sheilagh, both keen followers of racing form and the best of company.

In May 1979 Judy and I went alone to Chester, another beautiful Elizabethan town, where the lodgings, some say appropriately, are on the edge of the zoological gardens. We spent the weekend in the lodgings and visited my grandfather's house on Bangor racecourse and his grave at Wrexham, as well as driving over the beautiful country round Llangollen. We dined with the High Sheriff on the night of the general election and hurried home to watch the television results proclaiming a conservative victory for Margaret Thatcher.

Circuit enlarged my horizons in a way I would not have believed possible. As well as seeing much of England, which I would never otherwise have visited, I met people, both socially and professionally, from every part of the country. I learnt a great deal from them and I believe they learnt a good deal from the peripatetic judges from London. The circuit system provides a two-way interchange of ideas and attitudes between London and the provinces.

CHAPTER XXIV

The Family Division, 1971–80

In 1971 the Probate Divorce and Admiralty Division ceased to exist, after a life of nearly a hundred years, becoming the Family Division. Admiralty work was transferred to the Queen's Bench Division, although the Admiralty judge, Henry Brandon, refused to transfer, saying that he knew nothing of crime, and preferred, when he was not trying Admiralty, to try divorce of which he had five years experience. This did not please John Widgery, the Lord Chief Justice but as Henry was the only Admiralty specialist in the judiciary and was head and shoulders above any member of the Admiralty Bar, he got his way. I was sad, because it meant that I would try no more Admiralty, which I had found a welcome change from divorce. Contentious probate went to the Chancery Division, although the Family Division kept non-contentious probate, including responsibility for the Probate Registry at Somerset House. In return the wardship jurisdiction was transferred from the Chancery Division to the Family Division. As a result two leading silks from the Chancery Division were appointed judges in the Family Division: Arthur Bagnall and John Arnold. Arthur sadly died within a few years of appointment. He was a disappointment in the Division, as he took a rigid view of property rights. Tom Denning had growled, 'We don't want Bagnall in the Court of Appeal. He's too legalistic.' John Arnold had been Chairman of the Bar Council. I was surprised when he had been appointed to the Division, as he had himself been through the Divorce Court and, until then, no Divorce judge had ever been divorced. Indeed Kilmuir, when Lord Chancellor, had made John Marnan resign as a metropolitan magistrate after his divorce, since he exercised a matrimonial jurisdiction. I had often been against John Arnold when we were in silk and noticed that, although he could charm the birds off the trees, once in every case he would lose control of himself. This happened during the Selangor case and I was amused to see that neither the judge, nor any of the Chancery counsel involved, who all knew him well, took the slightest notice. After a few minutes the outburst subsided and the case continued as before. Once, in court, John threatened to report me to my Benchers for some imagined misdemeanour. The judge took no notice and when we adjourned at lunch time

John said, 'Come on Robin. Let's have lunch together in the Crypt.' So I wondered how John would fare on the Bench, although he was outstandingly able.

In 1974 Rose Heilbron was appointed to the Division. She had had a large practice, mostly in crime, on the Northern Circuit of which she had been leader before her appointment. She proved an excellent and most sympathetic judge. Whilst it was plainly desirable to have women judges in the Division there were, at that time, few possible candidates, since few women barristers had the necessary standing in the profession. It takes an average of twenty-five to thirty years in practice to reach the High Court Bench and there were few women who had practised for that length of time. This was because, until the fifties, there were law schools in only three universities, Oxford, Cambridge and London, and few women read law so that the pool from which women judges could be appointed was very small. Moreover, few women had quality practices. It was not until people like Clare Tritton broke into the fields of commercial and European law in the eighties that the city solicitors overcame their prejudice against briefing women counsel. Until then most women confined themselves to divorce and crime. There were several able women practising in the Family Division in my time and I noticed that they were particularly good at persuading some of their more intransigent female clients to see reason in cases which called for a compromise. But most, inevitably, took time off from their practices to bring up their families and some did not return. Margaret Higgins, wife of Nicholas Wilson who joined us in Queen Elizabeth Building and has recently become a High Court judge, told me that she liked her two children so much that she was not going to return to her large practice at the Divorce Bar. Even now, most women High Court judges have been Circuit judges before appointment, and the doyenne of them all, Elizabeth Butler-Sloss, now a Lord Justice and a highly respected judge, was a divorce registrar before her appointment. An exception was Margaret Booth who joined us in 1979, having been a silk specialising in the Family Division. She was David Moylan's pupil in Queen Elizabeth Building and, like Elizabeth, is a judge of the highest quality. So, I hope and expect, that as the pool of qualified women becomes larger more and more women will be appointed to the High Court Bench. But they must be appointed on merit and not just because they are women.

The procedural reforms which set up the Family Division were not wholly satisfactory. All undefended cases and their 'ancillary' matters relating to children and money were allocated to the County Court. As the reforms of the substantive law began to take effect, there were fewer and fewer defended divorce cases heard in the High Court and the real issues became custody of children and financial provision. These might be simple in a defended case and difficult in an undefended. But the latter were tried by County Court judges and the former by High Court judges. I wrote a paper for the Lord Chancellor's department suggesting that the matrimonial jurisdiction of the County Court should be amalgamated with the Family Division in a single court, analogous to the new Crown Court which had been set up for the criminal courts under the Courts Act 1971. The judges of this new court, which I suggested should be called the Family Court, would be the judges of the Family Division, the Circuit judges sitting in the County Courts and the registrars. The work would be categorised, as in the criminal courts, according to its difficulty and importance and allocated to the appropriate level of judge, regardless of whether the main suit was defended or undefended. This proposal was welcomed by the Lord Chancellor's department, but the majority of my brethren in the Family Division were opposed to it, saying that there would not be enough work for the High Court judges and so no action was taken. Their ground of opposition was of course right. I was underemployed throughout my time in the Family Division, trying many cases which could just as well have been tried by a Circuit judge, or even a registrar. But the remedy was either to reduce the number of Family Division judges by transferring a proportion who were qualified by their experience to the Queen's Bench Division or, as some suggested, by having a single list of High Court judges, with some specialising in particular fields of work, but all available to deal with cases as required. My own view was that Family work was of such public importance that it was necessary to maintain a specialised corps of judges to deal with the most difficult cases and to maintain standards, but there should be a rigorous administrative selection procedure to ensure that their time was not wasted on other, more straightforward cases. I hope that the procedural reforms of the nineties will achieve these results.

But more important than the procedural reforms were the reforms of the substantive divorce law itself. These represented a compromise between Church and State. Harry Phillimore in the fifties had been a member of a committee chaired by the Archbishop of York, which had produced a report entitled *Putting asunder,* which sought to maintain the idea of the 'matrimonial offence'. The government wished to introduce divorce by consent. The compromise was that the sole ground for divorce was to be 'breakdown of the marriage', but as the concept of breakdown was not justiciable it was to be evidenced by proof of conduct similar to the former matrimonial offences i.e. adultery, desertion and cruelty, although the latter was called 'unreasonable behaviour'. In addition there was to be divorce by consent after two years separation and, after five years separation, one party could divorce the other provided that proper financial provision was made for the latter. The old 'bars' of condonation and collusion were abolished.

Some of my more senior brethren thought that, apart from the abolition of the bars and the provisions based on separation, the reforms had changed nothing and wished to perpetuate the old technicalities of the divorce law particularly in the concept of 'unreasonable behaviour'. I tried one of the earliest behaviour cases, and said in my judgment that the question whether or not behaviour was so unreasonable that the other party could not be expected to tolerate it was a jury question and that the judge should approach it as such, taking into account all the circumstances, including the personalities of the parties and the length of the marriage and, applying that test, I granted the wife a decree. My friend Mary Bryn Davies, the Family

Division law reporter, and a keen follower of racing, wrote, 'The final word on behaviour. No need for another reported case.' Some of my brethren were critical, saying the decision made divorce too easy but, although there was no appeal, the Court of Appeal in a later case approved my judgment. Neville Faulks, after reading the judgment said, 'I don't know why you didn't just say that the man was a shit.' I replied that I preferred to let the facts speak for themselves.

The result of these reforms were that the courts became concerned, not so much with whether there should be a divorce, but with the consequences of divorce. Divorce law is a creature of statute. Parliament lays down the grounds for divorce and the financial remedies. These latter were set out in an act called the Matrimonial Proceedings and Property Act 1973. For the first time, to the great benefit of wives, a wide range of options was presented in the Act. The court could transfer property, order a lump sum payment or periodical payments and effectively readjust the family assets. Apart from certain matters to which the court was to have regard, complete discretion was left to the judge to put the parties in the same position in which they had been during the marriage, 'so far as it is practical and, having regard to their conduct, just to do so.' Of course in the great majority of cases it was not practical, so the judge did his best to make an order which was just and this later was achieved by an amendment to the statute. Almost all divorces, save for those of the very rich, involve a reduction in living standards for the whole family. Basically the judge had to balance the reasonable requirements of the wife and children against the financial resources of the husband. And it was this balancing provision which Parliament had left to the judges. There was no rule of thumb and no binding authority, although the ways in which other judges had dealt with similar situations were helpful. Hugh Griffiths, then a Queen's Bench judge and now a Law Lord, once told me that when on circuit he had found himself trying a Family Division property case. 'I have never found anything so difficult,' he said. 'I reckon I know whether the workman slipped on a pool of oil on the factory floor. But I am dashed if I know how to re-arrange the whole of a family's property.' 'For the first time,' I told him, 'you were required to exercise a little judicial discretion.'

In 1971 George Baker succeeded Jack Simon, who became a Law Lord, as President of the Family Division. George was the first puisne judge to have been appointed President and I felt that the appointment had been down-graded. Hitherto the President, like the Lord Chief Justice and the Master of the Rolls, had become a peer after his appointment. Not any more. Harry Phillimore should have been President, but was already ill with a fatal disease. A cousin of Harry's had been the first President and Harry was well qualified for the position. George was a sound judge, a good administrator and very supportive of his judges. But he did not have the vision required for the development of the law following the reforms of 1970. This fell to Roger Ormrod who, practically single-handed for twelve years, both in the Family Division and the Court of Appeal, revolutionised the whole approach to divorce law and moulded the present law of divorce. He refused to regard the Family

Division as a court of morals and was essentially concerned with the practical consequences of divorce: the custody of the children, the provision of a house and proper financial provision for the wife and children. The first difficulty was presented by the use of the word 'conduct' in the 1973 Property Act. At first time-consuming trials were held in chambers, where all property proceedings took place, akin to the former defended divorce cases. The purpose of these was to apportion blame for the breakdown of the marriage, rather on the lines of contributory negligence in an action for tort, so that the wife's share of the property could be reduced if she had been found to have been substantially to blame for the breakdown. I never heard it suggested that her share should be increased if the husband was to blame. As the financial cases were always heard after the decree, this sometimes gave rise to difficult questions of estoppel and resulted in many defended divorce cases which the reforms had been designed to prevent. But a more serious objection was that in almost all cases there was simply not enough money to go round and if a discount for conduct was made from the wife's share she would not have enough to support herself and the children. The judge had little enough room for manoeuvre as it was, without having to make some arbitrary deduction for 'conduct'. In 1973 in a case called Wachtel, Roger boldly announced, as was the fact, that in almost all cases both parties were to blame, usually in approximately equal shares, so that in financial proceedings conduct should be disregarded unless it was 'both obvious and gross'. This decision was upheld by the Court of Appeal and had a dramatic effect on subsequent financial proceedings. Matrimonial conduct could be ignored and the judges were able to concentrate on the practical problems facing the family after the divorce.

Roger did not confine his reforming zeal to financial considerations. Although for many years in children's cases the law had required that the first and paramount consideration was the welfare of the child, the judges had whittled this away by seeking also to do justice as between the parents and by giving weight to the wishes of an 'unimpeachable spouse'. When he was in the Court of Appeal Roger succeeded in sweeping away all these old cases, saying that there was no such thing as an unimpeachable spouse and that justice between the parties could only be done after an exhaustive inquiry into the marriage, which would not help the resolution of the issue of custody. As the years passed many began to say that the pendulum of reform had swung too far in favour of wives; that the courts were too biased in favour of wives being granted custody of their children; and that it was wrong that a promiscuous or nagging wife should have the same financial provision as a faithful loving wife. This criticism did not deter Roger, who had had nine years experience of trying defended divorce cases before the reforms and knew that in the great majority of cases the wife, whatever her defects of character, was the more suitable person to bring up the children, especially if they were young. It followed that she must be able to provide a home for them and must have sufficient financial provision to enable her to maintain as nearly as possible the standard of life which the family had previously enjoyed. He was not sympathetic to husbands who maintained that they could bring up the children as well as their wives, saying that such men usually either neglected their children or gave up their jobs and became so engrossed in the children that they grew up in an unnatural environment. Women, he maintained, were much better at combining their function of a mother with an ability to lead a normal life outside the family. As Roger and I had been in chambers together we were, naturally, close to one another and after I became a judge we would often lunch together in the Inner Temple and discuss our cases. I was much influenced by his ideas which I supported.

I found that the most satisfactory jurisdiction in the Family Division was wardship, an ancient jurisdiction which had been developed over centuries by the Chancery judges. Its origin was the exercise by the judges of the paternal powers of the Crown to protect minors and infants. At first it had been used to protect the property of minors from the depredations of grasping relatives and other ill-disposed people. But gradually it had been extended to include disputes between parents and others as to the upbringing and education of children. In theory there was no limit to the jurisdiction, but rules were gradually established as to the circumstances in which it should be exercised. The judge had the widest possible powers, not only as to who should appear before him, but also as to the conduct of the proceedings and the orders which he might make. So grandparents and other relatives or friends might appear before the court and the judge could make virtually any order which was in the interests of the ward. By the time that I became a judge wardship was a concurrent jurisdiction which ran in parallel with the statutory jurisdiction over children of the Family Division, the Divorce County Court and the magistrates and it was also a residual jurisdiction, since the judge in wardship had powers which went beyond those of judges and magistrates in other jurisdictions. The strength of wardship was its flexibility.

In those days the law relating to children was a jungle, in which only the expert could find his way and even he sometimes became lost. There were a number of Children Acts on the statute book, which had been amended piecemeal over the years, without any cohesive plan as to what was to be achieved. Consequently the same child might be subject to the jurisdiction of the High Court if the parents were engaged in defended divorce proceedings, of the County Court if the parents were engaged in undefended divorce proceedings, or of the magistrates if the parties were still married and there was a dispute about the custody of the children. But the most unsatisfactory aspect of all were the provisions for taking children into care. Local authorities are under a duty to protect children within their locality and had power in certain circumstances by resolution of their social services committees to take children into care for a limited period. But a long term care order could only be made by the magistrates sitting in the Juvenile Court under the provisions of the Children and Young Persons Act 1969. This act contained two quite different concepts of care orders. One set of grounds for making such an order was directed to protecting the child from ill-treatment or neglect by parents; another ground was that the child himself had committed a criminal offence or was delinquent. But all such proceedings were quasi-criminal in their nature, with no proper provisions for the representation of the parents and an unsatisfactory appeal structure. So an increasing number of local authorities used the wardship procedure to obtain care orders in ill-treatment or neglect cases and I tried many such cases. This had the great advantage that the wardship court had a wide range of options in making the orders, including adoption or long-care fostering if those were appropriate, with all parties represented before the court. But the cases were expensive and the large numbers threatened to swamp the resources of the Family Division, so in a case in which the Liverpool Corporation was involved the House of Lords severely restricted the exercise of the wardship jurisdiction in such cases, holding that unless some remedy not available to the magistrates was sought, the cases should be brought before the Juvenile Courts within the statutory system. Now there is a new Children's Act further limiting the wardship jurisdiction and giving increased powers to the magistrates. It will only work if the former procedural difficulties in the Juvenile Courts have been rationalised by separating its criminal and protective functions and allowing proper representation for the parents; and if the magistrates are sufficiently knowledgeable to be able to exercise the degree of flexibility of the court in wardship, which will put a heavy burden upon them. If not I fear that children will continue to suffer.

One wardship case which I tried, though not typical, illustrates the problems which could arise. A middle-aged, middle-class couple, who had spent their lives in philanthropic work in West Africa, determined as an experiment to bring up a black child in their middle-class white suburban environment in Surrey, sending her to a private school and encouraging her to have white middle-class friends. The mother of the child was of West Indian origin and had been fifteen years old when the child was born. She had fallen out with the black father, whom she had not married, and agreed to the child going to live with the white foster parents, though not to be adopted. She continued regularly to see the child and her relations with the foster parents were apparently good. She was intelligent and well-educated and apparently welcomed the prospect of her daughter being given advantages to which she could never aspire. Then she and the father married and said to the foster parents, 'We want our baby back.' The foster parents refused and made the child a ward of court. I soon decided in my own mind that the child should go back to her mother, but did not wish to give a judgment which might exacerbate relations between the parents and foster parents. So I employed a technique which I sometimes used saying, 'Although I have not finally made up my mind, it may help the parties if I indicate my preliminary views by thinking aloud,' and I told them the way my mind was working. The result was that the foster parents, with obvious reluctance, agreed to give up the child and I made an order vesting care and control in the mother, subject to a supervision order to the local authority, since the parents were still both very young. Some months later the case reappeared in my court on a Monday. The previous week, while I had been on circuit, a social worker had discovered what appeared to be bruises on one of the child's arms. As the parents had been uncooperative in the past and the social worker was not happy about the conditions in the home, she applied for and obtained from the magistrates a place of safety order so that the child could be taken temporarily into care until an application was made to me, since the child was still a ward of court. The order caused a near riot in the district in which the family lived: the social worker called the police, who advised against forcibly removing the child from the house, since it was surrounded by protesting black neighbours. But the parents agreed to bring the child to court on the Monday morning. The father appeared wearing a knitted cap, which I took as a protest, and there was a great deal of tension in court, with the social workers defending what I regarded as their rather heavy-handed action and the parents full of bitterness against them. I decided that the best course, instead of a formal confrontation in court, was to talk to the parents quietly in my room, since I had established good relations with the mother at the previous hearing. So I saw them, with the child, in the presence of my faithful usher Olive Moore, a motherly figure who had two sons, both successful clerks in the Temple. I pointed to the bruise on the child's arm and asked for an explanation. The father said, 'This child was naughty. When I was naughty my father hit me with a strap and I respected him for it. So when she is naughty I hit her with a strap.' I pointed out that this was not the right way to deal with a very young child (she was only two years old) and that if he did it again I would have to take the child away from them. I pointed out that I was on their side, as I had given them the child back previously, and would they both promise not to hit the child in future. They both said they would. So we went back into court and I gave a short judgment, in the course of which I said, 'The father has told me that when in the West Indies his father had hit him with a strap when he was naughty. He must understand that this sort of behaviour is not acceptable in England.' At that the mother jumped up in her place shouting, 'You bloody racist,' and advanced upon the Bench taking a knife from her handbag. Frank McGrath tried to restrain her and she shouted, 'Don't you touch me, I'm pregnant.' I deemed it expedient to retire through the door, which was fortunately immediately behind my chair, and she was eventually persuaded to calm down and leave court, but not before she had mutilated my notebook and the papers on the Bench. I returned to court (the parents had left with the child) and announced that I proposed to take no action for contempt of court, but that the case was to be brought back within 28 days. At the adjourned hearing the social worker gave a good report on the family and on the progress of the child. The mother was not in court, but the father was present, and after the case I asked to see him in my private room. He was not wearing his knitted cap. He said things were going well at home and that his wife was sorry for her outburst, 'She has been under a lot of pressure,' he said. I told him to give her my best wishes. I never heard any more about the case.

This case was one of many examples, well known to all judges, of the racial tensions which lie just below the surface in our country. A contemporary of mine, with a long and distinguished political career, said to me recently, 'Looking back, the one thing that I regret is the unrestricted immigration of people from the Commonwealth which occurred in the late forties and early fifties. Both political parties are to blame. We none of us foresaw the consequences.' I was surprised at this because Judy's cousin John Pilcher had told me that when he was at our embassy in Rome just after the war a proposal had been made that large numbers of workers from Italy, where there was massive unemployment, should be allowed into England, where at that time there was full employment, and more workers were required for the less skilled jobs such as porters on the railways and cleaners in hospitals. John said that the government of the day had taken the proposal seriously and a junior Minister had been sent to Rome to discuss it with the embassy, saying that if the Italians were allowed in as well as immigrants from the Commonwealth the labour market would be flooded. The embassy pointed out that Italians were preferable, since they would all return to Italy on retirement, whereas the Commonwealth immigrants would almost certainly remain, raise families and put down roots in England. The Minister replied, 'I see that. But we owe something to these people. They stood by us and fought for us in the war. Now there is great unemployment in the West Indies due to the removal of the sugar subsidies, which we can no longer afford. So the least we can do is to help them as they helped us.' So the flood started, but the country was never consulted and there has been a conspiracy of silence on the topic ever since. It has been left to the social workers, the police, the magistrates and the judiciary to deal with the consequences. Many of the immigrants and their descendants have accepted English social attitudes and English law and have flourished, especially Indians and Pakistanis. But many more, especially those who originated from the West Indies, have not, as I soon discovered when sitting in the great industrial towns where so many of the blacks are concentrated. Statistics show that a higher proportion of blacks than whites are sent to prison for similar offences. But this is not because of bias by the judges. On the contrary I always took even greater care than usual before sentencing a black man to prison. The truth is that many of those who were born here have become alienated from the whole of English culture and English ideas of law and order. The use of drugs is perhaps the best example. In the West Indies the use of cannabis is socially acceptable. In England it is a crime, but many young blacks do not see it as such and resent being labelled as criminals when they take drugs. Drugs give rise to other crimes, notably burglary, in order to obtain the money to buy the drugs and the users of drugs see nothing wrong in that or, if they are addicted, cannot resist the temptation to steal. Many young blacks in our towns and cities carry knives in order to protect themselves and many live rough. A young London policeman once told me that if, on his 'patch', he stopped and searched a young black he would almost certainly find drugs or a knife and probably both.

But the problems are not confined to blacks. Many of the Moslem community also have a quite different attitude to the position of women to that of the English. They originated from a polygamous society where women had few if any legal rights and were treated as chattels, although many had great influence behind the scenes. I was told that when the oil concession was being negotiated in Abu Dhabi the Sheikh's ladies were seated behind a curtain in the conference room. When a clause which was unacceptable to them was proposed, the Sheikh's mother, a formidable old lady, would emit a loud cough and nothing thereafter would persuade the Sheikh to agree. I tried several cases in which a Talaq, or Moslem decree of divorce, had been pronounced by the husband in Pakistan, the wife having no such right. The question was whether the decree would be recognised in England and whether, if so, the wife would be entitled to the property rights available to her after an English decree. The attitude of the parties to such matters was entirely different to the attitude of English couples to a divorce and they were reluctant to accept my decisions. I found most black and Asian women were good hard-working wives and mothers and many had jobs outside the home. But, in general, they were wholly subservient to their husbands, who were often violent and refused to accept any restraint on their behaviour to their wives or their style of life.

If there is a group of people, whatever their race or colour, who do not accept the standards of the society in which they live, then they are bound to come into conflict with the law and this is the tragedy of the present situation because many do not. There cannot be two codes of law whether criminal or civil in one country. Somehow everyone must be persuaded to accept the law as it has been established. This is not a question for the judges: their duty is to administer the law as it stands. But unless the problem is addressed society, especially in the large towns, is in danger of falling apart. Somehow the black and Moslem communities must be assimilated into the main stream of English life and their confidence and respect for English law must be restored.

The other reflection that I have upon my wardship case is that it was one of the very few child abuse cases, although of a relatively minor nature, that I tried during twelve years in the Family Division. Now I am told that Family Division judges spend a large proportion of their time trying such cases. They must always have existed and it must be only because of the vigilance of social workers that they are now coming to light in such numbers. In my time there were several scandals in which children had been killed or seriously injured by their parents and the social workers were blamed for not having discovered the situation in the family. They have indeed a thankless task. If they intervene and it is found that there has been no serious abuse, they are blamed for being officious and causing turmoil within the family. If they do not intervene and a child is seriously injured or neglected they are blamed even more for not performing their duties. So it is natural that they should be increasingly vigilant and this has happened over the years. Soon after I was appointed I sat next to Rayner Goddard at lunch in the Inner Temple, having just returned from Bristol. 'Was there much crime at Bristol?' asked the old man. 'Yes,' I replied. 'Mostly baby battering.' 'What's that?' said Rayner, having only retired about ten years before. By then the social workers were bringing many of the most serious cases before the criminal courts. Now the less serious and perhaps more subtle are going to the Family Division.

One of the most intractable problems facing a Family Division judge is presented by the child, usually a girl in her early teens, who refuses to see or speak to one parent, usually her father. A typical scenario was that there had been a history of violence against the mother, or drunkenness in the presence of the child, and in those cases one could understand her feelings. But in many cases the marriage had broken down for other reasons, causing great bitterness between the parents. The mother was granted custody, an order was made for access to the father, often by agreement, and then the child refused to see him. The mother's attitude was usually, 'I encouraged access, but she just would not go.' It was received wisdom in the Family Division, supported by the psychiatrists, that, although marriage could be dissolved, parenthood could not and that children should have the benefit of contact with both parents. Often, however, the mother had remarried, had children by her second husband and a new family unit had been built up in which the first husband had no part. Then it was said that the child of the first marriage was perfectly happy in the new family and that her only sign of distress was when she was obliged to see or visit her father. In some of those cases the father was jealous of the new family and his primary purpose in seeing the child was to disrupt the mother's life. But in many cases the mother was determined to exclude the father from the lives of the children, without any real reason, often using subtle means of suggestion why on a particular occasion they should not have access, while maintaining a position to the welfare officers and social workers that she was in favour of them maintaining contact with him. These were the most difficult cases. I once met the son of a Chancery judge who had been divorced before the war. He was a charming man, who enjoyed hunting and was a keen supporter of the Pegasus Club. But his ex-wife would not allow him to see their son, who told me that when he was at Cambridge he suddenly decided he would like to see this man whom he had not seen for over ten years and had been brought up to regard as an ogre. So he went, unannounced, to his father's chambers in Lincoln's Inn who took him out to lunch. He was immediately attracted to his father and thereafter they became great friends. He never forgave his mother. I used sometimes to tell this story to recalcitrant mothers, omitting the identity of the family concerned, in an effort to persuade them to allow contact between the children and their father. Persuasion of the mother was in the last resort the only means of achieving the desired result. It was unthinkable to order the tipstaff to take the child, kicking and screaming, to her father. If persuasion failed there was nothing effectively that the judge could do except transfer the custody to the father, which was usually impractical, but which I once did with dramatic effect. A week later the child was back with its mother, but thereafter access proceeded smoothly and happily.

The limits of the powers of Family Division judges was well illustrated by a case which I tried in the mid-seventies. It was a combined custody and property dispute, the custody issue involving two boys of prep school age. In the course of a long hearing I formed a most adverse view of the character of the husband, but both boys were adamant that they wished to live with him. Unusually I agreed to see them privately in my room. It is now a requirement of the law that, in deciding the custody of the children, the court shall give weight to their wishes. Of course, even before that statutory provision, we always did so. But I found that their true wishes were better expressed to a welfare officer in the familiar atmosphere of their own home, than to a judge in the awe-inspiring surroundings of the Law Courts. Moreover I felt that the trauma of the divorce of their parents put quite enough pressure on children, without them apparently having to choose, and be seen to choose, between mummy and daddy, where they should live. So I usually declined to see children myself, relying on the evidence of the welfare officers as to the wishes of the children. But in this case both parents urged me to see them, so I did.

Although both boys reaffirmed their wish to live with their father, I granted custody to the mother. Children I found are very suggestible, much influenced by the parent to whom they are closest and unwilling to hurt the feelings of a parent to whom they are attached. They gave no reason why they did not want to live with their mother, who was a sensible competent woman who had until then, like most mothers, looked after them on a day to day basis. The father, on the other hand, had shown a lack of understanding of the reality of the situation and was extremely persuasive. His masculine macho approach to life appealed to the boys, but I had no doubt that the mother was more likely to bring them up as decent responsible citizens, so I granted her the custody with access to the father. This meant that she had to stay in the matrimonial home and that the father would have to pay maintenance for her and the boys.

He refused to pay under the order for maintenance, although he never appealed. Eventually I appointed a receiver of the proceeds of his business, an unusual remedy which was gratifyingly effective, as ample money was forthcoming to meet the order. Meanwhile the father had used the access periods to turn the boys even more against their mother and they were becoming increasingly difficult at home. So I stopped all access, but it soon emerged that in defiance of my order the father had been having clandestine meetings with the boys. These continued after I had warned the father of the consequences of breaking orders of the court, so I committed him to prison for contempt. The next morning there was a banner headline in the *Daily Mail*, 'Loving father jailed by judge.' But it did not stop there. The father had told me at one hearing that he had referred the case to 'higher authority' and the following day his MP, having only heard the father's side of the case, put down a motion in the House of Commons for my removal as a judge. Since High Court judges can only be removed by a joint address to the Crown of both Houses of Parliament according to the Act of Settlement of 1703 passed in order to secure the independence of the judiciary, this move was unlikely to achieve its professed object.

It did of course cause more publicity, with detrimental effects on the family. About the only signatory to the motion was John Stonehouse MP, who at that time was on bail awaiting trial on charges of fraud after he had disappeared in circumstances which suggested suicide, so the motion was never even debated. Shortly thereafter, the father having apologised and promised to obey orders of the court in future, I released him from prison, at the request of the mother, granting limited access. But I made an order that neither parent was to communicate either 'directly or indirectly' with the press about the case. This was an order which I was entitled to make under the Administration of Justice Act 1960 and I made it because life in the family was quite difficult enough without having the further aggravation of press publicity.

About a month later the case came back to me, the mother complaining that she has been struck by the elder boy and that the father's influence was such that the boys were becoming unmanageable. She asked me to transfer the custody of the boys to the father, which I duly did. I gave a short judgment in open court, since the case had already attracted so much publicity, continuing the order restraining both parents from communicating with the press. The MP then applied to the Speaker of the House of Commons, alleging that my order was directed against him, since it inhibited him in his efforts on behalf of a constituent, that it constituted a contempt of Parliament and requesting that my conduct be referred to the Committee of Privileges. Perhaps the cap fitted. However, the Speaker pointed out that I was entitled to make the order and ruled that it did not constitute a contempt of Parliament and refused a reference to the Committee of Privileges. It is better that MPs should concentrate on their task of governing the country, rather than attempting to interfere with the administration of justice. I can think of only one thing worse than being ruled by judges and that is being judged by politicians. But in the last resort I was unable to help those boys or their mother or to protect them from the influence of their father. I have often wondered what happened to that unhappy family.

I was always surprised by the resilience of children whose parents were involved in divorce proceedings. Some tried to play off one parent against another, as in Nancy Mitford's classic novel *The Blessing*, required reading for any Family Division judge. But the great majority adopted a much more adult approach than either of their parents, were astonishingly philosophical about their situation and their school reports showed that they were virtually unaffected. There were of course many exceptions where children's work at school was seriously disrupted by the strife between their parents, but they were in the minority. One of the submissions of which I was always sceptical was that the mother had formed a 'stable relationship' with another man, who could provide a stable environment for the children. I could never forget that 40% of second marriages end in divorce. I also noticed how much support brothers and sisters derived from one another, very often a great deal more than they received from the parents. I never split a family.

The wide-reaching reforms of the Divorce Law did not apply to the domestic jurisdiction of the magistrates who, throughout the seventies, were operating the old law involving a finding of fault by one spouse before a financial order could be made. We were involved in this jurisdiction through sitting from time to time with the President in the Divisional Court of the Family Division, to which appeals came from the magistrates. This was an unsatisfactory jurisdiction because, unlike the Court of Appeal, there was no re-hearing, the magistrates 'stating a case' for the opinion of the court in which they set out their findings of fact and the reasons for their decision. The 'case' was drafted by the clerk to the magistrates and it was often difficult to go behind a well stated case, even when the decision was plainly wrong. This was particularly so in custody cases where, because they were still operating the old law, the magistrates sometimes paid more attention to the conduct of the parents than to the welfare of the children. However, we usually managed to do justice, although this often required some intellectual gymnastics in order to overcome the difficulties presented by the 'case'. I came to realise that one advantage of a knowledge of the law is the ability to avoid its technicalities in the pursuit of justice.

The Family Divisional Court did not hear appeals from the Juvenile Court, which lay to the Crown Court and the Divisional Court of the Queen's Bench Division, due to the 'delinquency' provisions of the Children's and Young Persons' Act. I repeatedly suggested to the Lord Chancellor's department that appeals from magistrates in care cases involving ill-treatment or neglect of the children by parents should lie to the Family Division, but nothing was done before my retirement in 1984. This is a much-needed reform, which I hope has been achieved in the new Children's Act.

But the most difficult and interesting aspect of the jurisdiction lay in its financial provisions. The magistrates were dealing with the lowest strata of society, living at or below subsistence level. There was literally no room for manoeuvre. Every penny counted. It was axiomatic that no order should be made, the consequence of which was to put the husband below subsistence level. So if the husband was himself receiving social security, which was by definition fixed at subsistence level, there was no money left for the wife and children. If he was in work, but qualified for income support so as to bring him up to subsistence level, the same situation applied. It was only if he was earning significantly more than required for basic subsistence that an order for the wife and children could be made. And even then husbands did not pay. The arrears under matrimonial orders in the magistrates courts were immense and enforcement was a nightmare. Many husbands either gave up work or indulged in 'moonlighting' and did not disclose their incomes. In one case a husband was seen walking near his house dressed in the white jacket and trousers of his previous occupation of a painter, while drawing social security. When asked for an explanation he said, 'These are the only clothes I have got and anyway I like wearing them.' Attachment of earnings orders could be made, but were largely ineffective since husbands changed their jobs or gave up work. This was the so-called 'poverty trap', in which it paid the husbands to go on social security rather than obtain well-paid work and pay maintenance for their wives and children. Many husbands were committed to prison for non-payment of maintenance, when it was proved that they had the ability to earn but refused to do so. As a result most wives gave up applying to the magistrates for maintenance and themselves applied for social security payments for themselves and their children. All this was fresh ground to me and I soon realised that if husbands were unable or unwilling to pay for the support of their wives and children, the state was obliged to shoulder the burden.

The whole situation was so unsatisfactory that in the seventies the government set up an inquiry into the problems of one-parent families under Maurice Finer, a recently appointed judge of the Family Division. Maurice, who died shortly after producing his report, was a highly intelligent man with a social conscience. His report was a remarkable and well-researched document, which went far beyond the narrow limits of his terms of reference and was in effect a blue print for the complete reorganisation of the domestic jurisdiction of the magistrates. His basic proposition was that it was wrong that there should be two support agencies, the Department of Social Security and the magistrates courts, for the same woman. He recommended that every woman with children whose father did not support them should have an absolute right to a 'single parent' allowance from social security and that the department should have the obligation to apply to the magistrates court to recover such sums as the father was able to pay. This recommendation was turned down out of hand by the Labour government of the day on the grounds of expense, but I do not believe that there was ever a comparative study of the costs of the Finer scheme, compared with the Legal Aid costs of applications by wives to the magistrates courts and the enormous cost of enforcing abortive orders. Moreover, Finer was critical of the way in which the magistrates exercised their domestic jurisdiction. He pointed out that they traditionally exercised a criminal jurisdiction and were bound by statute to follow strict rules of evidence and procedure. This was contrary to the more flexible approach required in Family Law and the magistrates had neither the experience nor the power necessary to adopt it. So he recommended that the domestic jurisdiction of the magistrates should be transferred to the County Court, where all such cases would be tried by a judge sitting with two magistrates. This recommendation was also rejected by the government.

My own view is that magistrates are not equipped to deal with the permanent situation which arises after a divorce and that it is putting too heavy a burden on them to expect them to do so. They are accustomed to dealing with people of comparatively small means and are not equipped to assess the evidence of accountants in cases of substantial assets. Nor should they have jurisdiction in adoption, than which there is nothing more permanent. Their concurrent adoption jurisdiction with the County Court and High Court sometimes gave rise to difficulties. One County Court judge wrestled for years to maintain contact between the father and the children, who were in the custody of the mother, who had re-married and who objected to access. She and her second husband then moved to a different part of the country and successfully applied to the magistrates to adopt the children. The jurisdiction of magistrates should be confined to the temporary situation which arises immediately on the breakdown of the marriage: interim custody and access; maintenance for the wife and children; and if necessary an ouster order to regulate the situation in the home. The permanent arrangements to be made after divorce should be dealt with by judges. But I fear that financial considerations have played a large part in the recent reforms of the law, whereby magistrates will play an increased rôle in Family Law. They will certainly require much more training and may in the process lose the advantage of their amateur status.

I sometimes pondered upon the future of the institution of marriage in our country. I read that marriage is more popular than ever. But it is not Christian marriage, the union for life of one man and one woman. What is the true nature of the bargain which men and women make when they marry today? Before the reforms of 1970 it could safely be said that the bargain was a conditional one: union for life subject to the other party not committing a matrimonial offence. But what are the terms of the bargain now? Perhaps to live together as man and wife until either party becomes bored with the arrangement or finds a preferable partner. The longer I sat in the Family Division the more convinced I became that marriage was originally intended for the protection of women, so that they might have a legal right of support by a man to enable them to bring up the children. Perhaps now that so many women are earning that protection is not so necessary. Whenever I go to a wedding, I am impressed by the extreme solemnity of the marriage vows. No bargain could be more formal or apparently more binding. Yet in one third of marriages those solemn vows are broken. Perhaps it is because most of those who take them do not believe in Christianity and only go to church for weddings and funerals. Whatever the reason, divorce remains a traumatic experience for those involved. A female client of mine at the Bar once said to me after her divorce, 'I feel as though I have been through a major operation. Like losing a limb.' All the judge, like the surgeon, can do is to perform the operation as efficiently and painlessly as possible. He cannot cure the malaise. It was difficult sometimes to remember that judges were not social workers. Their function was to decide issues.

I had mixed feelings about my eleven years in the Family Division. Feelings between the parties ran so high and one's decision meant so much to them and their children that the judge was inevitably under strain. There was seldom finality, as in the Queen's Bench Division, once the case was over. The life of the family went on and it was important that, as far as possible, the decisions should be accepted by all concerned because, as I have shown, in the last resort there was no effective sanction. Some of my brethren in the court of Appeal, especially a few from the Queen's Bench Division, thought that appeals from the Family Division were otiose because there was no right or wrong solution, only a more or less unsatisfactory one. I did not take that view. In very many cases I felt that I had been able to help the family in the best possible way, to resolve what had become, for them, an intolerable situation. And it was this that made the work satisfying. All the same it was a relief to go on circuit for a change of scene and to try civil actions and crime. I found the most deadening aspect of a judge's life was the repetition of the same class of work, whether divorce, crime or civil. To me variety was all and I would return to London refreshed after a stint of Queen's Bench work. I had the same feeling after a long stint of crime on circuit and have never been able to understand how the specialist judges at the Old Bailey can put up with spending their lives trying one criminal case after another. Criminals, on the whole, are so unattractive.

In 1974 an event occurred in our family which gave great delight to Judy and me. Janie married Rollo Clifford whose parents, Henriette and Peter, were old friends of ours. The Cliffords had lived at Frampton-on-Severn near Gloucester since the Norman Conquest and had achieved the remarkable feat of remaining on the same land for nearly a thousand years. The estate had just been handed over to Rollo, who had recently retired from the 14th/20th Hussars, and after her youthful travels round the Far East Janie settled down to become the lady of the manor and over the next ten years presented us with four splendid grandchildren. Allan, who had been a contemporary of Rollo's at Eton, had returned from Australia and set up a small National Hunt training establishment at Lynch, thus achieving his heart's desire. So our cup of happiness was full.

CHAPTER XXV

Presiding Judge, 1974–78

For six hundred years before 1971 the King's Bench judges had travelled the circuits usually in pairs, one trying crime, the other civil, sitting at the assize courts in each and every county in England and Wales. The circuit lasted for the whole of a legal term and the judges moved from one assize town to another. The arrangements for the judges' accommodation were the responsibility of the local authorities and varied over the country. The whole administration of the circuit was in the hands of two officials, the Clerk of Assize and the Clerk of Arraigns, both members of the Bar, who sat in the two courts as associates. Two or three typists and filing clerks completed the establishment of the circuit office and, at the conclusion of an assize, all the books and papers were packed into large wicker-work hampers and taken by train to the next assize town. The juries were called by the Under Sheriffs of each county, who were also responsible for executing civil judgments and orders and were solicitors in private practice. This system had worked well for centuries, but by the late fifties the increase of work, especially crime, was such that, especially in the larger towns the system in increasing measure became unable to cope. Conversely some of the smaller rural counties were unable to produce sufficient work to justify the presence of a High Court judge for a week three times a year. Rayner Goddard's solution had been the extension to all large towns of the system of Crown Courts, similar to those in Liverpool and Manchester. These comprised a full time recorder, the other judges being the local borough recorders and the chairmen and deputy chairmen of the local county Quarter Sessions. A High Court judge was permanently in attendance. This system worked well, as I discovered when I first went to Liverpool.

In the sixties, however, the government set up a Royal Commission on the assize system under Dr. Beeching, of which Harry Phillimore was a member. Beeching, in his report, adopted the same remedy as he had proposed previously for the reorganisation of the railway system. Just as he had closed many of the small branch lines, concentrating resources on the main inter-city lines, now he recommended that High Court judges should no longer visit many of the smaller counties and should be concentrated in the main centres of population. Perhaps his most far-reaching recommendation was that the whole administration of the courts, including the County Courts, should be nationalised and taken over by a new courts service under the Lord Chancellor's department.

This involved the creation of a vast and expensive bureaucracy, which in due course became unionised. Once, not on the Western Circuit, the Circuit Administrator came to me with tears in his eyes, saying that the following day there was to be a one day strike involving his whole staff throughout the circuit, but would I please sit as usual, as he could provide me with an associate but not an usher. I said my clerk would act as usher and drove to court next morning as usual in my wig and robes with my police outriders. Outside the court was a sheepish looking group of court officials carrying placards, to whom I bowed before walking in. We had managed to find two civil actions which were likely to settle. Both did and I was back in the lodgings by 11 am. But honour was satisfied and the strike was broken. Nobody shouted 'Scab'.

Each circuit had its Circuit Administrator, who on the Western Circuit had a well-staffed office in a large house on the Clifton Downs. The Western Circuit, like Gaul, was divided into three parts, each with a main centre at Bristol, Winchester and Exeter respectively. For each centre and its satellite courts there was a Courts Administrator with a staff. Each court complex, some comprising several courts in places such as Portsmouth, Southampton, Winchester, Bristol, Exeter and Plymouth, had its Chief Court Clerk with a staff including associates, ushers, listing clerks and clerks responsible for calling juries, as well as the County Court staffs. These had formerly belonged to the highly efficient County Court service, which had been administered in each court by the registrars, who now lost their administrative functions. In addition the courts service became responsible for the maintenance and upkeep of the court buildings and the provision of accommodation for the High Court judges, in most cases buying the lodgings from the local authorities. One politically-conscious Under Sheriff persuaded his MP to ask a question in the House of Commons comparing the cost to the Exchequer of the administration of the courts before and after the reforms. I cannot remember the figures, but the additional cost was enormous. All these reforms were incorporated into the Courts Act 1971 and there is no doubt that, after initial teething troubles, the courts were as a result able to give a better service to the public. I have, however, often wondered whether the same result could not have been achieved at far less cost if Rayner Goddard's proposed modifications to the assize system had been adopted. However, both Quintin Hailsham, the Lord Chancellor, and Hubert Parker, the Lord Chief Justice, were in favour of the reforms.

One of Beeching's recommendations, which was not incorporated into the Courts Act, was that for each circuit two High Court judges would be appointed as Presiding judges, one of whom would always be present on the circuit. The recommendation was accepted by the Lord Chancellor and the Lord Chief Justice and in 1974 I was appointed Presiding judge of the Western Circuit with Hugh Park, who with Fred

Lawton had set up the system in 1971. Hugh knew much more about the circuit than I did, his practice at the Bar having been predominantly a circuit practice, mostly in Devon and Cornwall. So I was glad of his help and advice for my first year as Presiding judge, when he was replaced by Desmond Ackner, with whom I worked for the next three years. Desmond always enjoyed having a target at which to shoot. When he was chairman of the Bar Council it was the Law Society; when a Presiding judge it was the Civil Service; when he became a Law Lord it was the Lord Chancellor; and throughout his career he never failed to attack the press. But underneath his love of combat he was pure gold. During all our time together we never had a serious disagreement. He never started shooting without consulting me first, so that I could if necessary deflect the fire or prevent it altogether. Although I made many professional friends amongst my brethren, Desmond and his wife Joan were amongst the very few who became real family friends.

In broad principle the Presiding judges were responsible for the judicial or operational side of the circuit, while the Circuit Administrator was responsible for the administrative support. But in practice the two overlapped and, as with so many English institutions, all depended on the personal relations and personalities of those at the top. Some of the Presiding judges took the view that, since judges were not trained administrators, it was better to leave all questions of administration to the Circuit Administrator. Desmond and I did not share that view, particularly with regard to the allocation of work to the different judges. There were twenty-seven Circuit judges who varied greatly in quality. Some were capable of trying serious crime or High Court civil actions; others were better kept in the County Court or trying Quarter Sessions type crime. There were the same numbers of recorders and Deputy Circuit judges, almost all members of the Bar, though there were by then also a few solicitors, who sat for a minimum of twenty-one days in each year. Desmond and I thought that we had more knowledge of the capabilities of all these people, and hence the work that could safely be allocated to them, than the Circuit Administrator and his staff. We also took a close interest in the listing of cases, especially in our own courts. Listing requires a balance between keeping the judges, whose time is of course expensive, fully occupied; and of not wasting the time of counsel, solicitors, litigants and witnesses including expert witnesses, whose time is also expensive. This involves knowledge of the probable length of cases and of whether they are likely to settle at the door of the court. Nothing causes more public dissatisfaction with the law than having to wait outside court for hours and then not to be heard that day for want of time. Judges by their experience are well equipped to estimate the probable length of cases in their own courts and in the early days especially the court staffs were hampered by lack of such experience.

Another, perhaps the most important, function of the Presiding judge was to recommend persons suitable for judicial and other appointments on the circuit. His patronage was immense and humbling and I felt it right that appointments as Presiding judge should be limited to four years, so that a fresh look could be given to the various candidates. All appointments except to the High Court bench were by application and lists were kept of all applicants in the different categories by the Lord Chancellor's department in London. The Circuit Administrator had no responsibility for appointments, although I discovered that court clerks kept notes of the performance of recorders and Deputy Circuit judges. When I protested about this, I was told that it was done for listing purposes, because there was so much variation between different judges in the expedition with which they dealt with their cases. I accepted this, making it clear that the notes should not attempt to make value judgments on the capacity of different judges. All Circuit judges and Deputy Circuit judges were effectively appointed by the Presiding judges from the lists kept at the Lord Chancellor's department. All applications for silk by members of the circuit were submitted to the Presiding judges, who were asked to put them into a 'batting order'. Our recommendations were never varied when the list of successful applicants was published.

These various responsibilities involved getting to know the people, especially the Circuit judges and the Bar, on the circuit. Of course I knew many of the Circuit judges and those of the Bar who appeared in my court and would consult with Peter Rawlinson who was the leader of the circuit. But only comparatively few of the more senior members of the circuit appeared before a High Court judge, so I consulted with Circuit judges whose judgment I felt I could trust. It took a year to go round the circuit, as we spent half of each term at one of the main centres. So I embarked upon a programme of entertainment in the lodgings. Almost every day we had a lunch party for members of the Bar appearing in my court or in the other High Court judge's court if there was one and for recorders and deputy judges sitting at the centre. We had a dinner party once a week, to which we invited the local Circuit judges and their wives to meet such local dignatories as the High Sheriff, the Bishop and the Chief Constable, as well as some of our own friends. Lunch especially was brief, barely an hour in the lodgings before we had to return to court, but these occasions gave me some opportunity of at least putting a face and a personality to the names and curricula vitae which I kept in my 'appointments' file. Judy, who was with me a great deal on the Western Circuit, was invaluable on these occasions, since she had the knack of making all feel at home and creating a relaxed atmosphere.

I soon became concerned about the quality of the Circuit judges. Except in Hampshire, where Raymond Stock at Southampton and Norman Brodrick at Portsmouth were judges of high quality, there were few to whom we could confidently release High Court civil cases or serious crime. So I saw six silks on the circuit and asked them to consider applying to be Circuit judges. I told them that, although I might be wrong, I did not think that they were likely to be appointed High Court judges, but that they would make admirable Circuit judges and that we could release them plenty of interesting work. With two exceptions they all declined the offer, some saying that they still had hopes of the High Court Bench and others that they had children to educate and could not afford a drop in income to a Circuit judge's salary. So I approached Elwyn Jones, then Lord Chancellor, and suggested that, in order to attract some leading silks to the Circuit Bench, a recorder, similar to the Recorders of Liverpool and Manchester, should be appointed at each main centre. He would only need to be paid an extra £1500 a year, but by wearing a red robe and being called 'My Lord' instead of 'Your Honour' his status would be enhanced. Elwyn said he was against two tiers of Circuit judge and that in any event the Treasury would never agree. So we had to do the best with what we had.

My other concern about the Circuit Bench was that at Bristol almost all the judges came from the Bristol Bar. This caused an incestuous and cosy atmosphere, so I decreed that any new appointment from Bristol should, at any rate initially, sit at one of the other centres. We had difficulty in finding suitable judges to sit in some of the more remote areas, such as Cornwall. When I mentioned this to Gerald Gardiner he said, 'The church has the same problem. When I asked the Archbishop of Canterbury how he dealt with it he replied, 'We put an advertisement in *Horse and Hound*.' But I was never allowed to do this.

I also visited the offices of all the courts in which I sat and, when I had an early day, would drive over to the outlying courts and visit their offices. My purpose was to meet the staff and discuss any problems they had with listing and the calling of jurors, another field of public dissatisfaction. I soon learnt that these visits were much appreciated, some clerks saying that they had never previously met a judge and that it was refreshing to discuss the consequences of their work from the receiving end. However, the Circuit Administrator gently chided me, saying that I was talking to too many junior people. I replied that in the army I had been taught to talk to everybody and that junior people often had useful ideas.

The Circuit Administrator was Ian Ashworth, a product of Manchester Grammar School and Queen's College, Oxford. After qualifying as a solicitor, he had entered local government and at an early age had become Town Clerk of Rugby. When the courts service was set up he had applied for, and been appointed, Circuit Administrator. I believe he had found the initial setting up of the system a challenge, but by the time it was running smoothly felt that it gave little scope for his talents. He was a Janeite and a highly intelligent and cultured man. Our personal relations remained excellent and he and his wife were regular guests at the lodgings whenever I was at Bristol. We each of us knew exactly the limits of our own powers and influence and were careful not to offend the other, or to trespass on his territory. But I suspect that he was relieved when Desmond and I were replaced by the more benign rule of our successors, Peter Bristow and Gerry Sheldon.

But the rôle of the Presiding judge was not confined in my view to the immediate work of the courts and the appointments of judges. Every year Desmond and I held a circuit sentencing conference attended by all Circuit judges, Deputy Circuit judges and recorders, to try to encourage a consistent approach to sentencing. I also held meetings of the registrars, whose jurisdiction in Family work had become increasingly important and who I felt had been excluded from the main stream of judicial thought. I addressed the magistrates of each county of the circuit, principally on their domestic and Juvenile court jurisdiction and encouraged discussion about their problems, especially the difficult question of bail, following the passing of the Bail Act which limited their powers. Many were worried that burglars, especially if granted bail, would commit as many burglaries as possible while awaiting trial, so as to provide themselves with some cash when they were released from prison. I held meetings of all the prosecuting solicitors at each centre, in those days mostly private practitioners who were instructed by the police, and tried to persuade them not to include too many counts in their indictments, since over-indicting was already causing problems. I visited every prison on the circuit and met all the governors. Finally, greatly daring, I held a conference for all Chief Constables and their deputies and assistants from every police force on the circuit. Many of the senior judiciary maintained that, in order to preserve the independence of the judiciary, there should be no contact between the judges and the police. I thought that the police played such a vital rôle in the administration of justice that there should be at least an exchange of views on subjects of common interest. At the outset of the conference I made it clear that I was not prepared to discuss questions, such as sentencing policy, which were solely a matter for the judges. But we did discuss such things as the waiting time between arrest and committal for trial by the magistrates, over-indicting and the charging of offences of conspiracy and affray where the charging of substantive offences would be appropriate. I also pointed out that much time in court was taken up by challenges by defendants to their written statements taken by the police and suggested that the police should improve their procedures either by recording verbatim the questions and answers as they were given, instead of writing up their notebooks subsequently, or of tape-recording the interviews. We had what diplomats call a 'full and frank discussion' on all these questions, although, from what I read in the newspapers, most of them still remain unresolved. But I am sure that the conference did nothing but good.

Each of our main centres on the circuit was quite different. The lodgings at Bristol were on Clifton Downs among the houses of the old haute bourgeoisie of Bristol and next door to the Mansion House. Judy owned a beautiful lurcher called Tessa, who always accompanied us on circuit.

It was at Bristol that I tried my only IRA case, amid tight security. The police insisted, when I went to Lynch for the weekend, that I should be accompanied by an armed escort from the police special branch. On the Saturday he came to the meet of the hounds in a police Landrover and followed the hounds all day, to his evident enjoyment. It was thought that I would be a difficult target so long as I kept on the move on my horse. Next day he came to church at Selworthy with Judy and me. As she left the church an old lady said to Judy, 'What a nice-looking young man that was sitting in your pew. Is he a friend of your children?' 'No,' said Judy, 'he had an automatic pistol strapped under his armpit.'

Once, when at Bristol, I spent a day at court in Gloucester where I had had a happy

CITY AND COUNTY OF

THE CITY OF GLOUCESTER

SUMMER

ASSIZES

1969

HAROLD KEITH FISHER, Esq., Sheriff

NOTICE IS HEREBY GIVEN

That on MONDAY, the 30th day of JUNE, 1969, the ASSIZES and GENERAL
GAOL DELIVERY for the said City and County are appointed to be holden at
the SHIRE HALL, GLOUCESTER

before THE HONOURABLE

SIR MAURICE LEGAT LYELL

and THE HONOURABLE

SIR ROBIN HORACE WALFORD DUNN, M.C.

Two of the Judges of the Supreme Court of Judicature.

THE COURT WILL PROCEED TO BUSINESS ON

TUESDAY, the 1st day of JULY, 1969

At 11 o'clock a.m., When all Justices of the Peace, Mayors, Coroners, Escheators, Jurors summoned
Prosecutors, Witnesses and others concerned, are required to give their attendance.

All matrimonial and civil causes for trial at these Assizes must be entered with the District
Registrar at the District Registry, Hillfield, London Road, Gloucester, not later than 14 days before the
said 30th day of June, 1969.

GORDON WILFRED LANGLEY-SMITH,

Solicitor, City Under-Sheriff.

City Sheriff's Office: Westgate Chambers, Berkeley Street, Gloucester.   1st June, 1969

John Jennings (Gloucester) Ltd.

Poster for Gloucester summer assizes, 1969.

time with Maurice Lyell at one of my first assizes. Now High Court judges no longer
go there regularly, but I wished to show the flag, so arranged a day of pleas of guilty.
However, as soon as they saw a red judge walk into court all the defendants pleaded
not guilty, so my day was wasted as no witnesses had been warned to be present. In
the evening I was invited to dine by the Gloucestershire Magistrates' Club at the old
lodgings where I had previously stayed in Gloucester. I was surprised to notice at
dinner that no women were present, as there is always a large proportion of women
on the Bench, and asked the chairman of the club for the reason. 'Oh,' he said, 'this
club is not open to all magistrates. Those considered suitable are invited by the
committee to join. And we never invite women.' This could only have happened in
Gloucestershire, as I made plain to the chairman.

In the summer we always went to Winchester and stayed in the beautiful Queen
Anne house in the Cathedral Close. Judy and I loved to go on a warm evening and
sit in the cool of the cathedral for choral evensong, sung by the cathedral choir. I
believe that people come to Winchester from Roman Catholic countries from all
over the world to listen to the pre-Reformation music, which they cannot hear in
their own countries. Tessa and I used to walk in the early mornings through the

college grounds, along the Itchen to the ancient hospital of St Cross, the origin of the hospital in Trollope's novel *The Warden*. Sometimes I returned carrying a squirrel or a rabbit caught by Tessa. My first cousin, Prudence Balfour, lived in a beautiful house about ten miles from Winchester and we spent many happy times there with her and her husband Colin, who had himself been High Sheriff. Prudence had all the Colvin brains and ability and was chairman of her local Bench, as well as doing all kinds of other work in the county. But the great attraction of Winchester to us was the fishing on the chalk streams. Francis Tuke, chairman of Barclays Bank, allowed Judy to fish his water at Wherwell on the Test, where she caught many fine fish, including two years running the best fish caught on the Upper Test. She would spend most of the days with Tessa on the river while I was in court, although sometimes in the evenings we would go down together for a picnic supper and fishing, either on the Test or on the Itchen where the Baring family kindly allowed us to fish their beats. These were magical times beside the deep swirling oily looking water, with the lush vegetation and teeming wildlife on the banks.

The courts at Winchester were I suppose the worst in the country. They had been built adjacent to the castle, the old assize court, in the sixties and were extremely ugly and grandiose. No advice had been taken by the architect as to the internal requirements for law courts. The judge was perched so high up the wall that he could not see counsel in the front row. The jury rooms were like airless cells so that the jurymen became claustrophobic. I never allowed them to be used in a difficult case where there was likely to be a long retirement, insisting that the jury should use the 'reception room', which had been constructed so that the judges might hold receptions after court, a quite unnecessary facility. Behind the courts the corridors were wide and the judges' rooms unnecessarily large, causing great wastage of space. The whole layout was a disaster and must have cost the rate-payers of Hampshire, who paid for the courts before the Courts Act, a fortune.

On my first visit to Winchester John Pelly was High Sheriff. The evening I arrived the Under Sheriff called on me in a great state saying, 'I understand that the High Sheriff was divorced by your sister. I do hope you will not be caused any embarrassment.' I reassured him and next morning John arrived looking very smart in his Coldstream Guards frock coat. After the formal presentations we moved together to one side of the room and John said, 'Well, Robin, old cock, I never expected to see you dressed up like Father Christmas.' Thereafter Judy and I saw John and his then wife Hazel, whom he had married while farming in Rhodesia after the war, whenever we went to Winchester, visiting his beautiful estate at Preshaw. It was a delight to us both when he remarried Barbara after Hazel's death.

One year when we were at Winchester a murder was committed in Dorset. Since I was assured that the case would last for at least a week, I decided that it should be tried at Dorchester with a Dorset jury instead of at Winchester. The lodgings were a few miles outside Dorchester in the middle of Hardy country in a house belonging to Peter Birley, who had been a dancing partner of Judy's in London before the war,

Peter and his wife moving out while we were in residence. It caused some amusement that soon after the judge's car left for court in the mornings, Peter would arrive to entertain the judge's wife. The case became known as the 'harpoon murder'. The wife of an army sergeant had left him and set up home with another sergeant in the same regiment. The husband bought a cross-bow which fired a metal harpoon, a lethal weapon, waited outside the house after dark and when the other man came out with the dog shot him in the chest. He died in hospital. The defence was diminished responsibility, which would have reduced the offence to manslaughter, although there was evidence that the killing was deliberate, since the defendant had had the cross-bow for some months and had even practised shooting it against his garage door. I summed up in the afternoon, breaking off so that the jury would not have to retire late, as I thought they might find the decision difficult, and sent them out soon after I had sat next morning. They took all day to reach a verdict and eventually by a majority returned a verdict of guilty of murder. The verdict was academic, since I had determined to pass a sentence of life imprisonment even if they had returned a verdict of guilty of manslaughter. I had formed the view that the defendant was an exceptionally dangerous man, who might re-offend if in the future he was subjected to stress. It was and is the practice for judges, when passing a sentence of life imprisonment, to write personally to the Home Secretary stating the determinate sentence he would have passed appropriate to the gravity of the offence. When the prisoner comes up for his periodic reviews the judge who tried the case is asked by the Home Office to comment for the Parole Board on the various reports from psychiatrists and prison officers on the prisoner's performance while in custody. I was interested in this case that the assessments of the various experts were similar to my own and he served a very long sentence.

There is no doubt that the mandatory life sentence for murder should be abolished and that judges should have a discretion to pass the appropriate sentence, as they do for all other offences. The mandatory life sentence was introduced when capital punishment was abolished to placate the capital punishment lobby. No judge today would be in favour of capital punishment. Even Rayner Goddard once said, 'Capital punishment does not matter. It is no deterrent. But we must keep the birch for the under twenty-ones.' However effective a deterrent the birch might be, its reintroduction would plainly be unacceptable today. But Rayner was right about capital punishment. After the Homicide Act was passed in 1957 creating two categories of murder (capital for murders in pursuit of crime and of the police, and non-capital for other murders) offences of capital murder increased and those of non-capital decreased. The vast majority of murders are family murders: I have never tried one which was not. They are usually committed after months or even years of friction and stress and the murderer loses control. Those who commit them do not think of the consequences, so hanging is no deterrent. To be obliged to pass the same sentence for those murders as for a case like my Dairy murder where the manager was shot down in cold blood by an armed robber, or for a terrorist who kills innocent civilians or policemen, is to make a mockery of justice. Judges are well accustomed to assess the gravity of a particular offence and should be allowed, if appropriate, to pass a determinate sentence for murder, as they are for manslaughter and rape, which both carry maximum sentences of life imprisonment.

One evening after court at Dorchester, the High Sheriff, who was also treasurer of the Cattistock Hunt, invited me to visit the kennels and judge the hounds. I replied that my only experience was of judging bitches in the Family Division, although I should perhaps have added mad dogs as well. However, we spent a pleasant hour in the kennels, which I found a welcome relief after a long day in court.

The lodgings at Exeter were the best in the country. Each judge had a suite, including a study where he could work in peace, instead of sitting at a table in the communal study shared with the other judge or judges. The house was a large Victorian mansion in a spacious garden overlooking the River Exe and the canal, close to the Maritime Museum. I used to walk Tessa along the canal bank before breakfast and Judy would take her out to the woods and moors while I was in court. When I had become a judge we decided, for the first time, that we must have two cars. So Judy bought a maroon Alfa Romeo sports car, as she loved to drive a fast car, leaving me the Volvo estate to carry the luggage on circuit. I always associate 'Alfie', as we called the car, with those times on circuit. We had many friends round Exeter, especially Anne and Anthony Goodall from Pegasus Club days, who lived at Moretonhampstead. Although Anthony had a first-class brain, he never had much practice at the Bar. Now he was the senior Circuit judge in Devon and a tower of strength. Anne had been a Chichester, an old Devon family, so that Anthony was ideally placed to represent the law in the county. Judy once said to me, 'Why can't we live a life like Anthony and Anne? He lives less than an hour's drive from all his courts and can dispense justice from his own bed, instead of moving continually round the country as we do.' Judy's mother sometimes stayed with us for a few days at Exeter and also Bristol, which she much enjoyed, saying how much more comfortable the lodgings were than when she had gone on circuit with Judy's father. We made friends with Eric, Bishop of Exeter. I do not know what happened to the bishops of my generation who were appointed after the war. I met many of them while on circuit and they seemed to have abandoned their traditional function of the cure of souls and to have taken up every transient and trendy fashion which caught their fancy. Some even seemed doubtful of the existence of God and the fundamentals of Christianity. It was as if a judge questioned the basis of the law. But Eric was an exception. He had served with distinction in the Light Infantry in the war and was a proper pastoral bishop.

One of the High Sheriffs of Devon in my time was Field Marshal Dick Hull, who had been Chief of the Defence Staff, and brought military distinction to the office. Once, when we were processing into the cathedral for the annual legal Sunday service, a man from the crowd shouted, 'You bastards. I hate to see the red judges in Exeter. God knows I've suffered enough from you,' and approached me menacingly. The High Sheriff, who was immediately in front of me, quickly turned round, his hand flying to the hilt of his sword. Fortunately a young policeman stepped quickly forward and defused the situation.

While at Exeter I tried a man named Norton for burglary. There were fourteen different counts of burglary at different country houses all over the south and west of England. Peter Rawlinson prosecuted and Robert Harman, an experienced criminal silk, defended Norton. After two or three days Norton dismissed Robert and insisted on defending himself. The result was a nightmare. Norton disputed every piece of evidence and insisted on all facts being strictly proved. The case lasted from 1st October until Christmas and was the longest case to have been tried at the Crown Court at Exeter. The prosecution evidence was overwhelming, especially as Norton's accomplice gave evidence for the Crown and I knew that the only thing that could go wrong was if I showed any bias against Norton or made a mistake in my summing up. The High Sheriff, Michael Holland-Hibbert, now Lord Knutsford, said to me during the case, 'I do not know how you can have such patience.' I replied that I had no alternative. I summed up for several days, dealing with the voluminous evidence on each count separately, and the jury returned unanimous verdicts of guilty on all counts. My summing up was not helped by my having a cold in the head. I sentenced Norton to fourteen years imprisonment, which the Court of Appeal reduced to ten. One Lord Justice who had been sitting said, 'We thought you must have given him ten years for the burglaries and four for wasting your time.' But Norton did not learn his lesson. Soon after he was released he was arrested for further burglaries and there was a second long trial in which he again defended himself with the same result. After being released from that sentence he was arrested a third time for a further series of burglaries and once again defended himself. I was surprised to read in the newspapers that in the course of that trial Norton had become uncontrollable and the judge had stopped the trial and directed the jury to return a verdict of 'not guilty', on the ground that Norton was under so much strain that he was unable to conduct his own defence properly. At my trial Norton and I always treated one another with courtesy and I have never heard of a trial being stopped on such grounds. In some of the IRA trials, when the defendants were disruptive in the dock, they were sent to cells which had been wired and proceedings were broadcast, so that they could hear what was happening in court and intervene if they wished. I do not see why a similar procedure could not have been adopted in Norton's third trial.

There were advantages to Norton in the course which he adopted. He received special privileges in prison while awaiting trial and then in custody pending his various appeals: a cell to himself and facilities for interviews with his solicitor and for legal books and papers to be available in his cell. But I believe his primary motivation was hatred of the police. Norton had objected at the outset to being tried at Exeter, saying that country juries were 'green' and did not know how the police worked. He demanded to be tried at the Old Bailey where, he said, the juries knew all about the police. I refused this, saying that almost all the witnesses came from the West Country where most of the burglaries had been committed and that was where the trial should take place.

Although an extreme case and quite exceptional, the Norton trial showed how our whole system of criminal justice could be almost brought to a halt if every defendant insisted on his rights. Under our procedure a defendant is entitled to insist on every fact and every document necessary for proof of the charge to be strictly proved and this can be a time-consuming process. Efforts were made by the use of pre-trial reviews to agree as many facts as possible, so that the jury could concentrate on the essential issues. But this depended on the cooperation of the defence and in its absence there was no sanction, as in civil procedure where the defence can be struck out if procedural orders are not complied with. Fred Lawton, probably the best criminal judge of my time, used to suggest in the presence of the jury that certain facts should be agreed and this put the defence in a difficulty because if they refused to agree they might lose the vital sympathy of the jury. But in the last resort nothing could be done. Only draconian legislation, probably unacceptable to parliament and public opinion, can resolve the problem.

In the course of the trial I learnt a good deal about the methods of professional burglars. After a successful burglary Norton would leave the West Country before dawn in his hired car and drive into London on the motorway during the morning rush hour. The bulk of the silver would be taken to a house in St John's Wood, where it would immediately be melted down and sold in bars. The rest, apart from easily identifiable articles which would be sold privately to a receiver, would be sold in the open market in Petticoat Lane. Lord Vestey's house, Stowell Park, had been burgled on a Wednesday and amongst other things a crested silver wine cooler was stolen. The wine cooler was sold on the Saturday in Petticoat Lane to a dealer from Birmingham, without any supporting documents evidencing the sale. The Birmingham dealer sold it over the weekend in a fully documented sale to a specialist silver dealer in Stow-on-the-Wold. He re-sold it on the Monday to a well-known jeweller and silversmith in Bond Street, who put it on display. Lady Vestey, visiting the shop a few days later to replace her stolen silver, saw it bearing her family crest and recognised it. I asked the manager of the Bond Street shop who gave evidence, 'Did you not make any inquiries before you bought it? After all it was crested.' He replied, 'If we made inquiries about every piece of crested silver we were offered we would never buy anything.' After the case I wrote to the Attorney General suggesting that stringent conditions, as for the sale of lead, should be introduced for the sale of silver, so that the parties to such sales could be more readily identified. He replied that such conditions would be impractical. Having been burgled myself three times during our marriage and lost all our family silver, I could not consider this reply satisfactory.

From Exeter we would move to Bodmin. Until the advent of the railways the Cornwall assizes were held at Launceston, just across the Tamar, to shorten the coach journey for the judges from Exeter. But when the railway was extended to Bodmin the assizes were moved there and an elegant court and judges' lodgings were built. It was the only place where the judges walked in their robes from the lodgings across the road to the court opposite. Now the courts have been moved to Truro, a spacious eighteenth-century county town, more accessible from Penzance. There was not much to see at Bodmin, except the depot of the Duke of Cornwall's Light Infantry and the old county lunatic asylum, a Victorian gothic building surrounded by a high wall. There were several acres of garden, where the inmates had grown their own vegetables and kept pigs and poultry, doing their own laundry and generally looking after themselves. It was a structured environment where the inmates were kept busy and could not hurt themselves or anyone else. Some spent their lives there. I thought how much better they were cared for than the misfits of our present society. There are many people today in prison who should not be there. They are inadequate people incapable of managing their own lives without committing criminal offences. It was, and I believe still is, extremely difficult to find a place in a secure hospital. There are very few such establishments in the country and beds are reserved for only the most dangerous offenders. so if a hospital order was made on the recommendation of two doctors, the offender was sent to an ordinary NHS psychiatric hospital, where there was no security and from which he could, and often did, simply walk out. In any event he would soon be discharged 'into the community' with probably a minimum of supervision and would almost certainly re-offend. So the only option for the protection of the public was to send him to prison, often for a long sentence. Like many other judges I complained to the Home Office about this lack of facilities with no result.

I once tried a hunting case at Bodmin where a lady sued a fellow member of the field whose horse had jumped on top of her after she had fallen at one of the Cornish banks while out hunting. I thoroughly enjoyed the case and behaved extremely badly. I gave most of the evidence myself, took over the final speeches and gave judgement for the defendant. However, Swinton Thomas, who appeared for one of the parties and became a popular Presiding judge of the Western Circuit, told me afterwards that everyone, including the plaintiff, had been happy at the result.

One year, when Arscott Molesworth-St Aubyn was High Sheriff, he entertained us to dinner at Pencarrow, his beautiful family home near Bodmin, which he opened specially for the occasion. He lived near Holsworthy on the Devon border, where one Saturday he asked me to shoot snipe. He showed me his family game books which went back two hundred years and recorded that year after year large numbers of snipe had settled in the same fields on almost exactly the same dates in December. The guns stood behind a Cornish stone-faced bank while the snipe were driven towards us by beaters. They came at high speed, jinking and swirling in the wind and were difficult to hit. It was very exciting and I was lucky to shoot one in the first drive, so honour was satisfied as I am not a good shot. I believe that Tetcott Manor is one of the very few places in the country where snipe are driven. The following week

Judy caught a salmon on the River Camel, where salmon fishing continues almost until Christmas. There must be few places where you can shoot a snipe and kill a salmon during the same week.

After Bodmin we usually went for a week to Plymouth, which had never been an assize town, although it was the largest town in Devon with great historical associations. However, the city fathers were most anxious that the High Court judges should visit Plymouth and offered us the use of Lady Astor's fine terraced house on the Hoe overlooking Plymouth Sound, which had been left to the city corporation on her death. The house was fully furnished, including many photographs of Lady Astor welcoming Winston Churchill and other leading figures to Plymouth when she was MP, the first woman MP in the country. We made friends with the Admiral, who was Commander-in-Chief of the Eastern Atlantic and kindly invited us to one of his morning briefings in front of an enormous screen showing the disposition of every Soviet ship and aircraft in the Atlantic and European waters.

During my time as Presiding judge I replaced a Queen's Bench judge while on circuit, so was engaged wholly on Queen's Bench work, mostly serious crime. It had been received wisdom that juries on the Western Circuit would not convict of rape if the defence was consent. There was always at least one middle-aged, middle-class woman on the jury who, if the victim had encouraged the man in any way, would say, 'She is no better than she should be,' and would persuade the jury to acquit. When the property qualifications for jurors were abolished and the minimum age reduced to eighteen, there was a dramatic change. The young jurors thought that just because a woman had invited a man to have coffee in her house, it did not mean that she wished to have sexual intercourse with him. So the rate of conviction rose sharply. Sentencing in rape cases was always difficult. Rape covers such a wide spectrum. There is a great difference between the criminality of a man who assaults a woman in a dark alley, or even enters her house, and rapes her, and that of the man who spends the evening alone with a woman friend, who allows some love-making and then when the man is thoroughly aroused refuses intercourse. But all are guilty of rape and the judge must decide the sentence. The campaign for sterner sentences for rape was just beginning when I was a High Court judge and I always made a point when passing what might appear, without a full knowledge of the facts, to be a lenient sentence, of explaining in detail the reasons for my sentence.

Arson was a crime which also caused sentencing problems. Pyromania is a recognised medical condition, one of the facets of which is that the fire-raiser cannot resist watching the blaze which he has caused. Many arsonists were arrested while watching the fire brigade fight the flames. Many already had several convictions for arson, so long sentences were often necessary.

But I found the most difficult crime for the sentencer was incest. In cases of children, or when there had been any force or coercion, long sentences were inevitable, which had to be served in solitary confinement or special prison wings for sexual offenders for their own protection from other prisoners. One senior headmistress of a comprehensive school once begged me never to allow bail to be granted to a man charged with incest, since his presence in the house after being charged had such a deplorable effect on the family. But there were many cases involving consenting adults, especially brothers and sisters or fathers and grown-up daughters who had taken over the rôle of their mothers after her death, where the criminality was minimal, although they were all equally guilty of incest. Once, at Birmingham, one of my brethren was faced with an unusual problem. One of the daughters of a large close-knit family was a nymphomaniac who had become a prostitute. In order to remove her from the streets the family all conferred together and persuaded her to allow herself to be serviced by their father. This continued satisfactorily for some time until an interested neighbour discovered what was happening and informed the police. After consulting with all his High Court brethren on the circuit and the Lord Chief Justice, the judge gave them both an absolute discharge.

There has been a great change in public attitudes to sexual offences during my time in the law and this is reflected in the length of sentences, since judges are sensitive to public opinion. I once sentenced a man at Plymouth, who had pleaded guilty to buggery of a boy under the age of consent. He had two previous convictions for buggery, both with consenting adults when such conduct constituted an offence. In both cases he had been sentenced to fourteen years imprisonment. I thought of the remark of Malcolm Hilbery, when sentencing a bugger at the Old Bailey, 'I'm not a dirty man myself and I don't like dirty men.' This reflected public opinion and the attitude of the judges in the fifties, although Judy's father always said that he felt sorry for the homosexuals who appeared before him since they could not help themselves, but felt obliged to pass long sentences.

In 1976 Frank McGrath retired as my clerk and found an excellent replacement in Neil Ferguson, also from the metropolitan police in which he had risen to the rank of inspector. Neil had been born in the Outer Hebrides and spoke only Gaelic until he was seven years old when he learnt to speak beautiful English with no trace of an accent. Like Frank he was a keen golfer and used to entertain us by dressing up in his highland costume and marching round the lodgings before dinner playing his bagpipes. Sadly he died of a sudden heart attack shortly after his retirement. He was a charming man and an excellent clerk.

My four years as Presiding judge were the happiest and most fulfilling of my time on the Bench. I enjoyed the variety of the work in court, I enjoyed running the circuit with Desmond and I enjoyed the social life with Judy in the different lodgings. We made many friends and we both look back to those times on the Western Circuit with great affection. After I retired Ian Ashworth wrote inviting me to sit on the circuit whenever I wanted, trying crime, civil or divorce, whichever I preferred and offering to open the lodgings at Bristol or Exeter for us whenever we wished. I was tempted, but Judy said, 'It would be like being ghosts at our own funerals. I could not bear to go back to those places where we have been so happy. We could never recapture the atmosphere.' So I refused. But I felt flat and deflated returning to the Family Division in 1978 and taking my turn on the circuit cab-rank, although it was not to last for long. After a year I received a letter from the Prime Minister inviting me to accept an appointment to the Court of Appeal. This was a genuine surprise. When Tom Denning had mentioned the possibility some months earlier I had said, 'I am not clever enough for the Court of Appeal. Anyway I believe I am better at dealing with witnesses than the law.' But when the offer came I accepted, remembering the military maxim, 'Never volunteer, and never refuse a good offer.'

CHAPTER XXVI

Lord Justice, 1980–84

The Court of Appeal is the best working men's club in the country. It is also the power house of the law of England. If you succeeded in passing the strict security to the Law Courts just before 10.30 am or 2 pm on a day when the court was sitting and gained entry to the high-ceilinged, red-carpeted corridor which runs behind the Appeal Courts, you would see small groups, each of three elderly men in wigs and black robes, standing in earnest discussion outside the door of each court. This is where the law is made. By 1980 the court was full of my friends and contemporaries, whom I had been against at the Bar and known well when we were High Court judges. Peter Oliver, who had preceded me as pupil to Harry Phillimore, had been a Chancery judge and was appointed on the same day as me. John Donaldson and Desmond Ackner had just been appointed. Ted Eveleigh had been appointed a couple of years before. Roger Ormrod and Roualeyn Cumming-Bruce were from the Family Division and Jo Stephenson, Fred Lawton, Sebag Shaw and George Waller were all old friends. We were joined shortly afterwards by Tasker Watkins, Patrick O'Connor, Hugh Griffiths and Michael Fox who had married Hazel. Someone once said, 'Nobody wants to be in the Court of Appeal until all their friends are there.' We were the wartime generation and when Tasker (VC) and Hugh (MC) were appointed shortly after me, a legal journal remarked, 'The trouble with the Court of Appeal, as at present constituted, is that more of its recent members were decorated for gallantry than received firsts in law at university.'

The court sat to hear civil appeals in five or six divisions and two or three Lords Justices presided in each of the courts of the Criminal Division. The senior Lord Justice always presided in each court: seniority means a great deal to the judiciary. When we processed on ceremonial occasions each grade of judge walked in strict seniority of appointment. The senior Lord Justice when I was appointed was John Megaw, who had sat in the Restrictive Practices Court and whom I knew well. Denys Buckley, who had also sat in the Restrictive Practices Court, presided in the court which heard appeals from the Chancery Division. As there were only eighteen Lords Justices, retired Lords Justices and often a puisne judge sat to make up the numbers.

But towering above us all was the Master of the Rolls, Tom Denning. He had first sat in the Court of Appeal in 1948 and, after a spell in the House of Lords, had become Master of the Rolls in 1962. He was, quite simply, a genius. He had the amazing facility of expressing complicated thoughts in clear simple English. He had a vast knowledge of the law, especially case law, which he used to enable him to do justice in the particular case. He had a passion for justice and at the same time an original mind which enabled him to make changes in the whole field of law, in a way which I believe had never been achieved by any previous judge, certainly not in this century. Some of his judgments, especially in the fifties and sixties, were classics. At the same time he was a kind and charming person, with a love of his fellow human beings. He never forgot a face or a name and knew everybody in the law: judges, barristers, solicitors, academics and students in whom he was specially interested. By the time that I was appointed he was a public figure and his views were frequently reported by the press and the media. This led to his downfall, since one of his very few weaknesses was a love of publicity.

The court changed its constitution every three weeks and, in accordance with precedent, I spent my first three weeks sitting in Tom's court. Judy came to court that first day and in the evening said, 'The speed of that old man! I could see you were miles behind him.' When I had been at the Bar each division of the court had heard appeals from a separate division of the High Court. But Tom changed that. His clerk arranged the lists and somehow all the most interesting and important cases found their way into Tom's court, regardless of their origin. Only Denys Buckley kept the Chancery appeals. When he retired there was no Chancery Lord Justice sufficiently senior to preside and it was suggested that an ex-Chancery judge should always preside on Chancery appeals, whatever his seniority. This, however, was overruled by the majority and Chancery appeals were listed like any other. The system was unfortunate for John Megaw, who, as senior Lord Justice, often found himself dealing with County Court and other appeals of less interest. John should have been a Law Lord but I do not think that Tom fully appreciated his great qualities.

On Monday mornings we heard applications by litigants in person (Mad Mondays they were called). Tom's unique method of dealing with these was an education. He would go straight to the heart of the matter and even when the applications were dismissed, as they usually were, the parties went away happy. Many were regular attenders, enjoying the opportunity of appearing before Tom. 'You here again Mrs. Snooks,' he would say. 'What can I do for you this morning?' His court was always crowded, especially by students and foreign lawyers and all felt that we were in the presence of a great judge dispensing justice.

But sitting in Tom's court was not all plain sailing. He seldom reserved judgment and when we clustered round his chair at the end of the case would mutter, 'We're all agreed there's nothing in this appeal, aren't we? Let's get rid of it.' He always gave the leading extempore judgment himself, in his characteristic way, making the facts come alive and linking the law to them in a way which was comprehensible to everyone. But we never quite knew on what grounds he would allow or dismiss the appeal. Sidney Templeman, who was sitting with us, said to me, 'Being number two in Tom's court is the hardest work in the Court of Appeal. You cannot just agree with Tom for fear of being party to some heresy which will become the law of England. You must listen like a lynx to every word he says. It is safer, even if you agree with the result, to give a short judgment stating your own ground for disposing of the appeal.' All continental courts deliver unanimous judgments, as does the criminal division of the Court of Appeal and the House of Lords adopts the same practice in many cases. It makes for certainty in the law, but inevitably involves compromise by the judges and some say is inconsistent with the judicial oath. Although in reserved judgments the Court of Appeal may deliver a judgment of the court, in many judgments Lords Justices give their own reasons and sometimes dissent from the majority. This practice over the years has helped the development of the common law, since some of the great dissenting judgments have, in a different context, enabled the law to be changed.

During the years before my appointment Tom had been reversed with increasing regularity by the House of Lords. Some of the more conventional Law Lords thought that in some cases Tom had gone too far in his passion for law reform. 'Tom has been naughty again,' they would say indulgently. Tom did not like this, especially since all the English Law Lords had in the past sat at his feet as Lords Justices and did not hesitate to say so publicly. This caused some ill-feeling between the Lords and the Court of Appeal and, on my appointment, one retired Lord Justice wrote, 'I hope you will be able to deal with those small-minded little men in the House of Lords.' Inevitably the Court of Appeal had much more influence than the Lords on the development of the law, simply because we heard so many more cases: fifteen hundred a year in the Court of Appeal, compared with ninety in the Lords. And many of the latter were tax cases and other specialised branches of the law. But occasionally the Lords would decide a case of general application by which we were all bound. If Tom did not approve, he would say so in trenchant terms and find a way of distinguishing the case. Nor did Tom like being overruled in his own court, which happened once when Patrick O'Connor and I were sitting with him. The case was about legal aid and, because of the wording of the certificate, the successful plaintiff was unable to recover his costs from the legal aid fund. He had clearly suffered an injustice, but nothing could be done because of the clear wording of the Legal Aid Act and the regulations, which provided that the certificate should be conclusive. Patrick and I could see no way out, but Tom refused to accept that an injustice could ever be upheld. So he dissented on a ground which neither of us could support. He said to us, 'I lay in bed all last night worrying about this poor man. The Legal Aid Committee must have made a mistake and I shall apply the Slip Rule.' This was a rule which enabled slips to be rectified when an order was drawn up which did not reflect the intention of the judge, as stated in his judgment. It was unfortunately not appropriate to the circumstances of our appeal. It was some months before Patrick or I sat with Tom again.

After so long in the backwater of the Family Division, interesting as it was, I was pleased to be back in the mainstream of the law, although the width of the stream and the speed of the current nearly submerged me. The Court of Appeal not only hears appeals from all divisions of the High Court and the County Court, but also from all manner of tribunals, including the Social Security Commissioners and the Employment Appeals Tribunal, which has established a jurisprudence of its own with two series of specialised law reports covering the whole field of employment law. The court also hears appeals in civil matters from the Divisional Court of the Queen's Bench Division, which deals with applications for judicial review. This, over the previous twenty years, had been developed from the ancient remedies stemming from the prerogative of the Crown. It enabled the courts to question the decisions of public authorities, government departments and local authorities and the jurisdiction exercised by the Divisional Court was the nearest thing we have to a continental administrative court. Indeed some academics thought that our remedies were more effective than those on the Continent. This jurisdiction had gradually been developed by Tom Denning and Scott Reid, the latter sitting in the Lords. A delicate balance had to be struck between the powers of the government and the powers of the courts. In general the courts were not concerned with the merits of the case, but were concerned to see that the proper procedures had been followed and that the decision was not wholly unreasonable. In one of my first cases, sitting with Tom, the Borough Council of Windsor had made an order under a particular section of the Highways Act prohibiting lorries from driving through the centre of that royal and ancient borough. I thought this was sensible, but there was doubt whether the order had been made under the right section and whether proper notices had been given. Tom said to me, 'I agree with you that this is a good idea. But we must keep an eye on these bureaucrats and make sure they have gone about it in the proper way.' This, to me, summed up the whole law of judicial review.

To Tom any minute not spent in court was wasted. If we finished an appeal at 4 pm we would go straight on to the next, even though only fifteen minutes of court time remained. Once, when Roger Ormrod had to go to Oxford to address some undergraduates, he asked if Tom would rise at 4 pm so that he might catch the train. 'Of course,' said Tom. But when they rose Tom announced, 'The court will sit at 10.15 tomorrow, as we have had to rise early.' This practice of Tom's meant that all reading of papers and Law Reports and the writing of reserved judgments had to be done outside court hours. Tom said, 'I like to come with an open mind to each case. So I never read anything about it, except glance at the judgment and the notice of appeal, before I go into court.' He was a great believer in the value of oral argument and certainly I found that the cut and thrust of argument, not only between counsel but also between the members of the court and counsel, helped me to clarify issues and to arrive at a conclusion. But it was a time-consuming exercise, not least because much time was spent by counsel reading the judgment, the documents and the transcripts of evidence, as well as citing verbatim from the various relevant cases in the Law Reports. But in Tom's court, especially, because of the speed with which he saw the point, we seemed to get through the cases with expedition and the waiting lists were not much if at all reduced when John Donaldson became Master of the Rolls and introduced reforms to the procedure.

In order to keep abreast of the work I found it necessary to do a good deal of background work, regularly reading the Weekly Law Reports and the various learned journals; otherwise I found it difficult to keep pace with counsel in cases dealing with branches of the law with which I was not familiar. In writing reserved judgments I found much time had to be spent unravelling the facts of the case, since it was the practice for the leading judgment at any rate to recite the facts in some detail. In the Criminal Division each judge was given a summary of the facts, prepared in the Criminal Appeals office, which was extremely accurate and well presented. So the judge giving judgment could concentrate on the arguments of counsel and the reasons for the decision. Some of the classic nineteenth- and early twentieth-century judgments are quite short, running to perhaps a couple of pages of the Law Reports and setting out clearly the principles of law to be applied. Nowadays judgments are becoming longer and longer, much of them taken up with an elaborate statement of the facts and many short on statements of principle.

Much of our work in the Court of Appeal consisted of analysing the various relevant decisions in an attempt to extract a principle which applied to our particular case. This was also a time-consuming process, involving consideration of perhaps twenty or more cases. It became even worse when computers began to be used which recorded all decisions of the courts on a particular topic and not just those which had been reported in the Law Reports. In the course of argument in one case I mentioned a case with which I had been concerned which seemed to me to bear on the subject under discussion. All I could remember was that the case concerned a sewage farm. Next morning counsel returned triumphant saying, "We put Lord Justice Dunn – Sewage" on the screen, which came up with your Lordship's case.' Such are the marvels of modern science. But the law reporters exercise an intelligent discretion in deciding which cases to report and many of the cases from the computer were unhelpful, simply adding to the length of the case.

I noticed that the performance of the Bar was, on the whole, better than at first instance. I think this is probably because at first instance they are moving on shifting sands: nobody knows until the end of the case what facts the judge will find, whereas in the Court of Appeal there is at least a firm basis of fact on which to found submissions.

At first I thought I would not like to sit with two others. I had enjoyed sitting in my own court and running it in my own way. But I soon discovered that, particularly in difficult cases, it was a relief to sit with others, to watch their reactions to the case and to discuss the problems with them after court. They were all people whose judgment I respected and, even if I did not always agree, it was helpful to have their views. Fortunately, in my time, we all got on very well together and this had a good deal to do with the personality of Tom and the atmosphere he created, treating his Lords Justices truly as a band of brothers. The problem usually was to do justice as between the parties in the particular case, without bending the law in such a way as to make it uncertain and contrary to previous decisions. This was a more acute problem than at first instance, when almost all cases turned on the facts, since our decisions of law were binding not only on all lower courts but also on future decisions of the Court of Appeal. One case I remember where we had as near a 'cold' point of law as possible, the construction of a commercial document. 'Tell me,' said Tom to counsel for the appellant. 'Have you any merits?' 'No, my Lord,' said counsel. He told me afterwards that he had realised that that honest answer had been the end of his appeal. He could perhaps have quoted a remark of F. E. Smith when asked the same question, 'This is a naked point of law. Clothe it with merits and it loses its beauty.'

We used to spend part of each term sitting in the Criminal Division with two Queen's Bench judges or sometimes a judge from the Family Division. I had occasionally sat there myself as a puisne judge so knew something of the work of the court. It was much better organised than the Civil Division, necessarily so as there was an ever greater volume of work. Leave to appeal was necessary and when on circuit all judges were sent batches of applications which had to be decided on paper. Most could be refused out of hand. If in doubt the single judge could refer the case for argument before the full court. Even if leave was refused the applicant could re-apply to the full court but ran the risk of an increase in his sentence if the appeal proved frivolous. This procedure provided a useful filter system which could well be adopted in the Civil Division. One of the principal reasons for the backlog of work in that division is the hopeless nature of many of the appeals, since no leave is required for any final appeal from the High Court. In the Criminal Division the cases are carefully prepared by the staff of the Registrar of Criminal Appeals, at that time David Thompson who had been Registrar since 1965 and had worked in the office since 1954. He was a member of the Bar and a man of outstanding ability who had built up an efficient organisation with a competent staff. As well as the summary of the facts, which was invaluable, there were often helpful notes on the law and the relevant cases.

All this involved the judges in a great deal of reading before going into court. The work for Mondays and Tuesdays was read over the previous weekend; Wednesdays were 'reading days' in preparation for the work on Thursdays and Fridays. Over 80% of the cases were appeals against sentence and the three judges would assemble in the Lord Justice's room at 10 am to discuss our list, having marked our papers with a provisional sentence. If we all agreed that the sentence should be reduced I would say to counsel in court, 'Do you think you can do better than (say) three years?' The answer was invariably, 'No, my Lord.' The office indicated on the papers which of the three judges, in rotation, should give the judgment so that, unlike the Civil Division, we knew which case was earmarked for each one of us. All this meant that a great deal less time was spent in court on the individual cases. Appeals against conviction were more time-consuming and often difficult. The criminal law defines the state of mind which has to be proved before an accused can be found guilty of a particular offence and this is often difficult to define in language which is understandable by a jury. There were also difficult questions to be decided on the admissibility of evidence. So in many appeals against conviction judgment had to be reserved. The powers of the Criminal Division are defined by statute and are much more limited than those of the Civil Division. There are effectively only three grounds for an appeal against conviction: a misdirection of law by the judge in his summing up; a 'material irregularity' in the trial, such as the admission of inadmissible evidence; or an 'unsafe or unsatisfactory' verdict. In addition the court has limited power to quash a conviction or order a retrial if fresh evidence is produced before it. Some thought that the Court of Appeal, if satisfied that the fresh evidence was cogent, should always order a retrial, since to quash the conviction would be to usurp the function of the jury. But in some cases the fresh evidence was so strong that the conviction could safely be quashed. In most cases the evidence was suspect and did not stand up to close examination when compared with the evidence which the prosecution had called before the jury and the applications to call the fresh evidence were refused. Basically it is the jury in a criminal trial who are the judges of the facts. They give no reasons and the court has no power to review the facts and quash the conviction, even if it thinks that the verdict was wrong. This is a consequence of our system of trial by jury and, so long as that exists, to enlarge the powers of the Court of Appeal would be to replace trial by jury by trial by the judges. I often reflected upon these matters, which are self-evident to lawyers, when reading in the newspapers about the few 'miscarriages of justice' which came to light after I retired.

Soon after I became a Lord Justice Geoffrey Lane was appointed Lord Chief Justice in place of John Widgery. Apart from Rayner Goddard, who towered above his contemporaries and whose methods would not have been acceptable in the eighties, Geoffrey was the best Lord Chief Justice since the war. His responsibilities were heavy. He was responsible for the work of the important Divisional Court of the Queen's Bench Division; he was responsible for the administration of the Queen's Bench Division, including the circuits; and he was responsible for the work of the Criminal Division of the Court of Appeal. The accumulated burden of these responsibilities had destroyed the health of both his predecessors, Hubert Parker and John Widgery, and led to their early deaths. On his appointment I wrote congratulating Geoffrey, saying that he would need as much luck as when he started his operational tour as a pilot in Bomber Command in the war when he had won the AFC. Geoffrey wrote back, 'The odds in Bomber Command in 1943 were variously 8 to 1 or 12 to 1 against survival depending on the type of aeroplane. I imagine they are about the same here, though I am hoping the flak will be less accurate in 1980.' Sadly both the flak and his assessment of the odds against survival proved all too accurate.

Geoffrey's first move was to decentralise the work. John Widgery had himself spent much time sitting in the Divisional Court which he called 'The Lord Chief Justice's court' and, as his powers began to fail, the arrears of work in the court increased. Geoffrey nominated John Donaldson, a recently appointed Lord Justice, to preside in the Divisional Court and reduce the arrears. John had been appointed a judge by Gerald Gardiner at the early age of forty-six. In 1971 he became the first President of the National Industrial Relations Court, set up by the Heath government to bring the trade unions within the rule of law. When the Labour government came to power in 1974 the court was dissolved and John was denied any further judicial preferment, despite his undoubted ability as a judge. This was the worst example of political interference in judicial appointments in my time and was ironic since John's politics were if anything to the left of centre. It was not until the Conservative government came to power in 1979 that he was rightly appointed a Lord Justice. John took a remarkable grip of the Divisional Court and within a year the arrears had been eliminated. Thereafter a Lord Justice always presided in that court.

Geoffrey also appointed Tasker Watkins Deputy Chief Justice to supervise the running of the circuits through the Presiding judges. Geoffrey himself always sat in the Criminal Division and took a firm hand in the development of the criminal law. For the first time sentencing guidelines for different offences were laid down so as to encourage uniformity of sentencing. Out of court Geoffrey was an unassuming person and no politician who had no time to spare for public communication, which in any event he did not regard as part of a judge's function. His appointment coincided with the beginning of a press campaign against the judiciary, led by a few extremely articulate and influential commentators. They wholly overlooked the work he was doing to improve the administration of justice and the fact that it was the judges, and only the judges, who stood between the ever-increasing powers of government and the freedom of the individual. What price the freedom of the press if it was left to the untrammelled power of the executive?

In 1982 Tom Denning retired at the age of eighty-three. Peter Oliver was the preferred candidate of most of the Lords Justices. There had been a tradition that the position of Master of the Rolls should alternate between Chancery and Queen's Bench judges, and Tom had come from the Queen's Bench. Peter, as well as being a successful Chancery judge, had chaired a committee which had just produced a well received report on the reorganisation of some of the archaic procedures of the Chancery Division which must have dated back to the days of *Bleak House*. The views of the Lords Justices were sent 'through the usual channels' to the Prime Minister who replied, 'Lords Justices are not self-elected. They do not even have a constitutional right to be consulted about appointments to the Court of Appeal. I shall appoint the man I consider best suited for the job.' She appointed John

Donaldson.

John, while as passionately interested in the pursuit of justice as Tom Denning, regarded himself as having been appointed for a particular purpose, namely to improve the efficiency of the organisation of the Court of Appeal, to increase its throughput and to reduce the arrears of cases awaiting trial, though these were far less than in most other civilised countries, notably the United States. He appointed a registrar whose function was to be similar to that of the successful Registrar of Criminal Appeals, although he did not succeed in finding a David Thompson. Peter Oliver and I were charged with the task of interviewing candidates for the post which was advertised. I think it might have been better to have appointed an experienced Chancery or Queen's Bench Master, but that course was vetoed by the Lord Chancellor's department on the ground that the primary requirement was for an administrator. John also took steps to eliminate pending appeals which were not being actively prosecuted and to reduce the time spent in court on individual cases. He introduced a system of 'skeleton arguments' to be read by the judges before they went into court, he allowed 'reading days' as in the criminal division and he decreed that reserved judgments should be handed down instead of being read aloud by the judges in open court. He also arranged for the installation of a computer to assist the listing of cases. Certainly, during my time, these reforms had little effect on the lists.

One of John's reforms with which I did not agree was that all interlocutory appeals and appeals from County Courts should be heard by two judges so that more judges would be available to man other courts. This meant that virtually all matrimonial appeals were heard by only two judges. Two-judge courts are unsatisfactory since there is a subconscious tendency for the judges to agree as there is no prospect of a majority decision. And if one is a puisne judge, as he often is, he will inevitably follow the lead of the Lord Justice. I had suggested to Tom Denning that a Family Division judge should sit on all appeals from the Family Division and from all Divorce County Courts which would at least release one Lord Justice, which he was pleased to agree. Now I suggested that all such appeals should be handed over to the President, who was an ex-officio member of the Court of Appeal, second in status only to the Master of the Rolls, who should sit permanently with two Family Division judges, as the Lord Chief Justice did in the Criminal Division. In that way the President would be able to exert a decisive influence on the development of family law, which in its way is as specialised as the criminal law, two Lords Justices would be available for the ordinary work of the Court of Appeal and two judge courts for family work would be avoided. Unfortunately my proposal was not accepted. It would, amongst other advantages, have provided more interesting work for the judges of the Family Division who I thought were under-employed. Apart from increasing the numbers of Lords Justices, which might devalue the currency since they are recruited from a comparatively small pool of High Court judges, not all of whom despite their qualities are suitable for the Court of Appeal, there are only two ways in which the work of the court could be accelerated. One is to require leave to appeal in all cases, the other to limit the time for oral argument in court, as in the Supreme Court and some other appellate courts in the United States. I would favour both reforms, though the latter would be unpopular at the Bar. The court might, however, have a discretion to increase the time limit for argument in a particularly difficult case. The costs of litigation have become so immense that something drastic must be done to reduce them.

The most difficult decision which I had to make in the Court of Appeal arose quite by chance and without warning. Sidney Templeman and I were judges 'on call' during the long vacation to deal with urgent appeals. Having finished our list by lunchtime, we were asked to take an appeal from the Family Division in the afternoon. No papers were available and we went into court not knowing what was before us. The case concerned a child who had recently been born with Down's Syndrome and suffered from a respiratory defect which could easily be cured by a simple operation. If there was no operation the child would die. The doctor had advised the parents not to agree to the operation, pointing out the difficulties of bring up a child with Down's Syndrome, and the parents had agreed. A nurse in the hospital discovered what was happening and reported to the local social security department who made the child a ward of court. The Official Solicitor applied on behalf of the child for the operation to proceed. The judge refused to make the order. The parents had sworn an affidavit saying that, even if the operation was successful, they could not face the prospect of bringing up a Mongol child, so she would have to be adopted if an adopter could be found. The difficulty was that there was no evidence of what it was like to suffer from Down's Syndrome. We were told that the expectation of life was about twenty-five years, that sufferers varied widely in their symptoms and that it was impossible to tell until the child was two years old whether she would be wholly incapacitated or able to live a more or less normal life. We were also told that sufferers were liable to outbursts of uncontrolled rage, but that in the intervals they were capable of great affection towards those close to them. Surprisingly there was a long list of people willing to adopt babies with Down's Syndrome. The case only lasted for less than two hours since there was very little evidence and the arguments on both sides did no more than state the obvious. At the end of the case Sidney and I retired into the corridor to decide what was to be done. His first words to me were, 'I don't know about you, Robin, but I am not prepared to kill this child.' I agreed, so we went back into court, allowed the appeal and ordered the operation. We heard afterwards that the parents subsequently decided to keep the child and bring her up themselves. All that summer a lively discussion continued in the correspondence columns of *The Times* as to whether we had made the right decision. Many said that it would have been better for the child and the parents to have let her die peacefully. They did not have to make the decision.

Another case which attracted a good deal of publicity was an appeal from Giles Best, one of my favourite Western Circuit judges from Dorset, who had granted a

"Is it Saturday already?"

husband a decree of divorce for unreasonable behaviour, the wife having refused
sexual intercourse more than once a week. The evidence showed that her husband
spent four nights a week with a lady friend, only returning home at weekends and
in those circumstances we thought that Giles had been unusually hard on the wife.
Roger Ormrod, with whom I was sitting, asked me to give the leading judgment and,
sensing that there might be some press interest, I was careful to confine my remarks
to the facts of the case and not to make any generalised comments. Roger, however,
had no such inhibitions. 'I have never,' he thundered, 'heard such an absurd
proposition that for a wife to limit sexual intercourse to once a week constitutes
unreasonable behaviour towards her husband.' The press reacted at once. That
evening, before I returned home, Judy had been rung up by a reporter and asked
for her reaction to the judgment. Wisely she replied, 'No comment.' Next morning
the story was all over the front pages and featured in the BBC news. JAK produced
a cartoon in the *Evening Standard* showing a group of robed, bewigged judges
running out of the Law Courts with a by-stander saying, 'Is it Saturday already?' JAK
sent me the original cartoon in return for a bottle of port and it now hangs in my
WC. The commentators had a field day, saying that this was yet another example of
how out of touch the judges were with the habits of 'ordinary people'. And there
was a sequel. One evening after dinner Janie rang up to say, 'Daddy, you are on
television.' So I switched on the set to see a famous impersonator apparently
interviewing myself. 'When you become a Law Lord, Sir Robin,' he asked, 'what title
will you take?' Then I heard my own voice reply, 'I shall never become a Law Lord.
Once a lord always a lord. But once a Knight is enough for me.' The resemblance
to my own voice was uncanny. He must have sat in court listening to me giving
judgment.

As I have explained, judges of the Family Division have a wide discretion in making
their decisions. There was a difference of opinion amongst the Lords Justices as to
the proper approach of the Court of Appeal to appeals from the discretion of judges,
especially in family cases. Some took a strict view, saying that the court should only
interfere where the judge had gone wrong in law or when he had taken into account

something he should not have taken into account, or failed to take into account something which he should have taken into account. This view, which was supported by some decisions of the House of Lords, had grown up in the context of interlocutory decisions involving the determination of procedural disputes which were within the discretion of the judge. Technically decisions as to the custody of children and matrimonial finance were interlocutory decisions in which the judge also had a discretion. So it was logical that the same rule should apply. Others in the Court of Appeal, including Roger Ormrod and myself, took a different view. We felt that nothing was more final than an order for custody or the redistribution of matrimonial property; and that in any event the parties had the right of appeal and the court should not fetter its powers by applying rules which had been established to meet quite different situations. What was the point of a right of appeal if the court could not do justice as it saw it? In every other class of appeal the court allows the appeal if it thinks that the judge's conclusion was wrong. Why should not the test be applied also to family appeals, the result of which are so vitally important to the parties and their children? By the time I retired it had been established that in such cases the court could act if satisfied that the judge was 'plainly wrong', though I could never understand the necessity for the word 'plainly'. To me a decision was either right or wrong, but then I was by my early training only a simple soldier.

Another difficulty I found was with libel appeals, especially the assessment of damages by juries. In several cases enormous sums had been awarded against newspapers which were quite out of line with awards made by judges for serious personal injuries. Damages for libel are supposed to be compensation for loss of reputation, but these awards must have contained a large punitive element which no doubt reflected the jury's dislike of the conduct of the newspaper. But there was nothing that we in the Court of Appeal could do, since there were at that time decisions of the House of Lords making it impossible to interfere with an award of damages by a jury, unless the judge had erred in his summing up. The whole law of libel is in an unsatisfactory state and I could never understand why no government has implemented the recommendations of my old friend Neville Faulks in a report in the seventies by a committee of which he was chairman. This, as well as suggesting many sensible reforms of the law of libel, also suggested that damages should be assessed by the judge, so as to introduce some conformity with personal injuries awards. Some of my brethren, however, did not agree, saying that the power of the press was such that damages should be left to juries as representing public opinion. In one libel case we had evidence of the practice at the editorial conferences of a periodical with a large circulation. A decision was made as to the 'target' for the next issue, against whom the most damaging allegation possible was to be made without any inquiry whatever as to its truth. If the victim did not deny the allegation it would be accepted as true and repeated with embellishments in subsequent issues. If he asked for a correction or threatened legal proceedings then journalists would be sent out to discover any dirt they could dig up about his private life. No wonder in such cases juries awarded large damages. Our history shows that any institution which abuses its power in this country is eventually humbled. In the Middle ages it was the Knights Templar; in the seventeenth century it was the monarchy; in this century it has been the trades unions; perhaps in the next century it will be the press.

While I was in the Court of Appeal I led a delegation of United Kingdom judges to the European Court of Justice at Luxembourg. We sat in court with judges from every other EC country to listen to the proceedings which I found alien to our tradition and foreign in every sense of the word. I was entertained by John Pierre Warner and his wife. John had succeeded Arthur Bagnall as junior counsel in the Restrictive Practices Court and was Advocate General of the European Court. He was bilingual in French and English, his mother having been French. I mentioned my misgivings from the English point of view about the procedures of the court. He replied that the English Bar, when they appeared before the court, adapted well, although they were inhibited by the time limit on oral argument. An orange light would show some minutes before the expiry of the allotted time and a red light marked the final limitation. He explained that the Advocate General was equivalent to the judge of first instance and not without reason expected to be appointed to the Court of Appeal when his appointment at Luxembourg finished. In the event he became a Chancery judge. On the last evening a dinner was held for all visiting judges at which I sat next to a distinguished member of the French Conseil D'Etat. I said that the whole procedure and atmosphere of the court seemed to be dominated by French influence. 'But of course,' he replied. 'I myself helped in the drafting of the Treaty of Rome and we made sure it would benefit France. If Great Britain had wished to influence our deliberations you should have joined at the outset.' Next morning, in accordance with custom, I made a short speech on behalf of all the visiting judges, thanking the court for their hospitality. I quoted from a judgment of Tom Denning's in which he had said that European law was like the tide, which was flowing inexorably up the creeks and rivers of the common law of England.

Another assignment which I had while in the Court of Appeal was to chair a working party which was to monitor research into mediation and conciliation in matrimonial proceedings. A charitable foundation had financed the research, to be done by Michael Murch, a sociologist at Bristol University, and the Lord Chancellor's department, in return for giving facilities to the researchers to attend court and see all relevant documents, wished the research to be monitored by a working party. When I was Presiding judge I had become interested in the subject. By the time that husband and wife visit solicitors there is virtually no hope of reconciliation between them or of rebuilding the marriage. But there is plenty of scope for conciliation over the practical consequences of divorce: the future of the children and of the home and the disposition of the family assets. The actual breakdown of the marriage, or the separation of husband and wife, is almost always a traumatic and emotional time for both of them. They are so overwhelmed by their own feelings of disappointment, remorse and often bitterness and even hatred towards the other that they find it almost impossible to think clearly about what has to be done about the practicalities of the future. This caused great wastage of time in court and an unnecessary increase in legal costs while the parties came to terms with their new situation. The senior registrar at Bristol, Geoffrey Parmiter, had enlisted the help of the probation service who were on circuit responsible for the work done by the Family Division welfare officers in London, interviewing the parties and their children and producing welfare reports for the judges. He had arranged that in any case which seemed to him appropriate he would refer the parties and their solicitors to a probation officer who would act as mediator and try to concentrate the minds of the parties on to the real issues in the case and perhaps even reach agreement. The system was working well in Bristol and as Presiding judge I had supported it as it reduced the work load of the registrars and increased the number of cases with which they could deal, since they were able to confine themselves to real issues. There were a few other such schemes in operation at other centres in different parts of the country and the terms of reference of our working party were to report on the research into the different schemes and make recommendations for a country-wide system of mediation. We eventually reported shortly before I retired and I do not know what, if anything, has been done. I became convinced that there is a future for mediation in matrimonial proceedings, so long as it is understood that the mediator is not a judge, can make no decisions and should not be part of the judicial system. Our research showed, however, that in many cases the mere opportunity of talking to some informed independent person helped the parties to adopt a more realistic approach to their problems and even to reach agreement on some of them. The cooperation of the solicitors was essential and this was achieved in Bristol where solicitors were glad to hive off some time-consuming and unproductive work. The figures produced by our researchers showed substantial reductions in the costs of legal aid cases where mediators had been used and this might be attractive to the government, though of course the mediators themselves had to be paid, though not as much as solicitors. The first question at our working party asked by the representative of the probation service, an official of the union NAPO, was, 'What resources will be available for this work?' When I replied that I did not know, she attended no further meetings.

It was with great sadness that I read, after my retirement, of the few cases in which the Court of Appeal, after hearing fresh evidence, had quashed convictions which the court had upheld years previously when the fresh evidence had not been available. These 'miscarriages of justice' have been used as part of the general attack on the judiciary and especially on Geoffrey Lane as Lord Chief Justice. Almost all these were IRA cases and the original decisions to convict had been made by juries in the seventies in towns where the various outrages had been committed and where as I remember feelings against the IRA were running high. As I have explained the powers of the Criminal Division of the Court of Appeal to quash convictions are limited by statute and, in the absence of cogent fresh evidence at the original appeals in these cases, it is not surprising that they were dismissed. Almost without exception the convictions were eventually quashed because recently introduced scientific tests had shown that some of the police evidence was unreliable and sometimes perjured. I had long formed the view that the police, as a body, had become frustrated by what they saw as too much bias in our criminal procedure in favour of the accused. Judy's father had once said, 'An English criminal trial is a conspiracy between the judge, counsel and the police to secure the acquittal of the accused.' The whole of the criminal law of evidence is directed to safeguarding and protecting the accused and, in some cases, the police undoubtedly manipulated the evidence where they were convinced the accused was guilty, but the laws of evidence prevented them from proving it. The most common example was the 'verbals' where in the police car immediately after arrest the accused was alleged to have said, 'It's a fair cop,' or words to that effect. I am convinced that if the law of evidence was reformed, so as to reduce some of the artificial safeguards which now exist, the police would not be so tempted to trim the evidence and would be more likely to accept the system. In my experience almost all the police are dedicated to their profession and see themselves as guardians of society. They also have a strong feeling of responsibility for bringing criminals to justice. They feel balked by the present state of the law.

Soon after I became a judge the Standing Criminal Law Revision committee, comprising judges, barristers and academics, had recommended two drastic changes in the law of evidence. The first was the modification of the accused's right of silence, so that the judge could comment to the jury on the fact that he had not given evidence. The second was that the judge should have a discretion to admit in evidence the criminal convictions of the accused where they were relevant to the charge. These recommendations were debated in parliament and rejected. Most of the major problems of our criminal procedure date from that decision, since the police became disheartened and disillusioned by the system. The inviolable right of silence is an historical anachronism, dating back to the time when no accused could give evidence in his own defence. It was only in 1896 that he was allowed to do so. Before that date the onus had been entirely on the prosecution to call evidence to establish guilt. It was not so much a right of silence as a prohibition against giving evidence. The change in the law meant that many accused convicted themselves out of their own mouths as soon as they went into the witness box. So the 'right of silence' grew up. Why should the judge not be able to say to the jury, 'There is only one person who knows what happened on that fatal day and that is the accused. Why has he chosen not to tell you?' The exclusion of previous convictions also dates back to the days when juries were mostly uneducated and thought to be unlikely to be able to assess the evidence properly. The consequences of a conviction, death by hanging, transportation and flogging, were also much more horrific than they are today. But now we have well educated sophisticated juries, who regularly watch television and are accustomed to make up their minds about all manner of issues in their daily lives. Logically, on a charge for instance of burglary, it must be relevant that the accused has previous convictions for that same offence and my knowledge of juries makes me confident that they could safely be told of that fact in appropriate cases. I believe that if these reforms had been made in 1970 the attitude of the police to evidence would have changed and the various miscarriages of justice would not have occurred.

It would be dangerous to increase the powers of the Criminal Division or to set up some kind of 'review body' with wide investigative powers to inquire into the facts of cases in which appeals had been dismissed. Although one miscarriage of justice is one too many, the proportion of miscarriages is tiny. Almost all cases are satisfactorily dealt with and it is difficult to see how cases considered appropriate for review could be identified. This in any event would replace trial by jury to trial by a review body and the former provides one of the basic constitutional rights of the subject. None of this prevented a whole series of ill-informed attacks on poor Geoffrey Lane after the various 'miscarriages of justice' cases which extended to the judiciary as a whole and indeed the whole system of criminal law. This is a sinister development because one of the best ways of destabilising a country is to undermine public confidence in its judicial system. This will not be cured by judges trying to be more 'user friendly' or abandoning their traditional dress.

My only doubt about jury trial is its suitability in its present form for serious fraud cases involving, as they frequently do, voluminous documentation and the customs of various markets. Eustace Roskill recommended shortly before I retired that such trials should be conducted by a judge and two lay assessors. I am doubtful about this, since in my experience juries almost always reach a sensible decision, provided that the case is presented to them clearly without a proliferation of different charges. Their verdicts may not always be strictly in accordance with the law but, when they are not, there is usually a good reason for it. Before 1945 fraud cases at the Old Bailey were tried by a City of London jury, drawn from people who worked in the city, and had experience of accounts and the workings of the markets. They were abolished, with special juries which had a high property qualification and sat in libel cases, by the Labour government. I do not see why City of London juries should not try serious fraud causes. It would be a true 'trial by peers'. And I would reduce the number of jurors from twelve to seven, as in the United States, with a possible majority verdict of 5 to 2.

Meanwhile the crime rate continues to increase and the courts and the police come under increasing pressure. 'Law and order' has become a political slogan, although the two words are not synonymous. Law is designed to prevent disorder and order cannot be created by judges, magistrates or the police, however strongly they enforce the law. The malaise lies much deeper in our society. Between the wars, when unemployment stood at over three million and there was in many places real deprivation of a kind which is unknown today, the crime rate was minimal compared to the present. Why was this? I believe that it was because of the gradual erosion of the Christian moral standards which existed throughout society. You have only to read *The Five Towns* by Arnold Bennett to see the very strict code of conduct which existed at the turn of the century amongst the working classes in the great industrial towns and the influence of the Church and especially the chapels. All that has gone. We live in a selfish hedonistic society with few moral restraints. We are all of us to blame for this, parents, schoolteachers and the churches. I see no prospect of an improvement during my lifetime, but sooner or later in one of those great movements which have occurred during our history there will I am sure be a return to Christian standards and values. It is true that judges see human nature at its worst. A prison governor once said to me, 'People do not understand that there are those who positively enjoy crime. They enjoy violence, they enjoy rape and they enjoy the excitement of a burglary. There is nothing that can be done with them except lock them up for a long time.' Such people have always existed. But their attitude is now more widespread and encouraged by television. I am I confess a strong believer in the doctrine of original sin but, with proper influences, the sin can be ameliorated. My contacts with the young whom I meet in the army, in the hunting field and the children of my own friends have always given me hope. Until the standards of the best of them are more generally accepted by society I fear the crime rate will continue to increase, and there is nothing that the forces of 'law and order' will be able to do about it.

By 1984 I had completed fifteen years on the Bench and qualified for my 'index-linked' pension. So it was time to go. Although the work was hard in the Court of Appeal, I did not feel under the same strain as when I was a leading silk. And I much enjoyed the company of my brethren in the court. But I felt no particular commitment to the law. Unlike most judges, who live in London and take an annual holiday abroad, Judy and I had always had one foot firmly placed on Exmoor. Had we been truly London-based I should no doubt have remained on the Bench for another nine years, listening to interesting arguments and lunching with my friends in the Inner Temple. But Exmoor beckoned. I had suggested to the Lord Chancellor's department that judges should retire at the age of 70 except for the House of Lords who should continue until 75. My reason was that all the regular presiders in the Court of Appeal were people who had been passed over for the Lords. Although they were very good they were not, by definition, the very best. If they retired at 70 there would be younger presiders in the Court of Appeal with a prospect of promotion. Life in the Lords is not so strenuous; they only sit four days a week and many Law Lords such as Scott Reid have produced some of their greatest work in their seventies. Now I read that the retiring age for all judges is to be reduced to 70, with a discretion in the Lord Chancellor to extend the appointment to 75. I think this will be invidious and that almost every judge will be granted an extension. It will not address the problem of elderly presiders in the Court of Appeal. Moreover judges are to serve twenty years before qualifying for a pension, so they will have to be appointed before the age of fifty in order to qualify in full. It is during their forties that most people reach their zenith at the Bar and if appointments are generally to be made from that age group it will dramatically weaken the Bar in its top echelon.

I would not have wished to become a judge in my forties when I felt full of vigour and at the height of my forensic powers. The life of a judge is less demanding and requires less energy and provided that there is no reduction in mental capacity the work can easily be done during the fifties, sixties and in some cases seventies. The reduction in retiring age linked to the pension provisions can only weaken the judiciary and must have been proposed by the Treasury.

When I told John Donaldson that I wished to retire he said, 'Of course you will come back regularly and help us out, like all the others.' I replied that I would not, since we were selling our London house and I had no wish to go to London for three weeks every term and live in my club. Moreover, I did not think that I would be able to cope with the work unless I was doing it regularly which I certainly did not intend to do. I would have no room, no clerk, no law reports and I felt that I would be a passenger. I have never regretted my decision.

So Judy and I returned to the country life we had always wanted. One of my judicial brethren wrote, 'I cannot think how you will occupy your time, except by reading Surtees.' But there is hunting in the winter, fishing and gardening in the summer and a visit to the Caribbean every February. Our grandchildren come to stay with all their ponies and we ride together over Exmoor where they learn about the habits of the deer. And I find myself deeply involved in the political battle to defend hunting. Sadly Judy has had two hip replacements so cannot now ride, but I still manage to mount my horse and ride to hounds. I still experience the old excitement when the pack is laid on and I feel the power of a good horse between my knees as we gallop over the heather, with the hounds in full cry beside us and the stag like a dancing midge on the horizon, although I can hardly see him because my eyes are watering so much. The war is a distant, though vivid memory and my years in the law seem no more than an interlude. The time seems to have passed so quickly.

APPENDICES

Dunkirk Diary 1940

Friday, May 10th – I felt as if I was going back to school, and my goodbyes to the Carpentiers with many embracings and promises to write, were most depressing.

At 9.55 pm my troop passed the church in Thumesnil, the regimental starting point.

Saturday, May 11th – As dawn broke I woke up feeling stiff and cramped. I had been driving every alternate two hours, following the vehicle in front, and now it was dawn. The column halted and I walked up to find Ashton with the cheerful news that we had gone wrong in the night and were now on the 1st Division route. We drove on as the day grew lighter and eventually came on the main road to Brussels. A squadron of German bombers passed overhead but ignored us. The road was full of private cars loaded to overflowing with people and property, all hurrying towards France. There were many expensive looking American cars with well bred, well fed looking people inside them. The road, the people, the buildings on either side were much like a by-pass near London at a summer's weekend. The whole effect was noticeably English after France. The number of men of military age standing about in plain clothes also contrasted forcibly with France.

We drove on through Brussels and I determined then and there to visit it after the war. I liked its cleanliness, its broad double track by-passes with trees in the middle, its dignified public buildings, its solid-looking private houses. The time was about 8 am and my troop were the first British guns to pass that way. People cheered and waved and threw flowers and fruit and sweets at us, as the guns bumped and rattled over the cobbles. The men, who had been tired after their drive, cheered up and grinned and waved in the traditional manner of the British tommy. I thought of Wellington's army moving out of that same city to Waterloo.

We eventually left Brussels behind and arrived at our harbour; a small village in a valley with convenient orchards. The countryside was rolling and green and wooded, a pleasant change from the industrial north of France. Just as we were tucking away our guns and vehicles, a German reconnaissance aeroplane flew low

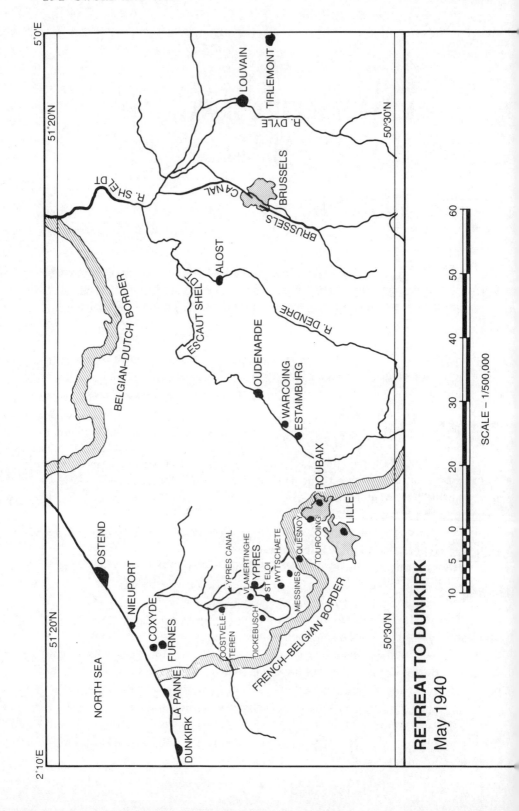

RETREAT TO DUNKIRK
May 1940

SCALE – 1/500,000

over our village. The bren gunners fired their guns, the riflemen blazed away with their rifles, everybody turned shining faces to the skies. A quarter of an hour later two aeroplanes came back and each dropped a bomb on the village. It was the best lesson we could have had. From that moment onwards, I never saw one of our men fire at an aeroplane with rifle or bren gun, both quite ineffective except at about fifty feet, or in fact, do anything except keep still or take cover.

The Belgian army at this time was still out in front of us, but we had no idea how long they would hold out. As soon as we had shaved and fed we began reconnoitring OPs and battery areas. In the meantime the battery moved to another harbour in a big wood.

At about 5.30 I was in this wood and saw the dive bombing attack on the bridge at Louvain. It was the most awe-inspiring sight. Calmly, unimpeded, the aeroplanes circled round, each one in turn diving with a high-pitched whine, which was followed by the four crashes of the bombs. I did not like it.

We were just sitting down to dinner in a monastery near our wood when we saw 12 enemy bombers overhead. Suddenly the silence was broken by a whistling noise, and 12 bombs burst round us. Several of the men were shaken, none hurt, but in general I think it did more good than harm, as nothing raises a man's morale like being bombed and shelled and getting away with it. This attack was followed by a despatch rider on a motor-cycle with a message to say that the cavalry had reported Germans seven miles from Louvain; we were to move back to another harbour at Coige, some five miles away, and be prepared for tanks. In fact, a thoroughly alarmist message. I listened to the German news in English on my wireless as we stood formed up waiting to move off and it sounded so sinister that I must confess my morale was lower at that moment than at any other for the next three weeks. For a moment I am going to digress to explain why. It was not the alarmist report; it was not the news of the Germans being across the Albert Canal; it was not the demoralised Belgians, some of whom had already started to trickle through to us. It was the feeling that those controlling our movements had lost their grip and this feeling was brought about entirely by the fact that our battery area had been changed twice in eight hours. I had often heard of 'order – counter order – disorder', but had never until this moment realised its terrible truth. I found all through this campaign that men will carry out any orders provided they are clear. They may be unreasonable, they may be suicidal; the men simply say, 'No doubt they're the best possible'; but if they are changed, doubt, fear of the unknown and loss of confidence begin to set in.

I went to bed at 1 o'clock, exhausted and unhappy.

May 12th – I was woken at 3.30 and ordered to go at once to Beerbohm to prepare a position for the guns. The position was along the front edge of some big woods and, leaving Marcel to prepare the technical side of it, I went back to fetch the guns. It was about 9 am before I got back to our harbour. The roads were completely blocked. The Belgians were in full retreat with stories of four German aeroplanes to every one of their machine-guns, of tanks, of bombs and shells. There was a continuous stream of Belgian refugees, a few in cars, some on enormous farm carts, some on bicycles, most on foot. All carried what they could and all had the same look of patient despair. They made it difficult to bring up the guns.

Having got the guns into action, I went up to choose an OP which I eventually found on a hill behind and to the left of Louvain, from which I could see in front of the town. I spent the afternoon drawing a panorama, digging a good funk hole in the bank and generally preparing things. At about 5 o'clock I drove through Louvain, over the Dyle and fixed a few targets in what would soon be Germany. The effect was extraordinary. The whole place was deserted. The bridge was untouched, but all round it houses were shattered and roads cratered. When I arrived back at my OP I found that the infantry had arrived and that my hill was to be held by the King's Company, 1st Grenadier Guards. Safe enough. They were full of rumours. The Americans and Italians had given Hitler forty-eight hours to get out of Belgium. Mussolini had shot himself; the King of Italy had abdicated. I went back to the gun position as dusk was falling.

May 13th – The night had been disturbed. We had been warned of parachutists and some of our young soldiers saw one behind every tree, and of course fired at them. In the end, I had to beat the wood with a lighted torch to convince them.

After breakfast I went round the infantry with John Dill. The Belgians were by now pouring back completely demoralised, shooting almost anything they saw. Louvain was deserted of civilians and a complete shambles from bombing. We marked the positions in on our maps and discussed things with the infantry, who seemed absolutely confident.

At lunchtime we heard that many more artillery had come up and we were to move again to make room for them. This, however, we did not mind as there seemed to be a reason for it. We moved as soon as it was dark to another and better position. It again was in a wood, but there was a very deep sunken road behind which would have suited admirably for digging mined dugouts. It took us some time to get the guns in as the men were not by then track-minded and one had to lead in almost every vehicle personally. There was much material to unload, much ammunition to dump.

I cannot dwell too much on the refugees and the terrible impression they left. As one of my most hard-boiled drivers said, 'It makes you want to f-ing weep sir,' and it did.

May 14th – I left for the OP before breakfast. News came through that the cavalry were in touch some ten miles beyond Louvain. There was great aerial activity over the OP all through the morning and the Belgians continued to move through. They appeared to be hurrying now and several batteries passed through at a brisk trot. About lunchtime some of our armoured cars passed. During the afternoon we received a message from the CRA to say that the cavalry were clear and registration could begin at once. At the same time, British shells began falling all over the front. I enjoyed directly the battery's first shoot in anger. As the evening drew on the Germans began to make themselves felt. I heard small arms fire in Louvain, an anti-tank gun was fired into a tower nearby which might have been used as an OP and shells were bursting in Louvain and just behind us. I left at 9 o'clock when it was too dark to see and realised that war had begun in earnest. The Germans were shelling a level-crossing I had to pass, but not often. Several houses were burning, but I felt supremely confident. We had had a clear day to prepare our new position, which I liked very much. So far all had gone according to plan. The Belgians had not held out as long as we had expected, but it had been exactly as we had practised countless times. All our OP information was fixed, the guns were in very well-concealed positions which were becoming stronger every hour. I slept dreamlessly and well.

May 15th – We fired a bit during the night – an SOS and a certain amount of harrassing fire. I left at 3 o'clock for the OP. The infantry had had a quiet night, except for the machine-gunners who had fired harrassing fire. The subaltern commanding them said he had been on the bridge at Louvain when it had been bombed. He had had two guns and their detachments for the defence of the bridge, thirty-six bombs had been dropped within eighty yards of them and nobody had been hurt, although they were only in a hole in the road.

During the morning a Horse Artillery subaltern drove up on to the top of my hill, about fifty yards from me, in a light tank. A light German gun immediately started to range on him and then to search the hill. Some of them were unpleasantly close. The infantry were furious. Meanwhile the German shellfire increased. I went forward to a platoon of the Grenadiers which commanded the bridge below, the only bridge which had not been blown. From here I saw my first Germans, running across the bridge and diving into the woods on either side. They were wearing greatcoats and looked heavily laden in the sun. The shelling had meanwhile increased considerably and my telephone line had been cut. I was just preparing to engage the Germans on the bridge when I got a message over the wireless ordering me to evacuate the forward OP at once and that the main OP some fifteen hundred yards back and more centrally placed was now manned by John Dill and ready to carry on. The Horse Artilleryman in the light tank put down fire on the bridge, I believe effectively.

I went straight back to the command post and told the Major all I knew. He told me that some enemy infantry had crept into Louvain during the night, had lain up in the town till morning and were now sniping from houses. A few had been seen by John coming out of the town, but he had fired on them and they had turned back.

I lunched with the Major and all of a sudden felt flat and tired, as I had never felt before. I also found I was shaking like an old man. I lay down and slept for four hours; when I woke up I had a complete wash down under the old pump and felt ready for anything. I have recorded this in some detail as it was the first time I had ever been shelled and I find the effect a curious one.

Marcel went up to the OP that night.

May 16th – It is time to stop mere description and try to give impressions. The first and most important impression I had was of the complete air superiority of the Germans. We seldom saw a British fighter and when a patrol went over it was always at a time when there were no German machines about. We usually had a Lysander army reconnaissance aircraft overhead, but they were obviously not for defence purposes. I saw one shot down over Louvain by two Messerschmidts. It was a pathetic sight, as watching any defenceless being attacked by greatly superior forces is apt to be.

My second impression was the terrible effect of war on a countryside. It is more vivid in town areas than in the country. One somehow associates open country with war, but towns developed for the pleasures and pursuits of peace present a terrible picture when bombed or shelled. I remember seeing a tram hurrying down the road from Louvain to Brussels with bombs bursting all round it. Broad boulevards with shady trees built for the delight of citizens on long warm summer evenings somehow look desolate out of all proportion to the damage done when they have been bombed or shelled. And of course the refugees with their patient faces, suffering eyes and eternal questions, 'Il y aura danger ici, monsieur?' War is not too bad for a soldier; he has his friends and weapons with which to hit back. But it is sheer horror for civilians in the battle area.

That day we began organising ourselves. The isolated attacks of the day before had been beaten off; they were obviously only to try our strength. A company from the reserve brigade was to go forward tonight to mop up in Louvain. We had unbounded confidence in our infantry; we were supporting the Ulster Rifles and our liaison officer with them. Storey, who got an MC for his work there, spoke of them in glowing terms. We expected the Germans to put in a terrific attack in a few days; in the meantime we made our preparations confidently. The gun pits were ready and roofs of timber and corrugated iron were being erected over them. I had put a miner in charge of a squad to make a mined dugout in our bank which was 30 feet high. The command post was in a farm and Humphrey Drew started organising it. It was in fact a depressing sight. Unmilked cows wandered about lowing sadly. We organised morning milking. The houses were left obviously at an hour's notice or less. Drawers open, clothes all over the floor, food still lying about. We took beams from the roofs of the barns and everything we could find to strengthen our position. We organised reliefs and an officer's mess. In the afternoon the Major went off to reconnoitre a more permanent cable route. At about 3 pm I had an order over the telephone, 'Target 578248, 20 rounds per gun per hour till further orders.' A quarter of an hour later, 'Double your rate of fire.' A quarter of an hour later we were given six targets and told to fire them, rate normal (three rounds per minute), until all our dumped ammunition was expended. I rang up Jimmie, our CPO (command post officer). He was rather short. 'I know no more than you,' he said, 'but those are my orders.' I continued firing, with a horrible feeling inside. We had about six hundred rounds per gun dumped. At this moment I saw the Major standing behind my no. 4 gun. I walked over and told him what had happened. He had heard nothing about it and rushed off to investigate. At about 5 o'clock he rang me up. The enemy had broken through on the right of the 1st Division. We were to withdraw to the River Dendre about ten miles the other side of Brussels – the regiment was moving at once. My troop was to remain in action till 8 pm when it would be under command of 8th Infantry Brigade which was the rearguard of the division. I was to report to the Brigadier personally in the armoured scout. I was amazed. The guns were red hot by this time; the gunners were working like slaves, stripped to the waist. They could not understand it when I told them we were to retreat. 'Why sir? Why? Why don't we advance? If they leave us here nothing will ever get through this.' I explained that nothing ever would but that it was elsewhere that things had gone wrong and that unless we went we would be cut off.

I drove up to the infantry and found them as usual unmoved. The Brigadier and his staff were having dinner. They directed me to Colonel Bull, 4th Royal Berkshires, whose battalion was covering the withdrawal of the brigade. I arrived in the middle of his conference. He gave me my orders. Stay here as long as you can. Fire an SOS here at midnight and then be prepared to cover me on the eastern outskirts of Brussels at 3 am. It was fun. We fired ten rounds per gun intense on each SOS then limbered up and away. We passed long columns of infantry on the road who cheered us saying, 'There go the boys who saved us at Louvain.' It was rather like that picture of Snaffles: 'The guns, thank God, the guns'. We dropped into action in a respectable little suburb of Brussels at 2.40. I went off to my Colonel Bull. No, they had not been impeded and had seen nothing of the enemy. I climbed up the chapel spire of a monastery but could see nothing. It smelt very frowsty.

May 17th – I remember at 7.30 I heard from a cavalry man that a few bodies of the enemy had been seen leaving Louvain at 5 am. We were to continue the retreat at 9, when I was to rejoin my regiment. I breakfasted off tea and bread and jam with the Berkshires and at 9 o'clock limbered up and drove through Brussels. It was a very different Brussels from that of a week before. The people were very kind and gave us food and drink, but they knew the Germans would be there in a few hours and they had hoped we would stop them. I felt depressed as I thought of German officers in the cafés and restaurants. I drove turn and turn about with my driver until I dropped off to sleep and ran into a refugee on a bicycle when my driver said, 'Come on, sir, let me take over!' We drove back over the Dendre. The roads were cluttered up with vehicles now that we had rejoined the main bodies. Eventually at about midday we arrived at the regimental rendezvous and I led my troop to harbour in an orchard. A meal was ready and after it we slept as we lay as the shadows lengthened under the trees. The regiment was moving into action that night, but my troop, as a special concession, was to have a good night's rest and move into action at dawn. I slept in a farmhouse on a real bed, between real sheets. Bliss.

May 18th – We moved out of harbour at 4 am and were in action by 6. The roads were narrow and were filled with guns and vehicles of all descriptions from the 4th Division who had held the line of the Brussels Canal during the night and were now going back through us.

Our new position was in some orchards on the outskirts of Wussel. My command post was in a café. We were now faced with a new problem. The area in which we had hitherto been fighting had been compulsorily evacuated, but our unforeseen retreat had brought us into an area still full of civilians. Many of them were German spies and arrows were found on several occasions cut in the grass and pointing towards headquarters, battery positions and so on. These were often bombed. It is a distressing but inevitable result of German fifth column methods that many should have to suffer for the few, and I am certain that many innocent peasants were arrested by us. But once the civilian population are involved, it is impossible to draw the line; it is all or none. Life was trying in this village, for every time a German aeroplane flew over, which was about every twenty minutes, the entire village crowded into the cellar of our café which was deep and strong and the main reason why we had selected the building. There they would huddle weeping and wailing and praying for deliverance. Finally I had to lock all the doors and forbid them to come in, as they made work impossible. We were now right in the centre of Flanders proper. The north of Belgium is practically Dutch, the south French, but this land of Flanders is neither and the people are as separate from either French or Dutch as possible. I found their language repulsive to the ear and quite unintelligible when spoken, although I could read it quite easily. It is a curious mixture of English and German with some Dutch thrown in. The men seemed strong and well built, but the women are magnificent. I understood why Ann of Cleeves was called the Flemish Mare. The women are very big of bone with broad high foreheads, flat noses, eyes set far apart and wonderful carriage. I will not say that the people were pro-German, but it seemed a matter of indifference to them whether a British or German army was in occupation. Their chief concern was whether or not the battle was to be fought over their land, a very natural point of view for people whose country has so often been devastated by war.

I bought a chicken off the farm nearby and we ate it with champagne and some ceremony for dinner. It had been a quiet day with little firing. We had a gun in the garden of our café and every time it fired a window would break and the glass fall with a tinkle on the floor. Trying.

After dinner we heard that we were to continue our retreat to the Scheldt. I was to man the OP from 4 am till 8. At 8 the troop was to move. John's troop was to cover the withdrawal leaving at 12. During the night we were disturbed by an officer of the RAMC hunting for spies. I was very rude to him. We fired harrassing fire all night.

May 19th – I arrived at the OP at 4 and went off to the 2nd Grenadiers who were holding the village just in front. They said our harrassing fire had been effective. They had had a quiet night, but had been sniped by civilians. I did some amusing shooting from the OP. During the morning I met a subaltern of the Skins (5th Inniskilling Dragoon Guards) who had been right up to the Belgian-German frontier in the early days. He said that as soon as any shells or bombs fell anywhere near, the Belgians had bolted.

I handed over to John at 8 and after a very quick breakfast limbered up and we started for the Scheldt. It was a glorious day and it was good to be bowling down the road with the noise of gun fire getting fainter. At this time, after a week of continuous fighting, everyone remarked on the curious state of their nerves. The whine of tyres going down a road, a petrol cooker starting up or any loud and sudden noise made one start involuntarily. It was noticeable how a good night's rest put this state of affairs right. We had an undisturbed drive as far as Oudenarde when the German bombers began to appear. Two flew towards our column very low and I realised they had spotted us. It was no use stopping so we kept quietly on and two bombs dropped about eighty yards from the road. Just beyond Oudenarde there was a traffic block caused by an AA battery coming into action beside the road and troop-carrying lorries going the other way to pick up infantry. A Messerschmidt chose this moment to machine-gun the column, but nobody was hurt. I thought of other British armies that had fought at Oudenarde and wondered if they had the same trials to contend with.

Eventually we approached Estaimburg where we were to cross the Scheldt. There were so many bombers about that I had increased our interval from a hundred and fifty yards between vehicles to four hundred. I never saw a British aeroplane all that day and I never saw so many Germans. As we drove into Estaimburg a scene of chaos greeted us. Every division in the army seemed to be using that particular bridge and the town was thick with vehicles of every regiment imaginable. To make matters worse, the place had just been bombed and three ammunition lorries had been hit and were going up in every direction. The whole scene was like the race traffic on Derby Day. I finally found the battery guide and was led out to our harbour, which was a few miles from the town.

This place brought the war home to me very much. It was a nice modern house standing in its own grounds. It has obviously been left in a hurry and it had also obviously contained children. The sight of toys and books in the rooms under such conditions moved me very much. We all washed, shaved and had a meal. I had a bath. The Major arrived at about 5.30 and said we were to go into action that night as forward troop in the village of Warcoing.

The position was once again in an orchard on the outskirts of the village, about eight hundred yards from the front line. We were soon in action and in bed.

May 20th – I went up to the OP at dawn. The Coldstream were holding the line here and said that no contact had yet been made with the enemy. I registered the troop and handed over to Storey at 9 am when I returned for breakfast.

It was a very quiet day. Storey shot one section during the afternoon at motor-cyclists and columns of MT which he could see moving towards the river. During the evening the enemy shelled the village with mortars and also ranged on the troop with air bursts, so as soon as it was dark we moved to an alternative position which had been prepared during the afternoon.

May 21st – I was at the OP at dawn to find that 4th Royal Berkshires had relieved the Coldstream. The enemy started shelling and dropping mortar bombs on Warcoing and this continued throughout the morning. The Major arrived at about 9 o'clock with John Dill, who was to relieve me. As he arrived they started ranging on the OP which was in the attic of a cottage and by general consent we adjourned to the cellar for a few minutes. As I left the OP John said, 'You haven't got a book of poetry you could lend me for the day, Robin, have you?' We returned to the troop to find that they were getting the overs from Warcoing and that one had gone through the roof of the barn we were using as a cookhouse. There was a canal which joined the Scheldt some five hundred yards to the left of where we were and ran back at an angle of about 45° to it. My troop was between the river and this canal and I asked permission to move over the canal, as the enemy bombardment was increasing and I did not want to get the troop cut off on the wrong side with the bridges blown. The Major agreed and we reconnoitred a position about a mile back in Le Trieu, a suburb of Dottigines. The move of the troop was unpleasant in the extreme. The Suffolks in Warcoing were having considerable casualties and the bridge was coming under machine-gun fire as we crossed it. To crown it all, one of my drivers missed the turning just after the bridge and while cutting across country to return on to the road, drove into a ditch. I very nearly burst into tears. Eventually I got into the seat myself and found the tractor came out quite easily. I was very much relieved when all guns and vehicles were reported in action at Le Trieu.

The remainder of the day was quiet and just before dark I received orders to go back to a place called Plavitout where the CRA was collecting under his direct command a mobile reserve of artillery, consisting of my troop, the forward troop of 9th/17th Battery, and the 2nd Regiment RHA. We dropped into action about midnight in and about a farm.

May 22nd – This was the quietest day we had had to date. We never fired a round and nobody fired at us.

By this time we all had a fair idea of how things had gone elsewhere. We knew that the Germans had cut our communications. We had been ordered to live off the country and that five rounds per gun per day was our limit for ordinary shooting. The Colonel had had a conference and had said that in his view the BEF would have to go for the sea and re-embark for England. This remark astonished us; it seemed inconceivable. We knew the French were putting in a counter-attack to close the gap. The Germans had nearly reached Amiens in March 1918; they were beaten by November. It was now May 1940; such was our feeling. We were told that that night we were to withdraw to the defences which we had prepared during the winter near Lille. We felt confident. It would be like playing a game on our home ground.

I shall take this opportunity to mention the German parachute tactics. I never saw a German parachutist nor met anyone who did; but there were always people, particularly some way behind the lines, who were ready to tell one of parachutists in the vicinity. I never saw any material damage done by a parachutist, but we had to have bigger guards at night and double sentries and this itself must have affected our efficiency when every hour's sleep was precious and every man rested a potential increase in strength.

After a day spent foraging for food we moved back in the dark through Tourcoing to a position prepared by artillery of 4th Division during the winter. We were back to the Lille line.

May 23rd – 25th – These days were so uneventful that I shall take them all together. They were days of preparation. The positions we occupied were the best I have ever seen and so I will describe them in some detail. They were based on a farm. One gun was in the garden of a cottage, one in an outhouse, a third in a barn and the fourth disguised as a rubbish heap in the farmyard. A road ran along the front of the guns so that tracks and blast marks did not enter into the picture. The command post was in a cellar and a telephone line was run to every gun. Some hundred yards from the position, under a dutch barn, we dug a dugout for the cookhouse and deep slit trenches for the men off duty. Our dump at Thumesnil was only a few miles away and with the material there we were able to make the position enormously strong without in any way interfering with its excellent natural camouflage. We propped up the roof of the cellar with enormous props, we roofed every gun pit with stout timber, corrugated iron and sandbags; we revetted everything. I do not think that we should ever had been spotted there and, if we had, nothing but a direct hit on each gun pit would have knocked us out.

As I have mentioned our communications were cut, but we had brought a pig with us from Belgium and in any case we were living on the farm. I requisitioned sixty eggs a day, milk, butter and five heifers to be killed as required. Bread was a problem, but we had brought two large sacks of flour and a bakery was near. We would not starve.

The wireless news was most depressing. The Germans were in Abbeville/ Boulogne, approaching Calais. But everyone seemed completely confident. The French would let the armoured divisions through and then they would close the gap and mop them up at their leisure. 'Will you walk into my parlour said the spider to

262 SWORD AND WIG

the fly.' The fly was to prove to be a wasp. I was ordered to turn one gun about facing our rear as tanks were reported to be behind us.

The civilian population here was a pathetic sight. It was almost like fighting at home, so well did we know this countryside. And we were pleased to be in France again. We did not like the Belgians; we could not understand their language. But France we knew. As we crossed the frontier my driver sniffed the air and said, 'Same old smell.' True it was the same old smell, but we had got used to it and it meant French courtesy and French coffee and things we understood and loved. I drove over to Thumesnil one afternoon. It was a pathetic sight. The Carpentiers on whom I had been billeted had, I am glad to say, got away but many had not. All were eager for news and all seemed to want to talk to me and ask my advice, as something that appeared stable in a world of instability. I did my best to cheer them, but it was not a cheerful prospect. Indeed the plight of these poor civilians in the Nord was desperate. They were surrounded with no communication with the outside world and, being an industrial area dependent on food supplies from without, very short of food. I drove very slowly through Lille and I thought of how I had so often seen it during the last eight months, streets and boulevards crowded, cafés full of British and French soldiers and their ladies. I passed the Carlton, Chez Freddy, the Bellevue Hotel, names as familiar to the officers of the BEF as the Berkeley, the 400 and the Ritz. Everywhere the shutters were up, the streets deserted except for a few unfortunates who had been too optimistic and stayed too long.

On the evening of the 25th I was ordered to relieve John Dill at the OP and to liaise that night with the East Yorkshires. The OP was on top of a water tower and I found John lying on his stomach with the inevitable book of poetry on one side and a bottle of burgundy on the other. He pointed out the landmarks from his panorama and then a gust of wind caught it and it blew over the edge and fluttered to the ground. Five minutes later three shells fell within fifty yards of us. I cursed John heartily. My signaller, who always came to the OP with me, merely said, 'Misfire at No. 4.' I left the OP about 8 and after an excellent dinner at Battalion Headquarters went to bed in a top room of the school which was the East Yorkshires Headquarters. Not a good place, particularly as a German mortar was firing harrassing fire on the road outside.

May 26th – This was one of the most boring days I have ever spent. I lay on the top of my tower from 4 am till 7 pm without seeing a move on the other side of the lines. At about 6 pm my tower was bombed. Four bombs fell round it, but no damage was done. A word about the bombing. I will not pretend that I ever got completely used to it, but it was so much a matter of luck and was so inaccurate that one lay in one's ditch or hole feeling reasonably happy. Shelling I disliked intensely to the end, for the Germans' predicted fire was very accurate and I knew as a gunner how accurate shelling could be; but I consider the bombing of troops a most uneconomical and unreliable way of inflicting casualties on them. The strategic bombing of towns, large dumps, ports, railway stations is a different matter; but for a British soldier of intelligence and high morale bombing should have few terrors, because he knows a hit is purely a matter of luck.

I handed over to John Lister at 7 pm and returned to my troop with thoughts of a good dinner and bed. As I arrived, Marcel said, 'Robin, the CO has got a conference at once.' I cursed roundly and drove out to RHQ. There I found all the troop commanders of the regiment with all the battery commanders and captains. The Major looked very depressed. 'A move?' I asked. He nodded gloomily.

The Colonel walked in with a 1/250,000 map of northern France put it up against the wall, turned to us and said, 'Gentlemen. My gloomy predictions of a few days ago have come true. The Commander-in-Chief has decided that the BEF's position is untenable. We are to move to the coast and re-embark for England. Personnel only can be saved. All equipment is to be rendered useless and left.' There was more in the same vein. We listened horrified. The worst had happened. Strange thoughts rushed through my mind; it was impossible to believe that what the Colonel said could be true. He continued, 'The Belgians have bolted on our left. The French counter-attack to close the gap has failed ...' I looked at the faces all around. I knew them all so well, Tony, John, Nigel, they all had the same look of bewildered depression. I thought of all our training, of all our high hopes and our confidence in our men. 'Robin, you will take your troop back at once to beyond Warnbrechies and will remain in action there to cover the withdrawal. John, you will stay in action here under command 8th Infantry Brigade. You will all remain in action until the last possible moment, when you will disable your guns and get away as best you can. On the way back you will shoot anyone on sight who tries to stop you, you will ... you will ...'. I drove back to my troop, my mind a turmoil. I gave, 'prepare to move' orders and sat down to dinner. When the troop was ready, I formed them up and told them what was going to happen and why. There was dead silence for about a minute, then a gunner stepped forward and said, 'It's not our fault sir, is it?' 'No, Newing, it's not our fault,' but somehow as I thought it over it made it worse; it was not our fault but we had to go.

Just as I was about to give 'cease firing' an order came through on the telephone: 'Stand fast. No move until further order.' The men slept in the vehicles, I slept by the telephone.

May 27th – I got up at 4 am after a disturbed, restless night and rang up for news. There was none. During the morning I walked round the position and was impressed once again by the excellence of the natural cover and of the strength which we had developed. It was a real tragedy to think that we were going to leave it without firing a shot.

At midday I was summoned again to RHQ. The retreat was to be an orderly rearguard action and not a race to the sea as originally intended. A bridgehead was to be formed round Dunkirk, at first large, then gradually becoming smaller. We were to hold the eastern edge of it to be exact, the Ypres canal to the north of Ypres. A mobile force consisting of some anti-tank guns, machine-guns, Nigel's troop and my troop was to go back at once to this line. The rest of the division was to move that night. In half an hour we were limbered up and away. We crossed the canal at Quesnoy, which had been bombed just before our arrival. We moved on north, through Messines and along the Messines ridge. Everywhere were war cemeteries and regimental and other war memorials of the 'war to end war'. And here we were, doing the same thing against the same people over the same ground, only twenty-five years later. I thought of the refugees, desolate homes, ruined towns and wondered, as I drove along Messines ridge, how to make sure that twenty-five years hence my son would not drive along the Messines ridge leading his troop into action in the same area against the same enemy.

It was no time for day dreams. Shells were falling on Wytschaete as we drove through and British batteries were firing on the left of the road which was full of infantry all looking east. They looked very tired and were caked with dust and sweat. They waved as we drove by. I must explain at this point that I had been ordered to go by Messines, Wytschaete, St. Eloi, Vlamertinghe, Oostverleteren. i approached St. Eloi where I found some infantry. I halted and went up to their officer. They were holding the canal south of Ypres. The Belgians had come back quicker than was expected and contact had been made. The enemy was in Ypres and over the canal at Hazebrouck, though only in small numbers. I told him where I wanted to go; he laughed and said, 'We've just sent a patrol down that road; there's the answer' – and he pointed at a tall German standing smoking a cigarette. 'He was part of a machine-gun detachment on that road.' He looked very like a guardsman – tall, slim and holding himself well. He looked tired but fit and was burnt a very good colour by the sun. I looked at the map; I would have to go back and make a detour. At that moment two traffic control police arrived to mark the route for the main body of our division. I told them the position and took them off with me. Fortunately there was a wide space in St. Eloi made by a cross-roads and there I told the guns to swing round and retrace their steps. As the last ammunition lorry pulled clear, four shells fell round the cross-roads, followed by four more, followed by four more. I stopped in Wytschaete, went into the headquarters of a medium regiment in action there and sent a message to HQ 3 Division via 1 Corps and 2 Corps to say that their route via St. Eloi was blocked, suggesting an alternative. I asked if anyone knew what was happening on their left, north of Ypres, as I did not want to drive into the front line again. No-one seemed to know, but the impression was that the Germans were still some way beyond the canal, so I drove on through Dickebusch back onto my original route. There were new shell holes all round but in our usual miraculously lucky way we got through without a shell falling near us.

We finally arrived in our area. We met some RASC men who were embarking that night who gave us 500,000 cigarettes they could not carry. We were in action along some hedges near a farm by dark. Marcel went off to liaise with the infantry and came back to say that the Germans were about five miles off, beyond the canal; in the meantime all the bridges had been blown up except one which was covered by two guns of the Middlesex machine-gunners and a gun of the 20th Anti-tank Regiment. The rest of the canal was held by the sappers, who had a post with a bren gun every thousand yards or so. This force, with my troop behind it, was responsible for the divisional front till the infantry should arrive at dawn. 'The Middlesex don't expect them to get up to the canal tonight,' said Marcel. 'I hope they don't,' said I, and told the NCO i/c guard to have our bren gun handy before I went to bed.

May 28th – I was to have a longer sleep than usual and it was not until 5 am that I was told that the commanding officer wished to see me. I found him looking tired and unshaven. The regiment had arrived and he wanted to know the situation. I told him as well as I could. This was another quiet day. The weather had been perfect up to date, but we had several thunderstorms that day. My chief recollection is of the unfortunate refugees who, not realising that we were surrounded, were moving in every direction. The Germans dropped some pamphlets during the morning showing how we were completely cut off and with the caption:

British soldiers!
Here is your true situation!
You are completely surrounded!
Lay down your arms!

This caused much merriment among the troops, whose morale at this time was magnificent. The French Light Mechanised Division (Division Légère Motorisée) was operating in the same area as us and I was impressed as always by their complete optimism and *sang froid*.

That evening we were told that the line was to be shortened and that we were to move a few miles to a position north of Oostverleteren. We pulled out of action at about 9 pm having previously sent off a troop to Nieuport to deal with a German tank attack which had been put in there and had had some success owing to the defection of the Belgians on our left.

Our new position was the worst we had yet occupied, along hedges in open fields. The wagon lines, command post and all administrative arrangements were collected in a farm, and if it had been bombed or shelled I do not like to contemplate the result.

May 29th – We found a large number of abandoned Belgian rifles and ammunition in the cellar of our farm and every man armed himself with one. All through the morning an almost continuous stream of traffic passed along the main Ypres-Furnes road moving to the coast. Poperinghe was heavily bombed as usual about 9 am. Just before lunch they started to shell Oostverleteren, which was a good target as it contained divisional HQ, our regimental HQ and the 9th/17th Battery in action. The latter was magnificent and kept up a spirited reply all the morning and afternoon with shells falling all round them. At about 1.30 the Colonel was brought in with a splinter in the thigh, but quite cheerful.

During the afternoon we received orders that we were to move back to our final bridgehead round Dunkirk, that we were to hold the line from Ooste Dunkirk to Furnes and that the guns were to move at 6 pm. The CRA wished it to be known that this was not simply a dive for the sea, that our division was to cover the embarkation of other divisions and that he thought we should have to fight very hard, possibly for several days. A cheerful prospect.

A word about the infantry. My admiration for them at this stage was unbounded. We did twenty-four hours at an OP and then returned to the comparative quiet of a gun position. They were there for days on end. We drove back from position to position in motor cars. They walked. Yet in spite of it all their dogged cheerfulness and courage seemed inexhaustible. Yet in this particular position the battalion we were behind failed. John Dill was with them and said it was the only time he saw infantry panic. The enemy was shelling hard and he was lying in a cellar which was platoon HQ. A man suddenly ran down the steps and shouted, 'The anti-tank guns have gone.' 'My God,' said the platoon sergeant-major, 'we'll go too.' And go they did. The rot was I believe started by a subaltern who was seen leading his company out of the line without orders. Fortunately for him he was killed.

We accordingly received the order to limber up at once and withdraw to our final position near Coxyde. We found the canal bridge had been blown and had to make a wide detour to get over the canal. Finally, however, we got back onto our route. During this drive I saw the only signs of disorder I had yet seen. There were many stragglers with torn uniforms shouting for lifts and soon our vehicles were crammed to overflowing and men were sitting on our guns and limbers. The road presented a chaotic scene, infantry moving down it, ditched and derelict vehicles on either side and shells bursting on most cross-roads. In the middle of all this we passed the 1st Grenadiers, a single line of men on either side of the road, their equipment complete, moving very slowly but all in step, back to their final line. It was a fine sight. As we approached Furnes the number of abandoned vehicles increased and our progress became very slow owing to the traffic blocks. There was terrific aerial activity overhead and many of the more undisciplined troops were firing their rifles into the air at the aeroplanes. Finally, however, we got through Furnes and arrived at Coxyde. Here we found artillery of 4th Division firing hard to try to stop a German attack which was being put in along the coast at Nieuport to try and cut us off from the coast. Troops were thick on the ground and our area was a very small and unsuitable one. At length, however, we got the guns into action in two dispersed sections, each in a farm. I went to the canal to reconnoitre an OP and found it held by the Welsh Guards who were handing over to our people that night. There was absolute inactivity there. I returned to the guns, had a good dinner and was soon in bed with every prospect of a good night's sleep.

May 30th – I was woken up at 1 am by Humphrey Fox, who was commanding the battery. He said that the 2nd Grenadiers had had a bad time in Furnes and were asking for artillery support. Their colonel and two other officers had been killed. Would I go up and do what I could. I arrived in Furnes to find all quiet, but signs of heavy shelling and houses on fire. I went to battalion HQ where I found some of the tiredest men I have ever seen. They were having trouble from snipers on the other side of the canal, would I quieten them? I said I would do what I could. As soon as it was light, I went up to their left forward company and was shown a house from where I could see the target. This house was on the canal bank and there was still an old woman living there. Poor soul, she was almost out of her mind with terror. I now started on a most difficult task. You must realise that we were fighting in country which nobody could have foreseen would ever have been fought over by us and of course there were no maps. I was faced with the task of doing a close shoot with a Michelin road map.However, I added five hundred yards for luck on to my estimated range, eventually saw a round and then all was well. I spent an amusing hour or so and then went back to battalion HQ for breakfast and a shave. Imagine my fury when I was rung up and told that the battery had moved and that my registration would have to be done again. All was now quiet, so I returned to my house and registered two defensive fire tasks in front of the Grenadiers. At this moment a dirty and unshaven captain of the 4th Royal Berkshires walked in and said that he was holding the line left of 2nd Grenadiers, that when they were moving back from the last position the Germans had started shelling them and that they now had five officers and a hundred men, that they had no gunners allotted to them so could I help. I crawled onto the canal bank and registered three defensive fire targets for them. These targets were to come in useful later. By this time the Germans had begun to shell the centre of Furnes with a battery of 5.9". I had a most excellent lunch with the forward company of the Grenadiers, pâté, bully stew, hock, port and cigars in a cellar. After lunch I returned to battalion headquarters which was being shelled hard. It was uncanny how they always seemed to know where headquarters were and take steps accordingly. Fortunately there were some very deep cellars and there we sat till 6 pm. Eventually the house came down on top of us, but fortunately did not block the entrance. Through it all a grandfather clock continued ticking. My admiration for the Guards, always high, became unbounded during that afternoon. We discussed everything under the sun except the war and the atmosphere of complete calm and self-control was marvellous.

At about 6 pm the bombardment reached an intensity previously unequalled. The commanding officer came in and said that he had just come from brigade HQ and that a smoke screen was being put down on the front of the Berkshires and an attack seemed to be imminent there. I asked if he wanted defensive fire. He said, 'Yes.' The wires were cut to bits and the wireless had a splinter through it, so I got into the car and drove back to the battery. This was I think the most unpleasant drive I have ever had. The exits to Furnes were being heavily shelled to stop I imagine this eventuality. It failed to do so. As soon as the SOS had been shot, I returned to the town and once again had a most unpleasant time before I finally entered the cellar. Reports were beginning to come back to say that that attack had been beaten off. My friends of the left forward company sent back, 'Intense shelling, all positions held, all platoons in good heart.'

The commanding officer told me that, although that attack had been beaten off, he expected another that night, but he expected it in front of the Berkshires. Would I make arrangements? I said I would and went back to the guns. There I found all quiet and collected a new wireless set. I had some stiff drinks and some bully beef. The adjutant said that he expected we would have to stay for about five days. I returned to Furnes convinced that we would never go.

At about 10 o'clock a message came through to say that bridging operations were in progress at the junction between the Grenadiers and the Berkshires. I brought defensive fire down and for about an hour all was indefinite. Defensive fire was called for again. Finally it transpired that some Germans had got across but had been counter-attacked by the Coldstream who had chased them back over the canal.

I was then recalled to the battery, where I found Humphrey Fox, John Dill, Jimmie and Ashton. Humphrey began, 'The Corps Commander saw the Prime Minister tonight and told him what a desperate plight we were in. Accordingly a tremendous effort is to be made to get the BEF away tonight. But a skeleton force is to be left for 24 hours. As far as we are concerned it is to be a section with three officers. I propose to toss up to decide whether it is to be found by your troop, Robin, or yours, John. Heads, Robin stays, tails, John.' We both sat with La Vie Parisienne between us trying to look unconcerned. He flicked up a ten franc piece. It spun on the floor for what seemed an eternity and finally dropped. Tails.

May 31st – In the early hours of the morning we abandoned our guns and, taking with us all our optical instruments and what kit we could carry, marched slowly off towards the sea with heavy hearts. We arrived on the beach just as dawn was breaking and marched down to the water where flat-bottomed boats were waiting. We had to wade up to our waists to get out to them, but quietly one man after another climbed in and we rowed out to the barges and small craft of all kind that were to take us back to England. I was lucky enough to be on board a destroyer and went down to the wardroom where I dozed in a chair, drank hot tea and did my best to dry my soaking clothes. We arrived at Dover at about 10 o'clock, were bundled into trains and by 10.30 were steaming through the Kentish countryside. We stopped at a station and were given hot tea and bread and marmalade. Never have I enjoyed a meal more. After that things became embarrassing. At every station where we stopped a mass of women appeared with cigarettes, sweet biscuits, lemonade and other delicacies. At one station a woman got into our carriage and insisted on feeding us and thanking us. I sat in my corner with twenty-four hours growth on my beard longing for the train to start. It was astonishing to be treated thus; we had expected the population to turn their backs on us, a beaten army. We went on – Redhill, Ash, Wokingham, Newbury, where could we be going? We finally stopped at Shrivenham, stumbled into waiting motor-cars which took us to a delightful house converted into a mess. A charming young man took charge of me, gave me a bath, razors, socks, underclothes. He treated me like a helpless child! We returned to the mess for dinner. As I walked into the hall, I glanced at the clock. 8.55 pm. Three weeks ago to the hour the leading gun of my troop had passed the church in Thumesnil on our way to Belgium.

Knightsbridge Diary 1942

Despite heavy bombing of Bir Hacheim during the night of the 26th/27th May, and reports from our armoured cars of tanks moving south of the Bir, 8th Army were taken completely by surprise when on the morning of the 27th the Afrika Corps moved north to the east of the minefield. 7th Armoured Division to our south were badly mauled before they could deploy to their battle positions and at 9 am we heard that a column of tanks was moving on Knightsbridge from the south. 2nd Armoured Brigade was concentrated about a mile east of the Box and we moved south about two miles, while 22nd Armoured Brigade moved north to deal with a column of tanks reported at Rigel north of the Box. By about midday we saw a long column of guns and vehicles, but no tanks, about four thousand yards to our west moving north. Its head bumped the Box and the Knightsbridge guns opened fire, the German guns quickly replying. It was difficult to see exactly what was happening, as the mirage was at its height and visibility was very poor. *My diary reads*:

The Brigade then swung right and began to advance against the mass of transport. Almost at once we were met by heavy and accurate shellfire. All the batteries were ordered into action and we started firing at the red flashes of the enemy guns. For perhaps half an hour the slogging match continued and then we could see some of the enemy batteries moving and their fire slackened. The brigade moved forward. I was ordered to go as FOO with the leading cruiser squadron and off we went for the enemy guns. The cruisers would advance perhaps four hundred yards at full speed, then halt and fire at the guns. We kept up a continuous barrage from the 25 pounders. The whole German position was a mass of bursting shells. It was impossible to distinguish one's own shells from the salvoes of other troops and the 75-mm shells of the General Grants. It seemed that nothing could live in that mass of corruption but still the tracer shell came flying down from the enemy position. We seemed to be irresistible. On every side the tanks were moving forward. Behind us our own guns barked and the shells whistled overhead. The tracer flying among us seemed to have no effect. We were filled with a feeling of invulnerability and I had to

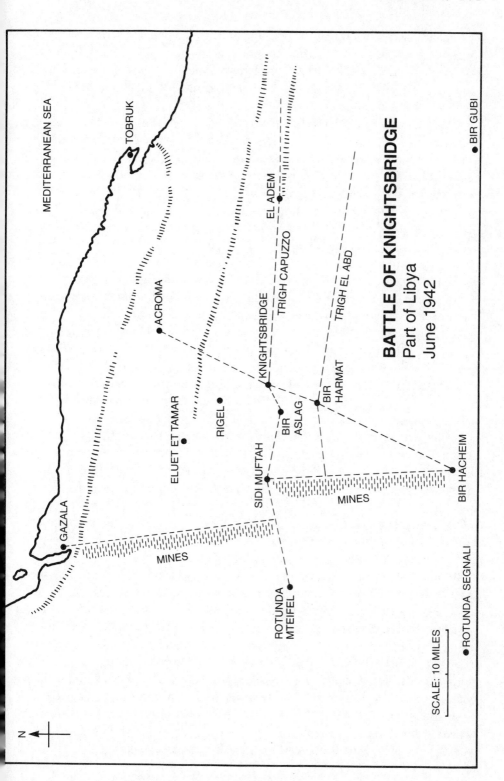

BATTLE OF KNIGHTSBRIDGE
Part of Libya
June 1942

reprimand my crew for opening the front visor to get a better view. By now several lorries were burning on the enemy position and the general mass of transport was hurrying away from us. Suddenly a few figures appeared through the smoke with their hands up and their helmets off. We were then about eight hundred yards from the guns.

The squadron I was with was ordered to go in among the guns. Off we went, the Bisa machine-guns stuttering and chattering as the cruisers raced for the guns. They went straight through them and then away in a right-handed semi-circle among the transport behind, while the Grants halted on the position and began to fire at the guns behind. The German gunners now left their guns and slit trenches and came shambling through our tanks with their hands up and their shoulders bent looking furtively about them – I was struck by how old many of them were and how pale-faced. They could not have been long in the desert sun. Meanwhile we were being met by accurate fire from a second position behind the first and I could see the Boche gunners feverishly serving their guns. I at once ranged my troop on to them, but they were very determined and continued to hold up any further advance. By this time the Grants had run out of ammunition and were withdrawn behind a small ridge to replenish. I found myself alone on the captured enemy position, but was so engrossed in shooting at the enemy guns and transport, which were wonderful targets, that I did not realise that I was being sniped by an anti-tank gun until two rounds fell just in front of the tank. I ordered the driver to reverse a few yards and lock over so to avoid the next round, but it was too late. The round hit the tank, penetrated the front armour and wounded my wireless operator in the face. I accordingly asked permission to withdraw and took him back to the nearest troop of guns, which had been moved close up behind us. We lifted him out – poor lad, he was unconscious and bleeding a lot, but I gather is now all right. I split a couple of bottles of beer with the other two members of the crew and we went back again to the firing line.

By now the light was failing fast. The Brigadier arrived among the leading tanks in his Blitzbug and held a conference of the commanding officers. It was decided that it was too late to assault the second position before dark. A small party consisting of Tommy Redfern's carriers, George Rich's troop and myself were sent out as soon as it was dark to destroy any enemy equipment that could not be salvaged and collect any stragglers. We counted sixteen guns, thirty-four lorries of various sorts and took over four hundred prisoners. Tommy found two very truculent German officers trying to make their way back to their own lines. He bundled them into his carrier. They were a very evil-looking pair, but the only two unwounded officers I saw. The rest had evidently made off before we arrived. We did some personal looting and I got a very nice Luger pistol. We then returned to the brigade, who had moved into close formation. At about 11 o'clock we drove back to our old leaguer area, leaving dozens of fires behind us to mark the battlefield. A good day, and when we got in we sat up for some time drinking whisky and discussing the fighting.

We learnt that we had been fighting 15th Panzer Division, whose tanks had reached Rigel where they had been attacked by 22nd Armoured Brigade. The column we had attacked had been their supporting lorried infantry and guns.

During the night there was an alarm. A German column moving west passed close to our leaguer, but neither side opened fire. At first light we opened out and moved south to the battlefield of the previous day, from where we could see a long column of guns and lorries to the west, stretching north and south as far as the eye could see. To our south columns were moving east along the Trigh El Abd. We spent the morning doing some desultory shooting and in the early afternoon received orders that the brigade was to attack the main concentration to our west. As the brigade started to move the first dive-bombing attack on the Knightsbridge Box went in. There were five dive-bombing attacks on the Box that afternoon, met in each case by a formidable barrage from our AA guns. In contrast to Dunkirk the Stukas did not press home their attacks as they had done when there was virtually no opposition. Instead of an almost vertical dive to within a few hundred feet of the ground, a small dip was enough for most of them before releasing their bombs. Occasionally a Messerschmidt 109F, queen of the Libyan skies, would go screaming low over the Box, its machine-guns glazing.

The Bays were in reserve as the brigade moved west and it soon became clear that the leading regiments were held up. We could see a hail of tracer coming from the German column. By this time the sun was sinking and we were ordered to halt and leaguer where we were, about a mile west of the Box.

May 29th was a busy day, according to my diary. As the first glow of light appeared John McDermid issued his orders. The whole brigade was to advance west and push the enemy back on to our minefield. I was to do FOO with George Streeter. We opened out and almost at once saw the Germans in the same place as they had been last night. The guns dropped into action at once and almost at the same moment shells started to drop among us. The Grant squadron was ordered to go straight for them, while a cruiser squadron was sent to the south round their flank. The Grants advanced in line, fifteen of them, moving forward, halting, firing, moving on again. They were stately and somehow rather feminine. I kept station with George Streeter and Bing Crosbie-Dawson, his second-in-command. We were being shelled heavily, but so far had suffered no casualties. I shouted to my crew to have the sausages ready because the affair would be over by breakfast time.

But an interesting situation was developing to the north. A column was hurrying towards us from the direction of Rigel and, as the light improved, we could make out forty German tanks for certain, with clouds of dust behind them and a column of vehicles and guns on the skyline. Tom Draffen (CO of the Bays) immediately sent out a flank guard, consisting of a cruiser squadron, the carriers and a troop of anti-tank guns all under Alex Barclay, his second-in-command. Our right rested on an escarpment, with some broken ground and wadis beyond, and it was hoped to delay them there long enough to allow us to overrun the guns and then face this new threat.

Meanwhile the attack was developing well and the leading cruisers were already on the position and darting in and out among the guns. Sorbo's platoon of the Rifle Brigade was sent forward to collect the prisoners. The enemy now began to shell the position themselves. A German officer went up to Sorbo, gave the Nazi salute and said, 'Heil Hitler! May I have permission to disperse my men?' Sorbo hit him hard between the eyes and replied, 'Only if you salute properly' – which he did.

The Grants now closed up on to the position and orders were given to continue the advance along the Trigh Capuzzo. The guns were limbered up and the brigade moved on. This order seemed to us rather rash at the time, but looking back the object presumably was to get across the gap in the minefield and stop the Boche withdrawing through it. But before we had gone more than a few yards fifteen Mark III tanks appeared to our right front, advancing at speed and keeping a very accurate fire. A troop of anti-tank guns was at once brought up to support the Grants and 9th Lancers came up on our left. The fire was now very hot and the German tanks were being reinforced every moment. My wireless aerial was shot away, which meant climbing out and fixing it in the middle of the battle. For some minutes the fight was very fierce and we were forced to withdraw a couple of hundred yards to conform with 9th Lancers and also to benefit from a small dip in the ground which gave some cover. But the line of Grants and 6-pounders broke the first shock of the German attack and they halted. George Streeter's squadron was withdrawn to replenish with ammunition.

But the position, although temporarily stabilised, was still very critical. The brigade had faced to its right. The Bays, originally on the right, were now in the centre, with 9th Lancers on the left and 10th Hussars had been brought up on the right. The flank guard was withdrawing. Our guns were in action still facing west. I was sent to our right-hand troop to find out their position and whether they were threatened by tanks and to take command there. I found them very exposed with the German tanks only a few hundred yards away, working up the wadis towards them. I at once suggested to John McDermid that they be withdrawn, covered by their protecting troop of anti-tank guns. This was done without loss under heavy machine-gun fire, but by the time the 25-pounders were safely away there was no chance of withdrawing the 6-pounders. In every case but one they were off their Portees and in very good positions commanding the wadis. Their subaltern was very worried, but we had some very amusing shooting and each gun accounted for one or two tanks before being put out itself. It was very heartening to see the tanks go up in flames. But the 50 mm guns on the Mark IV tanks were very accurate and one by one the guns received direct hits. The tanks were now very close so the anti-tank subaltern and I withdrew with the one remaining gun on its Portee. My Honey tank had had a glancing shot on the side, besides numerous machine-gun bullets, otherwise no damage.

On returning to the brigade I found that the Bays, having replenished, had taken up their old position on the left, the 9th were in the centre and the 10th on the right.

The German tanks were advancing steadily all along the line, with ours reversing slowly in front of them, firing as they went. The situation was difficult. We could count seventy-odd tanks to our front. But worse was to come. A column of tanks was reported to be advancing from the west and, shortly afterwards, another column was reported advancing from the south. Very soon both these columns were reported hostile and both as having about thirty or forty tanks. The 25-pounders of the brigade now formed a kind of rough square, pointing north, west and south. The tanks reversed slowly until they were sitting just behind the guns. We were surrounded on three sides – the Knightsbridge Box was on the fourth. We were in good positions, having a field of fire of about eight hundred yards. Our orders were not to fire until we could count their bogey wheels. The turrets of the leading German tanks appeared over the low crest. They halted. We waited. They did not come on. We still waited.

All the afternoon we sat opposite each other. We sniped their turrets with anti-tank guns. Their reply was very accurate and by the evening we had only two 6-pounders left. One or two of our tanks were hit. In return we could see several of their's burning behind the crest. They brought a machine-gun up, covered by the tanks, and machine-gunned my troop. It was very unpleasant as we could not spot them. During the afternoon John McDermid sent a message over the wireless, 'Tell the men to stick it. We have been promised reinforcements – you can't help larfin' can you?' 10th Hussars charged the tanks opposite them with a cruiser squadron, to try and relieve the pressure on their guns. Every tank was knocked out. It was the most unpleasant afternoon imaginable and on several occasions I felt very dry in the mouth. The troops were wonderfully good and furious at being made to hold their fire. We had sent all the gun towers well away from the gun positions. I think there was no doubt in anyone's mind that we intended to stay where we were – including the Germans.

Towards evening we expected the Germans to attack us from three sides at once. This was heightened by the arrival of the Stukas. The German tanks fired blue smoke to show their positions, but something must have gone wrong because to our delight they bombed the Italian column to our west. At last to our great relief darkness fell. We assembled for orders. John McDermid told us that the brigade formed a kind of wedge pushed into the German position, that the north end of the wedge was being cleared by some army tanks, and the south end by 4th Armoured Brigade, that at all costs we must sit tight where we were. To that end we must dig all night and be ready for anything tomorrow. He also said that poor Joe Baker of the Bays had had his head blown off in the first attack in the morning.

George Buchanan and I walked back to the troop. I changed the position by a few hundred yards – not so much because the other was bad, but because it held unpleasant associations for the men. I told the sergeant-major to rig up a light-proof lean-to against his lorry, so that one gun crew at a time could cook. We had had nothing to eat all day. We marked out gun pits. We sat and talked and drank whisky, and walked round the position and dug a bit to keep warm. At 3 am we heard the German tanks move off west. It seemed too good to be true.

The following morning (30th May) I was sent forward, with a section of carriers as escort, to the wadis where we had had the battle with the anti-tank guns, from where I was able to shell a large concentration on the Rigel feature. Their guns replied and shelled our guns and also my OP. At about 9 am I was relieved by Geoff Armstrong, who told me that the brigade was to continue its advance west, drive the enemy back against the minefield and block any gap in the mines to prevent further enemy withdrawal. He also told me that after yesterday's battle 10th Hussars had had only three tanks left. *My diary reads*:

The plan was that 9th Lancers supported by B and E Batteries of our regiment were to attack the enemy bridgehead frontally. Meanwhile the two cruiser squadrons of 3rd County of London Yeomanry were to sweep round the enemy's left or northern flank and get behind him. My troop was to support the Yeomanry and I was to get in touch at once with their CO. The Bays were to remain in reserve.

I found the CLY formed up on the Trigh Capuzzo near barrel 202. They were being fairly heavily shelled. I had some difficulty in finding the Colonel's tank. When I did find it, it was closed down. I jumped out of my Honey, climbed onto the turret and banged it. The Colonel poked his head out and I told him who I was and asked what he wanted. He said he was going straight along the Trigh for about a mile. He would then swing left-handed. By that time he hoped to have turned the enemy's flank. What he was afraid of was a threat to his right flank as he turned. Could I arrange for some smoke there? I said yes. I then motored up to the leading troop from where I had a better view.

The enemy bridgehead appeared to be held by about twenty-five Italian M13 tanks. They stood at regular intervals and shone very yellow in the sunlight. Their left rested on a gentle wadi. It was up this wadi that the CLY proposed to move. Behind the tanks were some lorries and guns. If the flanking movement was successful the CLY would be in among these, while the fifteen Grants would be more than a match for the twenty-five M13s.

I registered my smoke-screen very carefully and returned to the CO. At 11 o'clock the attack began. B & E crashed down on the guns and lorries behind the M13s. The enemy guns, including my northern friends of the morning, replied briskly. Shells were bursting all among our guns. At the same moment the line of Grants began to move slowly up the slope past Bir Aslag and the CLY cruisers dashed down the Trigh. I did not go with them but sat on a bit of high ground near a derelict armoured car. As the cruisers swung left in a cloud of dust I ordered 'fire'. The smoke-screen began to build up nicely on the flank. I moved forward to rejoin the cruisers. When I reached the CO I found him halted. I jumped out and ran across to him. He told me that the enemy left was protected by four 88-mm guns; that they were sited in the wadi, so that you could not see them until you were almost on top of them; that his leading squadron was held up and had suffered casualties. I motored up to the leading squadron-leader's tank to see if I could help. He told me that 9th Lancers, having pushed back the M13s, were held up by the enemy's guns; and that as the CLY were prevented from getting in amongst the guns the Brigadier had decided to break off the action. Then I received orders from the wireless, 'Disengage. Withdraw to previous position. Replenish. Brew up.'

At about 6 o'clock another attack went in. The noise was terrific as the shells from the forth-eight 25-pounders of the South Notts Hussars and 2nd RHA burst along the Aslag ridge. The smoke-screen was the longest and biggest I have ever seen. The whole ridge was wreathed in smoke with the M13s silhouetted against it. The Grants were climbing the hill slowly and laboriously. They halted and fired at the M13s. Then they moved on. The M13 edged back towards the smoke.

The CLY went along the Trigh Capuzzo with all the dash which made them famous in November. I raced along on their right flank. Tracer was flying and shells bursting among us, but it was difficult to see from where they came. After about two thousand yards we began to breast a low ridge. As we did so a line of eleven Mark III tanks appeared, hull down, in front of us. We were met by a fierce and accurate fire. The range was about one thousand yards. The 2-pounders of the CLY were at their worst range compared with the 50 mm of the Mark III. I at once halted. Fortunately I had the range pretty accurately to the ridge in front. I put down smoke at once. I thought perhaps the CO might decide to use it to allow his tanks to close. But the tanks had already had some casualties. Before the smoke became really effective the squadrons had wheeled outwards and rallied in a wadi a little behind my position. From there they kept up an unequal fire with the Mark IIIs. At this moment a message came from the Brigadier to say that the right flank was threatened, that the action was to be broken off and that the CLY were to rally behind the 25-pounders. After dark we formed close leaguer with the 9th Lancers.

During the night we were disturbed by sounds of battle about a mile away on the Trigh Capuzzo. We heard later that this was a column from the Box which had moved west down the Trigh during the night with orders to pursue 'the retreating enemy'. Instead they had run into a well-organised defensive position with mines, machine-guns and anti-tank guns, which had taken them completely by surprise. The column was dispersed losing about eighty men and five guns.

Next morning (31st May) I drove down the Trigh Capuzzo and joined a troop of armoured cars (the Royals) at Point 169, high ground which had been held only yesterday by the German tanks which had beaten off the CLY. From there I had a good view to my west and south of the German bridgehead over our minefield. I counted about seventy Italian tanks, with anti-tank guns dug in between them. Their left flank rested on the Trigh Capuzzo and was covered by anti-tank guns as far as the escarpment to the north. Behind the tanks guns were firing and in the distance

I could see about one thousand vehicles, presumably their supply echelon. *My diary adds*:

The mirage started at about 10 o'clock. Further shooting was a waste of ammunition. We were now on the battlefield of the previous two days. It was a mass of derelict tanks and lorries. We could see where the 10th Hussar squadron had been wiped out. Every tank was standing just as it had been hit, one on top of the other. They must have been caught coming round the shoulder of the escarpment into the wadi. I sent my crew to loot the German tanks. They all had a heavy, sticky smell about them. We lived for a week after that on German rations: meat and vegetable stew, very like ours but the meat stronger; slabs of thick heavy chocolate; ersatz jam; very good rivita called Knäckerbrot; best of all, lemons. The rations were all very clean and done up in cellophane paper. Several lorries had been abandoned merely through shortage of petrol. We searched several officers' kits. They contained the usual clothes and books. We also found masses of hair grease from Hamburg and Nivea cream and other skin foods. An interesting sidelight on the German character were several snapshots of blonde lady friends with no clothes on and in the most surprising attitudes. One letter began 'My sweetest darling' in English and then went on in German. I decided that everything German was unattractive, their food, their clothes and above all their smell and the hard ruthless lines of their tanks. I was fascinated by the tanks. Everything was so neat and well thought out: the ration boxes; the compartments for blankets; the escape hole for the driver in the floor; the commander's seat in the turret with thick bullet proof glass all the way round, giving him a great field of view. The log books in every case were kept right up to date. It was all so simple and efficient.

That evening in leaguer I heard that, due to heavy tank losses, the brigade was to be reorganised into a single composite regiment commanded by Tom Draffen, CO of the Bays, and his HQ. Our battery was to remain in the Bays Group. I also heard that there was to be a night attack by the infantry of 5th Indian Division on the enemy bridgehead over the minefield. This attack was postponed for twenty-four hours, as the Indians at Bir El Gubi were not informed until late in the afternoon and were unable to reach their start line till 4 am next morning.

On 1st June I went back to the OP at point 169 where I found Roy Seel of 2nd RHA with a section of carriers from the Coldstream and the armoured car troop of the Royals. *My diary continues*:

During the afternoon our CRA Frizz Fowler appeared in a jeep. He was very angry and blinking and snorting with rage. He asked what we were doing, where the nearest enemy were and in what strength. We showed him the four anti-tank guns about a mile up the Trigh. Asked why no guns had been moved up close behind us to silence the guns and push back the concentration still further. Said the armour was 'bloody sticky', that one determined squadron could deal with the anti-tank guns and then there was nothing to stop us. He finally disappeared in a cloud of dust.

We then decided to stage a little operation of our own. Roy Seel and I ranged our troops on the anti-tank guns. Under cover of this fire we and the carriers moved along the Trigh in some dead ground until we were about four hundred yards from the guns. We then poked our noses over a little rise. The carriers opened up with their bren guns and I opened up with my .37 and chased away a Mark II which was protecting the guns. Meanwhile the armoured car troop had moved below the escarpment to see what he could find, and perhaps work round behind. As soon as we opened fire the Germans replied quite briskly, so we withdrew. When we collected we found the Royals subaltern in high good humour. He had two dazed looking Italians sitting on his car. He had found them asleep in a lorry at the bottom of the escarpment, had shot up the lorry and captured them.

I returned to the battery to find, as I expected, that the attack had been postponed further. The troop had been shelled heavily all day. One had pitched in a gun pit, damaged the gun and wounded three men. George had had a chip out of his tin hat. Otherwise no casualties. So ended what we had all hoped would be a second 'Glorious First of June'.

This is perhaps a convenient moment to review the events of the first four days of the battle as they appeared to us at the time. After four days of stern and relentless fighting we had repulsed the first German attack. The enemy had been thrown back beyond the minefield, keeping however a bridgehead which so far had defeated all efforts to reduce it. We had captured many of his guns and hundreds of prisoners. Everywhere, except for the unfortunate 150th Brigade, our position was intact. Most important of all we had wrested the initiative from the enemy. The Armoured Brigade Group with its combination of General Grant tanks, 25-pounder and 6-pounder guns had proved itself a very formidable combination. Much of the success of 2nd Armoured Brigade was due to the fact that all the regimental groups had lived and trained together for three months. All the officers knew one another intimately and could appreciate what the other ones were likely to do. Although we all wore different badges we were all intensely loyal to the Bays Group.

2nd Armoured Brigade had been fighting offensively and defensively for four days and nights. The tank crews were tired and strained. The incessant noise of engines, the blare of the wireless, the dust, to say nothing of the strain of fighting superior equipment had blunted the keen offensive spirit of the brigade. After three days the enemy had been beaten back. It only required a final effort to destroy him utterly. If the attacks of the 30th had been pressed home this destruction would have been inevitable. But that effort was not forthcoming and the battle entered a different phase. Also it seemed that if the brigade had attacked even an hour earlier on the first day the 115th Lorried Infantry Regiment would have been entirely overrun, instead of only partially destroyed. The way would then have been open on the second day to advance and block the gap in the mines. None of the enemy would then have escaped. Such were our reflections.

The 2nd June was the first day since the battle had started that I did not man an OP, since my Honey tank went into the Light Aid Detachment for repairs to its throttle. So I spent the day trying to sleep on the gun position. Unfortunately the guns were shelled all day. On 3rd June we heard that 150th Brigade of 50th Division, who were holding part of the minefield at Sidi Muftah, had been overrun and we were ordered to Eluet El Tamar on the direct route to Tobruk to block any advance by the Germans in that direction. We stayed there, intermittently shelling the concentration at Sidi Muftah, until we moved on 5th June back to a position about five miles south and slightly east of Knightsbridge.

We were told that the Indians had attacked Bir Aslag at 3 am that morning with sticky bombs to blow up the enemy tanks and that they had everywhere reached their objectives. 22nd Armoured Brigade and 1st Army Tank Brigade were to exploit the success. We also heard that the Germans had made another gap in the minefield south of Bir Harmat, that tanks were reported moving through this gap and that we were to cover the left flank of the Indians. I was sent south towards this gap to try and locate these tanks, and after about five miles joined a patrol of 12th Lancers armoured cars. So far it was all very peaceful, although I could hear incessant gunfire from the direction of Aslag and Harmat. *My diary reads*:

At 2 o'clock I was told to return at once to the battery as they were moving. When I reached them I was given bad news. 22nd Armoured Brigade had been held up, were in difficulties and we must go to their help. We passed the headquarters of 5th Indian Division, which were being heavily dive-bombed. A subaltern taking ammunition forward told me that his battery were having a 'bloody awful time'. We passed the West Yorkshire Regiment, sitting about waiting for their transport. Their doctor told me that when they had reached their objectives that morning they had at once been counter-attacked by tanks and whole platoons had been wiped out.

The guns were now deployed in the low ground east of Aslag in very nearly the same positions that we had left for El Tamar. I was sent forward to find Frank Arkwright commanding 4th CLY and give him all the help I could. I drove up the Aslag ridge. Just below the crest was a line of British guns. They were the Divisional Artillery of 5th Indian Division. The guns were partly dug in, the ground was pitted with shell holes, empty cartridge cases lay everywhere, lorries were driving up and dumping ammunition by the guns, and a steady stream of wounded was walking back. Shells were bursting round the guns all along the ridge. The gunners worked and sweated at the guns stripped to the waist. A couple of thousand yards beyond, on the next ridge, were the tanks of 22nd Armoured Brigade. I drove up to them through the heaviest shelling that I had yet seen in this battle. There was a strong smell of cordite and the noise was terrific.

I found Frank Arkwright on the left of the brigade with his left on a minefield. The Gloucestershire Hussars were on his right, with a squadron of Valentines in between. He was having a slogging match with a line of German tanks about a thousand yards away. Neither side could advance. Frank Arkwright was withdrawing a troop at a time to replenish. The regiment had borne the heat and thunder of the day and Frank seemed tired and preoccupied as well he might. Shortly after I arrived one of those unaccountable lulls took place which always seem to happen in tank battles. Both sides, for no apparent reason, suddenly stop firing, and get out of their tanks to stretch their legs. Sometimes they even brew up. But that day we contented ourselves with Knäckerbrot, ersatz jam and some Boche lemons.

During this lull I saw a long column of lorries and guns moving south behind the Boche tanks. I engaged it and had a very good shot. Two lorries were set on fire and the column dispersed, but continued its southward movement. This column is to appear again later in a more sinister form.

John Scott, our brigade major, now appeared, took me to one side and said with the glorious *sang froid* of a cavalryman, 'Robin, these people are unhappy about their left flank, or think they are. If the Boche attacks down the minefield crash down as close in front of our tanks as ever you dare.' I said I would, but that it would not do much good. He said, 'Possibly not, but it will put heart into them, which they need badly' – and drove off in his Dingo (armoured scout car).

Soon after this nineteen German Mark III tanks began to advance towards the left of the CLY. Frank Arkwright moved his reserve Cruiser squadron round to support his Grants which were on that flank. I brought down my crashes and the thin CLY line held, gave a little bit but was not broken. The enemy fire was very fierce and he began to shell Frank's headquarters where I was. Some of the armour-piercing shot came very close, beating down anything in its way. It was very unpleasant to see the red flashes from the German tanks and to wonder for a second or two where the shot was going to go.

At this moment John McDermid ordered me to return to the guns. I cannot say that I was sorry. I drove back through the line of guns, some of whom were a bit quick on the trigger and shot at me thinking I was Boche. When I reached the battery the sun had already set. The Brigadier Raymond Briggs sent for me and asked me what the position was forward. I told him. He said that it was too late to do anything before dark. Meanwhile a column had appeared through the very gap which we had been watching and was striking north. He was going to march in the dark on Knightsbridge to avoid being cut off. He was very cool and as always in the battle I was much impressed.

The march was a nightmare. There was no moon, and we passed many shell holes and gun and vehicle pits into which several vehicles floundered. We moved in five long lines with the tanks in front, about twenty yards between lines and all vehicles closed right up. We made about 5 mph with long halts to collect stragglers. At 10 o'clock we were ordered to bivvy down, having marched 13 miles in 5 hours. I was very relieved to find my troop intact in its correct formation.

Next morning we found ourselves about a mile north of the Knightsbridge Box and were shelled by the German column which had moved north from Harmat the previous evening. We drove them off, and were joined by Brigadier Bill Carr and his HQ of 22nd Armoured Brigade, which he had managed to extricate from Aslag early that morning. But the guns were still where we had seen them the previous day and were in danger of being encircled by the southern column which I had shelled. *My diary continues:*

Meanwhile a column which was moving east down the Trigh Capuzzo threatened to close their sole remaining means of escape. I was sent to report on the column moving along the Trigh. I established myself just north of the Knightsbridge minefield. The column, of about twenty tanks, bumped the Box and then halted. The Box was heavily shelled.

2nd Armoured Brigade was now ordered to move against the German column from the north. Pinned as it was in front by the fire of the Box, it seemed that we had a good chance of taking it in flank, driving off the tanks and rescuing the guns at Aslag. Our battery was to move with the tanks and the other two batteries were to cover our advance. We had now the composite regiment of one Grant and two Cruiser squadrons, and also a Grant squadron of 8th Hussars, making a total of thirty Grants and forty Cruisers.

It was a stirring sight to see the leading Cruiser squadron, Humphrey Weld, work its way forward to my OP. The OP was on a kind of shoulder of the Knightsbridge ridge, which led down in front of us to a shallow wadi. After about a thousand yards this in turn rose steeply up the escarpment to the Trigh Capuzzo. The enemy's northern flank rested on the escarpment and as soon as the leading tanks bumped Knightsbridge anti-tank guns were put into action in the wadis running down from the escarpment. We shelled them as they came in, but they were very quick and soon tucked away. Consequently as soon as the Cruisers appeared round the shoulder of the ridge they were subjected to quite a heavy fire from the escarpment. It now became obvious that to storm the escarpment in face of determined opposition would be a costly and well nigh impossible operation, with the forces available. Accordingly, the 8th Hussar Grant squadron was sent straight over the Knightsbridge ridge against the enemy tanks. This meant that they would remain on high ground and would not have to scale the escarpment. It also meant that they would meet the German tanks to their left front, instead of cutting them off which would have occurred if the original plan had been successful. The squadron advanced straight across the open with great gallantry and determination. They were supported by the Bays' Grants, while the Cruisers demonstrated in the valley to draw the fire of the anti-tank guns. But twenty German tanks were too much for fifteen Grants and they were ordered to make a great right-handed wheel into the valley and rally behind the Cruisers. This they did and came out looking rather like hustled old ladies trying to preserve their dignity in a crowd, with the tracer flying all round them. But, although the attack had failed in its main object, it had forced the tanks attacking the Box to face left to meet this new threat. Further the converging fire of the Grants and the guns from the Box had forced the German tanks back with the loss of two, although they were not broken. It had also successfully removed any threat to the Box itself for the time being.

Meanwhile a great pall of smoke hung over Aslag. We could see many burning vehicles. There was increasing gunfire and little clouds of black smoke marked the German air bursts. During the afternoon I believe 4th Armoured Brigade made an attempt south of Knightsbridge to relieve the doomed batteries, but it was no more successful than ours. At 5 pm the firing stopped and we could see long black lines of men. The whole force, consisting of the South Notts Hussars, two or three field regiments and many anti-tank guns and infantry had surrendered. We heard afterwards that many gun crews were completely wiped out three times. Finally they ran out of ammunition and it was impossible to get any more to them.

When darkness fell the tanks leagured just behind the ridge and the guns remained where they were for the night.

The disastrous frontal attack on the bridgehead had had terrible consequences. If it had taken place five days earlier, as originally planned, it might well have been successful. The enemy was not properly established. He had his back to the minefield. He had had the worst of four days heavy fighting. But we had allowed ourselves to be lulled by the old cry that time was on our side. We had given him five precious days to dig himself in, to improve his supply arrangements through the mines, to repair and replenish his tanks and to organise himself thoroughly. Instead of straining every nerve and sinew to follow up our success we had allowed it to slip from our fingers. Then we attacked the enemy at his strongest point. We carried out a night attack, presumably to achieve surprise. But we sacrificed all surprise by a half-hour preliminary bombardment, so that the splendid Gurkhas struck at air. The enemy had very wisely withdrawn the bulk of his forces out of harm's way at the first sign of trouble. Then Rommel, with his brilliant opportunism, had not allowed the situation to rest there. He decided to benefit by our mistakes. To this end he threw the column round Harmat from the south and along the Trigh Capuzzo from the north. Thereby he succeeded not only in repelling but also destroying the attacking force.

Apart from consistent shelling of our guns during the morning, 7th June was uneventful until the afternoon.

At about 2 pm at the height of the mirage there was some movement among the German concentration and about twenty tanks advanced towards us. When they reached the edge of the escarpment they halted, took up hull down positions in the various accidents of ground there and began a long range desultory fire at our tanks. At the same time a heavy barrage came down on the Knightsbridge Box and on our guns behind it. Under cover of these two movements a column of troop carriers advanced at speed to within about a thousand yards of the Box. The infantry then dismounted from the troop carriers, which withdrew while the infantry advanced steadily towards the Box. The whole operation was so well timed and executed that it had happened almost before we realised that anything untoward was afoot. I at once brought down the fire of the whole battery onto the advancing infantry. I was surprised to see that there was no firing from the guns of the Box. When the German infantry seemed to be almost within the outer defences 2nd RHA spoke. I heard afterwards that the gunners had waited until the enemy were on the edge of the minefield, and had then fired a salvo over open sights. From where I was I could see the flashes of the guns followed immediately by the bursting shells. When the smoke cleared away there were many gaps in the infantry masses. They stood, hesitant, as if uncertain what to do next. 2nd RHA made up their minds for them. A second salvo crashed among them. This was enough. But their discipline was such that, instead of flying in confusion as any troops would have done, they remained where they were, digging themselves in frantically under 25-pounder fire, stiffened by the machine-guns and rifles of the Coldstream.

While this assault on the Box was taking place our divisional commander Herbert Lumsden appeared among the leading tanks and personally ordered the Brigadier to disengage and withdraw north of Rigel. Accordingly the guns limbered up and the tanks lumbered away over the Rigel feature. They were followed by a stream of invective over the wireless from Len Livingstone-Learmouth, who was commanding a battery of 2nd RHA inside the Box, ending with the words 'and you're a lot of yellow bastards, and I don't care who's listening!'

We spent two quiet days north of the Rigel ridge, a comparatively unspoilt part of the desert in stark contrast to the desolate battlefield south of Knightsbridge where we had spent the last fortnight. There the ground was torn up by shell and bomb craters, slit trenches and vehicle pits. The sand was everywhere churned up by tank tracks. Bits of equipment and steel helmets of both armies, biscuit and bully beef tins lay scattered around. There were so many derelict and burnt-out tanks and lorries of both sides that it was difficult to tell which were alive and which were not. There were many graves and over all hung the stench of death. It was a terrible and melancholy scene in what had come to be called 'the Cauldron'. We were therefore not pleased when at about 3 pm on 10th June, having spent the morning supporting an abortive attack by 4th Armoured Brigade west of Knightsbridge, we were ordered back south of the Box.

My OP assistant during the battle was John Tinsley. An Old Harrovian, he had joined the HAC before the war as a gunner. He was small in stature, very quiet and unassuming with charming manners. He had refused a commission in 1939 saying that he did not want the responsibility. He was a first-class OPA. I made him a lance-bombadier and felt privileged to have him with me.

During the afternoon of 11th June we heard that Bir Hacheim had fallen and that Rommel, always quick to exploit success, was pushing tanks north-east on Tobruk. 2nd Armoured Brigade moved east along the Trigh Capuzzo and, after about three miles, took up position on the left of 4th Armoured Brigade who were about a mile south of the Trigh, facing south. As we deployed under shellfire we could see the enemy column, like a long black snake of tanks, guns and lorries, about two miles away moving east. The light was fading fast as it does in the desert and it was obvious that there would be no major action that day. But it was also obvious to everyone that tomorrow would see a major tank battle. However, our armour was concentrated, we were in good positions along an escarpment and must be facing Rommel's last reserve. His move from Bir Hacheim was similar to the one we had defeated on the first day and we could do it again. So we went to bed full of confidence. *According to my diary*:

In the grey light of dawn we broke leaguer. The Bays took up their position on the escarpment on the left of 4th Armoured Brigade. Humphrey Weld's Cruiser squadron was thrown forward to occupy a low ridge about a thousand yards to their left front. The guns came into action about two thousand yards behind the tanks. As the day grew brighter I felt my way forward with a troop of armoured cars to make contact with the enemy. To the east we could hear heavy shellfire. This could only be an attack on the El Adem Box.

It was now fairly light and we could see the enemy about two thousand yards away. His tanks were deployed, facing us, in much the same position as yesterday. Behind them an unbroken line of guns and lorries was moving east. These we at once engaged and had some amusing shooting. The tactical reconnaissance aeroplanes now appeared overhead, diving and twisting above the enemy columns. Half an hour later their reports came over the air. A battle was in progress round the El Adem Box. No armour was engaged and so far our people seemed to have held their own. Indeed a slackening of the sounds of gunfire showed that the attack on the Box had been beaten off. Columns of armoured cars, guns, transport and tanks, the last totalling a hundred and fifty, were reported moving north-east from Bir Hacheim.

Meanwhile we sat inactive on the escarpment. We shelled the enemy columns and had breakfast. But neither side made any move until 9 am. At that time columns of field guns began to work round and harrass our left flank. Gerry was on this flank and engaged the guns with his troop. At the same time about thirty tanks, mostly Mark III, moved against the Bays. They advanced towards us in line about fifty yards apart. They advanced almost unopposed until they reached a ridge about a thousand yards from our position. As they breasted the ridge they were met by the fire of the Grant squadron. They replied to it, firing on the move. But the Grants' fire from their stationary platforms was more accurate. The line of Mark IIIs halted, reversed into hull down positions behind the ridge and began to return the fire of the Grants. At the same time three 88-mm guns were brought up with the greatest boldness and unlimbered just behind the crest. Here was the chance for the 25-pounders. I at once ranged on them and had the gratification of seeing all three limber up and withdraw. They tried to find other positions, but as soon as they dropped into action we drove them off, until in disgust one after the other withdrew. Meanwhile Gerry had been doing great work on the left flank. He had engaged the gun columns as soon as they had tried to establish themselves or become too bold. He kept them always on the move and at last they withdrew south-west.

The position on our front had now reached a stalemate. The Mark IIIs and Grants continued to snipe at one another, but we had beaten off the enemy and his first attempt to turn our left flank and cut our communications had failed. But the enemy brought several batteries into action on our front and the whole British line was, by 12 o'clock, subjected to a very heavy and accurate shellfire. Several tanks were hit and set on fire. Our batteries behind were included in this shelling and we began to have reports of casualties, among them Quentin Drage sightly wounded in the bottom! A medium battery came into action near us to try and deal with the enemy guns. But they were well hidden and I do not think its fire had much effect.

While the shelling was at its height the enemy launched fifty tanks against the centre of 4th Armoured Brigade. They advanced at speed, firing as they came. 4th Armoured Brigade, already shaken by the shellfire and having suffered some casualties, was pushed back by this fierce onslaught. They reversed slowly, returning the enemy's fire. They reversed until they reached the line of 25-pounders behind them, while the Mark IIIs climbed the escarpment. 4th Armoured Brigade now stood among the 25-pounders and halted the enemy on top of the escarpment. The Mark IIIs at once established themselves hull down behind the escarpment and began to machine-gun the crews of the 25-pounders. The situation was critical.

All this time the Bays had practically not been engaged and many of us on the spot thought that this was the moment for us to have launched a counter-attack on the enemy's flank. But it was not to be.

We received the order to disengage and withdraw four miles due north. It was said that 4th Armoured Brigade could not afford to lose any more tanks.

The guns limbered up under heavy machine-gun fire, but they withdrew without loss and in good order under their own smoke. Lorried infantry at once followed up our withdrawal very closely, machine-gunning as they came. A Cruiser squadron was sent to charge them and thereafter they kept their distance and showed us more respect. After going about two miles we were ordered to turn west and withdraw on Knightsbridge. By this move, although we allowed the enemy to cross our communications, we still remained a threat to his. 4th Armoured Brigade, however, never received the order and we last saw them going at speed for Tobruk.

When we arrived at the Box we found 22nd Armoured Brigade heavily engaged about Bir Bellefaa. They were being attacked from the south, their right on the Box.

They were supported by B & E Batteries of our regiment. The batteries had been dive-bombed just before we arrived and had suffered heavy casualties.

We were ordered to deploy on the left of 22nd Armoured Brigade, about a mile south of the Trigh Capuzzo and facing south. By the time we had completed this movement there was a lull in the battle and we brewed up. But a very unpleasant situation now arose. As it began to get dark the head of the pursuing German column approached along the Trigh Capuzzo from the east. A light gun was brought into action and began to shell 'E' Battery from their left rear, while the lorried infantry machine-gunned their wagon lines, setting several gun towers on fire. At the same time the Germans again attacked 22nd Armoured Brigade from the south. Humphrey Weld was sent to dislodge the lorried infantry and the light gun and to clarify the situation on that flank. I was sent with him to support him. It was now nearly dark. We succeeded in dislodging the gun by 25-pounder fire and George Rich took a troop to push back the lorried infantry enough to allow 'E' to extricate their wagon lines. But it was now too dark to do more than this.

We were ordered to leaguer near the Box. I could not find the battery on this confused battlefield, so received permission to leaguer with the Bays. At this juncture my faithful Honey refused to go another yard, so I was towed into leaguer by Humphrey Weld.

An echelon of sorts arrived with a little of the wrong sort of petrol, no food and worst of all no ammunition for the tanks. We were surrounded on three sides by the enemy's leaguer flares. Well might George Rich's driver say to him, 'Is that right, sir, the General said, 'Every man for himself'?' Humphrey Weld said to me, 'Robin, tomorrow will be the most bloody day you and I have ever spent.' We rolled ourselves up in our blankets in a depressed frame of mind.

When I am asked why the great tank battle on 12th June was lost I say, 'Because the enemy had higher morale and was in better tanks better handled.' Surely adequate reason.

Shortly before dawn on 13th June we broke leaguer. By working all night my Honey tank had been repaired. 22nd Armoured Brigade was to face south, with its right on the Knightsbridge Box; we were to face east, with our backs to the Box. I was to go with Humphrey Weld as FOO. We moved to very much the same position as we had occupied last night. Humphrey told his crew to cook breakfast, but I was looking through my glasses and saw a sight that very soon stopped all idea of breakfast. About a mile away a column was breaking leaguer. As we watched them we saw about thirty tanks open out and begin to move towards us in line. Behind them a long column of guns and lorries stretched down the Trigh Capuzzo. It was a horrible sight to see on an empty stomach at such an early hour. But fortunately for us the enemy only advanced slowly as the light improved. If he had advanced with his usual resolution things would have gone badly for us, for we were only half deployed. There seemed to be no threat from the south, so we all side-stepped to the left to meet the new situation. 22nd Armoured Brigade took our place astride the Trigh Capuzzo and we moved north of it. The enemy now advanced steadily towards us. We began shelling the long column behind and I think must have caused considerable damage because they were packed very closely together. At any rate we very soon established superiority over their artillery because we did not allow them to come into action and they practically never fired.

Meanwhile the enemy tanks with the 88 mm among them were slowly pushing back the Bays. The 88s were very well handled and made very good use of ground. The enemy also had the rising sun behind him, so that it was extremely difficult to see them. I left Humphrey and joined the Grant squadron who were being much worried by the 88s. George Streeter had been wounded the day before and the squadron was commanded by Bing Crosbie-Dawson. I succeeded in silencing one 88, but the sun made observation very difficult.

The Bays were truly in their hour of trial. The regiment was in a sort of half circle, the Grants in the centre and the two Cruiser squadrons dropped back on either flank. In the centre Tom Draffen and John Tatham-Warter sat on the turret of Tom's tank, calmly directing the battle under very heavy fire. We had now reversed for about a mile, 22nd Armoured Brigade had come back with us and we extended their left flank. Their right rested on the Box. We were near a blockhouse, about a mile north of Knightsbridge. Orders now came to halt and not to retire any further. John McDermid, however, moved the guns back to a new position. This position, although well covered from the front, was open to the rear. As the guns dropped into action they were at once heavily engaged from the rear by the guns at Aslag. The shelling was very accurate and in a very few minutes we suffered several casualties, including George Buchanan. John at once moved the battery to another position, but it had been an unpleasant and expensive few minutes.

John now told me to stop shelling the vehicles and to bring the whole battery down on the leading enemy tanks. This I did and they halted. The situation, temporarily at any rate, had eased considerably. We had succeeded in holding the enemy and a lull ensued.

A battalion of Matilda tanks now arrived to relieve the Bays, who were to replenish. The Matilda tanks were full of confidence and good cheer. They had come from Gazala where all was quiet. They said that we had only to finish off this bit of armour here and all would be well. They were clean and well-shaved and clear-eyed and we, tired and unshaven after the hard fighting of the last day and a half, felt rather resentful of them.

John McDermid told me that half an hour before they were relieved the Bays had run completely out of ammunition, which was why he had told us to shell the enemy tanks. If they had come on then nothing would have stopped them. We now moved the battery back some way, to join the other two batteries of the regiment, so as to have better anti-tank defence. The position seemed, for the time being at any rate, reasonably secure. We brewed up and washed. The enemy were bringing up more anti-tank guns and these we shelled. 22nd Armoured Brigade was on our right and our left rested on the escarpment. Gerry was sent with our remaining three 6-pounders to secure this left flank.

A sand storm now started and we sat in it, unable to see more than fifty yards. At about 3 pm we had bad news. Under cover of the sandstorm the enemy had crept up and overrun the outpost company of the Scots Guards, holding the Rigel Box. They had then put the prisoners in front of their tanks and had advanced with seventy tanks on the main Rigel position. This at present was still holding, but they had succeeded in establishing themselves there to a certain extent. The position, as so often, was obscure. 4th Armoured Brigade, returned from Tobruk, were to counter-attack supported by the Bays.

I was now sent off to help the Bays in their counter-attack. The rest of the regiment was supporting them, the battery's main job being to face east. But I was to go with the Bays to give them any support which could be spared. When I reached them I found that the attack was held up. 4th Armoured Brigade were going in from the north and the Bays along the Rigel feature. The Bays were coming under fairly heavy shellfire.

The sandstorm now cleared and the enemy began to attack the Matilda tanks from the east. They stood back out of range of the 2-pounders and picked them off with great accuracy. Gerry then did the only thing possible. He put down a smoke-screen about eight hundred yards in front of the Matilda tanks. The enemy refused to move through it. Gerry kept up the smoke for an hour and a half, until it was dark, thereby stopping the battle. At this time the batteries of the regiment were firing in entirely opposite directions, 'B' & 'E' due west and ourselves due east.

Just before dark the guns were machine-gunned by our own Kittihawks. Poor Tommy Redfern of the Rifle Brigade was so badly wounded in the leg by this attack that he died in hospital. The counter-attack on Rigel had failed. Darkness found us in the very unpleasant position of having enemy tank forces east and west of us and a strong position to the south.

I leaguered with the Bays. We heard that the inevitable was to happen. The Knightsbridge and Rigel Boxes were to be evacuated and an hour before dawn we were all to move north for six miles. We leaguered where we were on the Rigel feature, the Bays limping in by ones and twos from their unsuccessful counter-attacks. They had eleven cruisers and two Grants left when all complete. I talked to Tom Draffen and drank some whisky with him. He said how disappointing it was that things had turned out as they had after such a promising start. He was very tired.

At 4.30 am on 14th June we moved north for six miles, and when we arrived John McDermid gave his orders. At all costs the Gazala-Tobruk road, down which 1st South African Division were withdrawing, must be kept open. The remains of 1st Armoured Division, consisting of ourselves, 2nd Royal Horse Artillery, with forty-eight 25-pounders between us, together with the Rifle Brigade and the remaining anti-tank guns, with the thirteen tanks of the Bays in reserve, were to hold the gap between the Eluet-El-Tamar and Acroma Boxes, both of which still held. Mid-way between these two Boxes was a subsidiary Box held by a battalion of the Essex Regiment and a 25-pounder battery of 8th Field Regiment. This we called the Essex Box. There was also a minefield which ran west from the Acroma Box to join the main minefield running south from Gazala. It was on this minefield that we hoped to delay the enemy. The guns were in primarily anti-tank positions covering the mines.

After a quick breakfast I moved to an OP about a thousand yards north-east of the Tamar Box. *My diary continues*:

When I reached the top of the Tamar feature I saw a formidable sight. A mass of vehicles and guns was swarming east and north over the Rigel feature. The whole German army seemed to be on the move. The desert was covered with moving lorries. From where I sat it looked like a disturbed anthill. I engaged the mass, but it was such an enormous target that one hardly knew where to begin.

At this critical time my Honey tank was pulling very badly. Fortunately a replacement had just arrived, so I returned to the guns and we changed the wireless set and all our kit and stores into the new tank. I found the gunners frantically digging gun pits, some of them looking a little white about the gills, as well they might with seventy German tanks reported two miles away and more behind. I shaved, washed all over, put on clean clothes and had an excellent lunch. By this time my Honey was ready and I was ordered to relieve Gerry at his OP at point 180, near the Essex Box.

To get any sort of view here it was necessary to drive through the minefield. Beyond the mines was a gentle slope, up which I drove. I halted hull down behind the crest. Gerry told me it was as well not to be too conspicuous on the crest because the Boche were very close and had been sniping him and firing a machine-gun. He then went off.

The sand storm was very bad. Visibility only about fifty yards. I sat in the lee of my tank with John Tinsley and talked hunting. We ate a tin of fruit. It was a very miserable day.

At about 4 o'clock the sand storm lifted a bit. I was feeling very tired and rather casual. I climbed into the turret to have a look over the crest. I then turned round to have a look at the gap in the mines, which I was surprised to see was coming under fairly heavy shellfire. As I turned a bullet went through the top of my hat, grazing my head. It knocked me silly for a bit and was bleeding a good deal. So I rang up John and asked for permission to have it dressed. I set off through the gap in the mines. When we were about half way through I was horrified to see twelve German tanks about six hundred yards from the gap. I told my driver to go at full speed. When we were clear of the mines I turned hard left down them, feeling rather like a rabbit bolted from its hole. Tracer was flying all round us. I realised it was only a question of time before we were hit. Suddenly there was a crack on the side of the tank and a smashing noise inside. I looked down into the fighting compartment and saw a scene of chaos. Tinsley and Baskeyfield, my wireless operator, were both lying on the floor with grey faces. The wireless was smashed. The tank stopped. I picked up the speaking tube and said, 'Go on Finneron.' To my amazement we went on and were soon safely out of range! I then looked down and was mildly surprised to see a large hole on the inside of my left knee. I drove straight to John McDermid and told him what had happened. He told me to go to the ambulance. When we reached the ambulance Baskeyfield got up. He was very shaken but otherwise all right. Tinsley was hit in the chest and I did not like the look of him at all.

Poor Hoppy Hopkinson's armoured car now arrived, with Hoppy (commanding 'B' Battery) dead inside. Also wounded from the Essex Box kept trickling up. We were on the edge of an escarpment overlooking the battlefield. We seemed to be holding them, but shells were falling all round the ambulance so we moved a thousand yards back. I was now beginning to feel rather light-headed. I took a bottle of whisky from my tank and drank half of it neat. The doctor then gave me a shot of morphia and dressed my leg and put me in the ambulance. As it was getting dark we drove off.

We had a nightmare drive. The ambulance nearly turned over going down an escarpment on to the road. Once on the road we were jammed in the retreating columns of 1st South African Division. The road was being shelled. At last at 4 am we reached Tobruk hospital. The organisation was wonderful. We were carried into a room where there were rows and rows of stretchers. We were given a cup of tea. In a few minutes a doctor arrived and looked at my card. Half an hour after arriving I was carried into the X-ray room. I was X-rayed and carried into the theatre with the X-ray photograph on my chest. Within an hour of arriving I was laid on the slab. A surgeon, his face grey with fatigue, was standing beside me. We talked for a few minutes about the battle. He looked at the photograph. Then a man came up behind, said, 'All right, old man, here you go,' clapped a chloroform pad over my nose and that was the last I knew for some time.

I came round at about midday to find myself in a large airy ward in the former Italian hospital, with views over the harbour. My left leg was encased in a 'Tobruk splint' with metal rods on each side of the plaster to keep my leg rigid. An orderly came in and announced that all those fit to be moved would be evacuated that day, as the Germans were approaching Tobruk. I shall never forget the expression on the face of the man in the next bed, whose leg had just been amputated, when he heard this news.

We were soon carried on stretchers and loaded on to ambulances. Mine was the last to leave and was driven by two Americans, members of the Society of Friends. When we had been driving for an hour or two and must have been near Gambut, the former HQ of 8th Army, the ambulance stopped, the doors opened and the driver's mate said cheerfully, 'Say you guys, how about stopping for a brew?' The road was deserted, always a bad sign in a war zone, and I had visions of a German 8-wheeler armoured car appearing at any moment from the desert. I said, 'Don't you stop until we get down the Sollum Pass. Keep driving.' 'Just as you say, Captain,' he replied, as cheerful as before, slammed the doors and on we drove. I must say I felt relieved as the ambulance rolled slowly down the Sollum Pass.

We stopped that evening at a casualty clearing station at Bug Bug on the road to Sidi Barrani. This consisted of some large tents, into which we were carried on our stretchers, which were laid on the sand. We were each given two mess-tins, one containing stew, the other tea, and there we spent the night. Most of the patients were walking wounded, who passed the time talking and swearing and playing cards. I did not find it easy to sleep.

Next day we drove on to Mersa Matruh to a tented hospital with beds with clean sheets, and nurses in starched uniforms wearing the smart red capes of their service. Mine was a dragon. All I wanted to do was sleep, but that was not to be permitted. First I must be shaved, then given an unsuitable meal of fried eggs and sausages. Only when I was considered fit for inspection by the CO was I allowed to sleep.

Next day we were carried on our stretchers on to a hospital train en route for the Delta. Mine was a lower bunk so that I could not sit up, and I suffered more from indigestion than from my wound.

Meanwhile the HAC were retreating across the desert and arrived at Mersa Matruh some days later. There they were surrounded with their backs to the sea and obliged to fight their way out in the darkness, suffering heavy casualties in men and guns. All the majors were wounded, so Geoff Armstrong was given command of a composite battery of about eight guns and an assortment of vehicles. This battery did sterling work with the small force that held Ruweisat Ridge and finally stopped Rommel's drive to the Delta.

Our new colonel, who had succeeded 'Baron' Ebbels on his promotion to CRA 10th Armoured Division just before the battle, decided that this was an appropriate time to retire from the scene, since the regiment was reduced to one battery, and established himself in the Hotel Cecil in Alexandria, not returning to the regiment until they were withdrawn from the line to re-fit. This action, coupled with stories of the Colonel's conduct during the retreat and especially at Matruh, caused outrage in the regiment. The Colonel's reaction was to arrange for Geoff Armstrong to be posted without notice or reason to the base depot. This caused a near mutiny among the officers, all the original HAC officers of 'A' Battery applying for transfers to other regiments, which were granted. Fortunately all turned out well. Geoff was posted in command of a regular field battery, and the Colonel was soon replaced by Richard Goodbody who had been the popular HAC adjutant before the war, and ultimately became a general.

The HAC won their spurs at Knightsbridge. After their disastrous first action at Agheila they redeemed themselves during that long fluctuating battle. This must have been recognised by the authorities, for the HAC were the first RHA regiment to receive the new self-propelled guns, with which they took part in the battles of El Alamein and across North Africa into Italy. But they had suffered terribly. During those first six months in the desert the regiment lost 13 officers and 142 other ranks killed, 20 officers and 158 other ranks wounded and 10 officers and 241 other ranks taken prisoner. Few of those who sailed in the *Samaria* escaped unscathed. Among the killed was John Tinsley who died of his wounds on 14th June. Jamie Shiel and Frank Cook were both taken prisoner during the break-out from Matruh and spent the remainder of the war in POW camps.

Stag Hunting

The best way to see Exmoor is from a horse, and the best way to see the deer is to go hunting, since on hunting days the deer move from the wooded combes on to the open moor. If you like mile upon mile of heather go to Scotland. The charm of Exmoor is the contrast between the wooded combes, the green 'in-fields' and the heather moorland behind. And it is always changing. In the winter it is dark and forbidding, with the rain sometimes driven horizontally by the wind, so that it is difficult to stay on one's horse. But even then there are beautiful clear days with the light changing as the clouds scud across the sun and in the spring when the ferns begin to peep the moor comes alive, until it reaches its full glory when the heather comes out in August. Then, in the autumn, the bracken turns red and then yellow and the range of colours is superb.

To see the moor in its changing moods is one of the principal pleasures of hunting on Exmoor. But there is much more to it than that. Hunting on Exmoor, especially stag-hunting, is like first division football in Liverpool. It is the common interest of all classes of society and provides cohesion to the whole district. Go into any pub on a hunting day and the talk is exclusively of the day's hunting: where the stag was found, where it came up and whether the original stag was killed or whether the hounds changed on to another. More and more people now come from all over England to follow the hounds in cars and on motor-cycles, as well as on horseback, and it is now a major spectator sport. The huntsman is submitted to the same kind of adulation and criticism as the manager of a leading football club.

For many years there has been an increasing campaign to stop stag-hunting. This is not the place to enter into that argument, except to say that the campaign is based largely on ignorance and is an attempt by animal rights activists to persuade an urban majority to ban the traditional way of life of the rural minority. For example deer are not 'pulled down' by the hounds; they are cleanly shot at the end of the hunt. Deer must be culled and every independent inquiry has confirmed that hunting plays a vital rôle on Exmoor, which supports the healthiest herd of red deer in the United Kingdom and practically the only herd left in England. I was not brought up to stag-hunting, the technique of which is very different to fox-hunting. But I have grown to love it, although perhaps not so much as Judy who has sadly had to give up after an unsuccessful hip operation.

The stag-hunting season revolves round the annual life cycle of the deer. On Exmoor the three lowest points on a stag's horns are called his 'rights' - brow, bray and tray. As the stag grows older he will have more and longer points 'on top', so that a twelve pointer or Royal on Exmoor is described as having all his rights and three on top. Many of the older stags have a fine spread of antlers and then the head starts to decline as the stag 'goes back'. The stags drop their horns in April when hunting stops and grow new horns during the summer, suffering a good deal of discomfort in the process. The nascent horns are covered with a protective layer of 'velvet', which falls away in August when stag-hunting starts and the big stags which are past their prime or 'going back' are hunted until the rut in late October. The hunt employs a harbourer, always a local with knowledge of the deer, and often an experienced naturalist who, in conjunction with the local farmer, harbours a 'warrantable' stag the night before hunting. Initially the harbourer tracks or 'slots' the deer, the stag's foot being called a slot. The harbourer can tell from the slot mark not only the sex but also the age of the deer, and the huntsman will often slot the deer during a hunt when it has joined other deer, so as to keep the hounds on the hunted deer. Early next morning the harbourer watches the stag move out from the covert to his grazing ground where he settles, usually in a bunch of ferns. At that time of year they are amazingly difficult to see despite their size and it was a great treat to be allowed to go out with the harbourer before hunting. The harbourers notice everything in the countryside, the movement of pigeons or sheep, the call of a jay and other signs all of which can point to the presence of deer. The harbourer goes to the meet, tells the huntsman where the stag is lying and the tufters (about four couple of experienced hounds) are drawn, while the rest of the pack is kennelled, usually nowadays in the hound van. The tufters rouse the stag and then, when it is clear of the woods and other deer, the tufters are stopped and the pack laid on. The tufting can often take up to two hours and is watched by the mounted field and crowds of foot followers from some point of vantage. Nothing is more exciting than the laying on of the pack, which is brought up by a whipper-in and the second horsemen. The hunt servants change horses, the huntsman blows his horn, the hounds settle to the line and start to give tongue and everyone tightens their girths and sits down to ride as hard as they can over the heather. There is a great sense of urgency from the moment the pack arrives. It usually takes about twenty minutes from the time the tufters are stopped until the time the pack is laid on, so that the stag is given that amount of law.

When the rut starts stag-hunting stops, as the stags become exhausted by their labours and lose condition. They sometimes travel miles in search of a bunch of hinds. The rut is the time to see the deer, as they are on the move when the big stags are collecting their hinds. The best time to see them is in the evening when the stags roar or 'bell', an eerie sound almost like the roar of a lion. I once saw a cheeky young stag cover a hind while his lord and master was leading the hinds down into a combe in the gloaming. When the rut is over hind-hunting starts. The hinds will have dropped their calves in June, so that they are weaned by November and are hunted until the end of February. Although by then many will be pregnant, 75% of the growth of the foetus takes place in the last six weeks, so the foetus is tiny while the hinds are being hunted.

The technique of hind-hunting is quite different from stag-hunting. There is no harbouring. After the rut the stags leave their hinds (they are not good fathers) and the hinds congregate into herds of thirty or more. The tufters are laid straight on to a herd and the hunt servants and some young farmers try to cut out one or more hinds. The tufters may divide and settle onto one or two or even three single hinds. This is all confusing to the novice follower, who has to decide which group to follow often in mist and the moor riding wet and treacherous. The tufters are not stopped and the pack is laid on when the opportunity arises. This requires great skill and control by the hunt servants. Ideally, when one hind is killed, the pack will be laid on to another which has been hunted by perhaps a couple or more tufters. The primary purpose of hind-hunting is to cull the maximum number of hinds. Deer are herd animals and, unlike stags which usually run straight, hinds tend to run in large circles in an attempt to return to the herd.

Spring stag-hunting starts in early March and continues until the end of April. This is the best time for hunting on Exmoor and many people from 'up-country' bring their horses down after they have stopped fox-hunting, so that there are often meets of up to three hundred riders with the staghounds. In the spring the younger stags and those with misshapen heads are hunted. The run of a stag is fairly predictable, although it has changed over the years with the fencing of parts of Exmoor. Deer will fly over fences while being hunted, but while grazing they tend not to do so. They prefer to keep to the high ground where the going is good, so it is best for the rider to keep on the high ground, although Judy liked to follow as close to the hounds as she could. The autumn stags usually make a point where there are likely to be other deer, but the spring stags are more unpredictable and often provide great hunts. The best day's stag-hunting I ever had was on 25th April 1957 when we ran from Hawkridge near Dulverton straight over the moor to near Lynmouth when hounds were stopped as they were getting close to the town. It was a seventeen-mile point all over open country, and lasted two-and-a-half hours from the time the pack was laid on. We only crossed three roads. I rode Lincoln Lad, an ex-racehorse with doubtful legs and a horrible trick of dropping his shoulder, whipping round and putting you on the ground. But that day he excelled himself and we were with hounds all the way.

A blood horse is required on Exmoor if one is to keep anywhere near hounds when they run, preferably one with short legs as a big long-striding horse tends to knock its legs on the rough ground in the river valleys and combes. The ideal was

Judy's Collough, brought over for her from Ireland by Tony Collings at the price of £90. Collough was a 15-hand chestnut mare by Sun King by Hyperion, winner of the Triple Crown. Like her august grandsire she had lop ears and moved like a machine with bottomless stamina. She also pulled like a train. Once, climbing up Hangley Cleeve in the middle of a long hunt when all the horses were reduced to a walk by the steep gradient, Collough and Judy went bounding up and when they reached the top Collough threw a buck just to show how she felt. One year in the fifties, when Willy, our groom, was away with my horse at the Bar point-to point, the children persuaded Judy to run Collough in the hunt race at the Staghounds' point-to-point. By that time, after a hard season, Collough had been turned out to grass, so Judy caught her in, fed her, groomed her and put up Norman Williams, son of a neighbouring farmer, to ride her. She won, never being headed all the way. She would stick her neck out and just go, although she had little regard for the obstacles, and Norman did well to remain in the saddle. Thereafter she won several point-to-points until she finally decided she had had enough of racing and returned to the hunting field.

Deer are destructive animals. They will go into a field of roots and take a bite out of every swede or turnip, throwing them over their shoulders in disdain. The farmers accept this level of damage only because the overwhelming majority of them support stag-hunting. On Dartmoor, where the deer have never been hunted, the red deer are now practically extinct having been slaughtered by the farmers. But the Exmoor hill farmers preserve the deer, because their whole life-style revolves around hunting. 'No hunting, no deer' is not just a slogan. It is accepted as true by all independent observers. The hill farmers are the true aristocracy of Exmoor, their families having farmed there for generations. It is even now a hard and lonely life, especially in the winter, and the hunt provides the only relaxation and opportunity to socialise. Many of the hill farming families inter-marry, since it is difficult for someone not brought up on the moor to adapt to the peculiar way of life. The great 18th-century prosperity did not extend to Exmoor, so apart from a few large houses near Dulverton, such as Pixton Park, there were few houses of any size on the moor. There were the two big estates owned by the Fortescues and Aclands and their yeomen tenants and shepherds. It was not until this century that, attracted by the stag-hunting and helped by the railway, people with money started to build houses and settle on Exmoor. Until the second world war the hill farmers suffered from the general agricultural depression but still went hunting on their Exmoor shepherding ponies, their feet almost touching the ground. During and after the war, however, with the great revival of agriculture, many of the tenants bought their farms at knock-down prices and benefited from the general prosperity of farming. Now they ride thoroughbred horses which their sons and daughters point-to-point; and the latter look like princesses and are as well mounted.

During the war the staghounds were kept going by Flo Hancock and Biddy Abbot, who remained master for some years after the war. If she had been a man she would undoubtedly have been a successful general. She came from the great Quaker Fry family and devoted her considerable abilities to stag-hunting. Another of the same sort was Violet Lloyd, who later became master having founded an Exmoor dynasty. Her husband Ned had been secretary of the staghounds. Violet Lloyd's son Dick, although possessing qualities which would have ensured him a successful career in business like his twin brother Pat, or in the navy like his elder brother Bob, chose to devote his life to stag-hunting on Exmoor. He became manager of Bernard Waley-Cohen's fifteen hundred acre estate on the moor at Honeymead, as well as being secretary and later chairman of the staghounds. Dick and his wife Wynn both probably now know more than anyone of the habits of the deer and of stag-hunting. Bernard became Lord Mayor of London while still in his forties and was an unashamed protagonist of stag-hunting. For many years he was chairman of the hunt and was a fine horseman in spite of his size. One year he won the hunt race riding his good horse Benelux. I was in the unsaddling enclosure congratulating his wife Joyce when Bernard appeared from the weighing tent and said, 'I made the weight all right.' At that moment the loud speaker announced, 'Winner weighed in. Three stone over weight.' Joyce also took well to stag-hunting, as did their four children who were contemporaries of our children.

Another lady who gave her life and fortune to stag-hunting was Norah Harding, who was a popular master for many years and in her youth rode with great skill and dash over the moor. Her sister married into the Yandle family, enthusiastic stag-hunters for generations. There were other successful masters in the years after the war. One was Michael Murphy, an ex-Indian cavalryman who had been on Monty's Intelligence staff in the war. In his youth Michael and a brother officer used to do a 'William Tell' act at guest nights in the regimental mess. Michael would stand with an apple on his head which his partner would slice with a cavalry sabre. One evening, perhaps after a glass too much of port in the hot weather, the partner missed his cue and scalped Michael who thereafter bore an ugly scar on his forehead. But he took great trouble to learn about the deer and was a respected master of the staghounds. Nigel Hambro, who had left the family bank to come to Exmoor and had established a herd of Exmoor ponies, and Bob Nancekivell who had been born and bred near Lynton were joint masters for several seasons. Bob was a larger than life character known as the 'King of the Forest' who showed great sport during his mastership. Now we have Maurice and Diana Scott, with an exceptional young huntsman and two keen whippers-in who produce sport as good as I ever remember. If stag-hunting could be removed from politics the future would look bright.

Although I was brought up to fox-hunting I soon decided that on Exmoor I would concentrate on stag-hunting. It is a unique sport, whereas I did not enjoy fox-hunting on the moor as much as in enclosed country with fences to jump. But I always went out with the Exmoor Foxhounds (the Stars of the West) whenever they were nearby, and Judy's father increasingly enjoyed fox-hunting as he got older and was for many years chairman of the Exmoor Foxhounds. After the war Guy Jackson became master. He had commanded the Warwickshire Yeomanry in the desert and in Italy, winning the DSO. One day, partridge shooting behind the lines in Italy, he stepped on an anti-personnel mine and blew off his foot. Putting down the other he stepped on a second mine with the same result. Thereafter he wore two artificial legs which did not prevent him from hunting three days a week. Guy was a big man in every way, a born leader of men and much respected on Exmoor. He also knew a great deal about fox-hunting and had the uncanny knack of always knowing where the fox was. When Ronnie Wallace was master of the Heythrop, Guy invited him to bring his hounds to Exmoor to hunt in the spring and this continued for many years. Guy died comparatively young and in due course Ronnie, having married Rose Green who had been brought up on Exmoor, became master of the Exmoor and shows great sport with them.

In the twenties Judy's grandfather Allan Hughes and some others bought the deer park near Oare from Sir Edward Mountain and formed the Badgworthy Land Company to preserve the land for hunting. The company, of which I am now chairman, owns eleven thousand acres of Exmoor, the result of gifts and legacies from hunt supporters, together with the hunting rights over a further fifty thousand acres, all given voluntarily so that the company controls the hunting over about one hundred square miles. The National Trust also owns nearly ten thousand acres of moorland and woodland, subject to covenants or the wishes of donors that hunting shall continue on the land in perpetuity. So, short of legislation, hunting on Exmoor is probably more secure than anywhere else in the country.

Index